Crofters and Habitants

Settler Society, Economy, and Culture in a Quebec Township, 1848–1881

J.I. LITTLE

McGill-Queen's University Press
Montreal & Kingston • London • Buffalo

© McGill-Queen's University Press 1991
ISBN 0-7735-0807-4

Legal deposit 4th quarter 1991
Bibliothèque nationale du Québec

Printed in Canada on acid-free paper

This book has been published
with the help of a grant from the
Social Science Federation of Canada,
using funds provided by the
Social Sciences and Humanities
Research Council of Canada.
Funding has also been received
from Multiculturalism Canada.

Canadian Cataloguing in Publication Data

Little, J.I. (John Irvine), 1947–
    Crofters and habitants

(McGill-Queen's series on the history of Quebec)
Includes bibliographical references and index.
ISBN 0-7735-0807-4

1. Winslow (Quebec) – History.
2. Winslow (Quebec) – Social conditions.
I. Title. II. Series.

FC2945.W46L48 1991   971.4'69   C91-090226-7
F1054.W46L48 1991

Typeset in Baskerville 10/12 by Caractéra inc.,
Quebec City.

To Mark and Brett

Contents

Tables

Maps and Figures

FIGURES

Acknowledgments

While one might assume that an advantage to researching a small geographical area would be the concentration of material in a small number of proximate locations, such was far from the case for this study. In addition to records consulted in the various archives at Quebec City, Ottawa, Montreal, Sherbrooke, Toronto, and Edinburgh, a good deal of essential material was scattered in various non-archival repositories across the province of Quebec. Most of the reports relating to land grants were stored in the basement of the Ministry of Energy and Resources, though steps were apparently being taken to move them to the provincial archives. Simply working one's way through the byzantine system of nineteenth-century record-keeping was a challenge, and I am grateful for the patience of the ministry employees who provided assistance as well as free access to the material.[18]

All records dealing with private land transactions were in the notarial files, in locations as far apart as St Joseph de Beauce and Valleyfield, and in the invaluable registry volumes lying neglected in the Sherbrooke and Cookshire registry offices. Historical researchers working with registry records must pay prohibitive fees for consultation and photocopying, even though the old cadastral lines in the nineteenth-century registers make them of little use for current purposes. Even records as official as the Presbyterian registers remain in private hands, though they were microfilmed after my research was completed. Unfortunately, the first volume for the Winslow congregation has been destroyed, as apparently have all the local school and court records and most of the municipal records. In order to consult the one council minute book that did survive, I had to await the retirement of the unco-operative secretary-treasurer who had it in his keeping. If the writing of comprehensive local history is to be encouraged in Quebec, it is urgent that archives collect and preserve what remains of the routinely generated records from the early years of state bureaucratic expansion.

I am nevertheless grateful to the many kind people outside the official archives who assisted me in the midst of their busy work schedules. I am especially indebted to the curé of St Romain for providing me with free access to the very useful materials from his parish. As for the over-burdened employees of the various archives I visited, they were also unfailingly courteous and helpful. My particular thanks go to Gilles Héon of the Archives nationales du Québec in Quebec City and to Gilles Durand at the Sherbrooke branch, both of whom did everything in their power to assist me. Diane Couture provided invaluable assistance with the tedious research in the crown land records, registry volumes, and notary files, while Wendie Nelson did some genealogical work and Jeanne Williams and Marilyn Jantzen compiled much of the data. Without the assistance of these students, this project would never have been completed.

Thanks are owed also to JacLynne Campbell of the Simon Fraser Instructional Media Centre and to Susan Riddell for their painstaking work on the graphics, to John Parry for his fastidious editing, and to Duncan McLeod, who acted as my guide along the backroads of Winslow. Kris Inwood, Wendy Johnston, Guy Laperrière, Doug McCalla, Sharon Meen, Wendie Nelson, Françoise Noël, and Brian Young were kind enough to offer me their expert advice on earlier drafts of various chapters, and Angus MacLaren lent a willing ear to my questions after our weekly squash games.

The Social Sciences and Humanities Research Council provided me with the precious year's leave from teaching which made it possible to prepare the manuscript without interruption. Above all, however, my deepest appreciation goes to Andrea and the children for bearing with me once again through what must have seemed an endless project.

Merchant Colin Noble's house and store, Stornoway (author, 1989). While both halves of this building were built apparently in the 1850s, the dwelling (on the right) must be a little older, for it contains hand-hewn timbers.

The house (c. 1950) of the Stornoway hotel-keeper, stage-coach operator, and merchant Thomas Leonard (*Stornoway 1858/1983*, 10). The original part of this house is said to have been built in 1853. Few of the village's other early buildings have survived, and this one has been greatly altered since this photograph was taken.

Thomas Leonard's store, c. 1900; it was destroyed by fire in 1931 (*Stornoway 1858/1983*, 26). The size of Leonard's store suggests that it carried a larger stock than Colin Noble's. Noble nevertheless held the mortgages to many Scots farms, while Leonard and sons did not.

Virginie Legendre and her brothers, Prosper, Ferdinand, Ernest, Alphonse, Philippe, and Télésphore, c. 1910 (*Stornoway 1858/1883*, 10). The only French-Canadian family in Stornoway for many years, the Legendres were successful mill operators who were said to speak fluent Gaelic.

The Legendres' fulling and carding mill, with their saw mill in the background (*Stornoway 1858/1983*, 14). The original carding mill was destroyed by fire in 1883 and replaced by the building shown here.

The Legendres' grist mill (author, 1989). The only mill left in Winslow, this building also dates from after the 1883 fire.

Communion at Winslow Presbyterian Church, 1902 (Duncan McLeod, Scotstown). Built in 1878, this church closed its doors for the last time in 1923. Morning services were always in Gaelic, and hymns were sung without the accompaniment of a musical instrument.

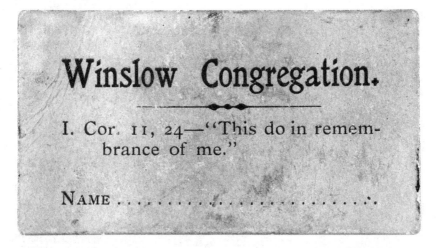

Winslow Congregation.

I. Cor. 11, 24—"This do in remembrance of me."

NAME . . . .

Communion ticket issued by kirk session elders (gift of Freeman Clowery). While all members of several neighbouring congregations were invited to participate in the five-day outdoor communion celebrations, only those judged worthy by the elders were permitted access to the communion table itself.

Hand-hewn headstone of an original settler, Ghisla cemetery (author, 1989). Note place of origin and religious symbols. The longevity recorded on this stone is typical of many in local cemeteries.

There are also many memorials to children, including this one to an infant who died at birth, Dell cemetery (author, 1989). Biblical verses are carved on many of the stones.

Gaelic inscriptions are also common, as on this memorial to a young accident victim, Stornoway cemetery (author, 1989).

Murdo Morrison and cabin, c. 1889. The Megantic Outlaw's ageing father is shown on the partially cleared lot near the southern tip of Winslow where he resettled after losing his homestead of many years to a local capitalist. Donald Morrison's captors were waiting at the corner of the cabin (number 1) when he emerged from the door shown here. Though wounded, he managed to reach the fence at Number 2 before being arrested. *Source*: La Société d'histoire de Sherbrooke

Crofters and Habitants

Introduction

Anyone visiting Winslow Township today might consider it a strange choice for the subject of a historical study as lengthy as this one. There are no more than thirty-five small farms and two cross-roads service centres within this heavily forested 113-square-mile area. Located on the northern edge of the Appalachian High Plateau, near the divide between the St Francis and Chaudière river systems (see Map 1), Winslow's altitude (1,000 to 1,300 feet) results in a growing season one month shorter than that of the Montreal region, with danger of frost in early June and late August. The average snowfall there is 165 inches, as compared with 95 inches for Sherbrooke, some 50 miles southwest.[1] Although the regional climate appears to have been warmer during the third quarter of the nineteenth century than it has been since the 1920s, there are frequent references to bad weather in the school inspectors' reports for the 1870s, and in 1881 Winslow's census enumerator reported that "les gelées ont fait beaucoup de mal partout l'an dernier."[2]

An equally severe constraint on agriculture has been lack of arable soil, for Winslow is one of the least fertile townships in a district of limited agriculture potential. A modern-day soil map classifies most of the township's surface at the lowest end of the scale, with no capability even for permanent pasture because of various combinations of adverse topography, lack of soil cover, stoniness, and excess water. The few arable pockets have soil capable of producing only perennial forage crops or a wider range of crops at low to fair rates of productivity (see Map 2). Finally, there is also the problem of isolation, particularly in the nineteenth century, when the stage-coach required more than twelve hours in midsummer to cover the fifty-one miles to Lennoxville, the closest centre of significant size.[3]

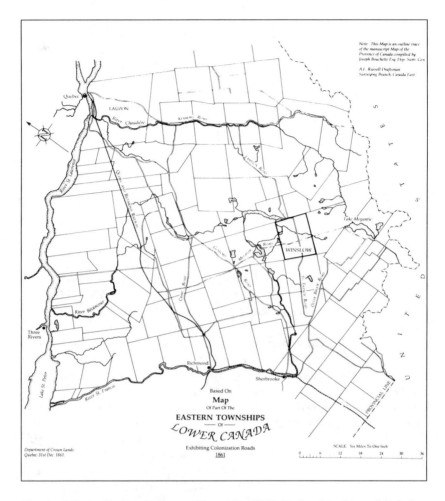

Map 1   Colonization Roads, Eastern Townships, 1861 (National Archives of Canada [NA], National Map Collection [NMC], VI/307/1861)

Though surveyed as a single township, Winslow is divided along a northwest-to-southeast axis by the Felton River, which empties into Lake St Francis near the northern tip of the township. Within a couple of years of the first settlers' arrival, the census enumerator recognized that there was slightly more arable land in the southern portion. Even there, however, it was "cut up a good deal by a swamp two miles in width & running north and south which separates one part of the settlers from the other."[4] These settlers were the northernmost contingent of the Gaelic-speaking, Protestant Highlanders who had claimed land beyond the American- and English-settled communities to the southwest. The northern part of the township, in contrast, was inhabited exclusively by French-speaking colonists who were at the forefront of the wave spreading southward from the St Lawrence seigneuries. Consequently, the Felton River was for a time as close to a physical boundary between British-origin and French-Canadian settlement as any that existed within the Eastern Townships (see Map 3).

The Highlanders may have been welcomed as reinforcements by English-speaking residents who had no inclination to colonize the inhospitable frontier themselves, but their very isolation ensured that the dissolution of the Gaelic culture would be a slower process than in most other North American regions. If that culture has all but disappeared today, it is primarily because the Scots descendants have scattered themselves across the continent. Winslow therefore represents essentially one environment settled by two distinct ethno-religious groups at almost precisely the same time, a situation rarely found in the local studies written by social historians and historical geographers. Consequently, we have a relatively clean laboratory for the study of ethnicity as a socioeconomic force. No doubt earlier and therefore less marginal settlements could have been found which approximated the same conditions, but the relatively late timing of Winslow's colonization offers one important compensating advantage: a wealth of historical documentation.

In 1931 M.C. MacLeod of New York City lamented that with the passing of his father's generation in the Lake Megantic area "many details of the early days ... are lost forever."[5] A few years later, the locally born Reverend Mr M.N. MacDonald of Edmonton echoed these same sentiments of irrevocable loss: "There was so much in connection with the experience of these pioneers that would be of interest to us today. The story in detail of the building of the first homes, their early successes and failures, as well as their joys and sorrows, would be of absorbing interest to their descendants for many generations. But much of that is lost forever, their unwritten history is largely buried with themselves."[6]

While it is certainly frustrating not to have found at least one good diary, memoir, or collection of letters written by a Winslow settler, these two descendants would have been pleasantly surprised by the abundance of material that does survive in the form of

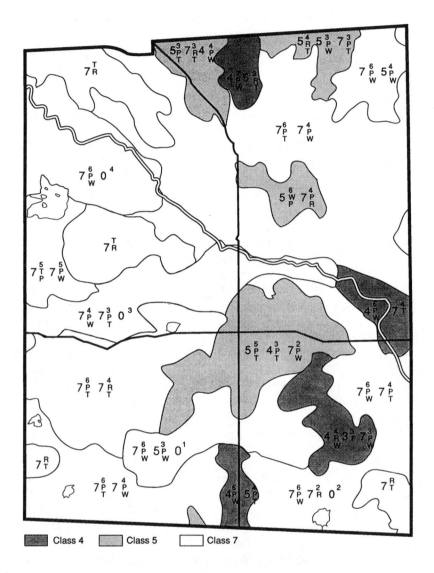

Map 2   Soil Map, Winslow Township, 1973 (Soil Capability for Agriculture, Canada Land Inventory, Sherbrooke 21ᴇ, Ottawa: Department of the Environment, 1973)

Class 4   Severe limitations restrict the range of crops or require special conservation practices or both.

Class 5   Very severe limitations restrict capability for producing perennial forage crops, and improvement practices are feasible.

Class 7   No capability for arable culture or permanent pasture.

O   Organic soils (not placed in capability classes).
Subclass P   Stoniness: stones interfere with tillage, planting, and harvesting.
Subclass R   Shallowness to solid bedrock: solid bedrock is less than three feet from the surface.
Subclass T   Adverse topography: steepness or pattern of slopes limits agricultural use.
Subclass W   Excess water other than from flooding limits use for agriculture. It may be caused by poor drainage, a high water table, seepage, or runoff from surrounding areas.

Large numerals denote capability classes. Small numerals placed after a class numeral give the approximate proportion of the class out of a total of 10. Letters placed after class numerals denote subclasses, i.e. limitations.

EXAMPLES   An area of class 7 land with topographic and depth of soil limitations is shown thus:

7^{T}_{R}

An area of class 5 land with excess water and stoniness limitations, and class 7 land with stoniness and depth of soil limitations, in the proportion of 5:7 is shown thus:

$5^{6}_{W_{P}} \; 7^{4}_{P_{R}}$

official records. One would not expect the much-studied winning of responsible government under Lord Elgin to have much to do with this examination of an obscure township, but responsible government helped to spawn the French-Canadian colonization movement and Canada's modern state bureaucracy.[7] It is no accident, therefore, that our story begins in 1848.

The original aim of this project was not to test a social-science theory or model, but simply to examine the people of a particular place at a particular time in as multifaceted a fashion as possible. In other words, there is no attempt here to focus on "single principles or features"; rather I shall explore "the causal impact of different dimensions of human experience on *one another*."[8] The approach is similar to that of the French practitioners of "histoire totale," but the period covered is certainly not that of the "longue durée." Even if access had not been closed to documents such as manuscript census lists and notarial records that were less than one hundred years old, the sheer volume of materials would have made it impractical for a single researcher to extend the study far beyond its thirty-plus years.

Michael Katz's examination of Hamilton and David Gagan's volume on Peel County cover a shorter period while including much larger populations than this study does, but expanding beyond

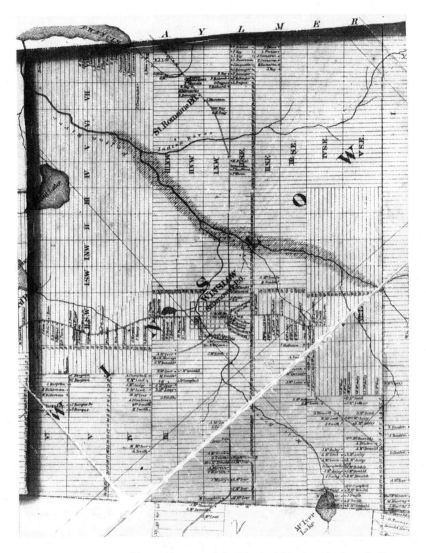

Map 3 Winslow Township, 1863 (Map of the District of St Francis, Canada East, From Surveys ... under the direction of O.W. Gray, Topographical Engr, published by Putnam and Gray, 1863. NA, NMC, H2/307/1863)

Winslow's geographical boundaries would again have led to problems of manageability without the extensive research teams of those two projects.[9] Fortunately, mobility rates were lower than those discovered by Katz and Gagan (perhaps, in part, because the lower population made manual linkages from several sources possible), with the result that a large proportion of the families could be traced across extended periods of time.[10] Although referring to a different historical context, Alan MacFarlane's recommendation that a study group should be 800 to 1,500 individuals per investigator proved to be valid in this case.[11] The combined French-Canadian and Scots population of Winslow was 1,571 in 1861, and somewhat more thereafter, but we shall see that the separate analyses for each group did lead to some problems in the case of the smaller Scots numbers.

In the absence of descriptive personal documents, any study that focuses on the family must depend largely on routinely generated historical materials which can be analysed statistically.[12] At the same time, however, it should be remembered that families did not respond mechanically to basic socioeconomic forces, nor did they develop in isolation from the surrounding community. Many of their cultural values were expressed through churches, schools, and municipal councils, and this study's examination of such institutions also provides insights into class structure and local response to outside agencies of "social control." An earlier volume studied the district within which Winslow is located from the point of view of external capitalist exploitation, but here we shall explore the relationship between settlers and agencies of capitalism in more detail.[13] This study will therefore adopt a dual method of analysis, with the earlier chapters focusing on the household and the later ones on the community. The organization is basically fourfold, with two chapters setting the stage, two focusing on society, two on economy, and two on culture, though most of the themes cannot be categorized so neatly.

The resulting overall picture is complex, but the main argument is that two stable, relatively independent, egalitarian, and mutually exclusive rural communities did emerge in Winslow Township. The similarities and differences between them were often subtle and not always predictable. Thus the limitations of the physical environment imposed a common system of intergenerational property transmission, even though the two groups developed rather different demographic patterns. The Scots had higher agricultural outputs, and they were less involved than the French Canadians in the forest economy, but both communities produced essentially for home consumption, and both depended to some extent on seasonal labour outside the township. We shall see, however, that it is far from easy to determine the exact degree to which either community of yeomen settlers became semi-proletarianized, particularly as strategies varied not only with the family cycle but also with the ups and downs of the international economy.[14]

While outside contacts eventually hastened the demise of one of the two communities, our examination of the first three decades reveals stronger cultural retention here than that described by most historians and geographers for other North American frontiers. It is not surprising that market forces would break down cultural differences more quickly in the less marginal and more ethnically mixed districts which have attracted most scholarly attention. This study suggests, however, that cultural background may have played a more subtle but none the less meaningful role in other settler societies than has been recognized by many historians, particularly by historical geographers.[15] Only more comprehensive local histories will reveal whether or not this is true.

In addition to rejecting environmental determinism, this study argues that there was more community-based autonomy in Winslow than historians of this country's still-dominant "social control" school would have anticipated. The strong degree of family/institutional independence discovered for Winslow may not seem surprising given the isolated nature of the district, but it was noted above that the settlers were not entirely independent from capitalist forces. They engaged in seasonal labour, often outside their district, which was itself exploited by large-scale, externally based lumber companies. One might even have expected their economically struggling communities to be weak and fragmented. Perhaps such indicators might be found in the divisive religious disputes among the Scots settlers, and, conversely, in the dominance of the curé over the French-speaking community, but these features actually emerged from the contrasting ecclesiastical structures and historical traditions of the two settlement groups. In other words, the frontier only exacerbated trends already taking place in the two home communities.

The main sources consulted for chapters 3, 4, and 5, on demographic trends, household structure, and domestic economy, were the parish registers of births, deaths, and marriages and the manuscript census reports for 1852, 1861, 1871, and 1881. Many of the data from the census were analysed through the computer-based Statistical Package for the Social Sciences (SPSS). The format used was essentially the same as that of Gagan's *Hopeful Travellers*, without the information on property acquisition and mortagages being entered, but with the addition of some extra information from the agricultural schedules.[16]

As noted above, families were linked manually from census to census in order to determine rates of persistence/mobility. These linkages were facilitated and verified by referring to the names and ages of all members of the family and by identifying farm locations from the agricultural schedules (1852–71), crown land records, Gray's 1863 map (see Map 1), and assessment lists from the early 1880s. Such a comprehensive approach was necessitated by the Scots' proclivity to identify themselves in English by a narrow range of first and last names, sorting themselves out informally through the use of Gaelic patronymics and nicknames which do not appear in the official records. (Thus one can find in a local merchant's accounts the names Angus, Donald, John, and Malcolm McLeod, all called Piper, to distinguish them from McLeods with the same Christian names in branches known as Chicken, Finger, Little, Megantic, Mountain, Penny, Pirate, Revach, Rugh, and Swamp.) This method also allowed us to make linkages for French-Canadian families that would have been missed otherwise because of the garbling of their names by English-speaking enumerators.[17] The census linkages were necessary not only to determine persistence rates but also to complement the parish registers in the reconstitution of families over such a short period of time.

Inheritance practices were examined through the use of notarial and land registry records, which also included the post-mortem inventories, mortgages, and property sales consulted for chapter 6, on the local bourgeoisie. The main sources for chapter 2, on the settlement process, were the crown land records, from which was compiled a lot-by-lot profile on the timing of instalments and issuing of official titles. While most of the documentation on conflicts over land titles has been destroyed over the years, there remains in the adjudications file of the former Ministry of Agriculture and Colonization a considerable number of detailed reports written by crown land agents. Chapter 7, on religion, is based principally on material in the Catholic presbytery at St Romain de Winslow, the chancellery of the Archdiocese of Sherbrooke, and the United Church of Canada Archives at Victoria College in Toronto and at Bishop's University. The principal sources for examination of schooling were the public education records at the Archives nationales du Québec at Quebec City, published reports in the province's *Sessional Papers*, and the literacy and school-enrolment columns of the manuscript census reports. The brief section on municipal government in chapter 8 was written primarily from the council's minute book for Winslow North. Finally, chapter 1, on the settlers' origins, is based largely on secondary sources, though published government reports and census data were consulted as well.

CHAPTER ONE

Crofters and Habitants

In order to understand the similarities and differences that we shall observe in the social, economic, and cultural responses of the Scots and French Canadians to the Winslow environment, it is necessary to examine where these people came from, why they left their places of origin, and how they happened to arrive where they did. While the Gaelic-speaking Presbyterian crofters and the French-speaking Catholic habitants may have been unlikely neighbours in many respects, the very fact that both local societies persisted as long as they did in such an inhospitable environment suggests that they shared certain fundamental characterstics. Not the least of these, as we shall see, was their mutual attachment to kin, community, and tradition. Both groups were forced by economic necessity to leave their home communities, and both moved to the upper St Francis frontier in search of the security offered not only by inexpensive land, but also by familiar customs and faces.

THE ISLE OF LEWIS

The Scottish settlers of Winslow originated almost exclusively from a treeless and peat-covered island, about sixty miles long and fifteen miles wide, lying at the northern end of the remote Outer Hebrides. By 1846 the population of Lewis had reached 18,400, of whom 15,200 lived in the rural districts and the remainder in the only town, Stornoway.[1] These peasants had become dependent on potatoes for a full two-thirds of their diet, when a series of blight-induced crop failures resulted in large-scale migration from the island, as from the Highlands in general.

Dependence on the potato, and even the very status of crofter, had emerged relatively recently in the Highlands, following elimination of the intermediary tribal links between tenant and landlord. Until the Battle of Culloden in 1746, clan chieftains had relied on large bodies of armed retainers. The extension of British-enforced law and order into the Highlands was accompanied by weakening of the hierarchical clan structure as the social status of the disarmed and increasingly assimilated chieftains began to reflect the growing amount of wealth at their disposal. At the same time as the retainers or tacksmen were becoming redundant, the commercialization of agriculture was being stimulated by industrialization in the Lowlands and England. Demand increased for the traditional market product, the small and hardy black cattle, as well as for two new commodities, wool and kelp.[2] The result, in historian James Hunter's words, was "a massive transformation" of the traditional communally oriented system of agriculture, with the emergence of the semi-agrarian crofting system on the northwestern seaboard and in the Hebrides.[3]

The commercial raising of sheep required large flocks, thereby placing it beyond the means of the small tenants who constituted the bulk of the Highlands' population.[4] Sheep encroached on cattle pastures until, in the 1790s, the landlord of Lewis began a policy of wholesale evictions from traditional settlements.[5] The aim of the Highland landlords was not to clear their estates, however, but to re-establish families on small, individually held "crofts" along the coastline, where large profits were to be made from the kelp industry. The alkaline extract known as kelp was produced by the burning of seaweed, then used (like Canadian potash) in the manufacture of soap and glass. Firmly established by the 1770s, the industry mushroomed two decades later when French military action cut off imports of Spanish barilla, its main rival as a source of industrial alkali.

The vast bulk of the profits from kelp production accrued to landlords – prior to 1799 the proprietor of Lewis cleared as much as £2,500 per year – who controlled access to the beaches as well as shipment to external markets.[6] The landlord was effectively able to avoid paying for his tenants' arduous summer labour simply by raising rents far beyond the level of the land's intrinsic value. The consequence, according to Hunter, was that he "was able to establish a degree of control over his work force which was quite unmatched by even the most tyrannical factory owner."[7]

The landlord's dominance was abetted by the breakdown of the traditional tenurial relationship caused by the spread of the crofting system. Farms had traditionally been held in common by joint tenants, often from tacksmen who paid only nominal rents to the chieftains in return for providing skilled soldiers from among the peasantry. At the turn of the century (around 1810 in Lewis), the

militarily redundant tacksmen began to be circumvented by the proprietors, who were reorganizing the scattered strips or "rigs" of arable
land into separate holdings or crofts. Each croft, averaging only two
to five acres in Lewis, was occupied by a single tenant or crofter who
would pay his rent directly to the landlord.[8] Rural improvers to the
south had long since identified the process of enclosure as central to
the commercialization of agricultural production. But in the Highlands, where tenants continued to lack security of tenure, the small
crofts increased dependence on potatoes, grown in "lazy-beds" on the
beaches, and on an outside source of income, whether from kelp, the
fishery, or seasonal labour.[9]

The impact of the kelp industry reveals itself dramatically in population statistics for the years between 1755 and 1831. In Scotland's
northern and northwestern counties as a whole, numbers increased
by 48 per cent during this period, while in the Outer Hebrides they
jumped by 139 per cent.[10] Well before the end of this period, however,
the conditions that had stimulated population expansion had disappeared. The end of the Napoleonic Wars brought opening of
trade, lowering of import duties, and, most important, abolition in
1825 of the tax on salt, a product increasingly used in the chemical
manufacture of alkali. The bottom fell completely out of the kelp
market in 1827. Production continued on the larger Hebridean
estates only because the kelping "wages" were essentially the rents
paid by many of their crofters.

The Lewis estate manager expressed the hope in 1833 that kelp
would soon be gathered only to fertilize the bear (a primitive form
of barley) being grown for the new distillery, but the distillery proved
no more successful than other projects attempted by the Earl of
Seaforth.[11] There were still patches of intense kelp-gathering in Lewis
during the 1840s, while the local white fishery (cod, ling, and tusk)
continued to supplement food supplies in some parishes.[12]

The Earl of Seaforth had attempted to establish a commercial fishery in Lewis, proposing in the early 1820s to evict up to a thousand
people from the southern upland parishes of Uig and Lochs which
were particularly well suited for the grazing of sheep. The tenants
were to be resettled on newly established crofts in the low-lying parishes of Stornoway and Barvas, to the north, where they would be
encouraged to engage in the fishery. Seaforth's trustees reminded
him that his finances were too limited to allow him to establish so
many crofts, let alone equip their inhabitants with boats and gear.
He managed, nevertheless, to clear a number of southern communities. The farm of Park in the eastern part of Lochs eliminated
twenty-eight settlements, resulting in the eviction before 1830 of over

a hundred families. One of Seaforth's factors reported in 1827 that those transported to waste land three miles north of the town of Stornoway found themselves in a situation "worse than anything I ever saw in Donegal where I always considered human wretchedness to have reached its very acme."[13] West of Lochs, in Uig, events took a similar course. Tenants around Loch Roag, the island's main kelping centre, were moved northward or accommodated in newly lotted townships on the coast. One of these coastal settlements was in turn converted to a sheep farm in 1836, with six of its tenants being crowded into a nearby township and the rest shipped off to North America.[14]

The Lewis report written for the *New Statistical Account of Scotland* in 1833 declared that the island was "a full century behind other parts of Scotland, in agricultural and domestic improvements, the town and inhabitants of Stornoway excepted, and a few tacksmen."[15] Even if crofters could have improved their holdings or increased their agricultural production, any added income would simply have been appropriated by the landlord. In Hunter's words, "apathy and hopelessness inevitably ensued ... And in such circumstances there grew up the myth of the ingrained idleness of the crofter that was to persist for many years to come."[16]

Certainly, the crofters' dwellings could not be described as anything but primitive. With no access to lumber, and no security of tenure, they continued to live in the traditional "black houses," which could be erected in a single day. The walls were inner and outer dry stone dykes, six or seven feet high and filled with earth and rubble; the roof consisted of old masts, oars, or driftwood, covered with turfs that were thatched with straw and secured against the Atlantic storms by heather ropes weighted with large stones. There were no eves or windows, and the smoke simply filtered through the roof from the peat fire in the middle of the earthen floor. The crofters' cows occupied one end of this dwelling, which had only one door. In the spring, the soot-covered thatch and manure were scattered over the tilled land with seaweed as fertilizer.[17]

The island's crofters had turned increasingly from kelping to labour on the fleet off the northeast coast of Scotland, but, with cattle prices in serious decline, rental debts accumulated.[18] The proprietor of Lewis remarked in 1823 that "all rentals since 1814 have been a mere joke."[19] As Seaforth's own debts increased, he became an increasingly strong supporter of large-scale emigration to North America. When redundant and disgruntled Highland tacksmen had begun to organize such a migration at the turn of the century, the government had responded with the Ship's Passenger Act of 1803, which forced the increase of fares beyond the limited means of even the more successful tenants.[20] Decline of the kelp industry brought a more "tolerant" attitude toward the overcrowding of emigrant vessels, but Seaforth's proposal for mass emigration still failed to win support from either his fellow landlords or the British government.[21] The removal in 1827 of all restrictions from the act did stimulate a sizeable movement to Cape Breton Island,[22] but only in 1838 does Seaforth appear to have become involved in an assisted emigration scheme.

Although no correspondence between Seaforth and the London-based British American Land Co. has been found, it is clear that an arrangement was reached between the two parties to send crofters to the company's recently acquired lands in the Eastern Townships of Lower Canada. The agent in charge was John Mackenzie of Stornoway, and in 1838 his son returned from Canada to guide some sixteen families to their new homes in the frontier townships of Bury and Lingwick.[23] In August, the Inverness *Herald* reported: "Although the emigrants have been detained six weeks longer than they expected, and in consequence, must arrive later in the season, there are houses provided for them by the Company, at the landing place, Port St Francis; also houses well supplied with stores for winter, at Sherbrooke, about forty miles from Port St Francis."[24]

Careful as the preparations may have been, the leave-taking of the crofters was not entirely voluntary, for Seaforth's Lewis factor later stated that he had provided the fares for fifteen families (seventy individuals) whose holdings were being converted to sheep walks. They were presumably from the township of Mealista in western Uig, most of whose tenants reportedly went to Canada when cleared from their crofts in 1838. Another, somewhat larger group was sent on the same ship from the mainland estate of Loch Broom, where conditions were still worse than in Lewis. The Inverness *Herald* stated that two hundred emigrants were on board the four-hundred ton *Energy* when it left Stornoway; on the western side of the Atlantic, the Quebec emigration agent reported receiving the same number of Highlanders in late September.

While all sixty families were sponsored by the British American Land Co., there is no indication that those from the mainland moved to the St Francis Tract.[25] They certainly attracted no subsequent immigration, in sharp contrast to the small group from Lewis, who were followed by many kin and former neighbours. The island's genealogist, William Lawson, has traced some four hundred Lewis families to Quebec, mostly from the northwest coast.[26]

The second group, of 223 Lewis crofters, again mostly from West Uig, joined their predecessors in Bury and Lingwick in 1841.[27] There is no indication that they were evictees, and they were certainly not assisted by the financially strapped land company, which left them dependent for survival during the first winter on donations from the citizens of Sherbrooke and Montreal.[28] Not surprisingly, few of the 1,194 emigrants who boarded ship at Stornoway the following year made their way to the St Francis Tract, though ninety-four people from the parish of Barvas were reported as destined for Lower Canada in 1843.[29]

Seaforth appears not to have had a direct hand in the later migrations.[30] He had all but accepted the imminent sale of his island as early as 1839, when he wrote from his post in Ceylon:

I cannot advert to this subject, I confess, without the very deepest pain; for I never had contemplated to live to see that last great remnant of the very extensive Estates of the Family sold; but the advice is so strong, and the enormous expense of the management by Edinburgh Agency is so destructive, and there is so little prospect of ourselves ever enjoying again the influence, or adding to the happiness of its population by residing in the Lewis, and I am afraid to add, the apparent indifference, at present at least, of our eldest son to the retention of this Great Property in the family ... I almost look to the measure as decided upon.[31]

In 1844 a purchaser was finally forthcoming in the person of James Matheson, MP. A friend of Seaforth's, Matheson had two years earlier returned to Britain after retiring as head of Jardine, Matheson and Co., the most important British firm in the Chinese tea and opium trade.[32] The new landlord could certainly afford to continue the modernizing investments begun by Seaforth, and for the first few years his plans apparently did not include mass emigration. There is no major movement recorded from Stornoway prior to 1849.[33]

The Lewis crofters were fortunate in acquiring Matheson as landlord when they did, for they were about to face one of the blackest periods in the history of the Highlands – the potato famine of the later 1840s. It had long been apparent to all concerned that the crofters' dependence on the potato placed them in a very precarious position indeed. As early as 1817 Seaforth had found himself holding a £6,000 bill for the grain provided by the British government after a bad harvest had been combined with the failure of the herring fishery, a fall in cattle prices, and the return of soldiers from wartime service.[34] Even in normal years the situation was tenuous, as Hunter describes: "Every summer there was provided – in the weeks or months between the exhausting of the old potatoes and the digging of the new ones – a miniature rehearsal of what would occur in the event of the staple crop being lost: the shores were ransacked for shellfish; while nettles, brambles and any other vaguely edible plants were uprooted, steamed and eaten."[35]

A full-dress rehearsal for the famine of the 1840s took place in 1836 and 1837, which no doubt explains Seaforth's involvement in the emigration movement of the following year. The minister of Barvas wrote in May 1836 that many cattle were dying of starvation, despite having consumed a great proportion of his parishioners' grain and meal: "The extreme severity of the weather continues unabated, more resembling the middle of Winter than the approach of Summer – the labour of Spring hardly commenced – a general scarcity of corn seed, and the little store of meal almost exhausted – no money – no employment, and no means of procuring subsistence."[36] A year later virtually everyone in the parishes of Barvas and Lochs was destitute, and the minister of Stornoway reported that some 2,000 of his 5,491 parishioners were in distress (see Appendix A).[37]

Once again disaster was avoided by governmental and charitable assistance, an estimated 26,400 bushels of meal being required for Lewis in 1837 alone.[38] The crops appear to have recovered that fall, but within a few years they failed more completely than ever. Lewis's potatoes were partially struck by blight in 1845, then in July and August 1846 the fungus quickly and thoroughly devastated the harvest throughout Scotland. It was estimated at the end of the year that at least three-quarters of the Highland and Hebridean population was entirely without food. Details on conditions in Lewis, as reported by the Free Church relief committee in 1847, are given in Appendix B. In the parish of Uig, to take one example, not only had the potato harvest "failed entirely," but the other crops of "a considerable number of families" had been destroyed by sea spray during a July storm. In the face of an unusually severe winter, many succumbed to sickness and disease, including typhus, cholera, scurvy, and dysentery from eating shellfish.[39] Serious as the consequences of the 1846 crop failure were, conditions became still more critical when the blight struck repeatedly over the next several years, destroying half the crop in Lewis as late as 1851. To make matters worse, the price for Highland black cattle dropped again after 1847, the Lewis herring catch reportedly declined by half between 1846 and 1847, and the buoyant labour market on the mainland collapsed with the onset of the commercial recession in late 1847.[40]

Widespread starvation in the western Highlands, and especially the Islands, was averted only by the generous public response to appeals for charitable donations, and by the prompt intervention of the government which had machinery already in existence for dealing with the distress in Ireland.[41] The state's assistance was not without strings attached, for proprietors were expected to pay cash for meal at Glasgow and Liverpool prices, then distribute it to their needy tenants in return for construction piece-work, or spinning and needle-work in the case of women. To ensure that only only those who were absolutely without resources of their own would be assisted, the allowance was limited in 1848 to a bare subsistence level – one pound of meal for one day's work.[42]

Fortunately, the new Lewis landlord, Matheson, not only sank some £102,000 into public buildings and improved harbour facilities at Stornoway while contributing £5,900 to education and charity, he also operated his own relief program in 1846 and 1847.[43] He did, however, recover through labour much of the £37,000 spent during these first two years of famine.[44] In 1848, after a July storm had destroyed much of Uig's crops once again, the Lewis proprietor finally requested that his island be included in the operations of the church-organized Central Board of Management.[45] During the next three years the board, which had taken over the government's relief role, distributed approximately 60,000 bushels of oatmeal and Indian corn to Lewis residents.[46]

Matheson's own preoccupation became the investment of a £50,000 Drainage Act loan in order to step up improvement measures on the island.[47] His main aim was to rationalize the croft leases by relotting townships so that no more than one family could occupy each holding. Subdivision was to be allowed only in the cases of aged or indigent couples incapable of cultivating a standard acreage, while surplus families were to be located on newly drained and trenched land, either contiguous to the existing arable or in the new settlement zones. When the expense of moving belongings, constructing access roads, and fencing the arable is added to the direct investment in land improvements, Matheson's investment in the crofting settlements reached approximately £15,000 by 1851, a sum which he would be a good many years in recovering from his rentals.[48] Matheson refused, however, to undertake any work-producing projects in Uig because he wished to shift many of its crofters northward to Ness in the parish of Barvas.[49] The degree to which people were uprooted by the landlord's project is reflected in the number of summonses for removal, which increased from sixty-six in 1847 to 121 in 1848, and 382 in 1849.[50]

Despite Matheson's investments, during one week in 1850 the number of aid recipients on Lewis reached as high as 12,829 out of a total population of some 19,000.[51] The situation was still critical, therefore, when the Central Board had to cease operations that same year because of the exhaustion of its funds. To make matters worse, Matheson too gave up on his unremunerative investments, having recognized, in one historian's words, "that the grand scheme of agricultural improvement had entirely failed to bring either an economic return to the estate or lasting material security to the people."[52] Matheson received a baronetcy for his efforts, but his tenants' future appeared to be as bleak as ever. In 1851 the island's four parochial boards warned the government that famine was expected before the fall harvest.[53]

If the landlords needed any further incentive to promote large-scale clearances of their estates, it was provided by the 1851 extension of the terms of the compulsory poor rate to cover the able-bodied victims of famine and destitution.[54] The Highlands and Islands Emigration Society became more active, subsidizing the passages of some 4,700 individuals to Australia between 1852 and 1855.[55] At the same time, disillusionment with the Central Board's failure to do more than prevent starvation during the crisis had finally aroused the interest of the government in publicly assisted emigration. The Emigration Advances Act of 1851 declared that funds originally voted under the Drainage Act could be directed toward subsidization of a voluntary exodus. Hunter estimates that between 1847 and 1857 at least 16,000 people emigrated from the northwestern Highlands, a figure which Flinn feels is a severe understatement. Relying on census statistics, Flinn calculates that fully one-third (60,000) of the pre-famine population of northwest Scotland departed between 1841 and 1861.[56]

As for Lewis, no more than twenty families took advantage of the free passages to Australia,[57] but Sir James himself offered considerable enticement for emigration to the more popular Canada. Cape Breton Island had been a frequent destination for Highlanders, including emigrants from Lewis, but its best land was settled by the late 1820s, and wheat fly and potato blight infestations were so severe between 1845 and 1851 that it became known as the "Ireland of Nova Scotia."[58] Matheson agreed to pay fares to any place in Canada East or Canada West, to forfeit all arrears in rent, to relinquish his right to hypothec over the livestock, to purchase that livestock at a fair price if other buyers could not be found, and to furnish clothing to those in need. If a substantial number agreed to accept the offer, Matheson also promised to provide a clergyman with fare and a one- or two-year stipend.[59]

With the carrot came the stick. Matheson was no Gordon of Cluny, whose tenants on the islands to the South of Lewis were hunted down with dogs before being bound and shipped off,[60] but the tenants of Lewis were given little freedom of choice. Estate chamberlain Munro

Mackenzie toured the island during the winter and early spring of 1851, selecting those who were to emigrate, those who were to remain, and those who were to be settled elsewhere on the estate. In the first category would be all families who owed two years' rent without what was judged to be a valid excuse and those in townships not conveniently located for fishing but suitable for grazing land. Conversely, communities in more promising areas were specifically excluded from emigration assistance. Mackenzie identified 518 families, the equivalent of about 2,500 individuals, whom he wished to send to Canada. When few of them expressed willingness to comply, they were served with formal notices of removal from their crofts. Also refused work on the estate, prohibited from cutting peat, threatened with confiscation of their cattle, and told that they could expect no assistance in seed or food, these families had little choice but to submit to Matheson's dictates.[61] It appears that once again the majority came from the western shore of the island.[62] Smout is clearly mistaken, then, when he states of Lewis that "there were no removals, except in the case of crofters who themselves petitioned to be shifted from townships of bad land to better."[63]

Between 1851 and 1855, 2,337 individuals from Lewis booked passage to Canada at a cost to the proprietor of over £10,000.[64] Of the 986 who arrived at Quebec in early July 1851, the majority headed for Toronto, but about 400 went to Sherbrooke, where the able-bodied were employed with a large number of Irish Catholics on construction of the St Lawrence and Atlantic Railway.[65] As promised, Matheson sent a clergyman to reside wherever the largest group should settle, but he instructed that the crofters should be dispersed "as the best means of eradicating those habits of indolence and inertness to which their impoverished condition must in some measure be attributed."[66] Contrary to Matheson's design, however, those who went to Toronto and then Hamilton immediately demanded land. Their final destination is not mentioned in the correspondence, but a large contingent from Lewis which had arrived at Quebec on 4 August is listed as having settled in Huron Township, Bruce County.[67] This township remained one of the few areas of homogeneous Scottish settlement in Ontario.[68]

As for the Sherbrooke contingent, all but ten families ignored the wishes of their pastor by leaving Brompton Township, near Sherbrooke, to join their fellow Lewismen in Lingwick and Winslow once the demand for railway labour had died for the winter.[69] Quebec immigration agent A.C. Buchanan claimed that all could have found steady employment in Sherbrooke but that he had succumbed to their wishes by paying for their transportation to the isolated settlement.[70] While glowing letters about the abundance of well-paid construction jobs appeared in the *Inverness Advertiser* in December, the following spring the Scots left these for the most part to the migrant Irish labourers.[71] The Lewis immigrants therefore represent a striking exception to the generalization made by by Mario Seccareccia that the pauper immigrants at mid-century either returned to towns to become chronically unemployed and dependent on charity or migrated to the United States because their lack of knowledge, skills, and capital prevented them from surviving on the land.[72]

Few, if any, of the 453 Lewis crofters assisted to emigrate in 1852 went to the Eastern Townships, and pressure to leave began to weaken thereafter as the potato blight ran its course, cattle prices began to rise, east coast fishermen established bases on Lewis, and renewed economic expansion in the south once again provided seasonal labour for the crofters.[73] Matheson nevertheless did pay the passage of 330 more emigrants in 1855, 200 of whom reportedly moved once again to the upper St Francis district of the Eastern Townships, primarily to the frontier townships of Winslow and Whitton.[74] Matheson had to be dissuaded from sending yet another large group the following year. After discussing "the great difficulties that hinder the progress of settlers in that part of the country," the delegates to the Montreal Presbytery of the Free Church of Scotland agreed in 1856 "to instruct the Clerk to write to Sir James and to represent that it is now for the interest of these emigrants that they be directed to more Western settlements."[75]

Henceforth, migration from Lewis, as from the Highlands as a whole, would be largely a matter of individual families making their own way to join relatives and friends in the colonies, but one final group migration of unknown size did arrive in the Winslow area in 1863.[76] It was caused by the failure of the oats crop in Galson, on the northwest coast of Lewis, as a result of heavy rains. When the chamberlain refused to advance seed for the spring planting, eight familes moved further south and the remainder emigrated to Canada. Mary Graham later recalled the six-and-a-half-week voyage from Belfast, after which she and her husband walked the 120 miles from Quebec to their Whitton lot with three small children. John Graham composed poems criticizing the harsh conditions of the land and reportedly died of homesickness in 1876, leaving Mary to raise seven children under the age of sixteen. When she died at the age of 101 in 1929, she still spoke no English and had never left the original homestead.[77]

Most of the Lewis emigrants came from the western shore, where fishing was next to impossible because of the lack of suitable harbours.[78] Lawson claims that those from the parish of Uig tended to migrate to the upper St Francis district, while those from further up the coast in Barvas gravitated toward Bruce County.[79] His *Register* nevertheless identifies a good many families in the Winslow area from Barvas. Indeed, a letter from one of the 1851 immigrants to the Townships states that "all that came from Barvas are here."[80] Furthermore, the Lewis place names that were transferred to the Winslow area as congregational subdistricts – Tolsta, Dell, Galson, and Gisla – were from the northwest coast of the island as well as from Uig.

Munro Mackenzie avoided including in his list of those slated for removal any families with several young children or those whose heads were deemed to be "too old,"[81] but, because whole communities were uprooted, it was not only independent young adults or recently married couples who crossed the Atlantic. In the spring of 1852 the Winslow enumerator recorded that only thirty-one (15 per cent) of the 203 resident Scots were between the ages of twenty-one and thirty. Thirty-three individuals were over forty-one, and one household actually consisted of four generations – the eighty-year-old Ann McLeod and the sixty-year-old Peter McLeod with his wife and three offspring, one of whom had a year-old infant.[82] Lawson's list of Lewis settlers in Quebec does not include kin ties in most cases, but the Highlanders clearly wished to preserve as many family bonds as possible in the new world. Thus the one-hundred-year-old Maryann Morrison remembered her family's departure from Harris (to the immediate south of Lewis) to join an uncle at Lake Megantic in 1888, long after the clearances: "There was lots of immigrants coming over with us. In our family there was my mother, father, sister, and myself, and my grandfather, and my auntie, and she had three children."[83]

Whether or not elements of the traditional clan structure were transferred across the Atlantic would be difficult to judge without extensive genealogical research.[84] The noted decline of the name McAulay in West Uig, and its ubiquity in Winslow, may suggest a selective process of migration, but twenty-two of the twenty-three most popular Lewis names appear in the Winslow records prior to 1881. The internal shifting about caused by the clearances resulted in surnames from one area of Lewis becoming mixed with others, while names of related lines tended to change. When the first contingent of Morrisons moved from Harris to Uig, for example, they adopted the name Smith as that of their hereditary trade. The second contingent became known as Mackinnons because their branch had the Christian name Ceathin, and the final group, who arrived in the 1850s, retained the name Morrison.[85] All three names were found in

Winslow. Indeed, it is quite possible that the traditional subclan links had been sufficiently eroded by clearances and the disappearance of the communal farming system that there was little beyond closely related kin networks left to transfer to the Winslow area at mid-century.[86]

Maureen Molloy suggests that as the impetus for clan-endogamous marriages decreased with the disappearance of jointly leased run-rig farms, families drew closer together with sibling-exchange marriages and marriages between cousins.[87] It appears clear that there was a process of kin-based chain migration taking place to the upper St Francis district. Lawson's *Register* reveals, for example, that eight of the thirty-one McIvers who settled in the area originated from the community of Lower Barvas, from where the original McIver emigrated in 1841. The second and third (one of whom was followed by a nephew) arrived in 1842, the fourth in 1843, the fifth in 1845, and the last three in 1851. Similarly, of the fifteen Murrays to migrate, eight were from Tolsta, the first arriving in 1841 and the last in 1883.

Tangible evidence that kin ties were transferred across the Atlantic to Winslow can also be found in the temporary living arrangements reported by the census enumerator in 1852. To take one example, living in a single cabin were the bachelors John and Murdo Smith with Kenneth McDonald and his wife Catherine Smith, evidently the sister of the first two men. In sum, one can safely conclude, as does Bruce Elliott for the Tipperary Irish in Ontario, that "the location of distant kin, more than soil capability, nearness of markets, and transportation routes influenced the choice of destination."[88]

But the Scots movement from Lewis to the upper St Francis district was not simply a voluntary process of chain migration. In that same cabin noted above one can also find evidence of the social upheaval caused by the evacuation process, for the three additional occupants were females with no resident male next-of-kin: Christy McLean, a sixty-five-year-old widow; Erick McLean, her unmarried twenty-eight-year-old daughter; and the eight-year-old Ann McRae.

Did the Lewis families who emigrated to the Eastern Townships come from a particular stratum within the island's crofter society? It is worth noting that the chamberlain chose families whose rents were furthest in arrears and that the thirty-eight families whom Lawson identifies as having settled in Winslow in 1851 originated from nineteen different communities. Furthermore, Table 1.1 suggests that the stock of those willing to emigrate was worth less than that of the

Table 1.1

Economic Status of Potential Emigrants from Lewis, 1851

	Willing to Emigrate	Not Willing
Number of families	112	184
Individuals	653	112
Average arrear per family	£6/0/0	£10/12/2
Average value of stock	£3/15/9	£5/17/6

Source: Report by the factors of Lewis in British Parliamentary Papers, xxvi (1851), Report to the Board of Supervision by Sir John M'Neill, G.C.B., on the Western Highlands and Islands (hereafter McNeill Report), 1,045.

average family, though it also reveals that they had smaller debts. In the final analysis there was probably little to distinguish the average emigrant from the norm within what was a remarkably homogeneous population. Referring to the Scottish northwest as a whole, economic historian Malcolm Gray writes: "Industry and agriculture intermingled in proportions varying from place to place, but the social pattern remained everywhere the same – that of a smallholding mass in which each man engaged in the combination of activities which happened to be characteristic of the particular locality; the peasantry did not here split its ranks either to provide an upper layer of larger farmers or to throw off a specialized industrial working class."[89]

In the Lewis of 1831, three-quarters of all males from twenty years of age upward occupied a leasehold, but only 2 or 3 per cent of them employed labour (see Appendix A). In 1841, according to the factor, 1,913 tenants paid between £3.3s.9d and £3.12s.3d in rent.[90] By 1851, the average rental for the 2,628 crofter families was only £2.12s.2d. As Table 1.2 shows, three-quarters of the ratepayers in Stornoway, Barvas, and Uig were in the under-£5 category. Another eight hundred householders did not have a lease, but many of these lived in the town of Stornoway, while only a relatively small number worked on large farms or sublet small patches of ground from the crofters. Furthermore, there was little social distinction between these cottars and the crofters who were their neighbours and kinsmen.[91]

At the very least, one can safely conclude that the Lewis emigrants brought little in the way of material resources or commercially oriented agricultural skills to Winslow Township. Furthermore, they were clearly imbued with a strong sense of peasant traditionalism. In 1838 Glasgow statisticians Allan Fullarton and Charles Baird reflected on observations made while administering the Highland relief fund during the previous two years:

Table 1.2
Categories of Ratepayers by Parish in Lewis, 1851

Rents	Stornoway	Barvas	Uig	Lochs	Totals	
Under £5	642	9	337	[no data]	988	(73%)
£5–£10	97	48	46		191	(14%)
£10–£20	65	1	1		67	(5%)
£20–£50	58	2	3		63	(5%)
£50–£100	23	1	6		30	(2%)
£100–£200	6	0	3		9	(1%)
	891	61	396		1,348	(100%)

Source: McNeill Report, 1,040, 1,047, 1,051.

Wherever we turn – let it be to contemplate the case of fine valleys inviting agricultural enterprise, but finding none – myriads of fish darting their way, without interruption, through every creek and channel of this piscatory region – a race of powerful and athletic men, wasting their time and their energies in plying the unwieldy casschrom, or of delicate and virtuous females bending under the pressure of the manure-filled hurdle – in all these cases we see that poverty is, and ever will be, its own aggravation, and that, till the energies of a people are roused and put in motion by the introduction of capital, no material improvement of their condition can be expected.[92]

What Fullarton and Baird failed to note was that capitalism, in the form of the kelp and wool industries, had long since invaded the Islands without adding to the local inhabitants' material welfare or even fundamentally altering their subsistence-oriented household economy.[93] Kelp may have stimulated population growth, but crofters were only a hindrance to sheep-raising, leaving many people with no choice but exile. Those who chose Winslow Township and environs as their destiny were seeking economic independence, but also the perpetuation of traditional social ties and cultural values.[94] In effect, they were rejecting the two basic alternatives that conformity to the norms of a modern capitalist society had to offer: to become either wage-earning proletarians or individualistic pioneers.

THE SEIGNEURIE OF LAUZON

In presenting his case that the historical analysis of the Highland clearances should be placed in a wider perspective, Eric Richards has written:

It is true that some of the circumstances associated with the clearances were very particular to the Scottish Highlands: these include the conditions of clan decline, of political and social humiliation after the defeat of the Jacobite Rebellion, and especially the radiating effects of the industrialization of the British economy in the south. But it is also true that the fundamental elements of the clearances – land hunger, over-population, landlordism, peasant recalcitrance, famine, the effects of modernization forces pitted against a traditional society, the clash of pastoral and arable economies – are all recurrent problems in modern history.[95]

While the St Lawrence Valley is not part of the European context alluded to by Richards, many of these same elements marked the socioeconomic development of its seigneuries after the British Conquest. The taking of Quebec, after all, postdated Culloden by only thirteen years, and the seigneurs did to a certain extent play the role of feudal landlords. Indeed there appears to have been considerable congruity in the timing of expansion and decline within the two economies, a cycle not entirely unrelated to their subordinate status within the British Empire.

Paradoxically, given the great amount of research undertaken into the socioeconomic history of Lower Canada, the question of expansion and contraction remains a very contentious one. Jean-Pierre Wallot and Gilles Paquet originally challenged Fernand Ouellet's claim that the agricultural decline began in the first decade of the nineteenth century, but the discourse has recently shifted to the question of whether there ever actually was an agrarian crisis or not.[96] All agree that wheat exports from Quebec to Great Britain and the West Indies increased rapidly during the years preceding American independence, as well as in the 1790s, and it is clear that there was no sharp drop during the following decade.[97] But Ouellet argues, albeit not entirely successfully, that after 1802 the lion's share of wheat exports came down the St Lawrence from Upper Canada.[98] Furthermore, his emphasis on the poor farming methods of the habitants loses its force in the context of the primitive farming practices characteristic of wheat producers elsewhere in North America.[99] Conceding that farmers to the west did gain an ever-increasing share of exports, Wallot and Paquet have argued that the Lower Canadians were simply turning to the less volatile internal market for oats, barley, and peas, the by-product of a greatly expanded timber industry.[100] More recently, Serge Courville has stressed the significance of the growing industrial village market during the first half of the nineteenth century.[101] Finally, in an attempt to demonstrate that there was increased agricultural commercialization during this period, Wallot and Paquet have analysed post-mortem inventories of Montreal- and Quebec-area habitants, demonstrating a steady upward trend in the value of movable property between 1807–12 and 1832–5.[102]

Quebec historians have yet to study the structural impact of the climatically induced crop failures of the 1810s or the decimation of the wheat harvests in the mid-1830s, but it is significant that the census reports demonstrate no marked increase in the potato ratio (about 46 per cent by volume) after 1827.[103] Instead, while wheat production dropped from 21 per cent of all crops in 1831 to 4 per cent in 1844, the oats ratio increased markedly, from 20 per cent in 1831 to 34 per cent in 1844.[104] Since there is no evidence to suggest that oats was a significant item in the habitants' diet, most of it was presumably destined for the market-place. The square-timber trade to Britain may have been on the decline, but the new American demand for lumber must have rescued the shanty market, and the government was employing hundreds of immigrants in a major program of canal construction.[105] With the increase in oats rather than potato production, the habitants could not only appease the curés and seigneurs by growing a commercial crop, but they could also avoid a further change in diet by using the cash from its sale to purchase wheat and flour from Upper Canada. Significantly, Lower Canada became the chief export market for Upper Canadian wheat during the 1830s.[106]

The habitants' rejection of subsistence agriculture was fortunate for them because the potato blight destroyed a large proportion of the province's crops in the mid-to-late 1840s.[107] In the fall of 1845, the Quebec Board of Trade requested that potatoes from the Maritimes be admitted duty-free throughout the following year, but, in their responses to an official questionnaire in the spring of 1846, the province's agricultural societies gave no indication of severe hardship.[108] It appears that the only petitions for government assistance came from the Gaspé region.[109] At the same time, with American cereal grains being imported duty-free after 1842, and with the Montreal price of oats fixed at no more than a third that of wheat, the 1830s and 1840s were obviously years of mounting debt for many.[110] In the words of geographer Serge Courville, "les malaises enregistrés par les chroniqueurs témoignent plus d'une crise du monde rural que d'une crise agricole comme telle."[111]

The seigneurs did not have the arbitrary eviction powers of Highland landlords, but the sudden exodus from the seigneuries during the 1840s is not difficult to explain, given the precarious economic situation of the rapidly growing population.[112] Between 1844 and 1849, some 20,000 Lower Canadians moved to the United States, a migration that would only accelerate as the century went on.[113] But the exodus was also a product of farm consolidation, particularly after the dramatic opening of the American market in 1849.[114] The average farm in Canada East grew dramatically, from 58.6 arpents in 1844 to 84.6 arpents in 1851, with cleared land increasing from 23.3 to 37.6 arpents.[115]

Who were the exiled families, and which ones moved south to the frontier townships rather than leaving the province entirely? A definitive answer would be impossible without a detailed genealogical study, but certain characteristics of the colonists are known or can be surmised. Within the colonization-roads zone of the Eastern Townships, most of the settlers in Wotton and Stratford were from South Shore parishes in the Trois-Rivières district, while the majority in Garthby were former Quebec City labourers pushed out by the disastrous depression in the timber market.[116] As for Winslow, the small group of francophones in the southern part of the township was an extension of the neighbouring Stratford settlement, largely from St Grégoire and of Acadian descent, while those in the north, according to the curé in 1874, came from "des paroisses qui avoisinent Québec."[117]

These Quebec-area parishes were on the South Shore of the St Lawrence River, which acted as a sharp dividing line between colonization on the northern and southern frontiers of the province. Thus, the majority of settlers in the Saguenay–Lac St Jean region originated in Charlevoix County, northeast of Quebec,[118] while Catholic marriage records identify most of the home parishes for Winslow North settlers to be located in what were then the counties of Dorchester and Bellechasse. They migrated to Winslow along the Lambton Road, built during the 1840s to link the upper St Francis district of the Eastern Townships with the Chaudière Valley and Quebec.[119] Of those thirty-two settlers in Winslow North in 1852 whose places of marriage could be located, twelve had been wed in the Dorchester seigneurie of Lauzon – all but one of these in younger, southern parishes – and an additional five further east in the neighbouring county of Bellechasse.

The remaining thirteen settlers had been married in the parish of Lambton, whose boundaries included Winslow North during the late 1840s (see Map 4). Genealogical records reveal the birthplaces of twenty-three of the partners in these thirteen marriages. Eighteen were born in Bellechasse, and five in the interior parish of St Henri de Lauzon.[120] It is likely that some of those who were natives of Bellechasse had as children accompanied their parents to the back country of Lauzon, before themselves continuing the southward

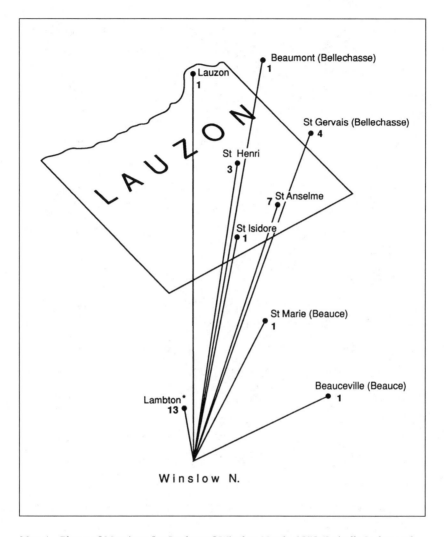

Map 4   Places of Marriage for Settlers of Winslow North, 1852 (Loiselle Index and Rivest Index, Montreal Bibliothèque nationale; Frère Eloi-Gérard, *Recueil de généalogies des comtés de Beauce-Dorchester-Frontenac 1625–1946*, Collège du Sacré Coeur, Beauceville, Quebec)
* Most of these individuals were living in Winslow because it was part of Lambton parish.

migration process. Certainly, Lauzon appears as the chief source of settlers when one identifies the places of residence for the parents of all those married in the parish of St Romain (Winslow North) between 1851 and 1870. Aside from the majority of parental couples

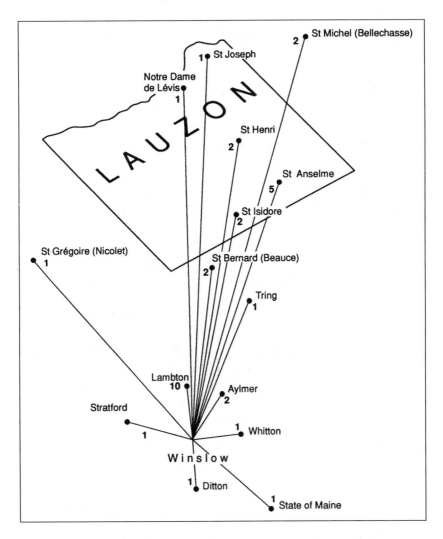

Map 5   External Parental Residences of Marriage Partners in St Romain de Winslow, 1851–70 (Parish Registers of St Vital de Lambton and St Romain de Winslow, Archives nationales du Québec à Sherbrooke)

who lived in Winslow and its neighbouring townships, eleven were recorded as residing in Lauzon, two in Bellechasse, and three further south in the Beauce district (see Map 5).[121]

The settlement of Lauzon, whose soil was considered to be of superior quality, dates back to the earliest years of the French régime.[122]

In 1636, the year after Champlain's death, the Company of New France granted the tract en seigneurie to Jean de Lauzon, an influential nobleman in the court of Louis XIII. Lauzon's energies were absorbed by his French intendancies until he was named governor of the struggling colony in 1651.[123] Only then did settlement of the seigneurie begin in earnest. By 1706, however, there were still only about 400 individuals in the seigneurie, and as late as 1723 less than a dozen families had settled on the second range parallel to the St Lawrence.[124] Colonization had nevertheless begun to move up the Etchemin and Chaudière valleys by the time of the Conquest, when Lauzon was purchased by Governor James Murray. The seigneurie's administration was neglected until it was leased by the energetic Major Henry Caldwell in 1774, but local unrest and military occupation during the American Revolution delayed development for yet another decade. Though he did not become proprietor until 1801, Caldwell pursued an ambitious colonization policy during the last fifteen years of the century.

According to the seigneurie's historian, J.-Edmond Roy, roads were built, rivers were channelled for log drives, saw and grist mills were established, and the growth of villages was stimulated. The population tripled between 1774 and 1801, a situation that Caldwell did not hesitate to take advantage of by raising the annual "rentes" on new grants and adding restrictions that contravened the spirit of the seigneurial system. In addition to enforcing the grist mill monopoly, he required all new grantees to clear four arpents a year for ten consecutive years; maintain perpetual residence on the land on pain of automatic retrocession; forfeit without recompense all lumber, rock, and other materials required for construction of ecclesiastical or manorial buildings; reserve all limestone and minerals for the seigneur; and surrender at its agricultural value any land up to six arpents required for mills or mines. After 1806 the censitaires' land titles were renewed only on condition that oak be reserved for export to British shipyards.[125] As one of the largest landholders in the province, Henry Caldwell clearly enjoyed playing the grand seigneur. Witnesses later recollected seeing his retinue of notary, surveyor, and domestics negotiating Lauzon's difficult roads in a custom-built carriage, fitted with triple springs and upholstered with soft cushions.[126]

More resentful than deferential, the censitaires of Lauzon were not immune to the revolutionary propaganda emanating from the Thirteen Colonies and France at this time. They turned a deaf ear to the militia muster in 1794 and forcefully resisted the reformed road laws in 1797. Because of the growth of the liberal-nationalist opposition, Henry's son John could no longer take for granted election to the legislative assembly, but he did replace his deceased father in the appointed legislative council in 1812.[127]

The younger Caldwell proved to be much more interested in business than in feudal trappings, prudently abandoning his father's unpopular English innovations of planting the May Pole and demanding two or three days of labour on the manor each year. John took over the management of Lauzon at the turn of the century, just when the square timber trade was beginning to boom. Like the Christies in the upper Richelieu, he focused his energies on that industry rather than on colonization, being particularly careful to horde all saw mill sites in the seigneurie despite the fact that this was illegal.[128] As a result, the granting of back-country land concessions slowed considerably, while in the old parish of Pointe-Lévis the commercial centres of New Liverpool and Aubigny (future Lévis) sprang up at the mouths of the Chaudière and Etchemin rivers, respectively.[129]

Having replaced his father as receiver-general for Lower Canada in 1808, Caldwell was able to finance his ambitious development projects with provincial revenues held in trust – a practice that landed him in trouble when timber prices declined and wheat crops failed in the early 1820s. In arrears by over £219,000, Caldwell was dismissed from office in 1823. The seigneurie of Lauzon was finally seized by the sheriff in 1826, but Caldwell's judicial appeals were not settled until 1833, and his claims were not finally dismissed until 1834.[130]

In the mean time, Caldwell continued to lease Lauzon at £2,000 per year. His aim was to recoup his financial solvency by pillaging crown timber in the unsettled townships to the rear of the seigneurie. Whether by design or not, the Government had conveniently made this timber available by appointing his partner and brother-in-law, John Davidson, superintendent of crown forests. According to Roy, Caldwell and Davidson stripped the pine all the way to the source of the Etchemin River, more than fifty miles from its mouth at the St Lawrence. This strategy collapsed, however, after Britain lowered its tariffs against the Baltic countries. In 1845, when the government purchased Lauzon at a sheriff's auction, it had to invest £6,200 to restore the mills to operating order.[131]

Not surprisingly, John Caldwell had become very exacting in his collection of the "rentes," which he raised substantially and made payable in wheat in order to take advantage of the inflation in prices. Whereas Henry Caldwell had charged 4 s. for each thirty arpents of land, by 1820 rents had increased to 1½ minots of wheat, worth 7½ s.[132] According to Courville's analysis of the 1831 census, Lauzon's "rentes" varied from an average of 3½ s. to slightly over 5 s. for thirty arpents, with no clear distinction between the St Lawrence parishes and those in the interior.[133] The census nevertheless does record sharp variations from lot to lot, even within the same ranges. The censitaires of St Nicholas parish were soon petitioning against the seigneurial system itself, arguing that they received nothing in return for their payments. Caldwell presumably lacked the finances to develop the rear concessions, particularly when it would take years to recoup such an investment from the additional ratepayers.[134] In 1830 Surveyor-General Bouchette reported that plenty of good land remained in the interior, yet farms were overcrowded at Pointe-Lévis and youths were taking long journeys from which few ever returned.[135] Settlement did begin to expand during the early 1830s, but Caldwell did not even bother to reconstitute the rent roll destroyed by fire in 1834.[136]

The growth of Lauzon's rural population can be traced in census reports from 1831 onward. Parish boundaries did shift considerably during the twenty years up to mid-century, but it appears that with one exception those boundaries remained confined within the seigneurie.[137] The major problem one encounters when attempting to compare data from the several census reports prior to mid-century is the absence of a distinct category for farmers or farming landholders. In 1831, 1842, and 1844, families were simply divided into proprietors and non-proprietors of real property, which is of no use whatever in any attempt to discover the characteristics of a typical agricultural unit. The 1852 census is much more helpful, with its categorization of occupants according to size of landholdings. The result is that one can determine the number of families actually on the land and even eliminate most non-farmers by subtracting the number holding ten arpents or less.[138]

The only way to acquire comparable statistics from previous census reports is to turn to the manuscript versions and add up the number of families listed with eleven arpents or more. Without resorting to the additional, time-consuming task of tracing and eliminating the acreages and agricultural production of all other families, one is left with slightly inflated figures for mean farm sizes and production, particularly in potatoes and livestock. Nevertheless, this method permits us to attribute at least some meaning to the resulting averages for 1831 and 1842 (the 1844 manuscript census no longer exists), which can be compared quite confidently with those of 1852. Farms on Quebec's South Shore had apparently been growing smaller after 1812, but one can see from Table 1.3 that this trend was not marked in Lauzon from 1831 onward, despite the steady increase in the num-

Table 1.3

The Family Farm in the Seigneurie of Lauzon, 1831, 1842, 1852

	1831	*1842*	*1852*
Occupants with more than 10 arpents	1,347	1,688	1,810
Land occupied (arpents)	107.3	94.0	99.1
Land improved (arpents)	38.1	38.5	46.8

Sources: Lower Canada/Canada, manuscript census, Lauzon parishes in Dorchester County, 1831, 1842, 1852.

ber of occupants with more than ten arpents.[139] Lauzon may have been a centrally located seigneurie, and nearly two centuries old, but its colonization actually accelerated during the 1830s and 1840s, when land under occupation increased by 24 per cent, and land under improvement by 65 per cent.

Table 1.4 demonstrates further that – as we saw for the province as a whole – there was no major shift to potatoes in response to the three consecutive wheat-crop failures beginning in the fall of 1831.[140] The average farm's loss of forty minots in wheat production between 1831 and 1842 was compensated by an increase of forty-four minots in oats and only twenty-three minots in potatoes. By 1852, potato production for the average farm was down to its 1831 level, but oats had increased by another forty-three minots, and wheat had recovered by fourteen-and-a-half minots. Cattle and sheep also registered a significant increase between 1842 and 1852.

The average Lauzon farm family was clearly in a better economic position in 1852 than it had been for quite some time. Oats may have sold for no more than one-third the cost of wheat on the urban market-place, but Table 1.5 demonstrates that it gave twice the yield. Most of the oats was presumably being sold for fodder in the timber shanties, because there was only one oatmeal mill listed for Lauzon in 1844. (The 1852 industrial schedules have been lost.) Production of potatoes and grains (with oats not included) was adequate to cover a diet equivalent to that of the average habitant family in the Lower Richelieu Valley, where adults consumed (in addition to meat) about fifteen minots of wheat and fifteen minots of potatoes per year.[141]

But does this picture of the "average" farm family actually have much meaning in a place where winter labour in the seigneur's lumber operations may have allowed some censitaires to maintain subsistence-oriented farms, while others were becoming increasingly market-oriented?[142] Certainly Table 1.6 demonstrates a broad range in

Table 1.4

Agricultural Production per Farm Family in Lauzon, 1831, 1842, 1852

	1831	1842	1852
Wheat (min.)	43.1	3.2	17.6
Oats (min.)	64.6	108.3	151.1
Barley (min.)	1.9	2.6	0.8
Rye (min.)	1.6	3.3	2.8
Peas (min.)	9.6	8.6	10.3
Buckwheat (min.)	0.1	0.7	0.3
Indian Corn (min.)	0	0	0
Potatoes (min.)	98.7	121.7	97.2
Turnips (min.)	–	–	0.8
Flax & Hemp (lb)	–	–	15.0
Hay (tons)*	–	–	9.4
Tobacco (lb)	–	–	0.4
Maple Sugar (lb)	–	14.9	22.4
Cattle	7.1	6.1	7.5
Horses	1.6	1.5	1.5
Sheep	9.9	5.9	7.2
Pigs	5.1	3.0	3.3
Butter	–	–	142.7

Sources: Lower Canada, *Journals of the Legislative Assembly*, XLI (1831–2), Appendix Oo; Canada, manuscript census, 1842; Canada, *Census Reports*, 1852.
*Calculated at one bundle = 16 lb.

the size of Lauzon's land units in 1852. However, acreage owned by peasants in many societies tended to fluctuate according to the developmental cycle of the family. Each household would attempt to acquire extra land at one stage in its history in order to provide for as many sons as possible once they reached maturity.[143] Thus Paquet and Wallot have found that between 1792 and 1835 larger families consistently had more land than did smaller ones.[144] Fifty arpents was probably close to the minimum required to support a family in most parishes, while one family's labour would not normally be able to exploit more than 250 arpents. According to Table 1.6, therefore, at least three-quarters of Lauzon's farms fell within the self-supportive, family-based range. It does not follow that they were indifferent to agricultural markets, but only 5 per cent of the farms had more than 200 arpents.

Sylvie Dépatie and Christian Dessureault report similar categorizations for pre-1781 Ile Jésus and pre-1815 St Hyacinthe, respec-

Table 1.5
Crop Yields (Minots/Arpent) in Lauzon, 1852

	Wheat	Barley	Rye	Peas	Oats	Buckwheat	Potatoes	Turnips
Yield	6.8	8.3	7.4	7.9	14.0	7.9	129.1	74.3

Source: Canada, Census Reports, 1852.

Table 1.6
Land Occupation by Size Category in Lauzon, 1852

Arpents	10−	10–20	20–50	50–100	100–200	200+	Total
Occupants	117	27	229	1,049	412	97	1,931
Ratio	6.1	1.4	11.9	54.3	21.3	5.0	100.0

Source: Canada, Census Reports, 1852.

tively, yet they posit a distinct hierarchy within these peasant societies. Dépatie bases her argument on the wide discrepancy in quantities of land under improvement, which to her demonstrates considerable disparities in production capacity within the agricultural community. She makes no attempt, however, to account for family life cycles or for the length of time the various parcels of land were under cultivation. Her data show that homogeneity in the number of arpents under production increased as the seigneurie's undeveloped arable land disappeared.[145] Dessureault does attempt to account for the family life cycles of his study group by measuring all assets (apart from land and buildings) recorded in post-mortem inventories and categorizing them according to number of years married at the time of death. That he would find a broad distribution of family fortunes within each of his length-of-marriage categories is not too surprising, however, given that half the average inheritance was based on grain stocks and cattle.[146] Holdings of these commodities would vary widely with the seasons, making a family appear much poorer in the spring than in the fall.[147]

If there was a strong trend toward economic polarization within habitant society, one would assume that the material range discovered by Dessureault for the young seigneurie of St Hyacinthe would be still wider some four decades later in an older, more centrally located seigneurie such as Lauzon. Detailed research in the notarial archives would be necessary to duplicate Dessureault's complex method, but it is a simple matter to check the manuscript agricultural census for those farmers who did not own draft animals, which Dessureault interprets as the key variable separating dependent from independent households.

Significantly, where half the St Hyacinthe peasants did not list oxen in their post-mortem inventories, and 17 per cent had no adult horses, the situation was very different in Lauzon at mid-century.[148] In the parish of St Henri, for example, two-thirds of the farm families reported owning oxen (steers and bulls are included in the category) *and* horses, while nearly all the others had one or more horses. While the average household had 4.1 draft animals, only thirteen of 336 (or 4 per cent) had none. Even accounting for animals too young to work, there appears to have been little distinction among St Henri's farm families in terms of access to these fundamental sources of labour power.

While he stresses that the average farm family aimed to market as much surplus production as possible, Dessureault does admit that the goal was also to keep purchases to a minimum: "Ce dernier objectif constitue en quelque sorte un frein à la spécialisation de l'exploitation paysanne et à son intégration dans l'économie englobante."[149] Thus, to return to Table 1.4, we see a remarkable stability in agricultural production over the twenty-one-year period from 1831 to 1852, apart from fluctuation in the "cash" crops of wheat and oats. We also observe significant production of maple syrup, tobacco, and flax, all products designed to preclude purchases of relatively expensive import items. Finally, in contrast to Lower Canada as a whole, there was a steady increase in homespun production, from 12.2 yards per family in 1842, to 18.7 yards in 1844 and 23.2 yards in 1852, despite the ready availability of imported textiles.[150]

Questionable though some census categorizations in Table 1.7 may be (note the fluctuation in numbers of paupers between 1842 and 1844), they do demonstrate the clear dominance of independent family production. Farm labourers were relatively few in number; indigence, even in this difficult economic period, was apparently exceptional; and four-fifths of the families owned their own farms. Furthermore, Greer has suggested that most tenant farmers in the communities he studied (where leasehold was much more common) were simply renting on a temporary basis as part of their inheritance settlement.

A more basic social distinction would have been found between the farmer and the village or town dweller.[151] As Table 1.8 suggests, it was primarily the non-rural population that was increasing in Lauzon during the 1840s. Between 1842 and 1852 the number of families with fewer than ten arpents grew by 296, which was 70 per cent of

Table 1.7

Non-Proprietors, Servants, and Paupers in Lauzon, 1831, 1842, 1844

	1831	1842	1844
Non-proprietors	342	577	528
Ratio of total families	18%	21%	21%
Male farm servants	0	186	102
Other servants – male	} 13	175	38
– female		239	109
Paupers	115	346	27
Total population	11,946	15,883	15,834

Sources: Lower Canada, *Journals of the Legislative Assembly*, XLI (1831–2), Appendix Oo; Canada, manuscript census, 1842; Province of Canada, *Journals of the Legislative Assembly*, V (1846), Appendix D.

the total expansion. Of the 1,330 familes who had less than ten arpents in 1852, only 117 are listed as occupants of agricultural units (see Table 1.6), making it clear that approximately 40 per cent of Lauzon's families held no more than town lots. The greatest population increase between 1842 and 1851 took place in the Lévis–St Jean Chrysostome parishes, which were directly across the river from the port of Quebec. The town of Lévis had been a shipbuilding centre since 1830, when the Davie dry docks had been established, but the move to free trade in Britain inevitably brought an employment crisis.

In the summer of 1848, at a meeting of the newly formed Association des Townships, P.J.O. Chauveau moved: "Que le manque actuel de travail et la famine déja commencé qui menacent d'envahir la société l'hiver prochain, rendent impérieux le besoin de coloniser les townships ou serait envoyé la partie de notre population qui manque de travail."[152] Chauveau's official committee to investigate emigration to the United States reported the following spring that an exodus was taking place from the rural area around Quebec City. [153] During the following five or six years, however, the town would experience a shipbuilding boom stimulated by gold rushes in California and Australia as well as by the Crimean War.[154]

While the recovery did not come soon enough to prevent Quebec ship labourers from colonizing Garthby Township, as noted above, it appears unlikely that many of Winslow's settlers came from the wage-earning sector of Lauzon society.[155] The young ages of the settlers enumerated in the 1852 census suggest that many were sons and daughters of established farmers, rather than wage-earners squeezed

Table 1.8
Families with Less than Ten Arpents, Lauzon, 1831, 1842, and 1852

	Total No. of Families	Families with 0–10 arpents
1831	1,941	594 (31%)
1842	2,722	1,034 (38%)
1852	3,144	1,330 (42%)

Sources: Lower Canada/Canada, manuscript census, Lauzon parishes in Dorchester County, 1831, 1842, 1852.

out by a faltering industrial economy. In sharp contrast to their Scots counterparts, only twenty-one of forty-eight French-Canadian married males were over thirty-one years of age, and thirty-two of fifty-nine families had no more than two children (see Table 1.9).[156]

We have already seen that the marriage records point to the rural interior parishes as the primary source of population. Antoine Roy's family would appear to have been typical. His ancestors gradually worked their way inland from the Ile d'Orleans, where the original immigrant couple had settled in the seventeenth century, to the South Shore in the early eighteenth century, and southward again to St Henri de Lauzon by the early nineteenth century. When Antoine married in 1851, he was living still further up the Etchemin River, at St Anselme de Lauzon, but a daughter was born in Winslow in 1860.[157] Whether the majority of the French-Canadian settlers came from the poorer segment of Lauzon's peasant society cannot be determined at this point, but social distinctions probably were not great, and even the more affluent peasant families would not have been able to establish all their offspring close to home.

Only a detailed genealogical study could establish the kinship ties of the French-Canadian pioneer families in Winslow, but an intricate web of cognatic and agnatic family ties is strongly suggested by the linkages between family names shown in Map 6. Had the enumerator listed maiden names for more than this particular section of the township, connections would clearly have been still more widespread.[158] The migration of closely related families must have facilitated mutual family assistance, thereby helping to explain how so many of the French Canadians were able to become colonists while their children were still too young to be of much assistance (almost two-thirds of the population was under ten years old).[159]

Despite their contrasting geographical and cultural backgrounds, the French Canadians and Highland Scots of Winslow Township did

Table 1.9
Family Characteristics of Scots and French Canadians in Winslow, 1852

	Age of Married Men						
	20–30	31–40	41–50	51–60	61+	Total	Average Age
Scots	6	7	11	5	1	30	42.1
French Canadian	27	10	5	4	2	48	33.8

	Number of Unmarried Offspring per Family						
	0	1–2	3–4	5–6	7–8	Total	Average
Scots	9	3	4	11	5	119	3.7
French Canadian	15	17	7	5	5	115	2.3

Source: Canada, manuscript census, 1852, Winslow Township.

share a strong sense of cultural conservatism. Both groups were involuntary exiles, in a sense, with little choice but to leave their native parishes once the wheat and potato crops began to fail. The Highlanders were joining relatives and friends in an isolated backwater, while the French Canadians were following a road that led directly from their home parishes and kept them in occasional contact with their former neighbours. The forces of modernization certainly clashed more brutally with traditional cultural values and social structures in the Hebrides than in the St Lawrence Valley. The French Canadians were not subjected to dispossession, they enjoyed freer access to the market-place, and they were successfully resisting increased dependence on potatoes even before the blight struck Canada East. It is also strenuously argued by the nationalist school of Quebec historians that the habitants had been effectively driven by market demand since before the start of the nineteenth century. The admittedly rather tentative analysis of the 1830s and 1840s presented here does suggest that the hard-pressed habitants rejected the path taken earlier by the Irish and the Scots Highlanders toward a more narrowly subsistence-oriented agriculture and that there was much greater diversification in the size of the habitants' land holdings, but also that at mid-century the rural economy of Lauzon was still characterized essentially by family-oriented production and consumption. Even the Highlanders had a long traditional link with the market place, raising cattle and harvesting kelp to pay for their rents, but it does not follow that they were commercially oriented producers.

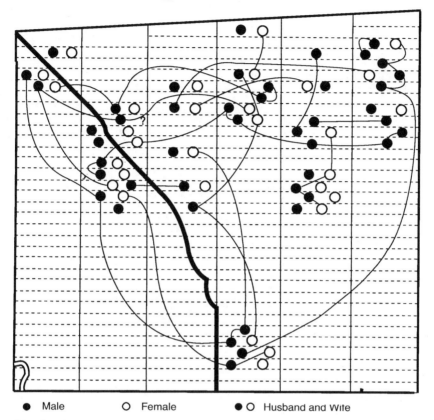

Map 6   Linkages between Family Names, Winslow North, 1852 (Canada, manuscript census, 1852)

Some of the crofters and habitants also participated in the wage-labour economy by engaging in the fishing and forest industries, respectively, but the seasonal nature of these occupations kept them tied to the land and to their cultural traditions. Furthermore, while the censitaires of Lower Canada enjoyed much stronger property rights than did the Highland tenants, the seigneurial system of tenure did perpetuate their exploitation within an essentially feudal framework. By mid-century the annual cens et rentes payable by the Lauzon censitaires amounted to approximately $5,550, and the mutation fines (lods et ventes) collected from July 1846 to December 1848 totalled $4,492.[160] Finally, the Lauzon seigneur's control over land appropriations and the operation of mills affected the pace of economic development.[161] That control would disappear in 1854, with the abolition of seigneurial tenure, by which time Lauzon's relatively large farms were in a good position to take advantage of the rapidly expanding local and American markets. The isle of Lewis would remain much more resistant to the forces of industrial capitalism. The following chapters will examine whether the same would hold true for the crofter settlers of Winslow vis-à-vis their French-Canadian neighbours.

CHAPTER TWO

Settlement

Winslow Township appears to have been the final destination for the majority of the 400 Scots who migrated to the Eastern Townships from Lewis in 1851. Most of them spent their first winter in neighbouring Lingwick, however, for the Scots had only begun to clear land in southern Winslow a year earlier. In the spring of 1852, the census enumerator found only 203 Scots in the township. As for the French Canadians, several families squatted at the northern tip of Winslow before it was officially opened to settlement, and in 1850 a few others began improving claims near the Stratford boundary to the southeast. They had arrived prior to the Scots, then, but French Canadians still numbered only 251 in the spring of 1852, according to the official census.

As of 1852, the two French-Canadian groups and the Scots were living beyond the termini of the colonization roads which they had followed from three different directions. These roads were the central focus of the government-and-church-sponsored colonization project which had been launched in 1848 to open up the large territory from Wotton Township to Lake St Francis and Lake Megantic. While the project was promoted with considerable nationalist fanfare as the solution to overcrowded conditions in the seigneuries, the reality for the settlers was more sobering. The local crown lands agent helped to keep them from starving, but he also enforced the misguided state policy of limiting free grants to fifty acres per family. Despite the arduous and restrictive conditions, the two ethnic groups nevertheless did manage to pursue somewhat different strategies of land acquisition, strategies that were linked to their respective roles in the local agri-forestry economy.

COLONIZATION ROADS

Winslow Township was in the hands of the crown when the settlement project of 1848 was conceived, but it had not been completely ignored by potential colonization agents. Americans had begun petitioning for the township as soon as the region as a whole had been officially opened to settlement in 1792. Two prospective township leaders, Theophilus Woodward and Bohurn Shepard from Fairhaven, Vermont, received a warrant of survey on the part of themselves and their associates in August 1792, but by 1794 they had still not advanced the survey money. A year later, after the oaths commissioners stationed at Missisquoi Bay on the Vermont border failed to recommend the two men as dependable prospects, their application was formally rejected.[1]

The next candidate was James Watson Jr, who justified his application as township leader by claiming that he had not been compensated for serving the British cause during the War of Independence. The oaths commissioners recommended Watson, but because they reported no knowledge of his thirty-nine associates, the executive council's land committee moved that he receive 1,200 acres, and his associates only 200 acres each, at least for the time being. Without a 1,200-acre grant for each of the forty applicants (the official limit an individual could claim), the leader would not be able to reclaim the thousand acres from each associate that would cover his expenses for lobbying, surveying, and establishing a rudimentary economic infrastructure in the township, not to mention his chances for a future profit on the speculation. In the end, Watson settled for a 200-acre lot in the much more advantageously located Hemmingford area, south of Montreal.[2]

In 1796, Treadway Thomas Odber of Quebec petitioned for Winslow, only to be informed that it was not vacant.[3] Though sizeable chunks of neighbouring townships were granted by the government around 1800, Odber's was the last private petition to be considered for Winslow.[4] In 1835 it became the northernmost township to be included in the British American Land Co.'s unsurveyed St Francis Tract. Because the company's ambitious but misdirected efforts in the isolated tract brought it close to bankruptcy, most of the territory, including Winslow, reverted to the crown in 1841.[5]

The British American Land Co.'s roads had not reached as far north as Winslow, while, from the other direction, the thirty-five-mile Lambton Road, built from the Chaudière Valley by the still-born Quebec and Megantic Land Co. had not reached quite this far south.[6] In 1841 Governor-General Poulet Thomson (later Lord Sydenham) sanctioned a grant to make the primitive Lambton Road passable for carts in the summer. Like his predecessor, Lord Durham, he assumed that the road would draw British immigrants to the frontier lying between the American-settled townships and the seigneuries south of Quebec. Thomson also offered free fifty-acre lots alongside the road, thereby setting aside his Wakefieldian belief that access to crown lands should be restricted to those with capital. Contrary to his imperialist design, however, the only permanent settlers to arrive were habitants from the overcrowded seigneurial parishes. In 1844 there were 123 French Canadians in Lambton and Forsyth townships, to the immediate north of Winslow. The thirty British colonists also enumerated that year had deserted the area by mid-century.

Their early departure is not surprising: in 1846, 221 petitioners complained that floods had destroyed much of the Lambton Road, that twelve to fifteen miles remained too narrow to preserve from rapid deterioration, and that rocks in other places made the route impracticable. The settlers stated that they had attempted repairs but that the task was too formidable because large barren sections would always remain uninhabited. Further, a bridge was needed to provide access to the Kennebec Road, the only Chaudière link to Quebec. The government rejected the petition, allowing road conditions to deteriorate: by 1850 families were reported to be subsisting on wild herbs and berries during most of the summer.

Their numbers nevertheless continued to grow, reaching 1,254 in Lambton, Forsyth, Aylmer, and Price by 1851. For two more years the government would remain deaf to their threats to emigrate en masse to the United States. It is difficult to assess whether the habitants felt that they had crossed a key threshold when moving from the seigneuries to the townships, but the new land-tenure system was clearly not in itself a major obstacle to expansion from Lauzon and Bellechasse to the Lake St Francis area. Indeed, the promise of freehold tenure was probably one of the main attractions for families moving into the district.

The failure of provincial authorities to respond to settlers' demands certainly did not reflect indifference toward expansion of settlement, for in 1848 Louis-Hyppolite LaFontaine's government had launched an ambitious colonization roads project just south of Lambton.[7] The government was initially stimulated by the political threat of a joint colonization venture between the Catholic church and the radical nationalist Institut canadien. The ultramontane Bishop Ignace Bourget of Montreal and anti-clerical members of the Institut may have made strange bedfellows, but their co-sponsorship of the Association pour l'établissement des Canadiens-français dans les Townships du Bas-Canada forced the hand of the ruling Reform party.

LaFontaine's lieutenants aggravated the political dissension which ultimately caused the association's downfall, while Governor-General Lord Elgin acquired a £20,000 grant from Britain as compensation for the expenses incurred in fighting the typhus epidemic among the previous year's immigrants. The Montreal branch of the Association des Townships did survive long enough to negotiate an agreement with the British American Land Co. whereby a successful colony was founded in the advantageously located Roxton Township. The less ideologically divided Quebec branch co-operated with the government instead in its project to colonize the isolated townships of the upper St Francis Valley.

The association's self-appointed role was to promote the project in the seigneurial parishes, build churches and schools, provide priests and teachers, and generally safeguard the colonists' moral interests. The goal of the government was to extend the Lambton Road nineteen miles southward from Lake St Francis to the terminus of the British American Land Co.'s Otter Brook Road in Hampden Township and to build a forty-two-mile artery from the Gosford Road, starting a few miles west of Lake Aylmer and heading eastward to Lake Megantic. These two roads would intersect in Winslow Township, at the site of the future village of Stornoway (see Map 1). Thus, at one blow, communications lines would be pushed into the most remote corner of the Eastern Townships.

In keeping with the earlier construction of the Lambton Road, the government was less concerned about quality than mileage covered. The new roads were supposed to be simply lines cleared of trees to a width of twelve yards, with bridges and causeways hastily constructed where necessary. Improvements were to be left to the settlers, who, again as with the Lambton Road, would be attracted by the offer of fifty free acres alongside the main arteries. Settlers also apparently had a five-year option to purchase an additional two lots at the standard price of eighty cents per acre, but only on the rear concessions.[8] Given the narrow survey pattern of each lot, even a fifty-acre extension would have been impracticable to operate. The government was clearly anticipating that lots on the back ranges would be taken by later arrivals, including the pioneers' own offspring, for it promised not to increase the price in the future (in fact it reduced the rate to sixty cents an acre). Its prospectus stated that "increase in the numbers of the people of the province, and the consequent rapid increase in the public strength and resources, are objects of more value than the price which can be derived from the sale of territory of the Crown."[9]

The immediate problem was the condition of the very trunk routes with which the new roads were to connect. The British American Land Co.'s Otter Brook Road simply ended in uninhabited wilderness, and eight to ten miles of its parallel St Francis Road to the village of Robinson (and thus to Sherbrooke) were not even negotiable on horseback. As for the links to Quebec, not only was the Lambton Road virtually impassable in many spots, as we have seen, but the section of the Gosford Road between Ireland and Dudswell townships traversed some forty miles of unsettled territory. The government colonization agent would complain that the condition of this principal access route made carters charge exorbitant prices to transport colonists' effects. The government was effectively leap-frogging the settlement frontier line on the principle that it should not contribute to the maintenance of roads in privately owned territory. However, the state lacked the will to tackle the non-resident proprietors directly, and it had still not devised an effective municipal system to raise local taxes from absentees as well as from residents in sparsely settled areas.[10] The result would be years of suffering and hardship for the land-hungry colonists attracted by the offer of free crown lots and the widespread publicity campaign of the Association des Townships.

In early August 1848, notices appeared in the press advertising free fifty-acre lots to settlers eighteen years and older. "Particularly invited" were "Canadians who cannot now obtain lands in the Seigniories." Settlers were to report to the resident agent, a surveyor and former MLA for Yamaska named Jean-Olivier Arcand. Arcand supervised the spending of slightly more than £1,000 on road work during the fall of 1848. A stretch of twelve miles was slashed from the Gosford Road to Lake Aylmer, and an eighteen-mile link was extended in the opposite direction to Shipton Township, where it joined the older Craig Road. This originally unplanned link would attract settlers from the Trois-Rivières district, as well as provide indirect access to Quebec, Montreal, and Sherbrooke. Primitive as the road lines were, by December they had attracted 230 families, half of whom were located in Wotton, the first township on the Craig–Gosford connection. With so many mouths to feed, Arcand had to devote the limited funds provided by the colonization society to seed grain rather than construction of chapels.

During the 1849 season an additional £2,600 was devoted to improving the rough-cut roads of the previous year. Arcand reported that completion of a road involved removing all roots and rocks, spreading gravel, digging a parallel three-foot ditch, clearing trees to a width of twenty-five feet on either side, and constructing bridges and causeways. The government had presumably come to realize the impracticality of its original plan to slash narrow paths into the wilderness.

Despite road improvements, settlement became still more sharply concentrated in Wotton, though Arcand reported with considerable displeasure that sixty of Winslow's lots had fallen to Highland Scots in October. These claimants must have still been living on British American Land Co. territory in neighbouring Lingwick and Bury, because the thirty-three Scots reported by Arcand in the fall of 1850 were all absentees.[11] Unfortunately for the settlers, the combination of June seeding and a late August frost destroyed most of their crops, leaving them dependent on the provisions that the agent had gathered for the following year's road work. Despite Arcand's prediction that the twenty-nine miles of new roads would be doubled in 1850, he managed to add only another twelve-and-a-half miles, extending the Megantic Road from Garthby eastward into Stratford (mistakenly identified as Thetford on Map 7).

At this point, the government's subsidization of the project stopped, at least for the time being. As a result, Winslow remained cut off from the Gosford Road to the east, the British American Land Co.'s roads to the south, and the Lambton Road to the north. In the fall of 1850 there were still only five recorded resident families, all living close to the Stratford boundary in Winslow South. They had cleared an average of 3.2 acres each and had harvested a total of only three bushels of grain and 125 bushels of potatoes to feed twenty-six individuals.[12] It would be difficult to obtain support from more established families nearby because early frosts and crop rust were stretching the district's resources to the limit. Nevertheless, the original five families were still present when the census enumerator called in the spring of 1852.

Despite continued isolation, Winslow's population grew rapidly during the initial years of settlement. By 1852 it had reached fifty-eight French-Canadian families and thirty-five Scots families, and they had produced enough grain and potatoes for the average household to subsist on for a year – about sixteen bushels per individual French Canadian and seventeen bushels for each Scot. The French Canadians owned enough horses to consume most of their oats, which would reduce their personal consumption of grain and potatoes to fourteen bushels, but the horses could certainly have earned their keep in the

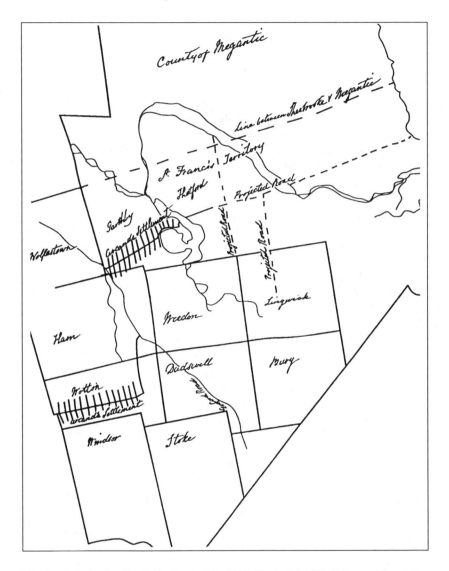

Map 7   Colonization Roads Project in July 1851 (Facsimile) (W.L. Felton to Hon. J.H.
Price, Sherbrooke, 14 July, 1851, Quebec, Ministère des Terres et Forêts, Vieux
dossiers, Correspondance, 1851 no. 686)

timber shanties during the winter. The average Scots farmer would
have still been better off, however, because he owned four cattle and
four sheep to only one of each for his French-speaking counterparts.

Averages may be useful for comparative purposes, but they can present
a misleading impression at the individual level, particularly in such

a young settlement. Even though considerable sharing would have taken place among the many related families, the enumerator reported serious hardship in Winslow. According to him, there were three main reasons for the inequality in harvests: "1st some lots of land are subject to early frosts. 2nd Many of the inhabitants sow *late*, so late that early frosts have, in some instances, totally destroyed their late sown crops. 3rd Some of the settlers sow on the same piece of land twice & in some instances *three times*." He should have added a fourth reason, even more important: wide discrepancies in acreage under cultivation. Thus Pascal Bélanger had sixteen acres in crops, while fourteen of the sixty-three French-Canadian occupants had arrived so recently that they had seeded no ground whatsoever.[13] Inevitably, then, some families suffered food shortages in the spring of 1852.

In April a dispirited Arcand wrote that "la misère est à son comble," and the project's priest, also stationed in Garthby, claimed that his tithe had practically all been distributed to "des supplicants affamés."[14] In early May the *Stanstead Journal* printed a graphic eye-witness account of French-Canadian women and children so starved that they did not have the strength to leave their beds.[15] Though the Association des Townships had long since disintegrated because of lack of public support, the archbishop of Quebec did manage to collect £28 for emergency provisions. Unfortunately, once the freight had reached the nearest rail station at Richmond, the colonists simply had no money to pay for its cartage to Lake Aylmer. To make matters worse, the priest and land agency moved to the less centrally located but more heavily settled Wotton Township, and no government road work was forthcoming again that summer.

Winslow's Scots farmers may have owned more livestock than the French Canadians, but hunger was also reported in their community, largely because of the substantial influx that had arrived in the district from Lewis in the fall of 1851. Nine of thirty-five families recorded in the 1852 census did not even appear in the agricultural schedule. Fortunately for them, they proved to have a considerably stronger external support base than did the French Canadians. As early as January a public meeting was held in Sherbrooke in order to assist the 300 recent arrivals, said to be "in a starving condition" in Lingwick Township. After subscribing £30, participants appointed a committee to raise more funds.

In its petition to the government, the committee claimed that the earlier settlers had given to such an extent that their supply of seed grain was becoming exhausted: "At this season of the year, individuals lately come from the old Country, unacquainted with the work, manners, and customs of this country can do but little towards the support of themselves and families; what they can do, your petitioners have already provided for by distributing those able to labour, around the neighbouring Townships, whence at least they will obtain shelter and food."[16]

The St Andrew's Society of Quebec also petitioned the government, claiming that its funds were "wholly inadequate to meet such an emergency." It had, however, forwarded £25 and was attempting to raise more by private subscription.[17] The Montreal branch of the society was less generous in its response. While some members opined that it would be "a shame if these poor Scotchmen were relieved entirely by Americans," Hugh Allan argued that they had been well provided for by Matheson and that jobs were readily available in the region. He moved that no funds be forthcoming, but a committee was struck to make further inquiries and to take up a subscription if necessary.[18]

Allan was not the only individual to take a critical stance toward the recent immigrants. In Quebec, emigration agent Buchanan complained: "Some ... separated from the main party have made a good settlement in Brompton Gore, and are prospering: but the remainder have by their own misconduct placed themselves and others in a most woful plight. Scarcely one continued working on the Railroad longer than six weeks, when it would seem, thinking that the great amount of wages they received would last them for an almost indefinite period, they all, the ablebodied as well as the helpless, have joined their countrymen in Lingwick." Buchanan recommended, none the less, that £50 be forwarded from the Emigration Fund for oatmeal to feed the women, children, and elderly or sickly men.[19]

The government complied with the Quebec agent's request,[20] but when a resident of the region named S.M. Taylor was sent to distribute the fund, he found the reports of distress to be greatly exaggerated. The recently arrived immigrants were widely dispersed in the settlement, and twenty families had proceeded as far as Winslow, twelve miles north of the village of Lingwick (Gould). Taylor had interviewed only those in Lingwick Township, but "from none of the people with whom I conversed, either the old settlers or those few of the new who could speak English, could I learn that there was then, or that there had been, any actual want, or apprehension of suffering from this cause." Although the earlier settlers "have been great losers by the introduction among them, in one season, of so many of their relations, ... several, both old and new, expressed annoyance that any public appeal had been made on their account." There had been three deaths, but Taylor claimed that there was no evidence to suggest that these had been caused by lack of food. There was still oatmeal in the two barrels that had arrived from Montreal, and there were 1,218 pounds of buckwheat, twenty-five barrels of oatmeal, and twenty-five barrels of flour waiting for distribution at various points between Sherbrooke and Bury. Most of these provisions were from outside the region, for the Sherbrooke committee had still not gathered the bulk of its subscriptions.[21]

The appeal had originated with the Lingwick pastor, Daniel Gordon, who was perhaps unfamiliar with the deprivations to which these crofters were accustomed.[22] That Gordon perceived of himself as a missionary dependent on outside support was made clear by a letter from his wife to the Free Kirk's newspaper in Edinburgh. She expressed hope that the crisis had passed but claimed that progress had been retarded for a year or two at least by the recent influx of immigrants: "The people have opened their hearts and houses to receive the strangers; but, owing to the failure of the potato crop, they must feel keenly the effect of their hospitality. Providence, however, in these circumstances, has provided relief for both parties. Abundance of employment, with good wages, are within their reach, a railway being in process of construction at a distance of fifty miles."[23]

There may have been plenty of jobs available on the St Lawrence and Atlantic road-bed during the summer of 1852, but Taylor was concerned that the Scots would not be re-engaged if other labourers could be obtained: "They are a very supine people, and exceedingly averse to continuous hard labour, such as is demanded in the public works." In his opinion, the government grant he was supposed to distribute should be directed toward helping the immigrants subsist on the land, but in Hampden Township rather than in Winslow, where they were being attracted by the free grants. Hampden was preferable, according to Taylor, because it was on the Otter Brook Road and therefore provided direct access to seasonal employment among the relatively prosperous farmers in Bury Township. Also, "it would obviate, in a great measure by its distance from Lingwick and Winslow, that congregation of an unmixed community which I believe is inimical to healthy progress." Taylor recommended that, rather than purchasing unneeded supplies, he should entice the Scots to Hampden by building a substantial house for their collective use and providing an axe and hoe for each family. Thus the government would "teach the lesson to all of confirmed pauperized habits that, for the future, in this country, they must depend upon themselves."[24]

A couple of months after his tour of inspection, Taylor did purchase six dozen axes, six dozen "grubhoes," and fourteen bushels of barley to distribute in the Lingwick-Winslow area,[25] but there was no chance that he could implement his plan to shift settlers to Hampden. Apart from the desire for communal ties that he would have had to overcome, the township of Hampden was outside the crown domain. The Lewis newcomers would certainly not have contemplated moving to another part of the British American Land Co.'s St Francis Tract when many of their predecessors were in the process of abandoning their Bury and Lingwick homesteads for Winslow and Whitton because of payments owed to that same company.[26] Lingwick's population would decline from 808 in 1852 to 564 in 1861.[27]

Settlers continued to struggle for survival in Winslow during the 1850s because of slow road construction. The isolation of the township had made a strong impression on the enumerator in the spring of 1852:

There is not a *foot of road made in the whole Township*. Those now settled there have suffered, and continue to suffer, great hardships for want of roads. The settlers on the east side of the township have no market nearer than Quebec, which is at a distance of *one hundred & ten miles* from them. The road which they have to travel to go thither intersects or joins the Kennebec road, thirty-six miles distant from the line of this Township & I am informed by the settlers that, for the greater part of the above mentioned 36 miles, the road is very bad. Most of the settlers on the west side of the township have to travel nine miles, four of which is through swamps, before they get to the road constructed by the B.A.L. Company in the adjoining township of Lingwick.[28]

The enumerator might have mentioned that two-and-a-half miles of the Megantic Road had been completed into Winslow as of the previous December, with another five miles suitable for winter travel,[29] but this northwest-running road provided a very indirect link to either Sherbrooke or Quebec.

T.F. McIlwraith has argued that improved roads were not a high priority for settlers in Upper Canada because of the ease of winter transportation, but, for the residents of the thinly settled upper St Fancis district, there remained the problem of swamps, rivers, and lack of traffic volume to pack the trails.[30] Thus the Winslow Scots complained in 1853 that their very lives were in danger because they were forced to carry their grain to distant mills "across unbridged rivers and thro woods inhabited by wild beasts."[31] The government had actually voted a £5,000 grant that year "for continuing and perfecting the improvements commenced under Mr. Arcand,"[32] and a year later it inaugurated a system of annual grants for colonization roads, but the Scots were slow to receive the benefits. A government inspector reported in 1854 that they were still "obliged to carry on their back along the narrow and swampy foot paths from the older settlements, their domestic and farming utensils and provisions and they have yet no other means of conveying their products to mill or market."[33] Finally, in 1855, the long-suffering Winslow settlers gained access to Sherbrooke via the St Francis Road, though a local merchant recalled walking nine miles to Lingwick with babe in arms in June 1856.[34] The Megantic Road was also linked more directly to the Craig Road in Chester Township, and by 1857 it had reached its eastern terminus in the wilderness at Lake Megantic, where Scots families had begun to settle a year earlier.

The hardships of the Scots were far from over, however, for their harvests continued to be depleted by frost and disease, and it appears that they earned little from the road construction in their neighbourhood. In September 1855 they submitted a petition with eleven signatures and ninety crosses claiming that not only were their grain crops frozen and their potatoes rotten, but they had not been hired as promised to work on the roads during the summer. In addition, they had recently been joined by two hundred more immigrants who had "received a free passage from that benevolent Landed Proprietor Sir J. Matheson." The newcomers would have to "go into the Bush farther back than we, and being aware that much of the lands are swampish and stony you may have some idea of the comforts of these families. They will be separated from one another. They will have no roads, no bridges, no mills, etc." To prevent starvation, the petitioners requested a grant of four dollars for each of the recent arrivals.[35] They were supported by a letter from their minister claiming that the roads overseers had refused to hire the latest immigrants "on the ground of unfitness for axe work to which they have not been hitherto accustomed." Reverend McLean repeated that the forty families would starve without public assistance, but none was forthcoming.[36] Aside from what summer employment they might be able to acquire from continuing road subsidies, Winslow's settlers were on their own as far as the government was concerned.

THE LAND-GRANTING PROCESS

The amount of free land each family could claim was supervised as closely as possible by the crown lands agent, who was located during the first few years in Garthby Township. He enjoyed considerable discretion as to who would or would not be granted a location ticket. Such a ticket was, prior to April 1852, simply an occupation permit but began to carry legally recognized property rights after that date.[37] Arcand wrote that he would issue permits only to those "qui ont prouvé par leur activité et leur travail, qu'ils sont bien déterminés à s'établir."[38] At the same time, Arcand's anxiety to see the district settled as quickly as possible led him to take liberties with government regulations. Even though the free grants were supposed to be limited to the main colonization arteries, he sanctioned them for settlers moving to the rear concessions as well.[39] This practice was discontinued by his successor, leading the Scots to protest in 1855. Their petition proclaimed that "to Grant lands to some poor families and not to others exhibits no principle. All these Townships should be made grants to poor people."[40] Agent J.T. LeBel was inclined to bend the rules at least for those who had settled on back ranges without receiving official permits during Arcand's tenure. Thus, in 1861, he successfully supported the claims of Angus McDonald and John McKinnon when they requested full title as free grants to two lots which they had occupied as early as 1851.[41]

Try as they might to persuade all settlers to conform to the letter of the regulations, LeBel and his successors were ultimately led to recognize squatters' rights, at least to the degree of declaring that all improvements had to be indemnified where there were conflicting claims to a lot. While the letters patent, or full official title, became rather meaningless after 1852, even the location ticket was not entirely necessary, given that settlers were able to sell their strictly informal claims to third parties. For example, Norman Murray and his son Donald never received location tickets for their two lots, yet they sold them as free-grant claims to Olivier Béliveau and Isaïi Bergeron when they moved to nearby Whitton in 1855. On the basis of these sales, the two French Canadians were granted letters patent in 1860.[42] In practice, then, location tickets were not even required prior to the issuing of full title to a lot. Of twenty-seven lots which LeBel listed for the granting of letters patent on one occasion, only nine had been issued location tickets.[43]

Official regulations provided a set of guidelines for crown land agents, but poverty and the rudimentary condition of communication links necessitated a good deal of discretion at the local level. The contentious Dion claim is a case in point. In 1853, Jean Dion and his three sons, originally of St Anselme in the seigneurie of Lauzon, protested the granting to third parties of four lots located where the Lambton–St Francis Road crosses the Lambton-Winslow boundary. The Dions had apparently arrived there while the Lambton Road project was under way in 1844. Their affidavit stated that they had cleared and sown about a hundred arpents, but there is no trace of them in the 1852 census. Joseph Laverrière, who had paid the first instalment on one of the lots in question, claimed that they had been absent during the preceding two years. It appears, however, that the Dions had indeed made considerable improvements, for Laverrière would not have had time to cultivate the thirty-four acres recorded with his name in the census, and this was the exact amount that the Dions later claimed to have cleared.[44]

The settlement community of northern Winslow was soon split into two opposing factions over the issue. Laverrière protested that the Dions were cutting his sugary after having forced two of his neighbours to abandon their claims "par les mauvaises traitements qu'ils leur faisaient souffrir."[45] Eighty-four residents of Lambton and Winslow, including a justice of the peace, petitioned the government that the Dions were permitting their livestock to destroy crops, cutting timber on crown land, and threatening to kill anyone who interfered with them. The petitioners wanted the offending family banished from the colony.[46] A rather different picture emerged from a petition sent by another group of settlers in defence of the Dions. Endorsed by the Chaudière crown lands agent, it claimed that Laverrière was shiftless and lazy and that he had started clearings on five lots, selling four for £275 without paying a cent to the crown.[47] The pro-Dion group appears to have been made up of settlers who had arrived with the construction of the Lambton Road in the early 1840s but failed to legalize their claims because of the distance from the nearest crown lands agent in the Chaudière Valley. In December 1853 the Dions and twenty-seven others wrote that they had settled before the surveys had been completed but that they had every intention of following official regulations.[48]

Squatters' "rights" on crown lands were traditionally strong enough, it appears, that this early group of settlers had not bothered to register its claims after 1848 when an agent had become available at Lake Aylmer. It is also possible that its members were not certain on which side of the township line they were located, for Lambton fell within the Chaudière agency and Winslow within the St Francis. The true cause for the sudden rise of concern in the area came not so much from the new wave of colonists, such as Laverrière, as from a group of outsiders interested in the mineral potential of the land at the head of Lake St Francis. Local settlers would want not only to protect their claims but presumably to ensure that they would be able to reap the benefits of the suddenly inflated land prices. It is quite possible that the Dions had become interested in lots they had abandoned only after they heard of the prospecting activities of the British American Mining Association, a subsidiary of the British American Land Co. formed in conjunction with three prominent residents of the Sherbrooke area. The association actually made no attempt to challenge squatters' rights, taking care to purchase the claims of settlers on both sides of the Lambton-Winslow border.[49]

In the spring of 1854, the local crown lands agent endorsed the transfer of ten lots to the mining company's principals, but it was Laverrière and not the Dion family who received $600 for the two lots he now claimed.[50] The Dions subsequently demanded the princely sum of $1,800 as compensation for their improvements. The company resorted to the courts in an attempt to gain possession of the lots, but its case was weakened by the fact that the location tickets had been destroyed in a fire at Quebec. Finally, in 1858, company commissioner Richard W. Heneker asked that the government either take back the two lots in question and return the $600 paid for the improvements or provide crown land of equivalent value elsewhere.[51] The Dions were certainly unwilling to pay the sum in question, but it appears that both sides agreed to a government-mediated settlement in 1860.[52] Despite the great demand created by the American Civil War, which stimulated a number of mines in the townships to the southwest, little if any copper appears to have been extracted in the isolated Lake St Francis area. The chief economic impact of the mining speculation was to freeze development of the over-priced lots during the next several decades.[53]

Aside from the interrelated problems of the early squatters and the mining speculators on the Lambton border, the crown lands authorities enjoyed a relatively harmonious relationship with the French-Canadian settlers of Winslow. The Scots were a different matter. One would expect the enclosures and evictions to have undermined the traditional Highland conception that the right to land was established by occupation and improvement, rather than by written contract, but squatting remained a common practice in Lewis.[54] A number of conflicts developed between Winslow's Scots and the local crown lands agents, caused in part by communication problems, but clearly exacerbated by the Scots' mistrust of officialdom and by the agents' lack of sympathy for the British Protestant intruders. Certainly, the general feeling among the Lewis immigrants was that they were being neglected "while the French have their claims and requests immediately attended to."[55]

The first controversies developed over the desirable locations on the St Francis Road adjacent to the village reserve in South Winslow. In the fall of 1851 Norman McLeod complained that three French Canadians had begun clearing land on three of these lots already claimed and occupied by himself. Whether he was aware of it or not, McLeod was actually residing on a neighbouring lot, which he did obtain as a free grant. A Murdoch McLeod, presumably his son, subsequently received one of the lots in question as a free grant and half another as a crown purchase.[56] The McLeods could not complain about their treatment by the crown lands office, but the other three lots adjacent to the road and the town site also became the subject of controversy. Norman and Angus McDonald settled on them, but in 1853 the newly appointed agent, Bazile Lupien, insisted that this land should have been part of the village reserve. It was becoming obvious that the surveyor had made a mistake in locating the reserve on only one side of the St Francis Road (see Map 8), for the more expensive village lots were being shunned by local merchants. Indeed, we shall see in chapter 6 that those who did eventually purchase several village blocks from the crown managed to subdivide and sell only a few acres of their investments.

Little, however, could be done to rectify the error once it had been made, and the McDonalds did receive free grant permits to two of the lots in question.[57] Donald McLeod was less fortunate. He was informed that he would have to quit the three short lots on the north side of the village site, even though he had built a house and barn and seeded some ground. As of 1881 the government had still not granted the lots in question to anyone. There were several other grievances focusing on the agent's refusal to recognize Scots' claims in 1853. Their spokesman complained that prompt registration of claims had not always been possible, given the time lapse between agents' appointments and the fact that they "never came to see us, in our dark situation."[58]

The following year Andrew Russell from the crown lands office did tour the Scottish settlements, and he became convinced that a Gaelic-speaking agent should be appointed.[59] Persistently making themselves available were two professedly trilingual candidates, merchant James Ross and innkeeper John Noble, both of the village of Gould in Lingwick.[60] When the opportunity for a new appointment finally arose in 1861, however, outside political interference attained it for William Farwell of Robinson in Bury Township.[61] The French-Canadian colonists were the only ones to object formally to the choice of a unilingual English Canadian, but the Scots would not benefit from any special favouritism on the part of Farwell.[62] He reported soon after his appointment that "I found them very poor and not disposed to make any payments to the department but I urged the necessity of them doing so as soon as possible as it was useless to settle on land unless they expected to pay ultimately."[63]

Farwell also echoed the complaint of his predecessors that the Scots appeared to be following their own set of rules as far as land claims were concerned. Such behaviour was consistent with their Highland heritage, for, to the degree that the clan system survived into the nineteenth century, it was as an unofficial device to enforce the traditional usufructory property rights of its members.[64] Furthermore, local Scots tradition in the upper St Francis district holds that the early settlers distributed lots among themselves by "singing the survey," that is, by walking through the woods in single file and marking the boundaries of each lot in turn after the Twenty-third Psalm had been sung a fixed number of times.[65] To his annoyance, Farwell found that many settlers were on lots other than those they had officially claimed and that transfers had not always been drafted when one party replaced another.[66]

The root of the problem was not transiency, as we shall see, but the Scots' desire to accumulate more lots than the authorities were willing to cede to individual settlers. Thus Farwell complained in 1869:

I am clearly of the opinion that the settlers of Winslow fully intend to get hold of all the land they can from the Government, and to pay as little as possible, until the Department compel them by some stringent measures. I am sorry to be obliged to make any such remarks, but all their movements show conclusively that such is their feeling toward the Government, especially in the Scotch Settlements of the Township of Winslow. I am fully of opinion that no part of the County has received so much assistance from the Government as the Township of Winslow during the past fifteen years.[67]

Sixteen years earlier, agent Lupien had arrived at a similar conclusion when he reported that the Scots had driven two youths from St Grégoire off lots for which they held permits on the Megantic Road. The reason they gave was that the land was reserved for relatives and friends arriving from Scotland in the spring. The irate agent warned that "ils veulent faire une nouvelle Guernsey." The government would have to make an example of this case or "les Canadiens de Winslow peuvent plier bagage."[68]

The Scots' aim, then, was not property speculation but to acquire enough land for offspring and future arrivals, particularly in the face of competition from French Canadians who were expanding eastward from Stratford Township. The family-based strategy can be illustrated with the case of the elderly John McLennan, who received lot 66, rang II sw, as a free grant in 1850, then apparently acquired a claim to neighbouring lot 67 shortly prior to his death in 1855. His intention, according to the son who had squatted on adjoining lots 66 and 67, rang III sw, was to ensure that his grand-

Table 2.1

Acreages Reported by Scots and French Canadians in Winslow, 1852 Census

	50	100	125	150	200
Scots	2	19	2	2	2
French Canadians	44	10	–	2	1

Source: Canada, manuscript census, 1852, Winslow Township.

sons (aged ten, eight, and one) would be able to settle near their father.[69]

There was nothing to prevent squatters' claims and location tickets from being transferred and therefore accumulated by certain individuals, but the land agents' complaints about Scots' acquisitiveness were legitimate only insofar as most families resisted being confined to a small fifty-acre lot. As Table 2.1 shows, while the majority of French-Canadian settlers reported to the 1852 census enumerator that they held fifty acres each, nearly all the Scots families reported one hundred acres.

The contrast between Scots and French-Canadian strategies for land acquisition can be accounted for partly by the Highlanders' being an older population with a higher ratio of maturing offspring when they arrived in Winslow – though adolescent sons were entitled to free grants even while living with their parents. Presumably, as well, the French Canadians were subject to greater land pressure because their continued influx was being encouraged by the proximity of their home parishes and by the strong endeavours of church and state to attract them to the district. The Lewis Scots, after all, had nothing to draw them but their kinfolk, and many from the island had settled elsewhere in North America.

Yet another explanation may well lie in the contrasting nature of land tenure in the two home communities. In the seigneuries, farmers avoided acquiring more land than they could exploit at any given time in order to keep their rents down.[70] This was a perfectly rational strategy under a tenure that strongly discouraged speculation and that officially made land available to censitaires on demand. The Scots could certainly not be said to have participated in a free land market on the isle of Lewis, owned as it was by a single family, but their appetite for land would presumably have been affected by bitter experience with short-term leases and community-wide evictions. Perhaps this helps explain why the Highland settlers of mainland Nova Scotia reputedly had "an extravagant desire" to own large parcels of land and why those on Cape Breton Island held larger lots, with higher portions not in cultivation, than did other ethnic groups within the same communities.[71]

Not only the Scots but also the smaller group of French-speaking settlers in Winslow South reported relatively large holdings to the 1852 enumerator. The three French Canadians shown in Table 2.1 with claims of 150 and 200 acres were among this group. They were probably reacting defensively to the Scots presence in the immediate area and perhaps compensating for the particularly poor quality of their land. Even their distant Acadian heritage may have been a factor: like that of the Scots, it was alien to the seigneurial system but not to the process of wholesale evictions.[72]

Whatever explains the contrasting behaviour of the Scots in Winslow South and the French Canadians in Winslow North when they first arrived in the township, there was a surprising similarity in their long-term land-claiming strategies. The family reconstitution files reveal that the seventy-one Scots who made their first claim in the 1850s would ultimately receive an average of seventy-seven acres in crown land, while their ninety-nine French-Canadian counterparts would claim seventy-four acres. Effectively, then, every second family of each group ultimately acquired a second fifty-acre lot from the government.[73] If we include all the 129 Scots who took out location tickets prior to 1880, we find that only 32 per cent made multiple claims during that period – not a great deal higher than the 25 per cent of their 158 French-Canadian counterparts who did so.

To understand further the settlers' land-acquisition strategies requires some familiarity with the settlement pattern. The standard township of ten miles by ten miles was divided into eleven ranges, with twenty-eight lots per range. Each 200-acre lot was therefore approximately twenty-three acres long by nine acres wide, a ratio that would change to about five-to-one when a lot was cut in half lengthwise. In the older townships, lots were often divided crosswise, and their rectangularity was also diminished by roads that meandered across concession lines, but the colonists on the crown lands of the upper St Francis district did not have this option. A denser settlement pattern emerged, not because the government drafted a more uniform survey grid, but because it offered its fifty-acre free grants in contiguous lots alongside the colonization roads (see Map 9). Furthermore, many of the larger lots on the side concessions were sold or granted as individual units to separate colonists (see Maps 10 and 11), with the result that the haphazard-looking, dispersed settlement in the old townships to the south was not replicated in the Winslow area. Gray's settlement map of 1863 (see Map 3) misses a large number of French-

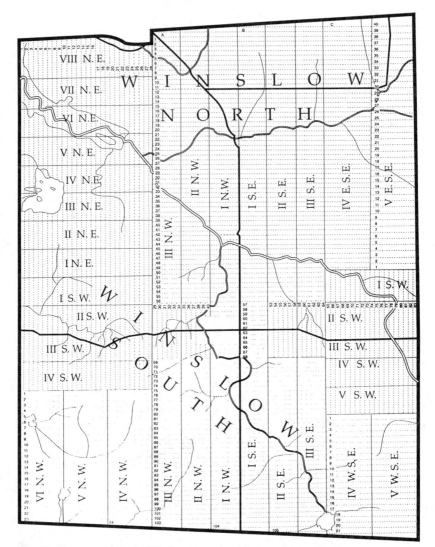

Map 8   Rangs and Lots in Winslow Township (Cadastral Map, Quebec, Ministère d'Énergie et Ressources, Service arpentage)

Canadian homesteads in Winslow, but it does demonstrate the township's pattern of densely settled, isolated pockets strung alongside short segments of the straight concession lines. Normand Séguin suggests that the narrow lots surveyed by the government in the province's townships represented an enlightened response to the need for mutual assistance in a subsistence-oriented economy, but in the upper

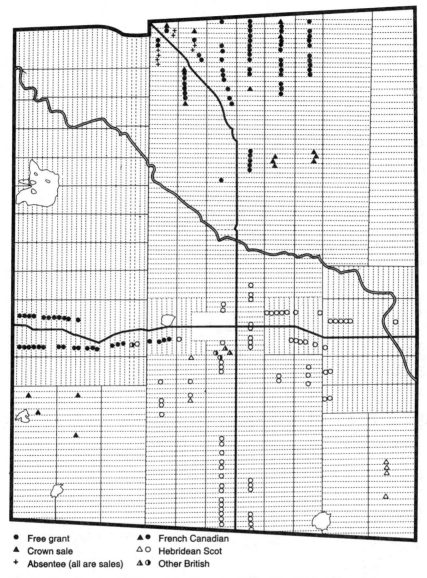

● Free grant
▲ Crown sale
✦ Absentee (all are sales)

▲● French Canadian
△○ Hebridean Scot
▲◑ Other British

Map 9 Free Grants and Crown Sales (Location Tickets) in Winslow Township, 1850–60

St Francis district they simply restricted settlers' access to a reasonably sized farmstead.[74]

When one examines the pockets of settlement more closely on a land claims map, one finds a denser pattern in the northern part of

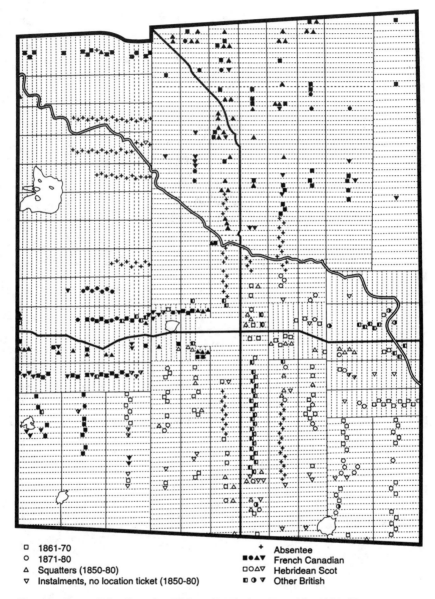

□	1861-70	+	Absentee
○	1871-80	■●▲▼	French Canadian
△	Squatters (1850-80)	□○△▽	Hebridean Scot
▽	Instalments, no location ticket (1850-80)	◨ ◑ ◩	Other British

Map 10   Crown Sales (Location Tickets) in Winslow Township, 1861–80

the township because the supplementary lots claimed by the French Canadians tended to be at a considerable distance from their original grants, presumably serving as sugar/wood lots in some cases. A larger number of Scots managed to obtain properties directly adjacent to,

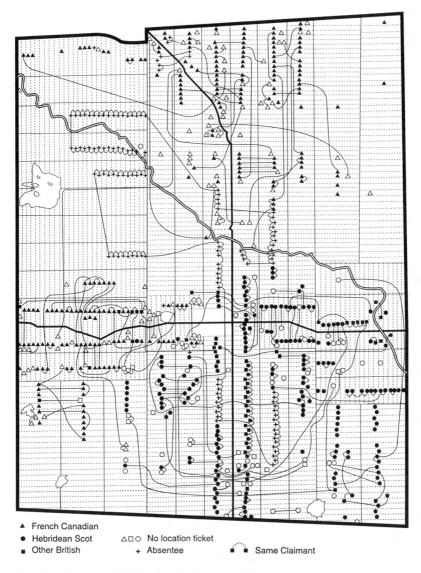

French Canadian
Hebridean Scot   △□○ No location ticket
Other British   +   Absentee   ⌒ Same Claimant

Map 11   Crown Land Claims in Winslow Township, 1850–80

or across the road from, their free grants (see Map 11).[75] To be precise, twenty-four Scots acquired additional crown lots adjoining their free grants, as compared with thirteen French Canadians. Most of these extra lots were purchased from third parties rather than claimed directly from the crown, for the land agents were diligent in refusing multiple free grants to single families. Of eighty-seven

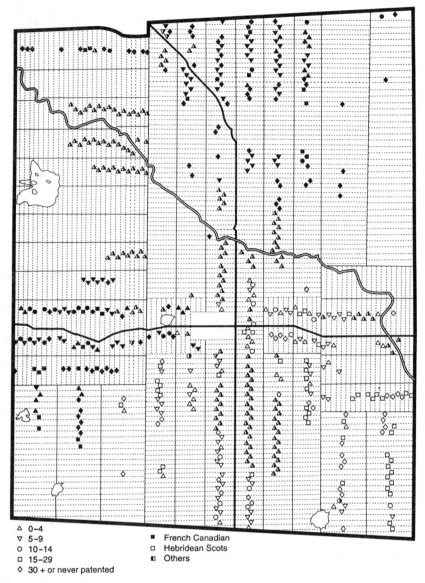

△ 0–4
▽ 5–9
○ 10–14
□ 15–29
◇ 30 + or never patented

■ French Canadian
□ Hebridean Scots
▣ Others

Map 12   Years from Location Ticket (1850–80) to Letters Patent, Winslow Township

French Canadians who received free grants directly from the government, only four obtained more than one, and the ratio for the Scots was two from a total of sixty-seven.

The strategy employed by a few of the Scots, however, was simply to squat on a second crown lot reserved as a free grant until a relative was ready to claim it.[76] Thus Donald Martin received the location

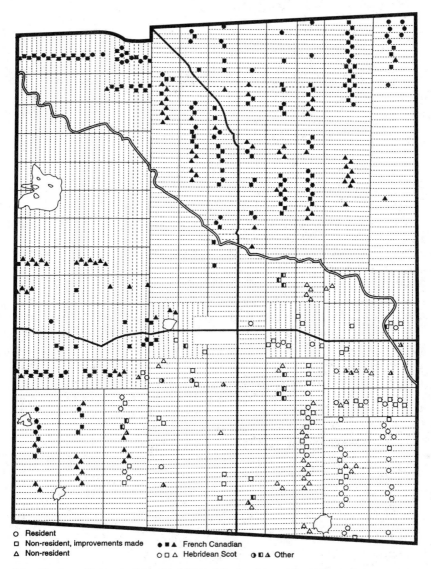

o   Resident
□   Non-resident, improvements made   ● ■ ▲ French Canadian
△   Non-resident   o □ △ Hebridean Scot   ◐ ◨ ▲ Other

Map 13   Lots Claimed without Full Title, Winslow Township, 1885 (Statement of
Inspection of Lands Unsold, or Sold but not Patented, May 1885, E21, Archives
nationales du Québec à Sherbrooke)

ticket to one lot in 1850 but was also recorded as occupying the lot
directly across the St Francis Road. Twenty years later his younger
brother, William, took out a location ticket for this second lot, and it
was finally patented by a George Martin in 1919. In another case,
the fifty-year-old Malcolm McIver squatted on a lot neighbouring his

Table 2.2
Squatters' Claims in Winslow, 1850–80

	(a) With l.t.to other lot(s)	Mean acres no l.t.	Total acres (mean)	(b) With no l.t.	Mean acres
French Canadian	19	48	104	36	60
Scots	19	49	119	10	57

Source: Terrier, Winslow Township, archives of the former Ministère des Terres et Forêts (MTF).

official claim in 1855, a lot that was sold by the crown in 1863 to Angus McIver, presumably Malcolm's son.[77]

Table 2.2 shows that a total of nineteen Scots, who legally claimed the mean of seventy acres each, were recorded with an additional average of forty-nine acres for which they personally did not acquire location tickets.[78] Similarly, nineteen French Canadians had laid unofficial claim to extra unregistered lots, but, unlike in the Scots cases, few of these lots were subsequently issued by the crown to offspring. Table 2.2 also reveals French Canadians as the most numerous among the group of squatters who had no land claims whatsoever in the township, outnumbering the Scots in this category by thirty-six to ten. It is possible that these individuals were interested only in cutting logs, for we shall see that the lumber industry played a more important role in the economy of Winslow North than in that of Winslow South.

Such was almost certainly the case for another category of individuals who, primarily during the latter years under study, paid location fees and even one or two instalments without receiving location tickets. This apparent oversight clearly contravened regulations which stated that a location ticket would be issued on payment of the first instalment of 20 per cent. Aside from illustrating the inadequacies of the nineteenth-century bureaucracy, however, it suggests that the individuals involved (thirty-six French Canadians, twenty-three Scots, and three of other British origin) were content to register a temporary claim to what were effectively isolated wood lots (see Map 10). Probably many crown lots were simply logged over by local individuals without even this formality, and the appearance of these unorthodox cases only during the later 1870s reflected closer protection of the timber licence as newly constructed railways and pulp mills increased the value of the wood supply.

Strictly speaking, then, many of the squatters and most of those who paid an instalment without bothering to claim a location ticket were the much-maligned "faux colons." However, they do not appear to have been either fronts for the lumber monopoly, which already held cutting rights to the township's crown lots, or full-time lumbermen.[79] Some were local farmers with an official claim to another lot, and others were young men attempting to accumulate some cash for a farm of their own. Thus, the twenty-four-year-old Damase Bouffard is recorded as having paid a single instalment of $7.20 on the northern half of lot 12, rang V ESE, in October 1878, seven months before he purchased a farm for $233, and ten months before his first child was born. Likewise, six months before his marriage in 1880, twenty-seven-year-old Norman McLean placed an instalment on lot 78, rang IV SW, but failed to receive a location ticket.

The final step to be taken in the land-claiming process was acquisition of letters patent. In addition to fulfilling settlement conditions, which effectively meant maintaining a residence on or near the lot in question, a claimant was supposed to pay five equal annual instalments, plus 6 per cent yearly interest.[80] Most of those purchasing a fifty-acre lot in Winslow would be expected to pay 60 cents an acre, plus $3.60 in interest over five years, a location fee of $1.00, and a patent fee of $2.00, for a total of $36.60. But very few paid the principal in five years, and so accumulated interest became a considerable burden on most lots, thereby establishing a vicious circle which further delayed the patenting process.

As early as 1856, crown lands agent LeBel remarked that a large number of colonists were not keeping up with their instalments. He was reminding them of their duty at the chapel doors but was reluctant to take a hard line because of the misery he saw around him. With very few having brought any capital with them, "ils doivent souffrir et manquer de stricte nécessaire, et ne peuvent procurer à leur famille, même, les premiers besoins de la vie, et en même temps de payer le fond de leurs terres."[81] As we have seen in the previous section, and as Map 12 illustrates, the government itself would remain reluctant to enforce payments long after the passing of these early years of settlement.

Table 2.3 reveals that although no price was attached to the land, only twelve of the eighty-three French-Canadian free grants, and eighteen of their sixty-seven Scots counterparts, were issued full title within four years.[82] The ratio increased to 70 per cent of the French Canadians and 85 per cent of the Scots before nine years had elapsed, but three of the French-Canadian lots were still unpatented at the turn of the century. As Table 2.4 shows, there was much more diversity in the time lapses between location tickets and letters patent for crown lots purchased. Though the Scots were twice as likely as

Table 2.3

Mean Years from Free-Grant Location Ticket to Letters Patent in Winslow
(Ratio in Parentheses)*

	0–4	5–9	10–14	15–29	30–49	50+	Total
French							
Canadians	12 (14.5)	46 (55.4)	18 (21.7)	3 (3.6)	1 (1.2)	3 (2.6)	83 (100%)
Scots	18 (26.9)	39 (58.2)	8 (11.9)	1 (1.5)	1 (1.5)		67 (100%)

Source: Terrier, Winslow Township, MTF.

*Excludes the few lots sold to individuals of another cultural background before
letters patent issued. Lots with no official location ticket are dated according to the
crown land agent's return, where its date is recorded, and assigned the date 1854
where it is not.

Table 2.4

Mean Years from Sales Location Tickets to Letters Patent in Winslow
(Ratio in Parentheses)*

	0–4	5–9	10–14	15–29	30–49	50+	Total
French							
Canadians	11 (8.7)	20 (15.9)	6 (4.8)	19 (15.1)	31 (24.6)	39 (31.0)	126 (100%)
Scots	19 (16.8)	10 (8.8)	7 (6.2)	44 (38.9)	24 (21.2)	9 (8.0)	113 (100%)

Source: Terrier, Winslow Township, MTF.

*Excludes the few lots sold to individuals of another cultural background before
letters patent issued.

the French Canadians to patent such lots within the first four years,
only about 30 per cent of each group had done so after fourteen
years. However, the Scots were much more inclined to take out their
patents than were the French Canadians during the next fourteen
years. Close to a third of the lots purchased by the latter group did
not receive full title within fifty years, in contrast to only 8 per cent
for those of the former group. In fact, eleven of the French-Canadian
lots were still not patented after eighty years![83]

One can only speculate as to why the Scots, despite their independent attitude toward officialdom, would tend to complete payments on their crown lots somewhat more quickly than did the French
Canadians. As we shall see in chapter 4, it is questionable that they
were able to accumulate significantly more material resources. Rather,
most of those lots not patented after twenty-nine years were undoubtedly exploited for their trees, because the French Canadians tended
to cut more wood and produce more maple sugar than the Scots.
One might speculate as well that the Scots shared a stronger collective
sense of insecurity, given their memories of dispossession in Lewis

and their minority status in a largely French-speaking province. An examination of private sales and mortgages suggests, however, that the Scots were no more inclined to pay attention to the official status of property involved in such transactions than were the French Canadians. Many lots were mortgaged, sold, and resold by both groups without letters patent, or even location tickets, while prior to 1880 only seventeen crown purchases were patented within a year of mortgage, sale, or transfer to an heir.

Glenn Lockwood states that in eastern Ontario's Montague Township the majority of the Irish settlers managed to acquire legal title to their farms after a twenty-year cycle and that the result was a major transformation in their living standard.[84] The dynamic in Winslow was somewhat different because farms were not generally confined to a single lot. Thus free grants could be patented without much delay, and there was no strong compulsive force to encourage claimants to make full payments on the sale lots. Even squatters were secure, despite legislation of 1859 that officially terminated their pre-emption rights.[85]

Only in the mid-1880s, when the rise of the pulp and paper industry brought renewed value to the logged-over district, did the government begin to take a close look at the status of claims to crown lots. In 1884 crown lands agent Charles Patton submitted a list of ninety-nine Winslow sales subject to cancellation, sixty of which were in the hands of French Canadians.[86] Fifteen of these were revoked a year later; in every case an instalment had been paid but no location ticket recorded. All but one of the claimants were non-residents on the lots in question, and the majority were listed as "able to pay." Meanwhile, Patton had added twenty-three more abandoned lots on which deposits had again been paid, mostly by French Canadians, again with no location ticket claimed.[87] One can assume that nearly all such lots had been exploited for their wood, however, by no means all unpatented lots were wood lots even at this late date. As Map 13 illustrates, a detailed report submitted by Patton in May 1885 revealed that a number of farmers residing in the most recently settled corners of the township had not acquired full title and that only some of the more isolated unoccupied lots had not had any improvements made. Once again, these lots were particularly prevalent in the French-Canadian sections of the township, where colonization was continuing, even at this late date.

Despite the timber leases of C.S. Clark and Co., the crown lands office also auctioned considerable blocks of unarable land to speculators and lumbermen. No settlement conditions were required, cash was always paid, and the price was usually ten-and-a-half cents per acre. In 1868 the Presbyterian minister, John McDonald, made the largest single purchase by a resident – nineteen lots (950 acres) of low-lying, swampy land between Stornoway and the Scots settlers to the south. McDonald probably failed to exploit all the timber on these lots, for in 1879 John Henry Pope, MP for Compton and former owner of Clark and Co., must have felt that they were worth the price of some local votes when he seized them through the courts.[88] Smaller speculative purchases of colonization road lots were made by Stornoway merchant Colin Noble, as well as by two local Irishmen, merchant Thomas Leonard and bailiff Peter Henry. By far the most active bidder, however, was Frederick Blodgett, the self-styled Eaton Township farmer who in 1870 purchased several remote blocks totalling 5,556 acres (see Map 11). Clark and Co. was soon in effective possession, however, through a mortgage signed in 1874.

There is no reason to believe that Blodgett or McDonald were fronts for C.S Clark, given that their purchases were not simply transferred but mortgaged and even seized through the courts by an individual associated with the company in the latter case. Certainly Clark would not have been in favour of crown land auctions because his company already controlled the lots in question through a long-term lease. There may be no coincidence that these auctions took place after Confederation, when Clark's associate, J.H. Pope, had moved to the dominion sphere and the newly formed provincial régime had adopted a less tolerant policy toward the lumber company. Contrary to what Séguin has suggested for Hébertville, there was no pretence that the sales here were for agricultural purposes.[89] To ensure its supply of timber, the company was itself forced to turn to large-scale private purchases in the early 1870s, a strategy that seems to have included the lots owned by Blodgett and McDonald.[90] It was able for a few more years to maintain a declining grip over Winslow and the district as a whole, but at a higher price than before Confederation.

Without descriptive documentary evidence, assessment of land-claiming strategies must remain a process of deduction and educated guesswork. I have suggested that if the Scots tended to acquire larger land claims at the outset, it was probably because of a combination of at least three factors. Their families were older, with more sons reaching maturity during the 1850s, they felt less early pressure to accommodate large numbers of families on the land, and they had experienced much greater insecurity with land-holding in their home communities. Most French-Canadian families ultimately caught up with the Scots in terms of crown land acreage claimed, but it does not follow that they actually cultivated similar-sized farms, given that they took longer to patent some of their lots and that more of these lots were located away from their homesteads. We shall see in the following chapters, moreover, that the question of how many acres supported each individual is not a simple one, for it depended as well on purchases of privately held land, inheritance customs, demographic growth rates, household structure, and even seasonal migration patterns. Thus a process that had been initiated and shaped in various ways by landlords, land companies, churches, and different levels of government soon took on a life of its own in each of the two new settler communities of Winslow Township.

CHAPTER THREE

Population Expansion and Mobility

The substantial immigration from Lewis and continuing influx from the seigneuries ensured that all the arable colonization road grants would rapidly be taken up by settlers. A visiting missionary-priest reported in 1857 that Winslow North was already overcrowded, but the French Canadians nevertheless continued to increase, from 853 in 1861 to 891 in 1871, and to an all-time high of 1,107 in 1881.[1] As for the Scots, even though migration from Lewis did not end in 1851, their population grew only marginally, from 718 in 1861 to 736 in 1871, and then declined to 669 in 1881. There were also several Irish- and English-descended families in the village of Stornoway, but their numbers were never high enough to affect significantly the dual cultural composition of the township. From just over half the population, the French Canadians climbed to more than 60 per cent by 1881.[2]

Although the Scots population was declining, however, land records reveal that none of the French-Canadian expansion took place on farms originally owned by Scots. Nor, as we shall see, were French Canadians subdividing holdings, most of which were too small from the start to support families without an outside source of income. Part of the expansion came from growth of the non-agricultural sector of the economy. From seven in 1861, French-Canadian non-farmer heads of family grew to fourteen in 1871 and thirty-two in 1881. But the number of farmers also jumped during the 1870s, after stabilizing in the 1860s. Thus the 132 French Canadians labelled as farmers in 1861 (127 are listed in the agricultural schedules) became 131 in 1871 (with 130 in the agricultural schedules), and 144 in 1881 (these agricultural schedules have been destroyed). In the final analysis, then, even though eighteen of the additional French-Canadian families in 1881 were non-farmers, the fact that there were also thirteen additional farmers suggests that the settlement process was continuing to add almost as many individuals to their numbers as was economic diversification.

Analysis of how the French Canadians could continue to expand on such a marginal frontier will have to await the following chapters, but the contrast in the Scots' behaviour suggests that Winslow family decisions to stay or leave were influenced by cultural as well as material considerations.[3] The number of Scots families declined by only four between 1871 and 1881, but this marked the beginning of a process that would see their complete disappearance from the township during the early twentieth century.[4] That the total Scots population was dropping faster than the number of families might appear to corroborate the widespread French-Canadian theory that "ces Écossais n'ont pas d'enfants,"[5] but, despite the nationalist myth of a "revanche des berceaux," a contrast in fertility does nothing to explain the demise of a population within a few short decades. Furthermore, the demographic analysis in this chapter will reveal that the Scots actually maintained a high birth rate throughout the period under study. In order to explain the contrasting population dynamics of the two groups, this chapter begins to explore the cultural and psychological dimensions of expansion and contraction in Winslow.

SOURCES

Official census reports can give us only decennial snapshots of any given community, but a good deal can be gleaned from them concerning family formation and development during the intervening years. The census, however, cannot identify those transients who came and went between enumerations, nor can it tell us which families dissolved because of deaths during the preceding decade. It even misses a significant number of deaths for the twelve months it was supposed to cover. Thus, of fifteen burials recorded in the St Romain parish records from mid-April 1870 to mid-April 1871, when the census was completed, only eleven can be linked to the manuscript census. The enumerator failed to report any fatalities in April 1870 as well as two infant deaths in February and early April 1871, while including two deaths in February and March 1870 that are not recorded in the parish registers. Not surprisingly, then, it appears that infant deaths as well as deaths furthest removed in the preceding year were the ones most likely to be missed. The census does, however, include cause of death – information generally not recorded in Winslow's parish registers, though the death schedules for 1881 have been destroyed.[6]

The lacunae in relation to migration and mortality are serious for any historian examining social development. An analysis of transience and death rates, particularly infant mortality, can provide valuable insights into a community's living conditions and economic development, as well as its cultural attitudes. Probably more important still for such purposes is the study of fertility rates. These can be estimated from the census alone, but only at the cost of neglecting the crucial factor of infant mortality. For these reasons, a reasonably accurate demographic profile depends on parish registers of births, deaths, and marriages, but manuscript census reports are useful supplements, especially for the pioneering years of a community's history.

The registers for Winslow North's Catholics are relatively complete only from the early 1860s onward. The colonists were served by the curé of nearby St Vital de Lambton until 1857, when a priest was appointed to neighbouring St Gabriel de Stratford. A year later Winslow North became a separate municipality and parish known as St Romain, but it did not receive a resident priest until 1863. Even then, the incumbent was instructed to continue serving Stratford, and so the registers of the two parishes were not recorded separately until 1868. Entries did distinguish between the two parishes, however: therefore records of baptisms, marriages, and burials become fairly comprehensive from at least as early as 1863. Unfortunately, for our purposes, the Catholics of Winslow South remained in the parish of St Gabriel, restricting analysis of the French-Canadian population to Winslow North.

For the Scots of Winslow South, not only were all records prior to March 1864 destroyed in a fire, but those from that date onward are lamentably incomplete.[7] To take one example, the minister recorded no baptisms from 16 August 1868 to 6 September 1871. In theory, the survivors born during these years would appear in later baptismal records, but the total number of births ultimately listed as having taken place in 1869 was much lower than for subsequent years. The general shortcoming of late baptisms should have been compensated to some extent by the infant burial records, but no deaths whatsoever are recorded from 1864 to 1877. Perhaps the congregation was perpetuating the Highland custom of performing burials without formal participation of the minister.[8] Certainly the Free Kirk cemeteries of the upper St Francis district are scattered throughout the countryside rather than confined to specific churches. Calculations of Scots fertility rates therefore can only be rough estimates, at best, dependent as they are on the manuscript census reports.

By reconstituting families with the aid of parish registers and the manuscript census, it is possible to gain a reasonably good estimate of how complete each set of records is.[9] The parish registers list 334 baptisms for Winslow North between 1861 and 1870, but a minimum of thirty-three additional births to local residents can be identified from the 1871 manuscript census.[10] Still more would have to be added to account for families leaving the parish before the 1871 enumeration. The register becomes much more complete in the 1870s, presumably because St Romain had its own curé throughout the decade. Only twelve children can be identified in the 1881 census as having been excluded from the list of 360 baptisms for 1871–80. The omissions for both decades could be a result of any of several factors. Refusal of parents to have a child baptized can be dismissed out of hand in this devoutly Catholic environment, and it is unlikely that the curé would neglect to record a baptism, but we shall see that some colonists were accustomed to attending the Lambton church before a resident curé was appointed to St Romain, and a small number of births and baptisms would have continued to take place outside the home parish while the mother was visiting relatives.[11] Between 1871 and 1880, eight baptisms were performed in St Romain for six apparently non-resident families, and in all but one of these cases the godparents were residents of St Romain, being kin in at least four instances.[12] For the purposes of calculating fertility rates in the later years, then, one can assume that baptisms missed through absenteeism were partially offset by baptisms performed for outsiders.

An accurate index of marriages is impossible to draw up for a single township because some of the men married women from outside their parish, and those marriages invariably occurred in the bride's church. By the same token, some women who married in St Romain would set up house outside the parish. Even if these two factors tended to balance each other out in the long run, they certainly would not do so on an annual basis. Consequently, no attempt will be made here to determine marriage rates, though St Romain unions that resulted in resident families will be examined.

For the French Canadians, the death records are the least problematic of the three sets of parish-based data. The high rate of deaths on the day of birth, accompanied by a very low number of recorded still-births, nevertheless suggests that the registers exaggerate the number of live births and therefore the mortality rates.[13] For St Romain the distortion appears closer to 10 per cent than the 1 per cent mentioned by Pouyez and Lavoie for the Saguenay region, but this is not a problem for purposes of comparison with other studies

Table 3.1

Births per 1000 population (Based on Three-Year Moving Averages),
Winslow North, Saguenay, and Province of Quebec, Selected Years, 1861–81

	Winslow North	Saguenay	Quebec
1861	49	58	50
1871	41	55	45
1872	42	55	45 (1871–5)
1877	40	51	
1879	41	50	47 (1876–80)
1880	40	48	
1881	44	48	44

Sources: Winslow North: Canada, manuscript census reports, 1861–81; St Romain
parish registers and reports, Archives nationales du Québec à Sherbrooke (ANQS);
Saguenay and Quebec: Pouyez and Lavoie, *Les Saguenayens,* 277, 279; Henripin and
Perron, "The Demographic Transition," 220.

on French Canada.[14] Indeed, for studying conception rates it is actually an asset.

The one remaining problem with demographic sources is the pau-
city of annual parish census records, which in turn limits the number
of years for which we can calculate rates of birth, death, and marriage. Researchers for the Saguenay project have concluded that the
annual parish reports are generally trustworthy, for population size,
and the numbers in those that exist for St Romain are certainly compatible with the dominion census reports.[15] However, the first parish
report was not submitted to the bishop until 1873, followed by a five-
year gap, with a consistent annual record only from 1878 onward.
For the calculation of ratios in the earlier period, we are therefore
limited to the years of the official census reports.

FERTILITY

Table 3.1 suggests that St Romain's crude annual birth rate was at
least as high as that for the province as a whole during the 1860s,
but that it dropped significantly vis-à-vis the provincial rate during
the 1870s. Particularly marked is the contrast with the Saguenay
region, where the frontier remained open long after that of the upper
St Francis district had closed. But crude birth rates reflect the fluc-
tuating size of the total population as much as they do female fertility
(see Appendix C), which Table 3.2 suggests did not actually decline
a great deal in St Romain during the 1870s.

Table 3.2
Births per Married Woman (Three-Year Moving
Average) Aged 15–49, Winslow, 1871, 1881

	French Canadians	Scots
1871	3.2	2.2
1881	3.0	1.9

Sources: St Romain and Winslow Presbyterian registers.

As for comparisons between Winslow's French-Canadian and Scots populations, Table 3.2 also suggests that even if one could account for the Scots births missed by Presbyterian baptismal records, there would nevertheless be a marked and consistent margin between the marital fertility rates of the two groups. To gain some insight into how these contrasting patterns developed, we must examine the spacing of births through reconstitution of family life cycles.

The pioneering historical demographers Henry and Gautier conceived of the family-reconstitution method for long chronological periods so that complete family histories for several generations could be traced, but the linking of parish registers to manuscript census data allows us to take a short-cut.[16] We can determine what rank a child's birth was in the family, even if it or earlier births took place before migration to the parish, simply by noting individual ages in the manuscript census reports. It is of course necessary to eliminate from the calculation all families whose older offspring might already have left the nest, but such cases are relatively few in Winslow. Another advantage to this method, in comparison to that which includes only families that have completed their entire life cycle in the parish, is that it includes a larger and more representative proportion of the total number of families in any given study area by not eliminating the more mobile segment of the population.[17] Canadian historians have therefore been too quick to reject family reconstitution for studying small areas of this country, at least for the period covered by available maunuscript census reports.[18] This method cannot account for child deaths prior to the arrival of a family in a given study area, but the impact for this study is minimal because I shall include intervals only for births recorded in the parish registers.

In eighteenth-century Canada the birth interval ranged from 21.1 months to 22.9 months for the first five conceptions and then increased rather sharply to 25.3 months. In St Romain, in contrast, the spacing of births remained very close and very regular right up

Table 3.3

Birth Interval in Months by Rank Order of Births for Farm Wives, Winslow, 1861–80

	Marr.–1	1–2	2–3	3–4	4–5	5–6	6–7	7–8	8–9	9–10	10+
FRENCH CANADIANS, 1861–80											
Interval	14.8	17.0	20.4	21.7	21.2	22.5	24.4	24.6	25.4	24.0	24.8
Cases	38	50	44	38	42	54	43	44	44	27	43
SCOTS, 1871–80											
Interval	12.8	25.3	27.4	26.8	31.8	29.8	31.5	25.3	–	–	–
Cases	12	15	13	8	16	12	10	12	–	–	–

to the tenth conception and beyond, comparing favourably with the unregulated fertility of twentieth-century Hutterite women.[19] The short intervals between births at the higher ranks might not seem significant, given that the women who produced the most births would necessarily have experienced the shortest intervals, but Table 3.3 reveals almost as many births registered at the higher ranks as at the lower. In other words, most married women in St Romain appear to have given birth every two years for most of their active reproductive lives. Analysis of the Scots birth intervals unfortunately had to be confined to a single decade – a very small population base. Table 3.3 demonstrates, nevertheless, that this limitation does not preclude reasonably balanced sampling of all the birth ranks. Nor does it prevent us from attaining a relatively consistent pattern of increased spacing as the birth rank increases (except in the last interval) – a pattern that contrasts markedly with that of the French Canadians. The result was that the seventh pregnancy for a Scots woman was retarded a full seven months longer than for her French-speaking neighbour.

Demographic historians point out that a woman's fecundity inevitably declines with age, but Table 3.4 reveals that – as with their seventeenth- and eighteenth-century forbears – the fertility of St Romain's women remained consistently high until they neared the age of forty.[20] Table 3.4 shows a small but steady decline in Scots fertility throughout the child-bearing years. Nevertheless, Scots women in their early forties were actually slightly more fecund than were their French-Canadian counterparts, though the latter were the only ones to give birth after the age of forty-five. Given an average age at last birth of 42.6 for Scots women and 43.1 for French Canadians – older in both cases than women in any of the natural fecund-

Table 3.4
Mean Number of Births by Age Cohort for Farm Wives, Winslow, 1861–80

	20–24	25–29	30–34	35–39	40–44	45–49
FRENCH CANADIANS, 1861–80						
Births	2.3	2.8	2.7	2.7	1.6	0.4
Women	56	64	57	50	29	14
SCOTS, 1871–80						
Births	2.6	2.4	2.1	2.0	1.8	–
Women	8	14	18	15	11	

ity studies reviewed by Charbonneau – it is clear that the difference in fecundity was not simply a matter of contrasting physiological conditioning.[21]

Some evidence suggests that Scots couples deliberately began to limit the size of their families. Within a population beginning voluntary birth control, the initial steps are usually taken by women in the later stages of childbearing.[22] Table 3.5 reveals a steady and marked decline in Scots births from one census to the next for the crucial cohort of married women aged thirty-five to thirty-nine, as well as a sharp drop for the forty-to-forty-four-year-olds between 1871 and 1881.[23] The decrease registered by Scots women in their twenties probably was a reflection of later marriages within those cohorts, as was the decline for the younger French-Canadian cohorts.[24] The accuracy of Table 3.5 in terms of measuring birth rates might be called into question, given the small number of married women it analyses, but the consistent rise and fall in the number of children recorded across the age cohorts for Scots as well as French Canadians suggests that it is a useful indicator of general fertility trends over time.

If birth control during the later years of marriage was starting to be practised by the Scots prior to 1881, it can nevertheless not be the main explanation for their lower fertility vis-à-vis the French Canadians. Among French Canadians, spacing was narrower for every birth after the first and fecundity was greater for every age cohort between twenty-four and forty. Historical demographers have as yet made little progress in explaining the great variety in fertility patterns from one society to another. Modell and Hareven, for example, offer no explanation why in nineteenth-century Essex County, Massachusetts, the fertility of native-born women should have peaked shortly after marriage, while that of the Canadian-born peaked in their late twenties, and the Irish in their early thirties.[25] The most that can be

Table 3.5

Children Not Yet Ten per Married Woman, by Age Cohort and Census Year, Winslow, 1861–81

Year	Age of Wife						
	15–19	20–24	25–29	30–34	35–39	40–44	45–49
SCOTS							
1861 (n = 76)	0	1.6	2.8	3.0	4.0	2.5	1.5
1871 (n = 67)	0	0.7	2.7	3.5	3.4	3.5	2.3
1881 (n = 51)	0	1.0	2.2	3.8	2.5	2.1	2.1
FRENCH CANADIANS							
1861 (n = 124)	1.0	1.7	3.1	3.8	3.4	3.3	1.3
1871 (n = 108)	0.6	1.0	3.3	3.5	4.0	3.4	1.5
1881 (n = 125)	0.6	1.4	3.1	3.7	4.0	3.3	1.9
PERCENTAGE CHANGE, 1861–81							
Scots	0	−60	−60	+80	−150	−40	+60
French Canadians	−40	−18	0	−3	+18	0	+46
PERCENTAGE CHANGE WOMEN AGED 15–24							
Scots	38						
French Canadians	26						

Source: Canada, manuscript census, 1861–81, Winslow Township.

said, it appears, is that some process of "unconscious rationality" was at play.[26] Whatever the reason for the contrasting fertility patterns of the two cultures in Winslow – and I shall suggest below that nursing practises were a crucial factor – the net result was that the average period between each birth for French Canadians was almost six months shorter than for Scots (28.3 months v. 22.6 months). The result – infant mortality rates and marriage age being equal – would be a completed family size 20 per cent greater for the former group.

MORTALITY

Nuptiality will be examined below, but first we must attempt to asssess the impact of mortality on the natural increase of the two populations. The rise of St Romain's three-year moving average to the level of the province as a whole by 1881 (as shown in Table 3.6) might suggest the ageing of an initially young population, especially in comparison with the Saguenay colonization zone. A closer examination nevertheless reveals very few elderly deaths in St Romain even

Table 3.6
Crude Mortality Rate (Deaths per 1,000 Inhabitants) (Three-Year Moving Average) in St Romain, Saguenay, and the Province of Quebec, by Census Year, 1861, 1871, 1881

	1861	1871	1881
St Romain	9	21	23
Saguenay	15	16	16
Quebec	22	25	23

Sources: Pouyez and Lavoie, Les Saguenayens, 293 (see Bibliography); St Romain parish registers, ANQS.

Table 3.7
Mortality by Age Cohort, St Romain, 1858–80

	0	1–9	10–39	40–69	70+
Deaths	123	75	39	22	15

by the late 1870s. Only two of twenty-seven people who died in 1880, for example, were older than thirty-nine years of age, and only four were older than the age of nine.

As Table 3.7 demonstrates, of the 283 deaths recorded in St Romain for the period 1858–80, almost half were infants less than a year old, and another quarter were children under ten.[27] Of the 790 infants born in the parish over this period, 17 per cent died before the first year was out, and 26 per cent died before reaching their tenth birthday. Though high by today's standards, St Romain's infant mortality rate, 167 per 1,000 births, was somewhat lower than the 193 per 1,000 for the rural parishes of New France, and on the low end of the 150-to-250 scale for Western pre-industrial populations.[28] Unfortunately, there are no figures available for Quebec during this period, and few standards of comparison for children under ten.

Sixty-five (53 per cent) of 123 infant deaths in St Romain took place during the first month after birth (forty-one during the first day), including the nine reported to be dead as soon as born, but not the five recorded as still-born. In this respect St Romain was quite similar to the early-nineteenth-century French-Canadian settlement in the upper St John Valley, where 47 per cent of infant deaths occurred during the first month.[29] Such deaths were caused primarily by endogenous factors, that is, conditions related to birthing complications and congenital malformations, though why these should have been so high is not clear from the demographic literature.

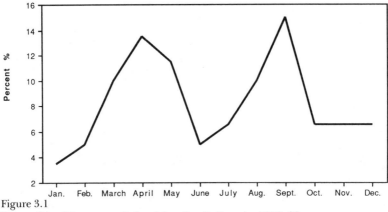

Figure 3.1
Seasonality of Exogenous Infant Mortality, St Romain, 1858–80

It is possible that undernourishment and heavy work by pregnant women played a role.[30] Certainly, Léon Gérin attributed the high rate of infant mortality in rural Quebec largely to "la vie trop laborieuse" of the mother "qui reste chargée d'une lourde besogne à la maison, et parfois aux champs."[31] Gérin's statement conjures up the image of European peasant women who reportedly tended to neglect their babies during the harvest season,[32] but Figure 3.1 reveals that the months of July and August were near the nadir for infant mortality in St Romain. A more reasonable explanation for the high rate of deaths above the age of one month lies with the recent studies that chiefly blame child-killing diseases. The April and September peaks shown in Figure 3.1 parallel those found for French-Canadian infants of the upper St John Valley and correspond to the higher incidence of infectious diseases during the early spring and early fall.[33]

More direct indicators of the impact of such diseases can be found in the manuscript census reports. As we have seen, enumerators were inclined to under-record infant mortality. Nevertheless six of seven French-Canadian deaths reported for 1852 were of children less than a year old. Causes of death were given only for older infants. A five-week-old girl had "water in the head," and a two-and-a-half-month-old girl died because of her mother's illness. For the Scots we find only two deaths reported for 1851–2, one of them a five-week old boy who had suffered from a bowel complaint. No infant deaths were recorded for either group in the 1861 census, even though two St Romain infants were buried in February of that year, but three young French Canadians and one young Scot died of croup, and a nine-year old French-Canadian boy was the victim of scarlet fever. It appears that the first two enumerations took place in years relatively free of infectious diseases.

The 1871 census lists seven French-Canadian infant deaths, with whooping cough and fever listed as the cause for two. Two slightly older children also died of whooping cough, and three of causes unknown. As for the Scots, a two-year-old child succumbed to fever and a ten-year-old to measles. Somewhat surprising, no child deaths were ascribed to the "Black Fever" which took five French-Canadian adults, three of them in one family. The curé of St Romain also noted causes of death in the parish registers for 1877 and 1878. The very young deaths were generally ascribed simply to "débilité," while smallpox (la picotte), croup, and consumption each claimed two children.

The curé's sermon note-book also reveals considerable trepidation about smallpox in the spring of 1875 and 1877, but analysis of the parish registers suggests that the traditional child-killing diseases hit the parish of St Romain particularly hard on three other occasions – the winter of 1863–4, the spring of 1870, and the spring of 1880.[34] The register records twenty-six burials between September 1863 and April 1864, as compared to only seven for the other sixteen months of 1863 and 1864. Twenty-two of the thirty-three deaths were of children under ten. In 1870, thirteen of eighteen deaths were likewise of children under ten, and in 1880 the ratio was twenty-three of twenty-seven.[35]

Unfortunately, similar analysis cannot be done for the Scots, but census enumerations do suggest an infant mortality rate considerably lower than the French Canadians'. There are only two infant deaths recorded in the three census reports for the former group, as compared with thirteen for the latter. Why Scots infants should have been more immune to disease than were those of the French Canadians – if indeed they were – is difficult to say, unless perhaps Scots mothers breast-fed for a longer period. Gérin's comment about the impact of the laborious life of French-Canadian mothers makes considerably more sense in this context, particularly since, as we shall see, St Romain's fathers commonly worked for extended periods off the farm.

The influence of breast-feeding on the timing of conception is a complex and contentious issue, though Henri Leridon claims that a year's lactation generally results in post-partum nonsusceptibilty for six to nine months, while doubling the breast-feeding period to two years also doubles the nonsusceptible period.[36] It is likely, then, that the longer Scots birth intervals reflected longer breast-feeding, especially given the common advice against sexual activity during the nursing period. A time lapse of only 9.9 months between first birth and second conception for the average French-Canadian mother in St Romain (considering only cases where the first child survived for at least a year) establishes the outer limit that she could have nursed, since milk production ceases with pregnancy. In fact, the average nursing period could have been no more than seven months, since that is the length of time by which birth intervals were shortened when an infant died at less than a month old.[37] Further, a mean interval between first and second births only 2.2 months longer than that between marriage and first birth suggests an even more limited nursing period, though initial pregnancies were doubtless delayed by the young ages of many brides.

The importance of breast-feeding to infant survival is stressed by Flandrin, who claims that infants in France were customarily nursed for two years and that those weaned before the age of one rarely survived because of the poor quality of their water and hygiene.[38] It appears that most infant deaths in nineteenth-century Quebec were caused by diarrhoea resulting from replacement of maternal milk by less nourishing broths — bread or corn starch mixed with contaminated cow's milk or well water.[39] Infants weaned early also become more susceptible to infectious diseases because they lost the protection of antibodies found in mothers' milk.[40] It is probably no accident, therefore, that the decline in St Romain's infant mortality after one month was interrupted briefly at the five-to-six-month stage when weaning would have taken place for many.[41]

A glance back at Table 3.3 reveals that the Scots' inter-birth intervals were more than adequate to allow for a lengthy nursing period. The mean interval between their first and second births was twelve and a half months longer than that between marriage and first birth, as opposed to the 2.2 months noted above for the French Canadians.[42] It does not necessarily follow that mothers took full advantage of this opportunity, for Maryann Morrison (who was married in 1894) recalled that when she tried to wean her youngest daughter, "She'd throw the bottle out, and throw it out, and ... I decided to give her the breast for the whole year." This statement suggests that Morrison usually nursed for less than twelve months — not surprising, since she raised thirteen children, but she did claim to have breast-fed one boy for three years.[43]

Inconclusive as our data may be on the Scots infant mortality rate, it is clear that one cannot adopt the assumption of Hareven and Vinovskis that differences in death rates among various ethnic and socioeconomic groups were not significant in the nineteenth century.[44] The higher French-Canadian birth rate suggests greater infant mortality: as already noted, birth intervals were shortened considerably by infant deaths. Flandrin suggests even that the higher birth rate in northern France as compared to the south might be the result of a higher ratio of infant deaths in the former region.[45] Recent studies have found that families with a higher incidence of infant mortality paradoxically also tended to have the most surviving children.[46] It is also likely that differences in infant mortality rates between ethnic groups of the same socioeconomic class, such as have been discovered for pre-industrial Montreal,[47] were caused by differing nursing practices, though this possibility appears to have been completely ignored by historians.

NUPTIALITY

If the link between infant mortality and the comparative reproductive rates of the French Canadians and Scots can be only guessed at because of the nature of the Scots' baptismal and burial records, their marriage registers do appear relatively complete, and marriage rates can be determined with the aid of the census reports. We shall see in this section, however, that the impact of nuptiality on general fertility rates is not easy to pin down.

A number of economists and cliometricians have observed that birth rates in North American rural areas tended to decline as population density and demand for land increased, but they generally do not attempt to identify whether that decline was the result primarily of delayed marriages or of a reduction in fertility within marriages.[48] Charles Tilley, in contrast, questions whether variations in opportunities to marry helped regulate fertility, and recent research has shown that women who marry later tend to be slightly more fecund than those who marry young.[49]

David Gagan states that delayed marriage was a much more significant force for the balancing of the rural population in nineteenth-century Peel County than was birth control within marriage, but his evidence suggests otherwise. Marriage ages for both sexes in Peel climbed by only two and a half years over a thirty-year period, which would presumably have eliminated little more than one conception per couple.[50] Furthermore, Gagan's hypothesis is not supported by the findings of sociologist Lorne Tepperman, who claims that most ethnocultural groups in Canada were practising some form of birth control by 1871.[51]

Tepperman does, however, specifically exclude Scots and French Canadians from his generalization. He claims that Scottish reproduction rates were relatively low throughout Canada in 1871 only because Scots women delayed marriage longer than those of any other major ethnic group. Visitors to the Highlands wrote that marriage ages had been lowered by introduction of the potato, but recent studies suggest that delayed marriages and an absence of birth control remained characteristic of the western parishes of Inverness and Ross counties (which included the island of Lewis), where during the first half of the nineteenth century women generally married in their later twenties.[52] As for the French Canadians, Tepperman finds that they married three to four years younger than the Scots, thereby avoiding family limitation almost entirely.[53]

I have already suggested that Winslow's Scots may have begun practising limited birth control within marriage during the study period, and, if Tepperman's generalizations about marriage ages hold up for this township, we should expect to find a significant margin between the two groups. Marriage registers begin too late to be of any use in tracing trends over time, but they do reveal a significant gap between the female first-time marriage ages of the Scots and French Canadians, even though both remained low as late as the 1870s. The average Scots bride was twenty-three – the lower limit of the European marriage pattern as defined by Hajnal – while the average French-Canadian bride was only nineteen.[54]

However, the index in Table 3.8 (based on manuscript census returns) does reveal a general pattern of later marriages as the settlement aged, a trend that was avoided in the Saguenay region until the 1880s.[55] The only exception to this trend in Winslow was French-Canadian men in the 1870s, which might seem puzzling, given the context of the 1873–8 recession. We have already noted, however, that the number of French-speaking families was expanding again during the 1870s, and we shall see that the period during which married men worked off the farm tended to increase during this decade. Thus it would appear that young French-Canadian men simply adapted to socioeconomic conditions in order to maintain their high nuptiality rate.[56] As for the Scots, there was a particularly marked increase between 1871 and 1881 in the ratio of men aged thirty to thirty-four who remained single, many of whom presumably never married at all. The reason, as we shall see once again in chapter 5, is that Scots offspring took up seasonal wage labour to help support their parental families.

Two of the poems published by local bard Angus MacKay (Oscar Dhu), who was born around 1865, suggest that bachelorhood remained common in the district at the end of the century. In "A Leap Year Ball at Lingwick," MacKay encourages the young women to sustain their efforts throughout the year:

Table 3.8
Ratio Unmarried by Age Cohort, Sex, and Ethnicity, Winslow, 1861–81

	Male		Female	
	Scots	French Canadians	Scots	French Canadians
1852				
15–19	100	100	100	54
20–24	79	67	60	18
25–29	50	26	14	17
30–34	–	–	–	–
35+	12	10	18	6
1861				
15–19	100	98	100	76
20–24	100	76	83	31
25–29	83	9	33	8
30–34	6	7	17	12
35+	7	9	24	10
1871				
15–19	100	98	97	90
20–24	100	83	67	49
25–29	82	37	75	34
30–34	17	24	24	17
35+	10	9	21	10
1881				
15–19	100	100	100	91
20–24	100	86	91	64
25–29	82	26	61	49
30–34	67	14	33	19
35+	16	17	31	20

And we beseech you throw your charms
Around the lonely mountain farms,
Where bachelors are up in arms
Against your luring spell.

And in "A Christmas Dream" he writes:

And bachelors (might they be fewer)!
I thought I'd see you single, sure,
But there they sit, at least a score,

On benches stuck;
Each one a wilted, lone flower
Awaiting pluck.[57]

Perhaps, then, the French-Canadian myth that the Scots were not reproducing themselves stems from observation of their declining marriage rates. Certainly Flinn points to this factor, rather than simply delayed marriages, as the chief means of controlling reproduction in the Highlands and, most notably, the Hebridean Islands. It was also a feature of society on Cape Breton Island, which suggests once again that cultural background in Scotland influenced settlers' response to changing environmental conditions in North America.[58]

COMPLETED FAMILY SIZE

While we cannot judge precisely the impact of nuptiality or infant mortality on rates of natural increase in Winslow, it is at least possible to estimate completed family sizes for the two populations. If we confine our analysis to the number of children enumerated in so-called completed families – whose wives were between the ages of thirty-five and forty-nine – the result is 6.2 offspring for the French Canadians in 1881, and 5.6 for the Scots. By way of comparison, there were only 5.2 children in such families in the Peel County of 1871.[59]

But such an index misses future births for women still in their thirties, as well as offspring already departed for women in their forties. A more comprehensive total can be arrived at from the family reconstitution records by counting the number of children in families that appear in the census before the wife reaches thirty-six and remain in the township until she is at least forty-five years old. Almost the only French-Canadian offspring missed by this method are those who died before the family migrated to the township, but most Scots children who died between census enumerations will fail to be counted. For the thirty-four French-Canadian families who fit the category as described, there was an average of 10.5 offspring, a family size similar to that of the Saguenay region.[60] For the twenty-eight Scots families in the same category there were 8.6 children, a large number by nearly any standard.

The demographic impact of nuptiality certainly cannot be dismissed. The increasing delay in Scots marriages would inevitably affect completed family sizes of the post-1880 period, and the ageing of Winslow's Scots population, as shown in Figure 3.2, was clearly a result partially of the declining marriage rate. Very dramatic is the

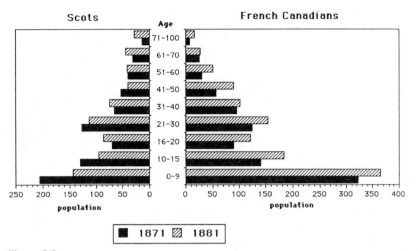

Figure 3.2
Population by Age, Winslow Township, 1871 and 1881

drop in the number of Scots children under sixteen between 1871 and 1881, but the decrease in size of two of the older cohorts also indicates another, more important cause of this ageing process: the onset of selective emigration from the township.

GEOGRAPHIC MOBILITY

We have already seen that Winslow's Scots population had reached its maximum size by the early 1860s, and Table 3.9 demonstrates that the French Canadians of Winslow North lost 74 per cent of their natural increase between 1861 and 1870. Even though the situation changed significantly during the seventies, when St Romain's loss of natural increase declined to 21 per cent, it would appear that there was little room for newcomers after the first few years of settlement – unless there was a steady exodus of settlers out of the township, such as Bouchard found for Laterrière.

Bouchard suggests that during the 1850s and 1860s Laterrière was essentially a transition point, with mature families heading toward the Lac St Jean frontier and being replaced by younger families from the south. Thus 47 per cent of all families identified in the township in 1852 were no longer there in 1861, and 61 per cent of the 1861 families had disappeared by 1871.[61] Not all upper Saguenay townships had such transient populations, however, for Marc St-Hilaire has found much more stability in St Fulgence, a condition he attributes to the parish's poor soil in comparison with Laterrière and the

Table 3.9
Loss of Natural Population Increase
in St Romain, 1861–80

	1861–70	1871–80
Births – deaths	334 – 122	360 – 147
= Natural increase	212	213
– Actual increase	55	168
= Net loss	157	45

neighbouring area.[62] Paradoxically, then, Winslow's poor soil and lack of access to a wider frontier may have made its population considerably more persistent than Laterrière's. Table 3.10 shows that the depression-ridden 1870s witnessed a particularly low ratio (22 per cent) of Scots and French-Canadian families uprooting themselves. Further, the decline in immigration from Lewis might help to explain the Scots' generally higher persistence rates.

The turn-over for Winslow's French Canadians was, indeed, far from insubstantial during the 1850s and 1860s, particularly when compared to that for the Scots. Table 3.10 does not provide a complete image of emigration rates because the census reports fail to capture those families who came and went between enumerations. For example, Benoit Bouffard was listed only in 1881, when he was fifty-eight years old, though he had received a free grant as early as 1850. He identified himself on a notarized contract in 1860 as a Winslow farmer, in 1863 as a farmer in St Joseph de la Pointe Lévis, and in 1870 as a "commercant et charretier" in the same parish. By 1880 he was back in Winslow where he purchased a lot, apparently intending to establish a mill.

Crown records and notarial deeds for Winslow North indicate a total of 341 resident heads of household who claimed, mortgaged, or alienated property between 1850 and 1881. Family reconstitution from census reports and parish registers for the shorter period 1861–81 produces a compatible total of 274 families who spent some time in the parish, even if only to marry and leave before the birth of the first child. In a parish with only 118 families in 1871, these figures suggest considerable mobility.[63] It is clear, nevertheless, that Winslow did not function as a transitional zone for settlers migrating from the seigneuries to destinations beyond. As we shall see, relatively few new families entered the township after the initial period of colonization. Emigration was largely a function of a resident population hiving off the equivalent of much of its natural increase, either as older families who wished to maintain close geographic ties with maturing off-

Table 3.10
Ratio (Percentage) of Farm Families Not Present in Succeeding Census,
Winslow, Laterrière, and Peel County, 1852, 1861, 1871

	1852	1861	1871
Winslow French Canadians	40	47	22
Winslow Scots	19	29	22
Laterrière (includes non-farmers)	47	61	–
Peel	47	60	–

Sources: Canada, manuscript census, 1852–71, Winslow Township; Bouchard, "Family
Structures," 363; Gagan, *Hopeful Travellers,* 110. In contrast to Bouchard and Gagan,
I count inheriting householders as persistent, but Gagan (p. 117) has apparently
provided for the impact of mortality in his mobility calculations.

spring or as young individuals and couples seeking better economic
opportunities elsewhere.

The family emigration figures presented in Table 3.10 show the
high persistence ratios of farm families on this marginal frontier
when compared to those in fertile and centrally located Peel County.
In addition, decennial rates of out-migration tend to exaggerate transiency: most rural communities contained a substantial core of families who remained on their homesteads for generations. Thus
Herbert Mays states of Toronto Gore Township in Peel County that
by 1850 almost half the householders had forged links "that would
continue, in one way or another, until the end of the century."[64] Similarly, in the Ottawa Valley's Alfred Township, 52 per cent of British-
origin individuals who were persistent from 1852 to 1861 were so
again during the following decade, and 31 per cent reappeared in
the 1881 census.[65]

Winslow's population was still more persistent, at least at the household level. Table 3.11 reveals that, of the fifty-two French-Canadian
families located by linkage of the 1852 agricultural census schedules
and crown land records, thirty-one (including heirs) appear again in
1861, twenty-eight in 1871, and twenty-five in 1881. In other words,
a persistence rate of only 60 per cent the first decade becomes a
much more notable 54 per cent over two decades, and a rather
remarkable 48 per cent over a thirty-year period. In conformity with
the pattern noted by many other studies of colonization communities,
the families who followed those established in Winslow as of 1852
would prove much less persistent.[66]

By 1861 the French-Canadian population had increased to 143
families, of whom 127 were listed in the agricultural census. Of the
ninety-six newcomer families, only thirty-nine would still be present

Table 3.11
Persistence and Transience of French-Canadian Landholding Family Lines
in Winslow, 1852–81

Years Resident	1852	1861	1871	1881
0–9	53 (100%)	96 (76%)	63 (48%)	44 (30%)
10–19	–	31 (24%)	39 (30%)	46 (32%)
20–29	–	–	28 (22%)	30 (21%)
30+	–	–	–	25 (17%)
Total	53 (100%)	127 (100%)	130 (100%)	145 (100%)

a decade later, and thirty-four in 1881. However, for reasons looked at below, the accelerated population growth of the 1870s saw a high rate of persistence even for the twenty-eight new families recorded in 1871. As of 1881 twenty-five of them were still present. By the end of our study period, then, 17 per cent of French-Canadian farm households had been on their properties for thirty years and more; 23 per cent for between twenty and twenty-nine years; 31 per cent for ten to nineteen years; and 28 per cent for less than a decade. Strictly speaking, these calculations are based not on individual families but on households whose composition may have changed entirely as the succeeding generation took over. To reckon otherwise, however, would be to exaggerate farmers' transiency, especially for the longer time frame.[67]

Considering the relatively high persistence ratios, and the small supply of even marginally arable land in the township, the establishment of forty-four new (that is, not inheriting homesteads) French-Canadian farm families during the 1870s appears remarkable. Only thirteen of them could have been absorbed by the increase in the number of farms, so most were clearly replacing the thirty-five families who left the township. Such a high rate of population turn-over might suggest a process of through-migration similar to that described by Bouchard for Laterrière, but closer examination of the forty-four families in question through parish registers and notary files indicates that the majority were actually not newcomers to the township.

Approximately twenty-four of the forty-four families appear to have been headed by young sons of local farmers, and four had simply not been enumerated in 1871, even though they had been in the township prior to that date. (Only one of these four families had been absent for a prolonged period.) The Laurent Corriveau family,

Table 3.12
Persistence and Transience of Scots Landholding Family Lines in Winslow,
1852–81

Years Resident	1852	1861	1871	1881
0–9	27 (100%)	84 (79%)	32 (30%)	14 (15%)
10–19	–	22 (21%)	53 (50%)	18 (19%)
20–29	–	–	22 (21%)	47 (51%)
29+	–	–	–	14 (15%)
Total	27 (100%)	106 (100%)	107 (100%)	93 (100%)

for example, may not appear in the 1871 census, but it baptized its first child locally in 1863, with others following in steady succession through 1870 and 1872. Only eight household heads could be positively identified as having originated outside Winslow (though one headed a "persistent" household by marrying a local widow), and all but one of these were from nearby parishes. The remaining eight may or may not have had earlier roots in the township.[68] It appears that a process of kin consolidation was well under way in French-speaking Winslow during the 1870s, with local kin networks expanding to take the place of families who were leaving the township.[69] Thus we have an explanation as to why marriage ages remained low during that decade.

The consolidation process also explains the varying persistence rates observed for each new cohort. As noted above, French-Canadian families first enumerated in the 1871 census lost only 27 per cent of their number by 1881, as compared with 60 per cent for the 1861 cohort during its initial decade, and 40 per cent for the pioneer cohort between 1852 and 1861. Apparently many of the latest cohort were local settlers' sons who were coming of age and able to acquire homesteads already established by out-migrants.

Given the common conditions they faced, one would expect the Scots to have developed the same pattern of mobility as the French Canadians, yet they failed to do so. Thus, Table 3.12 shows that the Scots families who first appeared in the 1871 census were less persistent than the preceding cohort. Two circumstances would seem to explain this contrast without invalidating our hypothesis concerning the second generation of French Canadians. First, because of their cultural isolation and mutual dependence, early Scots arrivals were much more persistent than their French-speaking counterparts, thereby leaving less opportunity for sons who did not inherit homesteads to acquire cleared farms or even reasonably arable land. Second, while the French-Canadian population was making a resurgence during the 1870s, the Scots were on the decline for the first time. In this context, the younger, less-established generation would be the first to leave. The fact that only ten of the families recorded in the 1881 census had not been resident ten years earlier helps to explain the ageing of the Scots community noted earlier in the chapter.

The failure of more Scots families to establish themselves in the township certainly did not stem from lack of potential recruits, for between 1871 and 1881 the marriages of twenty-seven Winslow males were recorded in the parish registers of Winslow, Lingwick, and Hampden. An examination of family formation through the parish registers reveals that of the 172 Scots families who lived in Winslow at some point during the period 1871–81, fifty-nine had disappeared by the time of the 1881 census. Twenty-three of those emigrating families consisted of young couples with either a single infant or no children whatsoever. We have already observed in Figure 3.2 the results of this differential emigration on the age-composition of the population. Between 1871 and 1881 there was a slight decline in the twenty-to-thirty-year cohort, which was echoed by a sharp drop in the number of children. Figure 3.2 also reveals a decline in the number of Scots between forty and sixty years of age. Some emigrating young couples were accompanied by parents, for Table 3.12 reveals that the pioneer cohort of 1852 experienced an unprecedented 36-per-cent drop in numbers between 1871 and 1881.

One example of such kin-migration was the household of John and Effie McIver. In 1852 they were forty-six and thirty-seven years old, respectively, and had five children aged twelve to two. In 1869 eldest son Murdoch received the farm, encumbered by a mortgage, in return for supporting his parents. In 1874 he sold it to a younger brother, Peter, who renewed the mortgage, but in 1880 Peter's widow lost the farm at a sherriff's sale. John and Effie must have left the township with one or more of their offspring, for they do not appear in the 1881 census. If the 1852 pioneer cohort became quite mobile during the 1870s, the 1861 cohort was less so, perhaps because its offspring were still too young to be looking for land.

In short, because the French-Canadian population was growing during the 1870s, pioneer families tended to expand at the expense of later arrivals, but, because the Scots were on the decline, pioneer couples tended to join their emigrating offspring. French-Canadian and Scots population movements may not have followed the same dynamics, but intergenerational ties nevertheless influenced decisions

Table 3.13
Mean Farm Values (Dollars) in Winslow, 1861

	Future Persisters	All Farms
Scots	599	563
French Canadians	602	494

on which families of each group would emigrate and which would stay behind.

Was it the less successful who tended to emigrate? North American studies generally find that families with smaller farms were inclined to sell to larger operators and leave the community.[70] This process was a natural one in an environment of increasing commercialization, but one might expect that it would be the more ambitious who would leave a marginal area such as Winslow. Indeed, Béatrice Craig states that it was the most economically advantaged families who emigrated from the isolated but much more arable upper St John Valley.[71] Such does not appear to have been the case in Winslow. Table 3.13 shows that families who remained in the township for at least a decade after 1861 owned more valuable farms than did those who failed to appear in the 1871 census, which essentially reflects the greater persistence of longer-established farmers noted above.

Where were the migrants moving to? Some crown land was still available in the district, for the provincial government was fostering another colonization drive to the south and east of Winslow during the 1870s. Sales deeds of those who had moved elsewhere before selling their properties show that the relatively undeveloped townships of Weedon and Whitton each took one French-Canadian family, and Marston on the shores of Lake Megantic claimed three, but five others simply moved to neighbouring Stratford and Lambton where land would have been at least as expensive as in Winslow.[72]

The migration toward the Lake Megantic frontier was certainly more substantial than these figures suggest, simply because few of the newly formed families who left in the 1870s would have had farms to sell. In contrast to Laterrière in the Saguenay region, however, Winslow was clearly not serving as a way-station for continuing step-by-step migration from the seigneuries to the frontier. Not only was the arable acreage on the upper St Francis frontier much more limited in scope than that of Lac St Jean, but the provincial government's various colonization projects were directed at establishing families

Table 3.14
Migration to the United States from St Romain de Winslow, 1878–90

	1878	1879	1880	1881	1882	1883	1884
Families	8	–	–	–	1	1	–
Youths	–	10*	–	–	–	13	–

	1885	1886	1887	1888	1889	1890	1891
Families	1	3	5	–	missing	1	1
Youths	–	–	22	3	–	–	

Source: Rapports sur les Paroisses et Missions, St Romain de Winslow, Archives de l'archevêché de Sherbrooke.
* "Seulement le temps des chantiers."

from the seigneuries and the New England mill towns directly on its crown lands.[73]

The sales deeds also suggest that few of St Romain's emigrants were heading to the United States. While farmers may have been likely to sell their land before moving such a distance, thereby leaving no trace of their destinations, only one deed indicates an American destination. The curé's annual reports corroborate this evidence. In 1873 he wrote that several youths had gone to the United States and returned after a few months "dans des conditions assez favorables." In addition, two families had emigrated for a few years to earn money but now spoke of returning "n'étant pas plus riches qu'auparavant."[74] No mention was made of emigration the following year, and the next available reports unfortunately begin only in 1878 (see Table 3.14). The reports reveal, however, that few individuals were heading across the border even though the parish's population had ceased to grow, the local frontier was essentially closed, and New England's textile industry had recovered from the depression of the later 1870s. More youths than families were migrating, but the curé continued to report that they were absent only for a few months.

A good illustration of the bonds that remained even for those who did emigrate to New England is the case of Féréol Roy, who had taken up residence in Lawrence, Massachusetts, anglicized his name to Jerry King, and styled himself an "artiste." On his father's death in 1869 Roy inherited a cow, but, rather than simply sell the animal, he placed it in the care of his father-in-law. The latter was to have the benefit of all the ensuing profits as long as the cow was in his possession, but if Roy were to die before reclaiming it, his father-in-law would be obliged to commission masses for the repose of his soul.

Those masses were to be worth half the value of the cow as determined by two independent experts. The cow clearly represented a link for Roy to his home parish, as well as a gesture of good will toward his wife's family. It also provided him with a double insurance policy in the dangerous economic and moral environment of Massachusetts, for it represented something tangible to fall back on in case of financial problems, and it would help to ensure the entry of his semi-assimilated soul into heaven.[75]

For the Scots, given that extended families were uprooting themselves from Winslow, we might expect to find common migration paths such as observed for Cape Breton Highlanders and other Nova Scotians, as well as French Canadians and Ontario Irish Protestants in the nineteenth century.[76] As relative newcomers to North America, the Tipperary Irish developed particularly strong migratory links between the Ottawa Valley and the London area of the province, yet few Compton Scots joined their Lewis compatriots in Huron Township, Ontario. The 1861 and 1881 census manuscripts for Huron include only a couple of families with offspring born in Lower Canada. The Lewis Scots had immigrated considerably later than the Tipperary Irish, when there was little arable land left on the Upper Canadian frontier, but they also failed to congregate together elsewhere on the continent. In 1931 M.C. MacLeod of New York City noted that the descendants of his grandfather's generation "are scattered far and wide, in the United States, the Canadian Northwest, nearly everywhere. I believe one is in New Zealand."[77]

Evidence from the nineteenth century suggests that MacLeod was not exaggerating. Of the four men who sold their farms, and identified new residences outside the immediate area prior to 1881, one had moved to Australia or New Zealand, one to Massachusetts, one to Dakota Territory, and one to Eaton Township in southern Compton County. Nearly all marriage partners came from within a narrow radius of Winslow, but one woman married a man from Saco, Maine.

The genealogy (*The Family Tree*) prepared by the Reverend M.N. MacDonald represents a particularly strong indication of how widely dispersed Winslow descendants had become by the third generation. The outline in Table 3.15 follows only those family lines that left the Winslow area, and these are followed no further than the first generation to leave. In other words, third-generation individuals are not included when it is known that their parents had themselves emigrated.

The similarity of pattern in all the branches of this family tree suggests that they were typical of the community as a whole.[78] It illustrates the dramatic transition from second to third generation,

Table 3.15

Migration of Three Generations of Winslow-Whitton Families

1 LEWIS–WINSLOW	2 LEWIS–WINSLOW	3 LEWIS–WINSLOW–WHITTON	4 LEWIS–WINSLOW
(a) Winslow	(a) Klondike	(a) Winslow or Whitton	(a) Winslow
(i) Boston–St Louis, Mo.	(b) Winslow (?)	(i) United States	(i) St Johnsbury, Vt
(ii) Alberta–Dixie, Wash.	(i) Littleton, NH	(ii) United States	(ii) Detroit, Mich.
(iv) Manchester, NH	(ii) Corinth, Vt	(iii) United States	(iii) St Johnsbury, Vt
(v) Edmonton, Alta	(iv) Littleton, NH	(iv) Alberta	(iv) Egerton, Alta
(b) Fitchburg, Mass.	(v) Barre, Vt	(v) Alberta	(b) Winslow (?)
(c) Seattle, Wash.	(vi) Toronto, Ont.	(b) Whitton (?)	(i) Western United States
	(vii) Corinth, Vt	(i) Keith, Que.	(ii) Seattle, Wash.
	(c) Winslow (?)	(ii) Barre, Vt	(iii) Sherbrooke, Que.
	(i) Montreal, Que.	(c) Glover, Vt	(c) New Hampshire
	(ii) Detroit, Mich.	(d) Graniteville, Vt	(d) Coaticook, Que.
	(iii) Detroit, Mich.	(e) Whitton	
	(d) Winslow (?)	(i) Alberta	
	(i) Cranbrook, BC	(ii) Reedsville, Que.	
	(ii) St Elmo, Colo.	(iii) Edmonton, Alta	
	(iv) Barre, Vt	(iv) Edmonton, Alta	
	(v) Forgan, Sask.		
	(vi) Portland, Ore.		
	(e) Winslow (?)		
	(i) Portland, Me		
	(ii) Portland, Me		

Source: MacDonald, *The Family Tree.*

with grandchildren of the pioneers scattering themselves widely throughout the continent. Northern New England (particularly the granite-producing centres of Vermont) and the western frontier were favoured destinations, but surprisingly few emigrating siblings settled close to each other.

The timing of the exodus was clearly crucial. French-Canadian and Maritime migratory patterns to specific New England towns were well established prior to the extension of the rail network across the continent. As Elliott points out for the later Irish emigrants from the Ottawa Valley, by the time Winslow's Scots began to move in large numbers, cheap railway excursions were available to the west. Thus intending settlers could scout out desirable locations for themselves, rather than depending on letters from relatives who had gone before them.[79]

Angus MacKay (Oscar Dhu) comments in "Guard the Gaelic" on the American destinations of many emigrants, as well as on the consequences for cultural survival:

Pity the disloyal clown
Who will dwell awhile in town
And returning wear a frown
If he hears the Gaelic.

Some gay natives of the soil
Cross 'the Line' a little while
And returning, deem it 'style'
To deny the Gaelic.

Lads and lassies in their teens
Wearing airs of kings and queens
Just a taste of Boston beans
Makes them lose their Gaelic!

They return with finer clothes,
Speaking 'Yankee' through their nose!
That's the way the Gaelic goes –
Pop! Goes the Gaelic![80]

To MacKay, who himself spent his last years in Seattle, emigration clearly exacted an emotional toll. He was a people's poet, not given to obscure symbolic imagery, but the Arizona desert takes on biblical significance in "The Alkali Land":

I left my home and my friends in the East
Ambitious to better my fortunes, forsooth;
and seek amid scenes of the strenuous West,
The gold which had gilded the dreams of my youth.

...

Yes, on as I plodded the limitless range,
In that land of hot sand and clear skies,
How oft in my thirst did I long for a change
To my own native hills, where the watersprings rise!

O Compton beloved! what visions arose,
Of thy hills and dark vales and thy cold mountain streams!
And each fountain-like fuadhran which bubbles and flows,
On the farm back at home in the land of my dreams![81]

The Scots communities of Winslow and the surrounding area have long since disappeared – way-stations to the North American melting pot for an Old World society still clinging to many of its traditional customs. But MacKay's laments are one indication that the journey was taken with some reluctance, and it certainly required more than one generation to complete. Table 3.10 reveals a level of persistence in the earlier years of Winslow's history higher than that noted by most other studies for the post-1852 period, yet the disappearance of the Scots community was obviously not caused by a low fertility rate.[82]

Rather, the Scots began to respond to population pressure during the 1870s by selective migration of multigenerational families, the same process as followed by the French Canadians. However, the departing French Canadians were replaced by the sons and daughters of those who remained behind, while Scots farms were simply abandoned as the younger generation began to postpone marriage. The following chapters, on family and community, will examine more closely the ties that held the Scots and French Canadians to Winslow, as well as the forces – such as internal religious dissension – that pushed many of them out during the first thirty years of settlement.

CHAPTER FOUR

The Family

The preceding chapters have already demonstrated the fundamental role of the single-household family in Winslow, but they have also suggested that broader kinship ties affected the process of migration and colonization. In this chapter we shall see that even if married siblings never lived under the same roof in Winslow after the initial pioneering period, family loyalties among the Scots delayed the departure of offspring for unusually long periods of time. Basic similarities in household structure between the Scots and French Canadians therefore mask a fundamental difference in the evolution of their families.

While studies of European peasant societies stress that the structural development of families was determined by inheritance custom, Winslow's two cultural communities followed essentially the same strategy of intergenerational property transfer. Scots parents, however, tended to transfer their patrimonies when they were older than their French-speaking counterparts. But rather than causing the late departure of their offspring, such delays were more likely a result of strong cohesive forces within the Scots family. European-inspired typologies of inheritance and household structure therefore do not help much in analysing the family dynamics of Winslow's two cultural communities. In the final section of this chapter, however, I shall apply the traditional/modern continuum as defined by cultural historians of the family in an attempt to explore the psychology of the Scots and French-Canadian families.

HOUSEHOLD STRUCTURE

Social scientists have been intrigued by the different categories of household structure since the work of Frederic LePlay in the second half of the nineteenth century. Thus demographic historians are now debating about Peter Laslett's generalization that the simple-family household has long been the dominant type in western Europe. Lutz Berkner has pointed out that even in regions where the nuclear structure dominated most of a peasant household's life cycle, that household might well haved passed through a three-generational or stem-family stage when one or both grandparents lived with the inheriting son, his wife, and their children. The stem structure of any particular household might not have lasted long because of the shorter life expectancy in pre-industrial societies, but it would be repeated in the next generation. Thus, even where the nuclear-family structure was the more visible one, the stem-family organization may well have existed.[1]

In the final analysis, the ratio of households that would experience such a multi-generational stage in a given area would depend on the timing of intergenerational property transfers and the number of adult offspring and newcomers who settled in that area. Thus, if farms were passed on to the succeeding generation while the parents were still relatively young, if all but the inheriting sons moved elsewhere, and if no new families settled in the area, most households would include one or more grandparents at one point in their developmental cycle. A high proportion of nuclear families, interpreted by LePlay as a sign of individualism, might instead reflect the propensity of offspring to settle near their parental families. In other words, family structure was less the determining sociocultural variable envisaged by LePlay than a product of other social, economic, and cultural variables.[2]

For this reason Gérard Bouchard and certain American historians of the family have rejected the validity of all sociological models for the North American context. What Bouchard perhaps inappropriately calls the structural approach attempts to discover how social, economic, cultural, geographic, and demographic factors combine to produce a particular family structure, but he warns that these factors may well be more important in themselves than was the actual structure of the pre-industrial family. Thus classifications and typologies are less helpful to an understanding of the family than is comprehensive knowledge of the historical context. Bouchard feels that this is especially true of North America because of its less densely populated environment.[3] Likewise, John J. Waters argues that the taxonomic approach to the study of the family must be replaced by a holistic view which follows "the flow of life experience through time."[4] Nevertheless, historians will presumably continue to study the size and composition of the household as it changed over time as an

Table 4.1
Household Structure and Size, Winslow, 1852–81

	1852	1861	1871	1881
MEAN HOUSEHOLD SIZE				
Scots	6.8	6.6	6.5	6.8
French Canadian	5.4	6.9	6.5	6.7
PERCENTAGE WITH CONJUGAL FAMILY UNIT PLUS NO EXTRAS				
Scots	68.6	65.5	84.2	69.0
French Canadian	58.6	73.4	79.9	80.7
PERCENTAGE WITH FAMILY UNIT PLUS relatives, boarders, or visitors:				
Scots	2.9	16.8	5.0	9.5
French Canadian	17.2	11.2	9.4	9.4
servants, employees, or other children:				
Scots	11.4	8.0	4.2	4.3
French Canadian	5.2	4.2	2.0	1.1
relatives, boarders, or visitors and servants, employees, or other children:				
Scots	2.9	4.4	0.8	1.7
French Canadian	5.2	–	0.7	1.1
second family:*				
Scots	14.3	5.3	5.8	15.5
French Canadian	13.8	11.2	8.1	7.7
PERCENTAGE OF ALL HOUSEHOLDS WITH MULTIPLE FAMILIES AND/OR "EXTRAS":				
Scots	31.4	34.5	15.8	31.0
French Canadian	41.4	26.6	20.2	19.3
MEAN NO. OF "EXTRAS" PER HOUSEHOLD WITH "EXTRAS"				
Scots	2.6	1.8	1.7	1.3
French Canadian	1.7	1.3	1.8	1.4

* May also include "relatives, boarders, or visitors" and/or "servants, employees, or other children."

important part of the life experience and as a significant distinguishing feature of various societies.[5]

As far as the size of Winslow's households was concerned, Table 4.1 reveals a surprising similarity between the Scots and the French Canadians, given that we saw in chapter 3 that the latter tended to produce more children. Elimination of the "extra," or non-family, members of the household brings the average sizes for the two groups closer together in 1852 and slightly further apart in 1861 and makes little difference in 1871 and 1881. As we shall see, the Scots offspring simply tended to remain at home longer than those of the French Canadians. As for the identity of the "extras," the census does not define individual status within the household, and the categories in Table 4.1 are designed to take all possibilities into account. For our purposes, however, they could have been reduced to "relatives" and "other children," with all two-family households (except for some temporary arrangements in 1852) representing two married generations of the same family.[6]

For the French Canadians, the ratio of nuclear-family households tended to increase steadily until it reached 80 per cent in 1871, where it stabilized. In contrast, the Scots nuclear-household structure fluctuated, reaching a high of 84 per cent in 1871 and dropping again to 69 per cent in 1881.[7] There was a noticeable jump in Scots two-family households in 1881, perhaps because of the ageing of the population. 47 per cent of married individuals were over fifty years of age, a significant increase from the 32 per cent a decade earlier. As we have already seen, the French-Canadian community was at the same time rejuvenating itself. In 1881 only 22 per cent of its spouses were over fifty years old. It would appear, then, that the marginal differences observed in the household structure of the two groups were governed largely by contrasting migration rates rather than by different social customs per se. As Table 4.2 shows, Scots households that remained in Winslow for at least twenty years were only slightly more inclined to have included a second family at some point (31.1 per cent) than were their French-Canadian counterparts (25.6 per cent).

The persistent Scots were rather more inclined than the French Canadians to have had, at some point, other "extras" in their households. It seems somewhat paradoxical that the Scots would have had more outside help as well as more extended kin in their households, but close examination of the census reveals that most of the former were teen-aged girls living with families whose offspring were still too young to be of much assistance. Thus, Maryann Morrison recalled that at the age of twelve she worked for a couple "taking care of a boy and a girl they had," while the mother worked in the fields.[8] In 1861, eighteen Scots households included non-family girls as young as fourteen, only five of whom were listed as servants. Eight were said to be residents of neighbouring townships, testifying to the temporary nature of their stay in Winslow. As for the male "help," one sixteen-year-old boy was living with a young married woman

Table 4.2
Distribution (Percentage) of Persistent Householders in Winslow by
Frequency of Presence of Extras in Households, 1861–81

	Never had	Ever had	Had once	Had twice	Had always
SCOTS (n = 45)					
Extras*	57.8	42.2	33.3	6.7	2.2
Hired help†	75.6	24.4	24.4	–	–
Relatives/boarders/visitors	71.1	28.9	24.4	2.2	2.2
Other families	68.9	31.1	22.2	8.9	–
FRENCH CANADIANS (n = 39)					
Extras*	74.4	25.6	25.6	–	–
Hired help†	92.3	7.7	7.7	–	–
Relatives/boarders/visitors	82.1	17.9	17.9	–	–
Other families	74.4	25.6	25.6	–	–

* Does not include extra couples.
† Includes non-family children ten years old and over.
Adding horizontally, "ever had" + "never had" = 100%, "once" + "twice" + "always"
= "ever had."

whose husband was absent at the time of the census, and two villagers
each employed a male servant, but there were only two other households with men who might have been hired workers. Both these
households had three such men, ranging in age from sixteen to
twenty-seven, and in each case two of them appear to have been
brothers. It is likely, therefore, that they were providing temporary
assistance in some particularly demanding task, such as raising a
barn or clearing some land. Presumably, only in the hectic haying or
harvesting seasons (long after the spring census enumeration) might
one expect to find boys being delegated by mature families to join
those whose offspring were still too young to do arduous work.

Still more striking than the Scots' independence from non-family
male labour was that of the French Canadians, for Table 4.2 reveals
that only 8 per cent of those families that had been persistent
through three census enumerations ever reported outside help of
either gender. As Léon Gérin noted in 1896, "l'habitant répugne à
envoyer ses enfants en service sur les terres du voisinage."[9] Long-
term sharing of labour within the same "moral order" was clearly
less common in Winslow than among the subsistence-oriented peasants of Europe, testifying once again to the strength of the North
American nuclear family as a social unit.[10]

Table 4.3

Unmarried Adults per Household (Unmarried Adult Offspring in Parentheses), Winslow and Laterrière, 1852–81*

Year	Winslow Scots	Winslow French Canadians	Laterrière
1852	0.70 (0.26)	0.43 (0.03)	0.60
1861	0.82 (0.48)	0.40 (0.17)	0.63
1871	0.88 (0.76)	0.60 (0.32)	0.66
1881	1.54 (0.98)	0.78 (0.44)	0.63

* Adult status is fixed at twenty years for Laterrière and twenty-one years for Winslow. The statistics for Laterrière are from Bouchard, "Family Structures," 359.

If the Scots were more inclined than the French Canadians to include outside help in their households, it was perhaps because of their Old World roots, as well as the somewhat smaller size of their families. But the contrast between Scots and French Canadians remains much less significant than that between Winslow and the farmers of market-oriented Peel County, where many of the "extras" truly were agricultural labourers. Whereas the maximum ratio of Scots households that included "servants, employees, or other children" was less than 12 per cent, in Peel the ratio was 22 per cent for both 1852 and 1861.[11] In fact, 59 per cent of all persistent households in Peel included "hired help" during at least one of the three census years from 1852 to 1871, in comparison to the 24 per cent noted for their Winslow Scots counterparts between 1861 and 1881.[12] There was a sharp decline in the ratio of Peel families with hired help in 1871 because mature offspring were increasingly inclined to stay at home. As we are about to see, there was a parallel development among Winslow's Scots offspring, which no doubt again explains the 1871 drop in the ratio of households that included the extras in question.

In contrast to what Hareven and Vinovskis declare to be the American norm for the nineteenth century, Winslow's families clearly did not prefer to share their household space with strangers as opposed to their own kin.[13] Although only a few households had "extra" residents at any given time in Winslow, Table 4.3 reveals a steady increase in the number of unmarried adult offspring remaining with their families. This number approximately doubled for the households among both the Scots and French Canadians between 1852 and 1881, but the Scots numbers were in turn persistently close to double those for the French Canadians. It was for this reason, and not because they included more outsiders, that Scots

Table 4.4
Number of Adult Offspring in Families with Adult Offspring (Ratio to Total Families in Parentheses) in Winslow, 1852–81

	1	2	3	4	5	Total
FRENCH CANADIANS (WINSLOW NORTH)						
1852	1	–	–	–	–	1 (3%)
1861	1	1	–	1	–	3 (3%)
1871	8	7	–	–	–	15 (13%)
1881	17	9	4	1	1	32 (24%)
SCOTS						
1852	6	–	1	–	–	7 (20%)
1861	12	7	2	3	1	25 (22%)
1871	15	12	8	6	1	42 (35%)
1881	16	17	11	5	2	51 (44%)

Table 4.5
Age Distribution of Dependent French-Canadian and Scots Adult Offspring (Ratio to Total Offspring in Parentheses) in Winslow, 1881

	21–23	24–26	27–29	30–32	33–35	36+	Total
FRENCH CANADIAN							
Male	17	5	5	1	1	3	32 (9.2%)
Female	22	13	7	3	2	1	48 (12.8%)
SCOTS							
Male	25	13	9	10	5	2	64 (27.4%)
Female	16	17	6	3	–	6	48 (24.0%)

households were as large as those of the French Canadians in 1871 and 1881 (see Table 4.1). Part of this phenomenon simply reflects the ageing of the population, but Table 4.3 also reveals how population turn-over in a maturing colonization parish such as Laterrière, in the Lac St Jean region, could obviate the problem of overcrowded households.

For all families to average more than one adult offspring at home, as with the Scots in 1881, most mature families must have actually included several sons and daughters over the age of twenty-one. Table 4.4, while not focused on families at any particular stage of development, demonstrates that not only did the ratio with adult offspring increase over time, but also the number of such offspring per family.

Finally, it also reveals how distinctively Scots was such a family structure. By 1881 close to half of all Scots families included at least one adult unmarried son or daughter, reflecting a stable population's ageing process, since most rural families would house a single adult heir at one stage of their development. But the presence of three, four, and even five mature offspring – some of them in their mid-to-late thirties (as we can see from Table 4.5) – was clearly unusual for almost any society.[14] Indeed, by 1881 one-quarter of all unmarried Scots offspring were over the age of twenty-one. The majority of these mature Scots offspring were male, while the reverse was the case for the French Canadians. Young Scots women were not much more likely to remain with their parental families than were their French-speaking counterparts.

Whether the Scots' apparent reluctance to leave the family permanently reflected a deep-seated cultural tradition is difficult to say because there are no detailed historical analyses of household structure for the Scottish Highlands. We have already noted that marriages tended to be delayed, and one rather jaundiced observer commented in the early nineteenth century that Hebrideans preferred: "having their children about them in the most miserable state imaginable, to the hardship, (or what they are pleased to call such) of driving them into service, either on their own island or any where else. It is a common sight, on entering the cottage of one of those subtenants, to find five or six grown individuals, half-naked and savage-looking, around a peat fire, watching a pot of potatoes, (their sole food for nine months of the year) without any idea or wish of changing their manner of life."[15]

Census enumerators rarely listed more than one Scots son as a farmer, even in 1871, when enumerators were instructed to record all sons working on their father's farm. Most older sons were generally identified as farm labourers of simply labourers, with only one listed as a lumberman and one said to work at home. A number of the daughters were recorded as servants. Presumably, then, they and their labourer brothers lived at home only part of the year. Indeed, they may have been away at the time of the census, since the enumerator's instructions of 1861 dictated the entry of "members of the family who are temporarily absent, but whose usual residence it is."[16]

In the following chapter we shall attempt to determine the nature of the migratory labouring economy, as well as establish whether or not there was a rational economic basis to the composition of the Winslow Scots households. First, however, we must turn to the role of inheritance practices in determining that composition.

INHERITANCE

As many Scots offspring remained at home after they had reached adulthood, one would anticipate considerable pressure to divide the family inheritance into several portions. Though no studies appear to have been published on Highland inheritance practices, Youngson claims that crofter holdings tended to become smaller because of the ancient Celtic practice of sharing land with children or other near-relations.[17] As for French Canada, even before the partible inheritance requirement of the Coutume de Paris had been eliminated by the Conquest, patrimonies were commonly reassembled by one of the heirs.[18] The assistance of offspring nevertheless remained crucial enough in pre-industrial North America that some sort of settlement was generally provided for each son and daughter.[19] Bouchard suggests further that, while the North American frontier was still open, most farmers were able to assist older sons in the acquisition of land before the family farm was passed on to the so-called inheriting son.[20]

Bouchard's strong emphasis on the equalizing influence of migration to the frontier runs counter to Easterlin's claim that strong population pressure quickly developed on agricultural land as communities were settled.[21] Certainly in Winslow any predisposition to provide land for more than one son was hindered by the small size of the original crown grants (particularly for the French Canadians), by the rapid early influx of settlers, and by the short supply of arable land. Furthermore, the farm population of Winslow was too stable to offer a great deal of opportunity to purchase the farms of departing neighbours, and, as Sylvie Dépatie has pointed out, the accumulation of improved lots would require means not normally associated with the inhabitants of a colonization zone.[22] We saw in the previous chapter that some second-generation French Canadians clearly did acquire land from out-migrants during the 1870s, but it is doubtful that the average persistent family in Winslow would have been able to establish as many as two to three sons locally, as Bouchard states was the nineteenth-century norm for the upper Saguenay region.[23]

A precise ratio is impossible to arrive at in this study because of the narrow scope of its geographical and temporal boundaries. Most sons settling in nearby townships are missed, and many pioneer families still had sons at home as late as 1881. But we can find some important clues by examining the thirty-five married couples who had resided in St Romain for at least twenty years prior to 1881 (one childless couple is omitted). These families had a total of twenty-six sons settled in the parish (not all of whom were farmers) and another

from the three or four who moved to the young colony of Piopolis on the shores of Lake Megantic, probably rather few settled close by. Evidence for this hypothesis can be found in the destinations of the mature daughters, who, because they seldom inherited a farm, would presumably have been more inclined than sons to have settled outside the township. St Romain's marriage records reveal that twenty of the persistent cohort's daughters had married local men by 1881, sixteen had apparently emigrated as singles, and only fourteen had chosen partners outside the parish but within the general district.[24]

Still, with as many sons settled in the parish as outside it, and most of the homesteads yet to be turned over to the chief heir, St Romain's thirty-five persistent families might appear to have been well on their way to establishing an average of two to three sons locally. Given that the French-Canadian population of Winslow had expanded considerably in the 1870s and would begin to decline in the 1880s, however, this would certainly become a more difficult task where the younger offspring were concerned. There would be no local frontier to relieve land pressure, unless a number of mature families moved to the burgeoning new railway town of Lake Megantic. In addition, even the success of the 1870s was far from being shared equally by the thirty-five families in question. Joachim and Angélique Hallé had five sons married and living in the township, and Paul and Catherine Richard had four – though one was a blacksmith and another a merchant – in addition to a fifth who had farmed in the parish for at least twelve years before leaving. Both the Hallés and the Richards had arrived in St Romain when their families were relatively mature; by 1881 Joachim was seventy years of age, and Paul sixty-seven. If more than a handful of their neighbours ever came close to emulating their success, the rate at which others uprooted themselves must have accelerated considerably during the 1880s.

Table 4.6 suggests that rather than expanding properties significantly as sons matured most French-Canadian and Scots families had to struggle simply to acquire enough arable land to constitute a viable homestead. This table would have been more useful had it not included as persisters those families whose farms had passed on to the chief inheriting son, but such cases were still quite infrequent by 1871. Further, the notary and registry records of the township reveal only two "donations à fin d'établissement" (grants of land to offspring not inheriting the homestead) and few sales of land by fathers to sons. Also, the deeds in gift generally transferred only the basic homestead (See Table 4.7).[25]

It appears that deeds in gift – typical means of intergenerational transfer for both groups in Winslow – were not customary in com-

Table 4.6
Acreage in Winslow Owned by French-Canadian
and Scots Landowners Persistent 1852–71

	1852	1861	1871
FRENCH-CANADIAN			
Mean	64.9	85.2	82.0
Median	58.1	73.0	73.0
SCOTS			
Mean	109.6	113.3	99.2
Median	102.8	100.6	99.8

munities where packages of land were sold to sons as they came of age. Among the German settlers of Minnesota, for example, the son who eventually took over the homestead generally paid a low price on easy terms, just as his older brothers had for the land they had acquired through the family.[26] Séguin suggests a similar pattern for Hébertville in the Saguenay region during the last half of the nineteenth century,[27] but in Winslow, even when a rare farmer such as Paul Richard managed to establish several sons in the parish, he did so by formally distributing the various packages of land with a single deed in gift.

Richard had acquired a free grant in 1850, paid the location fees on another lot in 1855, and purchased two privately held lots in 1862 and 1870. In 1866 he and his wife mortgaged the free grant as security for one son's rental of a blacksmith shop, and in 1872 they divided their four lots among three other sons and a son-in-law in return for a small annual payment in cash from each son and payment in kind from the son-in-law. The deed in gift made no mention of the blacksmith or the eldest son, who had first married in 1860 only to lose his wife and three of their children through an accident in 1869. Why the unlucky Paul Jr was discriminated against by his parents is not clear, but in the 1871 agricultural census he is listed with only a quarter-acre of potatoes, and an inventory taken a year later includes only a horse, a cow, two sheep, and three pigs. Debts outweighed assets by $81.97. The 1872 distribution of the patrimony was clearly a very significant event for the family, because Paul Jr moved to a neighbouring township after marrying for a third time in 1874, while the three brothers who inherited land went on to expand their holdings significantly during the 1870s.[28]

Table 4.7
Selected Summary Data from Wills and Deeds in Gift, Winslow, 1860–80

	Partible/Impartible	Impartible	Partible
SCOTS FARMERS			
No. of settlements	3	14	3
Mean no. of acres owned	152.5	74.4	107.5*
Mean no. of heirs	4.5	1.0	2.3
No. designating spouse as heir	–	–	–
Mean no. of offspring inheriting real property	1.0	1.0	2.0
FRENCH-CANADIAN FARMERS			
Wills			
No. of settlements	1	32	–
Mean no. of acres owned	(recorded in only one case)		
Mean no. of heirs	all offspring	1.0	–
No. designating spouse as heir	–	27	–
Mean no. of offspring inheriting real property	1.0	1.0	–
Deeds in Gift			
No. of settlements	4	19	6
Mean no. of acres owned	82.8	80.8	175.8
Mean no. of heirs†	3.7	1.0	4.0
Mean no. of offspring inheriting real property	1.0	1.0	2.2

* Only two cases record number of acres.
† Does not include spouses.

Table 4.7 demonstrates not only how atypical the Richards' experience of partible settlement was for both the French-Canadian and Scots communities, but also that the so-called Canadian system of partible/impartible inheritance was even less common.[29] Between 1860 and 1880, fifteen of twenty notarized Scots wills and deeds in gift were for impartible settlements. (One donation to a single son was accompanied by the sale of one-third of the property to his brother, but he appears to have paid the approximate market value). Of the five remaining cases, two split the land equally among two sons, and three divided a small amount of cash or livestock among several offspring (see Table 4.8).

Even with partible and semi-partible settlements, then, most Scots offspring received only a relatively small part of the estate. The same

Table 4.8
Principal Obligations of Primary Heir(s) to Each Identified Sibling with
Partible* and Semi-Partible Settlements, Winslow, 1860–80

No.	Siblings	Livestock	Cash	"Lit garni"	Spinning Wheel
SCOTS					
1	4 bro., 1 sis.	–	$123.47	–	–
2	1 sister	1 cow	$50	–	–
3	1 bro., 3 sis.	–	$20	–	–
4	2 bro., 2 sis.	–	$50	–	–
FRENCH CANADIANS					
1	?	1 ewe	–	–	–
2	1 sister	1 cow, 2 sheep	–	yes	–
3	5 sisters	1 cow, pig, ewe, & lamb	$50	yes	yes
4	1 brother	–	$50	–	–
	2 sisters	–	$25	–	–
5	?	1 cow, 1 ewe	–	–	–
6	2 sisters	–	£0.5.0	–	–
7	2 sisters	–	5 livres	–	–
8	2 sisters	1 cow, ewe, lamb	$25	yes	yes
9	3 brothers	1 cow, 2 ewes, 1 pig	–	–	–
	1 sister	1 cow	–	yes	yes

*Partible settlements are included only when they provide for offspring other than
those inheriting the landed estate.

was true of Winslow's French Canadians, for whom nineteen of
twenty-nine deeds in gift specified impartible inheritances. There
were obviously more members of the second generation acquiring
land in Winslow than there were deeds in gift, which suggests that
some sons may have been assisted informally by their parents. However, many of them may also have earned the first instalment needed
by engaging in off-farm labour, for we saw in chapter 2 that young
men were apparently preparing to establish families of their own by
cutting timber on crown lots.

More French-speaking farmers than Scots had notaries draw up
wills, but most of these documents simply designated the other
spouse as heir. Because Quebec law divided intestate inheritances
among all family survivors, wills guaranteed that the patrimony
would not be fragmented before the chosen son could take it over.
The small number of post-mortem inventories testifies to the infre-
quency of such fragmentation. No inventory has been found for Scots

farmers, and only six for French Canadians prior to 1881. Even when the father died intestate, arrangements were made to preserve the integrity of the homestead. Thus, with the death of Antoine Roy in 1875, the inheritance had to be divided between his widow, two sons who were of age, and seven minor children, but all the goods were purchased by one of the older sons at the auction held a few weeks later. Within a few months, his mother had granted this son her share of the homestead.[30]

The domestic situations at the time the wills were drafted demonstrate the typically temporary nature of most of them. Of the twenty-five cases where spouses were named as sole heirs (in two additional cases the family could not be reconstituted from the St Romain records), in fourteen the eldest son was still too young to take over the farm. In another instance, the widow transferred the farm to a son shortly after her husband's death. Four more were cases where the couple was either infertile or the children had all died in infancy. An additional five wills resulted from a widowed male's remarriage, and, in three of these situations, there were again no older sons. In cases related to remarriage, the new wife was protecting her share of the patrimony from the husband's first family. Thus Vitaline Aubé had Dieudonné Boulanger sign a will to her benefit nine days before their wedding! Only one farmer notarized a will to his wife after the family farm had been transferred inter vivos.

The nature of these wills suggests that married women in Winslow exercised more authority than one might have expected, given the deterioration of their property rights after the British Conquest. Husbands may have gained complete testamentary freedom under the new régime, thereby depriving widows of their inalienable usufructory right to half the communal estate, but Winslow's wills generally transferred absolute control of the whole inheritance to the surviving spouse. In effect, then, French-Canadian widows appear to have held a higher status than their counterparts in other British jurisdictions, such as colonial Massachusetts, where widows were granted "sustenance but not economic freedom": a Massachusetts widow might manage the estate, but she was effectively holding it in trust for the succeeding generation.[31] In the one Winslow case that specified that the widow of a French-speaking farmer would have to pass the estate on to one of the offspring, the choice of heirs was to be hers, and her husband was restricted by the same clause in her will. In two more of these reciprocal wills, each child was to receive a small cash settlement on coming of age. Widowers with children in Quebec did not enjoy unencumbered authority over the family estate, which explains why wills in Winslow were invariably drafted by wives at the same time as their husbands.[32] In one case where a mother died intestate, an inventory was drawn up immediately prior to her husband's remarriage two years later, clearly in order to protect the offspring of the first marriage.[33]

In sharp contrast to regions that have been examined outside Quebec, no mention was made in any will in Winslow of "cutting off" a widow should she remarry.[34] Indeed, when the widow Marguerite Royer remarried a year after she had transferred the family farm to her son, he ceded part of the land back to her, presumably because he would no longer have to deliver the annual "pension alimentaire" to his mentally handicapped sister.[35] Perhaps the low value of the land in Winslow helps to explain the lack of restrictions on widows' property rights, but recent studies suggest the same situation in other areas of French Canada.[36]

The control ensured to Winslow's French-Canadian widows over the family farm would seem to presuppose some sharing of responsibility in its operation prior to the husband's death.[37] Under these conditions there would be little need for the wife to maintain the additional protection of a douaire, which represented certain rights over real property owned by the husband before marriage or subsequently acquired by him.[38] Since this was a privileged claim that might interfere with sale or mortgage of the farm, it is not surprising that fourteen of the sixteen brides-to-be who signed community-of-goods contracts in Winslow simply renounced their dower rights. The other two limited these to $100, while a seventeenth contract specified separation of goods. The only other provision for the surviving spouse mentioned in most marriage contracts was a fixed mutual settlement known as the "préciput" which – in addition to personal items of bed, clothing, and jewellery or guns – ranged in value from $25 to $50. Rather than transferring wealth from one generation to the next,[39] Winslow's marriage contracts removed an encumberance to future disposal of real property. If more couples did not sign such contracts, it was probably because the new Civil Code ended wives' automatic dower rights in 1866.[40]

While the study on widows in colonial Massachusetts demonstrates that they found it difficult to find a second spouse, one might expect the widows of Winslow to have remarried relatively quickly. There were relatively few adult deaths in the township prior to 1881 to test this hypothesis, but the interval from bereavement to remarriage can be traced for eight St Romain widows and five widowers. The latter, who averaged thirty-one years of age at the time their spouses died (the range was from twenty-six to forty-two), remarried between sixteen and twenty-six months later, with the mean being twenty-two months. The average widow, who lost her spouse at the similar age of thirty-three years (but ranging from twenty-five to fifty-seven), remarried after the much longer delay of forty-four months. However, if one excepts the anomalous case of the thirty-two-year-old widow who remarried more than fifteen years after her first husband's death, the mean interval becomes very similar to that for the men – twenty-four months.[41] Most of St Romain's widows apparently had little more difficulty finding a second spouse than did the widowers.

No marriage contracts and only two wills were uncovered for the Scots. Married women in Britain held none of the legal claims over the family estate traditionally enjoyed by their French counterparts, so perhaps it is not surprising that the two Scots wills did include certain restrictive clauses. In contrast to the French-Canadian wills, they named specific sons as the ultimate heirs, but they allowed the widows to hold full usufructory rights over the estates until they died. The fact that the Scots did not notarize more wills suggests that women widowed before the farm was transferred would enjoy an essentially free hand in its operation, since the community of goods could be perpetuated with the permission of the children. A significant number of the Scots household heads listed in the census reports were widows – 9 per cent in 1861, 6 per cent in 1871, and 9 percent in 1881, as compared to 1, 3, and 4 per cent, respectively, for the French Canadians – but most parents in both groups transferred their farms to the succeeding generation before either spouse died. The will was therefore only a transitional step in intergenerational transmission. Once that transfer was made, the retired father would have no more authority over the patrimony than would his wife.

Not only did most of the deeds in gift drafted within both communities specify strictly impartible settlements, but even semi-partible transfers provided rather small rewards for the remaining offspring. In addition, all but one of the six partible cases settled land on only two offspring each. The partible settlements were clearly made possible by greater-than-average accumulations of land, but Table 4.7 (above) shows that for the French Canadians a patrimony's acreage had no relationship to the distinction between impartible and semi-partible settlements.

There was little reason for semi-partible settlements to require more land, because, as we can see from Table 4.8 (above), they provided for relatively small endowments. Most appear to have represented the marriage or coming-of-age settlements of younger offspring.[42] For example, when Paul Roy's two daughters reached their majority, each was to receive $25, plus a bed, spinning wheel, cow, ewe, and lamb. A third married daughter was said to have already received enough. Maryann Morrison recalled that on her marriage in 1894: "My father gave me two cows and and one sheep – two sheeps. And his [her husband's] father gave him one cow and two sheep. So we had four sheep and three cows. So we were very rich, mind you. It isn't everyone that got that much in those days ... A cousin of mine gave me one sheet, and another one gave me a pair of pillow cases. That was all – except my grandmother, blankets, of course, that she made herself."[43]

Dowries constituted recognition of a daughter's right to some share in the parental estate but were clearly too small to obligate most grooms to sign a marriage contract with certain guarantees for their bride's future well-being.[44] Table 4.8 reveals that French-Canadian dependent siblings were sisters more often than not; however, all able-bodied members of the household were expected to contribute toward their keep. Twenty-six-year-old Marie Cormier, for example, was to be allowed to earn money elsewhere, but if she returned to the family fold she would have to relinquish all her savings to her brother and continue to work at home.[45] The status of daughters was clearly subservient, with little hope of inheriting landed property and no control over the fruits of their labour as long as they remained with the parental family. Much the same could be said for most sons, however, and once a property was transferred they often had the right to remain at home only until they reached their majority, while daughters could generally stay until they married.[46]

More potentially onerous than the obligation to care for younger siblings was the requirement invariably attached to Winslow deeds in gift to lodge and provide for ageing parents. The cost of this task would depend largely on how long the parents lived after the inheriting son took over the farm. Certainly, filial duties were not to be taken lightly. In order to ensure that the terms of agreement were fulfilled, the patrimony was mortgaged in the parents' names, and in most cases their permission would be required before selling the farm or burdening it with an additional hypothec. Deeds in gift often spelled out in detail the chief heir's obligations to his parents.

In the eighteen Scots contracts, requirements were basically as follows: in seventeen, provision of a doctor's services when needed; in twelve, access to church services; again in twelve, Christian burial; and in ten, washing, mending, and renewal of clothing. One self-styled gentleman required a cash payment of six dollars every year and a suit of homemade cloth every second year. Another parental

couple reserved the right to exploit one of two lots, while three contracts set aside several sheep, and four mentioned the use of one or
two cows.

French-Canadian deeds in gift were more specific. In addition to
access to medical and spiritual services, for example, many reserved
use of a horse and carriage outside the busy season. Eighteen of
twenty-nine agreements also required that the parents have a separate
living space, generally a room, with kitchen utensils, stove, bed, and
bedding. Eleven reserved part of the garden, and ten specified an
annual cash payment ranging from $1.50 to $5.00. Finally, in sharp
contrast to Scots practice, fourteen listed annual food provisions to
be given to the parents (the "pension alimentaire"), and seven itemized the required clothing.[47]

The contrasting nature of Scots and French-Canadian donation
agreements cannot be attributed to the notaries who drafted them,
because the French Canadians patronized several different ones, and
the Scots generally resorted to J.I. Mackie in Cookshire, himself a
French Canadian despite his name. The list of conditions was clearly
thought out carefully by the clients rather than being drawn up arbitrarily or as mere formalities,[48] but the Highlanders were less legal-
istic in all aspects of their social relations. Lawrence Stone and James
Lemon, among others, have assumed that the painstakingly detailed
deeds in gift suggest lack of confidence in a son's sense of filial obligation, but strains were more likely to develop in relations between a
mother and a daughter-in-law who had imbibed another woman's
ideas on how to run a household.[49] Concern about the possibility of
domestic strife would also explain the commonly stated provision
that, in case of conflict, either a separate room with cooking utensils
or new lodgings would be provided.

No matter where lay the greater potential for conflict, the lack of
detailed specifications in the Winslow Scots' agreements left them
more dependent on the good will of the inheriting son and his wife.
Does dependence explain why Scots parents were in no hurry to
transfer their properties to the next generation? Table 4.9 reveals
that the mean age of the fourteen male donors was sixty-eight.[50] Not
surprising, the five Scots widows were somewhat younger, at an average age of sixty-two, but the fact that these widows were in charge
of the family estates testifies to parental hesitation in choosing an
heir. Thus, those receiving the family farm from widows were on
average five years older than those receiving it from their fathers.

The tendency for Scots sons to remain at home until well past
maturity may be partly explained by the late property transfers. The
preponderance of impartible intergenerational transfers suggests

Table 4.9
Timing of Scots and French-Canadian Deeds in
Gift, Winslow

	Age of Donor	*Age of Donee*
SCOTS		
Male	68 (14 cases)	28 (15 cases)
Female	62 (5 cases)	33 (5 cases)
FRENCH CANADIANS		
Male	63 (24 cases)	25 (28 cases)
Female	53 (2 cases)	22 (2 cases)

that most sons were not anticipating shares of the family inheritance, though they may have been waiting for the father to choose his successor. The reverse is at least as likely, however – that the transfer could not be made while a number of sons were still subsidizing the parental family economy with their seasonal labour. Rather than indicating hesitation to place their fate in the hands of an inheriting son, as Shorter suggests for the peasants of Europe, delayed transfers here probably reflect a strong sense of filial obligation.[51]

Whether or not parents in the seigneuries typically delayed intergenerational transfers, in Winslow the average French-Canadian father "retired" five years earlier than his Scots counterpart, at sixty-three years, and there were only two widows among the twenty-six grantors.[52] The relatively young ages of these women and their chosen successors testify to the premature deaths of their husbands. The French-Canadian grantees were also generally younger than their Scots counterparts – twenty-five years of age versus twenty-eight.[53] The contrast would have been greater if we could have included the two French-speaking recipients identified only as minors. Early transfer of farms by French Canadians suggests that their youths may have been more inclined to seek alternative means of livelihood.[54] Significantly, eight of twenty-nine (28 per cent) French-Canadian deeds in gift were formally retroceded, as compared to only three of nineteen (16 per cent) for the Scots. An examination of three of these cases reveals the difficulties that some parents experienced in finding a stable successor to take charge of the homestead and support them in their old age.

In 1864, Magloire and Angelle Audet redrafted a property transfer arrangement made three years earlier with son Pierre in order to add the proviso that he was to provide each of his siblings with five shillings and keep his two younger sisters until they reached eighteen years of age. Six months later, yet another agreement had to be notarized "pour terminer certaines difficultés qui se sont élevées entre eux au sujet de la rente alimentaire." This time the annual supply of food was itemized, but two months later Pierre extricated himself from his obligations by trading them, with the farm, for a lot in a more isolated and barren part of the township. Within a few more months, the new owner and Pierre's parents had settled accounts, and, by the following census, all of the Audet dit Lapointe family had left the township.[55]

Even a more prosperous farmer, such as Alexis Gosselin, had some difficulty with the patrimonial succession. With three of their four sons gone by 1877, Alexis and his wife attempted to keep Placide at home by transferring their 150-acre farm to him when he was twenty-four years of age. But Alexis himself was only fifty-four, and he maintained effective control by forbidding sale of land or cattle without his consent and by offering to forsake the "rente viagère" for as long as he was allowed to manage the farm. Perhaps spurred by having to help support five sisters, Placide gave up the succession in 1880.[56] The 1881 census found Alexis and his wife living with four daughters and no sons.[57]

As for Scots sons, the lack of detail in their parents' maintenance agreements attests to the strong affective relations between the two generations, as does the advanced age at which transfers took place, the relatively few retrocessions, and the reluctance of mature offspring to leave home. These bonds represented a component of the Scots' cultural background that was protected for a time in the new homeland because of their status as immigrant-outsiders in an isolated and marginal district. Clearly, then, the reason Winslow's Scots population was beginning to decline in the 1870s was not because of weakening family ties.

While the foregoing evidence suggests that familial bonds were tighter among the Scots than the French Canadians, we saw in the last chapter that the young francophones succeeded to a greater degree than the Scots in finding alternative means of support within the township. In other words, for the French Canadians, relinquishing the homestead did not necessarily mean exile from the community. The following chapter will attempt to explain how they supported themselves, and the next section of this chapter will examine the psychological aspects of the family more closely, but it should be reiterated that the similarities in the Scots and French-Canadian systems of inheritance were greater than the differences.

Contrary to the generous system of property transmission that Bouchard describes as typical of the era when frontier land was still available, intergenerational transmission for both of Winslow's cultural communities was basically impartible, and even the French Canadians had to witness the migration of a high proportion of their offspring.[58] In this respect, the upper St Francis district resembled overcrowded late-eighteenth-century New England more closely than it did the "open" America of the nineteenth century.[59] Bouchard's emphasis on the impact of material conditions as opposed to cultural traditions nevertheless remains quite appropriate. While Berkner and Mendels claim that impartible inheritance led to stem-family households, celibacy, and out-migration in European peasant communities – which it did to a certain extent in Winslow as well – here the intergenerational transfer system was itself largely a response to a specific physical environment.[60]

PSYCHOLOGY OF THE FAMILY

According to Lawrence Stone, four primary characteristics typify the "modern" or "bourgeois" type of family: "a greater emotional bonding between spouses, as marriage became a matter of choice based on personal affection and sexual attraction"; a "shift from an exploitative to a nurturant attitude toward the child"; "the slow evolution of the concept of privacy, the withdrawal from public rooms and promiscuous bedrooms"; and a change of the nuclear family "from a porous and outward-looking institution to a closed and inward-turned one." Paradoxically, the new expectations for married love have led to an increase in the divorce rate, and the emergence of a child-oriented society led to contraception, "since the quality of the children produced became more highly prized than the quantity."[61] While it is important to avoid an overly present-minded conception of sentiment, Stone's analysis – and the four characteristics that he posted – will serve as a useful reference point in our attempt to probe beneath the level of structures in the Winslow family.

While the family had not evolved in either of the Winslow communities to the point that marriages were dissolved or births controlled artificially, there is considerable evidence that conjugal and parental love were not insignificant forces. To start with "greater emotional bonding between spouses," traditional peasant marriages are said to have been mercenary arrangements, arrived at between parents, but we have seen that there were few marriage contracts drafted for Winslow and that they were rather perfunctory in nature. Also, only two families in Winslow North were linked by a double marriage prior to 1880, suggesting that land-owning strategies did not play a decisive role in the choice of conjugal partners. Parents could no doubt influence the choice of wife made by the son who would assume the homestead, since his marriage usually took place before or shortly after the transfer, but in Winslow there would be little material reason to constrain the choices of the other offspring.[62]

If sexual attraction played a role before a wedding, as suggested by the poems of Oscar Dhu ("The lively Galson girls were there, With dancing eyes and wavy hair") and by the curé's frequent fulminations against gatherings of young people in his parish, what of the status and treatment of the wife thereafter?[63] Contemporary accounts certainly deplore the burdens imposed on women in the Highlands. In 1847, for example, a Major Haliday reported from Portree on the Isle of Skye that "I have repeatedly seen tall stout young men walking along side six or seven females, some of them little girls, each of them laden like a pack-horse with turf or bags of meal, while the men stalked with nothing heavier than stick in hand."[64] Two years later, another observer wrote that "the females seemed no better than slaves, working hard at out-door labour, carrying manure on creels on their backs, and doing work which is elsewhere that of the lower animals."[65] Joseph Howe made a similar comment about the Cape Breton Highlanders' treatment of their wives, and a correspondent from Lingwick wrote less censoriously in 1841: "I like ... to see the robust hearty example of healthful field labour these Highland lasses give to our more effeminate American house women."[66] The Scots women's tradition of heavy outdoor labour would certainly help to explain why their families were able to persist in the upper St Francis district, but we should not be overly influenced by the moralization of bourgeois observers who had their own circumscribed vision of a woman's natural role.[67]

As for the French-Canadian women, their lives could not have been any easier than those of the Scots, given their more frequent births and their husbands' seasonal absences. We saw in the previous section, however, that the French Canadians apparently enjoyed more authority as widows than their counterparts did in English-speaking North America.

Turning to Stone's statement about parental attitudes toward their offspring, historians have noted how the French Canadians appeared to accept their high infant mortality rate as unavoidable, tied to the high level of natality.[68] Thus, Gauldrée-Boileau was informed at St Irénée in 1860 that "on se réjouit plutôt qu'on ne s'afflige de la mort d'un enfant en bas âge, parce que c'est un ange acquis au ciel."[69] Of course, stoic acceptance of death does not represent indifference, and the care taken to have infants baptized soon after birth suggests genuine concern for their souls.[70] Whereas it was common in some areas of France for only a priest and a sacristan to be present at the burial of children less than four or five years old,[71] in St Romain fathers and grandfathers commonly signed the death register for young children. Witnesses were not recorded in the Presbyterian register, but the Scots' sentiments are revealed by the homilies carved on the numerous nineteenth-century tombstones marking their children's graves. Indeed, while the *Rituel* for the Diocese of Québec recommended that a special section of each cemetery be reserved for the burial of children,[72] sizeable stones in Ghisla's Presbyterian cemetery commemorate infants who had yet to be named.

Shorter suggests, nevertheless, that the peasant custom of passing a dead child's name on to a later offspring reflects a certain sense of emotional detachment.[73] The Scots' headstones reveal that they followed this practice, at least to some extent, while, in St Romain, more than one child in three of each sex had its name transferred, in whole or in part, when death was followed by the birth of an infant of the same gender. It seems every bit as likely, however, that the transfer of a dead child's name was a mark of affection for that child. Certainly, one could reach such a conclusion in the case of ten-year-old Élise Giroux, whose name was assigned not only to an infant sister three months after her death, but to her brother's first-born child three years later.[74]

As for the emotional control parents were able to exercise over maturing offspring, we saw that French-Canadian sons apparently acted with greater calculative instrumentality (to use Michael Anderson's phrase) than did those of the Scots.[75] Scots sons tended to remain within the household, at least on a seasonal basis, long after their own economic well-being would have dictated otherwise, while French-Canadian parents sometimes found it difficult to find a successor who would support them and the younger offspring.

Indirect evidence, based on the marriage ranking of sisters within each family, suggests that French-Canadian daughters, as well, exercised some independence vis-à-vis their parents. Thus Daniel Scott Smith found in Hingham, Massachusetts, a long-standing tendency for daughters to be wed according to their birth order, a tradition that grew weaker after the middle-eighteenth century. Parents presumably would try to prevent a younger daughter from marrying before her older sister because this might advertise some deficiency in the latter, thereby making her less attractive to suitors.[76]

The high nuptiality rates and early marriage ages of French-Canadian women made it inevitable that the majority would follow their older sisters to the altar, and it is therefore significant that of the thirty-six St Romain daughters who married either after or before an older sister prior to 1881 fourteen preceded that older sister. In two of the fourteen cases the weddings were separated by only a few months, and, in a third, the older sister was identified as dumb; however, we did not add a number of daughters to this category whose older, and presumably unmarried, sisters were absent by the following census enumeration. These older sisters may have left the parish before the wedding in question and therefore could not be considered as potential impediments to the marriage, but their departure may in some cases have been triggered by the younger sister's betrothal. It would appear, then, that parental authority had definite limits in determining when a French-Canadian daughter of St Romain would marry. One might have expected the same pattern for Scots daughters, given that their dowries could not have been much larger, but the same analysis cannot be made from the Presbyterian marriage records because these fail to identify the names of parents.

Insights into family sentiments can also be gained from the examination of practices and ceremonies relating to the dead. For the French Canadians, the cult of Purgatory stimulated the offering of prayers and masses by the living to hasten the journey of souls to Heaven. Preoccupation with the fate of deceased relatives reached an annual climax on All Saints' Day and during the first days of the month of the dead in November.[77] Furthermore, wills commonly imposed the obligation of paying for masses for the repose of souls, a burden that may have led to a certain amount of resentment, as Natalie Davis has speculated, but that nevertheless must have fostered the concept of mutual responsibility and mystical unity within the family.[78]

As Calvinists, the Scots believed that such intercession was superstitious nonsense because the souls of the departed went straight to Heaven or Hell. This probably helps to explain why, during most of our study period, the Presbyterian minister ignored the law that required him to record burials. Yet the Scots' community-based ceremonies and local district cemeteries must have added to their sense of intimacy with the dead. Davis suggests that the rejection of Purgatory and ritual mourning by the Protestants may have left them "less removed from their parents, more alone with their memories, more vulnerable to the prick of the past, more open to the family's future."[79] Perhaps this explains why ghost stories make up such a significant part of the Compton Scots' oral tradition.[80] Certainly, the symbols, scriptural quotes, and biographical information engraved on Scots tombstones can be interpreted as evidence of a psychological individualization of death and a rejection of the void that it created in the family.[81]

Another of the major characteristics of modern families, according to Stone, is withdrawal "to private bedrooms behind locked doors." Certainly the wooden houses of Winslow provided greater opportunity for privacy than did the "black" houses of Lewis, where, according to Segalen's definition, the couple would virtually "not exist" because it had no space dedicated to it.[82] French-Canadian deeds in gift commonly mention separate rooms reserved for the use of the older couple. But given the large size of the families, and the small dimensions of the houses, privacy was obviously severely restricted by today's standards. According to an inventory taken for all non-patented lots in 1885, frame dwellings were still relatively uncommon. Of the fifty-eight buildings resided in by French Canadians, forty-nine were "block houses," most of which were only twenty feet wide by twenty-four or twenty-five feet long. The space available for each member of the average French-speaking household in 1881 would have been slightly more than seven feet by ten feet in such a dwelling. Eight other francophone families still lived in log cabins in 1885, averaging seventeen feet by twenty feet, and only one (a member of a saw-milling family) owned a frame house.

Scots' dwelling types were slightly more varied, with twenty-five of thirty-seven being block houses of essentially the same dimensions as those belonging to French Canadians, plus nine frame houses not much larger (generally twenty-four feet by thirty feet) and three log cabins. Those who had patented their land, and were therefore not included in this survey, were probably more likely to build larger frame houses, but we saw in chapter 2 that acquisition of letters patent was not a major preoccupation in Winslow. Moreover, the inventory does cover approximately one-third of the families in each community.[83]

Given the abundance of timber, as well as the availability of local saw mills, it would appear that more frame houses could have been built without great material sacrifice, had families felt strong enough desire for them. Certainly, the 1885 inventory reveals that almost all the French Canadians, and all but one of the Scots, erected considerably larger barns of frame construction. Parents may well have had their own bedrooms, even in the log cabins, but throughout North America the construction of large farm houses did not prevent the kitchen from long remaining the room where the family spent nearly all its indoor waking hours.[84]

Stone points out also that not only have members of the modern family increasingly sought individual privacy within the home, but the family itself has become more exclusively nuclear-oriented. We have seen that most of Winslow's Scots and French-Canadian households included only parents and offspring most of the time but that the older generation and younger unmarried siblings commonly spent a few years with the family of the successor to the homestead. The broader kin network was inevitably reduced in size if not in scope by the process of migration, but the geographically restricted origin of the settlers suggests strongly that significant fragments were transferred to Winslow. While relatively few families in either community were able to settle several sons within the township, the lack of new blood would soon result in a tight web of kin ties produced through intermarriage and selective emigration. During the 1870s, five French-Canadian marriages in St Romain required special dispensation because they involved second and third cousins.[85]

The institution of godparenting also helped the French Canadians to forge ties beyond the immediate family, particularly with extended kin. The blood relationship (if any) of godparents and infants was generally not recorded in the St Romain registers, but two-thirds of all those baptized between 1854 and 1880 did have a sponsor with the same family name. Some of these sponsors were older siblings or grandparents, but most appear to have been uncles or aunts. The result was that ties with in-laws were strengthened because the role of godparent was shared with a spouse in the great majority of cases.[86] Bonds with a godparent could be further sealed by transferring his/her first name to the infant, as was done for 53 per cent of the boys and 39 per cent of the girls in pre-conquest Canada.[87] This practice was considerably less common in St Romain, however, where only 30 per cent of the boys and 22 per cent of the girls baptized between 1858 and 1870 shared one name with the godparent of their gender. One reason, as we shall see in chapter 7, is that increasing priority was given to a wide variety of saints' names.

Extensive genealogical research would be needed to determine whether the Scots followed the pattern of close-cousin and sibling-exchange marriages discovered by Maureen Molloy for the West Highland settlers of Cape Breton Island and New Zealand.[88] It is quite possible that their community was sufficiently small and close-knit to make such additional ties unnecessary. The Scots may not have had the custom of godparenting to assist in the process of social cohesion, but, for both groups, traditional ties outside the household did include neighbours who were not necessarily kin. We have seen, for example, the unusual number of adolescent neighbourhood girls in Scots households at the time of the 1871 census. That same year, several French Canadians reported large quantities of square timber, which suggests that men in the community must have worked together in the woods for extended periods throughout the winter. There were also building bees, fulling and carding bees, and the annual road corvées. Nearly all this extra-familial activity took place at the level of the local range, an important subcommunity in its own right, as we shall see in chapter 8.

The importance of extra-familial social ties during earlier times is movingly described in a Gaelic lament ("Lonely Strife") composed by Donald Morrison of Tolsta district in Winslow:

1. When I am in my lonely strife
   Thinking to myself
   How different people are today,
   How terrible the heavens are
   In the light of our fathers' generation.
   As you all know,
   They were always charitable
   In the community and with one another.

2. Although they were poor and happy,
   They were neighbourly to one another.
   Cordially the stranger would get
   His keep for a night in their own houses,
   Although the food and staples were
   Quite scarce in relation to the need.
   But although they were short of necessities,
   They wouldn't refuse that itself.

3. When the time of harvest came
   They would all be out;
   Their custom at that time was
   To reap with sickles.
   You would see them so sympathetic
   To a poor lad in need,
   Being helped without wages,
   And treated like themselves.

...

7. Today you're not worth asking about
   Unless you're in high style,
   Your jacket like a dandy,
   A rig which shines from the bottom.
   If you don't have English,
   That's proof enough.
   If you go out at night with a lady,
   You won't get near her.

8. But I'm not asking
   To interfere with the young
   Since they themselves are so satisfied.
   They never saw their true destiny.
   What I meant to do
   Was to laud the heroes
   Who came before these; they were worthy of that.
   They were properly satisfied.[89]

What, then, are we to conclude about the nature of the family in Winslow? We have uncovered no evidence of major distinctions between the two cultural communities, but toward which end of Stone's traditional–modern continuum did the ninteenth-century Winslow family lie? The communal socioeconomic structure of Lewis had already been largely destroyed by the crofting system prior to emigration, and St Lawrence Valley society had been strongly oriented to the single-family farmstead ever since settlement began in the seventeenth century.[90] This same pattern was transferred to Winslow Township, but one would nevertheless expect the subsistence-oriented economy described in the following chapter to have hindered development of what Stone perceives to be bourgeois family traits. Certainly, we found evidence of significant kin and neighbourhood loyalties, themes discussed in greater detail in chapters 7 and 8. But what of the unmistakeable signs of emotional ties within the nuclear family itself? There is some evidence to suggest that intergenerational bonds were stronger among the Scots than among the French Canadians, but evidence as well that these were part of the Highland tradition rather than a manifestation of the family's "modernization." Perhaps immediate family and broader community loyalties were not as mutually exclusive as Stone's model would suggest. Certainly, whether bonds between family members were significantly weaker in nineteenth-century Winslow than they would be today is difficult to say, because such intangibles cannot be measured and because, as Flandrin has pointed out, it is necessary to avoid the false dichotomy formulated by historians who have their own bourgeois biases.[91]

CHAPTER FIVE

Farm Production
and Labour

For some years now a debate has been waged among American historians concerning the nature of the pre-industrial rural economy. Were farmers primarily oriented toward family self-sufficiency, exchanging only a relatively small surplus for the few necessities that they could not produce themselves, or were they essentially market-driven and imbued with a deep-seated desire to accumulate economic surpluses?[1] As we saw in chapter 1, essentially the same question has generated a good deal of passion in Quebec, where it has been intimately associated with the issue of national identity. Reacting to the stereotypical image of a recalcitrant and impoverished peasantry turning its back on the agricultural improvements made by its Anglo-Protestant neighbours, nationalist historians are attempting to demonstrate that rural society in the late eighteenth and early nineteenth centuries was market-oriented and economically stratified.[2]

No such claim has been made for the Lewis crofters, but one famine relief agent did remark in 1849 that because of the repeated failure of the potato crop, and the example of new means of cultivation being impressed on them, "the habits of life established for centuries have been brought into question."[3] The shock of the famine may therefore have psychologically prepared the emigrants for adaptation to the socioeconomic imperatives of the New World, but the very nature of their destination indicates the strength of their traditional cultural and community-based ties.

Unfortunately for our purposes, little detailed work has been done on rural society in post-1850 Quebec. One can assume that as agriculture became more market-oriented, socioeconomic differentiation became more pronounced.[4] Gauldrée-Boileau could nevertheless still write of Ste Irénée de Charlevoix in 1861–2 that "tous les habitants sont d'égale condition et possèdent une fortune à peu près semblable.

Il n'y a point ici de petites ni de grands propriétaires."[5] As we shall see, the same was essentially true for Winslow, with its short-growing season, rock-strewn soils, and isolation from external markets.

Industrial capitalism certainly manifested itself in the upper St Francis district through the operation of large-scale lumber companies and extension of the rail network, but it did little to stimulate commercially oriented agriculture. Farmers operated within a constrained economic framework, without the luxury of choice implied by the debate on the nature of the pre-industrial rural economy. Their main options were either to uproot themselves once again or to become more and more dependent on off-farm income. By the end of our study period, the Scots were leaning toward the former alternative and the French Canadians toward the latter, but there were more basic factors involved than the development of contrasting "mentalités." Perhaps most important, only the Scots had left their native land in moving to Winslow, and only they had begun to adopt the language of the continent outside Quebec as their mother tongue.

The basis of the family economy was, of course, land. We saw in chapter 2 that Scots settlers attempted to acquire as much crown land as possible at the outset, while the French Canadians tended to add lots as they were needed. Consequently, the census reports record a slight difference in the average farm size of the two groups as late as 1871 (see Table 5.2).[6] James Lemon argues that the accumulation of property was a paramount socioeconomic drive in colonial America, one which stemmed from a strong market-oriented individualism, but the evolution of farm sizes in Winslow does not suggest extensive marketing of privately held land.[7] Table 5.1 reveals that, to a still greater degree than in the seigneurie of Lauzon at mid-century (see Table 1.6 above), Winslow's farms were rather uniform in size. Over half those belonging to Scots remained within the 51-to-100-acre range, with another third lying between 101 and 200 acres. There were never more than 11 per cent of the Scots farmers holding fewer than fifty acres, and never more than 1 per cent with more than 200 acres. In fact, our categories exaggerate the impression of diversity: most of the farms lay close to one side or the other of the 100–acre dividing line.

The French Canadians exhibited greater differentiation, with a significant number owning farms of fifty acres or less, but over time they concentrated increasingly in the 51-to-100-acre category, where most of the Scots farms were located. There was also a slight rise by 1871 in the number of French-Canadian landowners with ten acres or less, reflecting the beginnings of a village centre at St Romain.

Table 5.1

Distribution (Percentage) of Land Ownership (Acres), Winslow, 1852, 1861, 1871

	Land			Landowners		
	1852	1861	1871	1852	1861	1871
SCOTS						
10 or less	–	0.1	–	–	0.9	–
11–50	3.4	5.0	3.7	7.4	11.3	8.4
51–100	64.4	61.4	61.1	70.4	67.9	69.1
101–200	32.2	31.3	32.5	22.2	18.9	21.5
200+	–	2.2	2.6	–	0.9	0.9
Totals	100	100	100	100	100	100
FRENCH CANADIANS						
10 or less	–	0.1	0.1	–	0.8	3.8
11–50	59.5	22.3	20.9	77.2	38.3	37.4
51–100	27.0	42.1	56.0	17.5	43.0	48.9
101–200	13.5	29.5	18.6	5.3	16.4	8.4
200+	–	6.0	4.4	–	1.6	1.5
Totals	100	100	100	100	100	100

Unfortunately, it is impossible to compare Scots and French Canadians for 1881, because of the destruction of all the agricultural schedules in the manuscript census.

In long-settled, fertile regions, the difference between a fifty-acre farm and one of 100 or 150 acres would certainly be significant, but, on a thin-soiled frontier such as Winslow, the more important variable would have been the size of a property's arable acreage. Map 2 (above) reveals that even though most of the soil in Winslow is not even suited for pasture by today's standards, the Scots did have a slight advantage in this respect, perhaps explaining why, as we shall see, they were able to concentrate more fully on agricultural production, though neither group could survive on farming alone.[8]

Even though the amount of land under cultivation on each farm was certainly limited by the extent of its arable soil, acreage in crop during the early years of settlement would be determined largely by the amount of labour applied to the arduous and time-consuming task of removing trees and rocks. Table 5.2 shows that during the 1850s the French Canadians made slower progress than the less experi-

Table 5.2

Exploitation of Land (Acres) on Average French-Canadian and Scots Farms
(11+ Acres), Winslow, 1852, 1861, 1871

	1852		1861		1871	
	F.C.	Scots	F.C.	Scots	F.C.	Scots
No. of farmers	50*	24†	127	104	127	105‡
Size of holdings	73.9§	116.7	84.6	108.7	82.9	106.7
In pasture	4.4	1.3	5.9	4.7	13.0	12.2
In crops	6.1	6.7	16.3	22.7	22.9	27.4
Oats	1.3	1.5	2.0	2.1	n.d.	n.d.
Barley	1.1	2.7	2.1	3.2	n.d.	n.d.
Wheat	0.7	0.3	0.2	–	0.6	0.2
Buckwheat	–	0.1	0.5	0.5	n.d.	n.d.
Rye	1.6	–	1.6	–	n.d.	n.d.
Corn	–	–	–	–	n.d.	n.d.
Peas	0.3	–	0.4	–	n.d.	n.d.
Potatoes	0.9	1.8	1.0	1.4	0.8	1.2
Turnips	–	0.4	0.1	0.4	n.d.	n.d.
Hay#	0.2	0	8.4	15.1	12.9	15.9

* Seven others had no land improved.

† Three others had no land improved.

‡ Excludes two major Scots landholders, merchant Colin Noble and the Reverend
  Macdonald.

§ Does not include six squatters who had improved land but reported no acreage in
  possession.

Not recorded in 1852 and 1861 census reports; calculated by subtracting acreage
  in other crops from total acreage in crop.

enced Scots in clearing their land, probably in large part because of
the more mature stage of family development that characterized the
pioneer Scots. Because of the limit to the acreage that could be
improved on the small, stony farms of Winslow, the gap between the
two groups did narrow by 1871, even though there were still a few
French Canadians establishing new farms during that decade. The
impact of the constraints to the expansion of cultivated acreage by
1871 is demonstrated by Table 5.3, which reveals that families with
one son over the age of thirteen had as much acreage cleared as
those with two, three, and more.

Table 5.4 demonstrates that as of 1871 those families who had
arrived before 1861 had on average more land cleared than those
who had arrived later; it suggests also a link between the amount of
land cleared and future persistence. Thus families in both commu-

Table 5.3
Acreage Improved per Household Correlated
with Number of Sons Aged 13–25 (Number of
Households in Parentheses), Winslow, 1871

Sons	French Canadians	Scots
0	25.9 (98)	31.5 (57)
1	38.9 (26)	40.8 (29)
2	44.5 (13)	39.6 (13)
3+	40.7 (12)	38.2 (21)

Table 5.4
Acreage Owned and Improved as Factors in Persistence / Mobility, Winslow,
1871

	Acres Owned	Acres Improved
SCOTS		
Arrived after 1861, left before 1881 (18 cases)	81.4	29.4
Arrived after 1861, stayed until 1881 (17 cases)	119.0	35.2
Present in 1861 and 1871, but not in 1881 (21 cases)	102.8	36.7
Present 1861–81 (45 cases)	111.3	45.1
FRENCH CANADIANS		
Arrived after 1861, left before 1881 (29 cases)	60.1	22.4
Arrived after 1861, stayed until 1881 (38 cases)	77.4	30.7
Present in 1861 and 1871, but not in 1881 (17 cases)	97.6	39.9
Present 1861–81 (41 cases)	92.2	44.2

nities who had arrived after 1861 and would persist until 1881 had
more land improved in 1871 than their counterparts who would leave
within the next decade. In fact, the cohort of persistent Scots families
which had arrived after 1861 owned larger farms in 1871 than (and
had improved nearly as much land as) the non-persistent cohort that
had arrived prior to 1861.

As noted in chapter 3, it was not the more successful farmers who
left, but by 1871, after more than twenty years of settlement, only
three or four farms stood out as obvious commercially oriented producers.[9] Louis Bouffard, with thirty-seven sheep, was the only farmer
in the township to specialize to some extent in one area of farming.
Bouffard had 150 acres improved, half of which were in crop, while

Table 5.5

Yields on the Average French-Canadian and Scots Farm, Winslow, 1852, 1861, 1871

	1852		1861		1871	
Crop	F.C.	Scots	F.C.	Scots	F.C.	Scots
Oats (bu/a)	11.2	11.2	16.4	21.5	n.d.	n.d.
Barley (bu/a)	9.9	12.0	16.9	35.6	n.d.	n.d.
Wheat (bu/a)	8.4	10.4	10.9	17.8	8.7	8.7
Buckwheat (bu/a)	5.2	15.1	14.2	22.5	n.d.	n.d.
Rye (bu/a)	8.9	16.0	6.1	–	n.d.	n.d.
Peas (bu/a)	6.8	–	8.5	–	n.d.	n.d.
Potatoes (bu/a)	47.0	42.2	91.7	74.2	116.4	108.2
Turnips (bu/a)	9.8	26.9	44.4	84.8	n.d.	n.d.
Hay (tons/a)	n.d.	n.d.	0.4	0.4	0.6	0.7
Butter & cheese (lb/cow)	16.3	17.4	26.8	51.5	33.2	37.4
All crops except wheat, potatoes, and hay	9.7	13.0	13.9	26.9	11.1	14.7

two other French Canadians each reported 100 acres improved, but with agricultural production not significantly greater than that of many of their neighbours. As for the Scots, no farmer operated on as large a scale as the minister, John McDonald, with his seventy acres in crop and his ten head of cattle sold or slaughtered in the fall of 1870, when no other Scot marketed more than three.

As Table 5.6 shows, the consistent, if rather narrow margin between Scots and French Canadians in land ownership and improvement was reflected in agricultural production. French Canadians may have instinctively reported their crop volumes in minots rather than bushels, but the result would be only a 10-per-cent underestimation of their harvests. If they also reported their areas in crop as arpents, their yields shown in Table 5.5 would have to be increased by 24 per cent, but they probably measured land in acres, since property sizes were obviously recorded in conformity with the English survey.[10] It appears that the Scots generally held an advantage in yields, as in areas under cultivation.

Farming in Winslow nevertheless remained an uncertain occupation for all families. As we have seen, the 1852 enumerator commented on the unequal yields within both the Scots and French-

Table 5.6

Agricultural Production on the Average French-Canadian and Scots Farm
(11+ Acres), Winslow, 1852, 1861, 1871

	1852		1861		1871	
Crop	F.C.	Scots	F.C.	Scots	F.C.	Scots
Oats (bu)	14.1	17.2	33.6	45.8	42.5	58.0
Barley (bu)	11.1	31.9	35.2	114.1	15.6	46.7
Wheat (bu)	5.5	2.9	2.0	0.6	5.3	1.6
Buckwheat (bu)	0.1	1.1	7.7	11.3	21.8	33.2
Rye (bu)	13.8	0.3	9.8	–	10.0	–
Corn (bu)	–	–	–	–	1.5	–
Peas (bu)	1.8	–	3.1	–	4.2	0.3
Potatoes (bu)	44.2	77.2	89.5	107.0	93.6	127.8
Turnips (bu)	0.4	9.5	4.2	35.9	1.0	2.8
Hay (tons)	0.9	0.1(?)	3.3	5.5	7.4	11.8
Flax and hemp (lb)	2.3	–	1.3	0.2	9.3	–
Tobacco (lb)	–	–	n.d.	n.d.	4.0	–
Maple sugar (lb)	141.9	80.3	264.9	27.5	242.4	34.0
Wool (lb)	1.7	8.4	4.8	12.1	14.0	33.4
Butter (lb)	11.1	26.8	38.0	119.7	67.8	106.5
Cheese (lb)	–	–	–	1.3	–	–
Beef (lb)	27	74	40	48	79*	120*
Pork (lb)	120	30	340	420	137*	96*
Mutton (lb)	n.d.	n.d.	n.d.	n.d.	26*	46*

* Estimated from the number of animals killed or sold at 350 pounds dressed weight
for each beef animal, 146 pounds for each pig, and 37 pounds for each sheep. See
Bittermann, "Middle River", 195, 198.

Canadian communities: some lots seemed particularly susceptible to
frost, crops sown too late had been damaged by early frosts, and
some farmers had already sown on the same piece of land two or
three times. Three years later the Scots claimed that much of their
grain had been frozen and their potatoes rotted, and in the fall of
1861 crops were reported to have failed again.[11]

The previous year, however, both communities had quite respect-
able yields when compared to the contemporary standards of the
northern United States.[12] The major weakness in Winslow concerned
hay – it had less than half the average American yield; the Scots in
particular must have been handicapped because they had twice the
French-Canadian acreage in this crop. Hay is quite susceptible to
climatic fluctuations, and at least two enumerators in the region com-

mented that the yield had been reduced by one-third to one-half in 1860 as a result of excessively dry summer weather.[13] But the problem with hay was not entirely environmental. During the early nineteenth century the recommended seed ratio was three bushels per acre, but the Scots reported saving only one-tenth of a bushel per acre in 1861 and 1871, and the French Canadians only twice that amount. Given the high cost, it is doubtful that seed purchases came near to closing the gap.[14] Consequently, hay yields remained lower than one ton per acre in 1871. Settlers elsewhere were relatively indifferent to the scientific cultivation of this crop, but both groups in Winslow were particularly ill-prepared by their pre-settlement backgrounds. The seigneuries had an essentially cereal-producing economy, and Highlanders traditionally treated hay production as an after-thought.[15]

Tables 5.2 and 5.6 reveal little difference between Winslow's two communities in terms of concentration on basic crops such as oats, potatoes, and buckwheat, which was consumed by the Scots as "slapochean" or slaps.[16] The short growing season ensured that neither group grew the popular pioneer crop of corn, which would have produced food during the early years without plowing, threshing, or milling.[17] But even in such a physically restrictive environment, cultural preferences led to certain persistent differences in focus. In contrast to the French Canadians, the Scots planted no rye or tobacco and virtually no peas or flax; in 1861 they avoided wheat almost entirely. In keeping with their Highland heritage, they gave barley and potatoes pride of place.[18]

The cultural exclusiveness of some crops suggests that they were destined for the home table rather than the market. But what of the major crops – those that might have found a demand in the local logging shanties: oats and hay for the draft animals, and potatoes and peas for the workers? In order to determine how much surplus produce could have been available for the market, we must first estimate farm consumption. The "pensions alimentaires" for French-Canadian couples are of limited use because of the wide variety of food quantities specified. The more generous settlements were presumably designed to provide the retired couple with a surplus for sale – and no doubt some of their stated goals were not commonly met.[19] Furthermore, the Scots did not draft any of these documents.

I will therefore adopt the consumption scale for major food items constructed by Marvin McInnis from the 1871 Ontario census and modified for families in the Canada West of 1861. This standard assumes that the average adult male's yearly diet included seven bushels of wheat consumed as flour, fourteen bushels of potatoes, sixty-

Table 5.7
Food Production Surplus / Deficit per Farm Family, Winslow, 1861, 1871

	1861		1871	
	Scots	*F.C.*	*Scots*	*F.C.*
Grain (bu)*	+89	−17	+37	+18
Potatoes (bu)	+33	+21	+52	+19
Peas (bu)	−5	−2	−5	−1
Meat (lb)	−59	−107	−281	−293

* Excludes oats.

two-and-a-half pounds of beef, ninety-five pounds of pork, twenty pounds of mutton, and fifty-two pounds of butter, cheese, and milk consumed as butter.[20]

These volumes are within the range of most of the fourteen "pensions" found for the French Canadians of Winslow, though the flour sometimes included rye, barley, and/or buckwheat, and the quantity of meat was generally lower. Although beef or mutton was mentioned in only three cases, pork was generally restricted to one hundred pounds or half a pig per person. Since the diet calculated by McInnis is rather generous in calories, and since some wild game would still have been available in Winslow, we could reduce the meat component of the township's standard adult male diet to one hundred pounds. We shall also test for surplus pea production, since this was a crop consumed in the shanty market; most Winslow "pensions" mentioned one to one-and-a-half minots per couple. We shall assume, therefore, a consumption rate of one bushel per adult male, though the Scots' production, and presumably consumption, were negligible.[21]

By converting the total population to adult male equivalents, and applying our dietary estimates to the harvests and meat production for 1860 and 1870, we arrive at small but consistent surpluses in grain and potatoes, though not in peas, for both groups. The Scots are slightly ahead for the first two categories in both years (see Table 5.7).[22] From these surpluses, however, we should subtract at least 10 per cent for seed requirements, up to 4 per cent for the tithe (for the French Canadians only), and another portion for the miller.[23] And, even though we have assumed that livestock fodder included all the oats or its equivalent, the supplementary feeding estimates provided by Atack and Bateman would suggest that the average Scots farm was consistently short by about ten bushels of oats, and the French-Canadian farm by sixteen to twenty bushels.[24] The Scots shortfall

would have been more than compensated in 1861 by turnip production, and, despite low hay yields, both groups reported cutting considerably more than what their livestock would have required,
according to Atack and Bateman's standard of a half-ton per head
of cattle and horses.[25]

Winters in Winslow, however, were considerably longer and more
severe than those in the American study area. Indeed, the hay-feed-
ing estimates of Lewis and McInnis for Lower Canada in 1851 are
more than three times higher than those provided by Atack and
Bateman for the northern United States in 1860.[26] Lewis and
McInnis's standards would result in a one-ton shortfall per Scots farm,
and one-and-a-half tons per French-Canadian farm, even for 1870–
1, when the hay harvest for each group had doubled over the previous
decade. It appears, therefore, that some of the potatoes and grain
in addition to oats may have been fed to the livestock, wiping out
apparent surpluses, most notably for the average French-Canadian
farm. Apparent surpluses did not actually increase from 1861 to
1871, despite more acreage being placed under cultivation.

Judging from the large shortfall in meat production, Winslow's
settlers would have had to consume more of their calories in grain
and potatoes than did McInnis's Ontario farmers. Economic historians assume, however, that the census underestimates the number of
livestock slaughtered or sold throughout the year, though they do not
explain why this should have been more difficult for farmers to recall
than the volume of grain they had harvested the previous fall. By
adopting the method of Lewis and McInnis, based on live pigs and
cattle reported in the spring, we obtain lower production of meat for
both groups in 1861, though a higher one in 1871.[27]

To add to the uncertainties of the above calculations, part of Winslow's population worked seasonly outside the township, thereby significantly diminishing consumption of local produce, especially in
Scots households, with their larger numbers of mature offspring.
Thus surpluses were undoubtedly larger than I have estimated, but
a glance at Table 5.8 nevertheless reveals that the number of livestock
reported on the average farm did not increase much beyond a subsistence level between 1861 and 1871. If the memoirs of a local resident are accurate in the claim that the Scots responded eagerly to
New England's demand for cattle during the US Civil War, the post-
Reciprocity market slump had clearly been damaging.[28]

Many farmers in northern Maine turned to specialization in potato
production when the railway arrived in the 1870s, but their climate
and soil conditions were superior to those of the upper St Francis
district.[29] Farmers in eastern Canada increasingly switched to dairy

Table 5.8

Livestock Ownership on Average French-Canadian and Scots Farms
(11+ Acres), Winslow, 1852, 1861, 1871

	1852		1861		1871	
	F.C.	*Scots*	*F.C.*	*Scots*	*F.C.*	*Scots*
Bulls, oxen, steers	0.1	1.3	0.5	0.9	1.0	1.6
Milch cows	0.7	1.5	1.4	2.3	2.0	2.8
Calves, heifers*	0.3	1.3	1.7	3.4	2.0	3.2
Horses	0.7	0.1	0.8	0.6	1.0	0.7
Sheep	1.0	4.5	3.2	4.5	5.0	11.1
Pigs	1.1	0.9	2.1	1.6	1.8	2.0

* This category changes slightly from calves and heifers in 1852 to heifers and steers under three years of age in 1861.

production, but in the Winslow area the growing urban and British market for butter and cheese would long remain essentially inaccessible.[30] Virtually no cheese production was reported by the Winslow enumerator, the French Canadians made only a small quantity of butter, and Scots butter production declined slightly in 1871, despite the increase in their average number of milch cows. While even the smallest of New England farms produced a butter surplus, none of the peak Scots production of 120 pounds in 1861 would have gone to market if each individual consumed as little as three-quarters of the thirty pounds calculated by Lewis and McInnis for the average Lower Canadian diet in 1852.[31]

McInnis found that the main determinants for an agricultural surplus in the Canada West of 1861 were farm size, length of settlement, and proximity to major transportation arteries.[32] Winslow was obviously a recently settled township by most Canadian standards, but the key factor to note is that, while cleared acreages did expand considerably between 1861 and 1871, agricultural surpluses did not. In Canada West, even the smaller farms produced surpluses if they had access to markets, and for the majority those markets appear to have been relatively close at hand. In McInnis's words, they consisted of "the nonagricultural population of nearby towns, villages, rural craftsmen, and functionaries."[33]

Was it scarcity of non-farm consumers nearby or poor growing conditions that prevented the average Winslow farmer from producing a significant surplus? Given that the township did not record a surplus in peas and pork, even though a major lumber company was operating in the district, we might assume that the farmers were incapable of supplying the market at hand. Perhaps C.S. Clark and Co. would not have operated a thousand-acre farm near Sherbrooke, nor purchased large quantities of flour from Lennoxville merchants, had there been dependable suppliers closer to shanty crews.[34]

Competition from outside the district, however, clearly discouraged local production. The major shortfall in Winslow was in livestock, which can be fed on land not suited to most crops, so one must assume that the local farmers lacked the market incentive to raise more cattle and pigs. The local shanty market was obviously no substitute for the urban and small town markets available to farmers in Canada West. During the 1870s, the railway would break the lumber monopoly and give birth to a number of saw mill towns in the upper St Francis district, but it would also bring supplies from larger producers located outside the district. Even in neighbouring Maine, the prices of items used by lumbermen dropped by nearly 50 per cent during the 1870s and 1880s.[35] We cannot judge Winslow's response in detail without the 1881 agricultural schedules, but we have already seen that the number of Scots farmers began to decline, while the French Canadians increased more than they had during the 1860s. The latter group was tied more closely than the former to the exploitation of local forests.

Another indicator of the failure by Winslow farmers to become integrated into the agricultural market economy was the increase in domestic textile production. This trend had been growing rather than diminishing in Lewis where, during the late 1840s, women had been provided with hemp and wool to manufacture into nets, coarse blankets, and checked shirts, in order to help earn food relief for their families.[36] Although the Scots kept more sheep than did the French Canadians, especially in 1871, textile production for the two groups was quite comparable, because the French Canadians consistently produced more "fulled cloth" and flannel per individual sheep, and they alone spun flax for linen cloth (see Table 5.9). Stimulated by the appearance of two carding mills during the 1860s, woollen cloth production reached 21.7 yards for the average French-Canadian household in 1871, and 35.4 yards for the Scots.

The Scots were producing one-and-a-half times the provincial farm average, but it is difficult to judge how much cloth they were marketing because there appears to be no estimate as to the quantities of homespun the average rural person would need in a year.[37] Logging crews presumably required large quantities of heavy blankets and clothing, but Table 5.10 reveals that Winslow families with one

Table 5.9
Domestic Textile Production (Yards) of Average French-Canadian and Scots
Farm Families, 1852, 1861, 1871

	1852		1861		1871	
	F.C.	Scots	F.C.	Scots	F.C.	Scots
Fulled cloth	2.1	2.5	5.4	5.2	} 21.7	35.4
Flannel	1.5	3.9	4.4	2.7		
Linen	1.0	0.2	2.4	–	10.3	–
Total	4.6	6.6	12.2	7.9	32.0	35.4

Table 5.10
Daughters Aged 13–25 Correlated with Domestic Cloth Production
(Number of Households in Parentheses), Winslow, 1871

Daughters	F.C.	Scots
0	23.2 (104)	26.3 (64)
1	36.7 (21)	36.5 (25)
2	33.5 (14)	33.5 (26)
3+	33.2 (10)	48.4 (5)
Mean	26.8 (149)	30.9 (120)

daughter in her teens or older generally produced as much cloth as
did those with two or more.[38] The one exceptional category was the
Scots households with three or more maturing/mature daughters, but
there were only five in this group.

The Civil War had created a temporary shortage of cotton, but the
market in the Eastern Townships must have been well supplied with
woollen cloth after Canada's largest woollen mill opened its doors in
Sherbrooke in 1866.[39] The best explanation for the increase in Winslow's textile production – apart from the fact that cleared grazing
land was expanding – is therefore provided by Grant and Inwood:
eastern farm families who were unable to adjust to western competition in grains by turning to a commercial livestock economy
"responded by retreating into self-sufficiency in various ways including domestic manufacturing."[40] We shall see in the next chapter that
Winslow's own families were not entirely immune to the temptations
of factory-produced cottons, but they bought little ready-
made clothing.[41]

Table 5.11
Value (Dollars) of Property on Average
French-Canadian and Scots Farms (11+ Acres),
Winslow, 1861

	F.C.	Scots
Land and buildings	501.06	567.69
Implements	15.46	22.32
Horses older than three	45.24	25.96
Other livestock	62.26	136.08
Pleasure carriages	7.35	3.96
Total	634.37	756.01

As of 1861, the majority of the Scots and French-Canadian families in Winslow still lived in log cabins, and farm investment of all kinds remained rather minimal. Whereas the average fixed capital in land, machinery, and livestock for the Canada East was $1,936, that for Winslow's Scots was only $756, and for its French Canadians $634 (see Table 5.11).[42] Thus implements on the average Winslow farm were worth only a fraction of the $100 estimated by Atack and Bateman as necessary for an operating unit in the northern United States of 1860.[43] In 1861 Scots estimated their implements somewhat higher than the French Canadians, but ten years later the French Canadians recorded the more impressive inventory of farm machinery. The 107 Scots farmers reported only eighty ploughs and cultivators, with twelve fanning mills, but the 127 French Canadians had eighty-three ploughs and cultivators, twenty-eight fanning mills, twenty machines in the reaper-mower category, and one threshing machine.[44]

The Scots' agriculture must have been very labour-intensive, for their average farmer had over twenty-seven acres in crop by 1871. According to Graeme Wynn, the cultivation of more than twelve or fifteen acres in the pre-mechanization era required labour beyond that of the average farmer and his family.[45] It becomes clearer, therefore, why an increasing number of adult Scots sons were remaining at home, or at least returning on a seasonal basis. The French Canadians not only owned more horses (see Table 5.8), on which effective operation of the new machines depended, but they also valued them more highly. A perhaps extreme example can be found in Antoine Roy's post-mortem inventory, which lists a single mare at $100, the same price as his nine cattle, eighteen sheep and lambs, two pigs, and nine chickens all combined.[46] The French Canadians' reputed passion for fast trotters may have influenced the relatively high sums they invested in horses. In 1871 the Scots reported only one carriage and sleigh for every two households, while the French Canadians had 1.3 of these vehicles per farm. But horses also played a major role in winter logging operations, an activity that the French Canadians pursued more than did the Scots.[47]

As of 1871 the major source of cash income for the French Canadians of Winslow was apparently seasonal off-farm labour involving the forest. To begin with, they were still trapping a few animals, for the census listed nineteen muskrats, nineteen mink, four martins, two foxes, and two other non-specified fur-bearing animals, all taken by French Canadians. The manufacture of maple sugar was much more significant and involved mostly women and children, if Winslow's pattern was similar to that of backwoods Upper Canada.[48] The enumerator for Newport Township, south of Winslow, had complained about the lack of market for maple sugar in 1861, but twelve years earlier a priest investigating a possible church site for Winslow and Stratford had reported that one recommended lot included fifty acres of "gros érables dont le produit surpasse celui d'une égale quantité d'acres de terre semés en blé."[49]

The average French-Canadian farmer in Winslow produced about 250 pounds of maple sugar in 1861 and again in 1871 (see Table 5.6, above), as compared with only about one hundred pounds per Newport farmer in 1861. One hundred pounds was close to the consumption level of the typical family, judging by Winslow's "pensions alimentaires," and so the French Canadians in the township were probably marketing considerable quantities. The Scots, in contrast, saw production decline from eighty pounds per household in 1852 to only twenty-eight pounds in 1861, and thirty-four pounds in 1871, presumably far below their own needs. The manuscript census reveals, moreover, that many farm families did not make sugar, which strongly suggests a system of internal exchange.

There is no record in the census reports of Winslow settlers resorting to the practice of burning trees to sell the ashes for production of lye, though some potash and pearlash was produced in neighbouring townships.[50] The one local resource that did find a ready external market was the district's spruce and pine timber, which could be floated down the St Francis River to the rail lines in the Sherbrooke area. C.S. Clark and Co., holder of virtually all the crown timber limits in the upper St Francis watershed from mid-century, shipped lumber and lumber products from its mill outside the district via the Grand Trunk Railway to Portland, Maine.[51]

The extent of settlers' involvement in the lumber industry is not easy to determine, but in 1866 the provincial immigration agent at Sherbrooke did comment on the significance of lumbering in Winslow, and the 1871 census records timber cut by a number of farmers.[52] Forty-two of the 127 French-Canadian farmers were reported with an average of sixty logs (mostly spruce) each. At the rate of 25¢ per log, as generally reported by local saw mills, sixty logs would represent $15 per active family. Even though the Scots had more adult sons in the average household, only twenty-one of their 105 farm families reported cutting logs, an average of forty-nine each, for the equivalent of approximately $12 per active family.[53]

The equivalent of almost half the 3,587 logs cut during the winter of 1870–1 in Winslow South was processed by two mills in the village of Stornoway, presumably for local use. Clearly, then, the Scots settlers were quite independent of Clark and Co. Indeed, they did not even sign the French-Canadian protest petitions against this district monopolist. Winslow North, however, lay at the very tip of Lake St Francis, and in 1871 only 822 of its 4,335 saw-logs were processed by mills in the community. An example of local dependence on Clark and Co. is to be found in Ferdinand Ruel's mortgage to a nearby farmer in 1860. Ruel was to repay half the £15 debt the following spring, if the timber company paid in cash; otherwise, he would make an instalment of £10 in July, £4 the following April, and the remainder a year later.[54] There is no indication, however, that company scrip circulated widely in the upper St Francis district, as it did in the Aroostook Valley of Maine.[55]

Whether Ruel had planned to sell logs to Clark or join his workforce in the woods is not clear, but it appears likely that Winslow North's farmers had little choice but to sell their logs to Clark as long as the upper St Francis River remained the only viable outlet to the timber market. Clark could presumably tolerate poaching on the company's crown berths as long as he effectively fixed the local price for logs. The local farmers' position as suppliers was also weakened by the fact that many of the approximately 150 mill-workers in Brompton Falls were shifted to the company's timber operations during the winter months. Thus, the 1861 census records that most of the crew of thirty-two in Garthby, and twenty-nine in neighbouring Stratford, were from outside the district. Indeed, sixteen were either American-born or residents of the United States. There were no sizeable shanty crews listed in the district in 1871, perhaps because the names of such workers were recorded only at their permanent residence. Thus Dominique Morin appears in the Winslow census for that year as a "conducteur" with 3,500 logs and thirty-four unnamed "hommes tous domiciliés ailleurs."

Insofar as local farmers participated as employees rather than "independent" operators in the logging industry, they appear to have joined small groups of no more than a dozen individuals hired by local sub-contractors. There were nine such crews in Lambton Township in 1861, mostly young single men whose occupation was listed as "serviteurs." One of these groups included a seventy-one-year-old "bourgeois" who was presumably the sub-contractor. The local notary records contain no contracts related to woods labour or supply, but Clark reported for the 1857–8 season that twelve contractors had delivered 6,945 spruce logs while his own crews had cut 27,200 pine.[56] Presumably there were no sub-contractors living in Winslow, but the 1871 census records that colonists in neighbouring Whitton chopped 13,008 spruce and pine logs "under the orders of Dominick Morin of Lambton for Clark & Co.," and we have seen that Morin claimed another 3,500 logs in Winslow North.[57] In Winslow South, apart from the small quantities cut by the Scots settlers, there was a total of only 760 logs reported by three local residents – a saw mill operator, a merchant, and the Presbyterian minister.

One indirect indicator of such seasonal off-farm labour in a community is the cycle of marriages, conceptions, and, in some cases, deaths. Thus, in the seigneurie of Petite Nation during the 1830s and 1840s, January brought a sharp peak in the number of marriages because men had returned for a mid-winter break from the shanties. A rapid decline followed until March, then came a slow rise (dampened in the spring by the Lenten restrictions of the Catholic church) to a second smaller peak in November, prior to the seasonal departures for the woods. The January peak in marriages is not matched by the conception curve, which declined steadily from October to March, but this trajectory, followed by the sharp rise in conceptions during April, was also clearly linked to the seasonal nature of the logging industry.[58]

Figure 5.1 reveals rather different patterns for Winslow. The variation in St Romain's marriage curve is much less marked than that of Petite Nation, with the most significant dips appearing in the proscribed seasons of Lent and Advent. The Scots' marriage curve fluctuates still less, reflecting the lack of religious restrictions for their wedding dates. The Presbyterian records are inadequate for the measurement of births and deaths, which might have shed some light on the unusual conception curve of the French Canadians. Where Petite Nation's conceptions declined from October to March, those of St Romain increased from November to January, before dropping

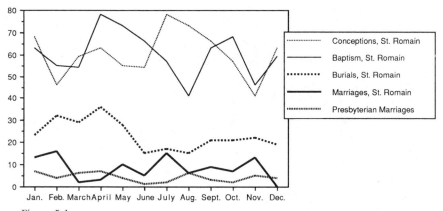

Figure 5.1
Seasonal Movements of Births, Deaths, and Marriages, Winslow, 1859–80

sharply in February and then rising again in March. The February decline can suggest only that married men spent a relatively short period of time away from home during the winter months. Perhaps extra workers and horses were needed by the lumber company to haul logs to streams in preparation for the spring drive.[59] Another possibility suggested by the November and February nadirs in St Romain's conceptions is that farmers were working on their own wood lots (or trespassing on company limits), for T.R. Roach notes that wood lot owners in early-twentieth-century eastern Canada cut and piled their logs late in the fall before the snow fell, returning only in the new year to haul them to loading points.[60] Given the density of the settlement pockets in Winslow, it is likely that many wood lots were far enough removed to necessitate sleeping away from home, particularly during the hauling season.

There is also more evidence of increasing independence from Clark and Co. The census of 1871 reveals that twelve French Canadians from Winslow North had cut square timber only, a product that would not have been destined for Clark's saw mill. In total, they were recorded with 20,000 cubic feet of pine, while one of them alone reported 48,000 cubic feet of maple, and three others a remarkable 1,780,616 cubic feet of tamarack, a species commonly found in thin-soiled, swampy areas such as Winslow. If the average gang of five could cut 10,000 cubic feet per month, this amount of tamarack would have required 178 men during a five-month period.[61] Much of the square timber was probably being sold to the railway companies then pushing two new lines into the district, for tamarack is well suited for rail ties[62] – a welcome market at a time when the interna-

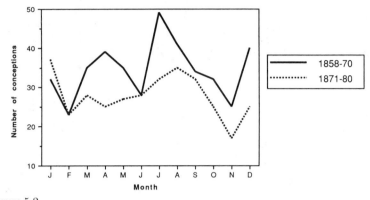

Figure 5.2
Monthly Conceptions in St Romain, 1858–70, 1871–80

tional recession severely depressed the district's lumber production. Clark and Co. reported processing only 80,000 pine and spruce logs at its mill in 1871, while Winslow's tamarack cut alone would have represented over 50,000 trees.[63]

The impact of railway construction was far from fleeting, for work on the Quebec Central and the International waxed and waned for over a decade. Begun at Lennoxville in 1869, the latter line reached Lake Megantic only in 1879, and the Maine border in 1885. In addition, there was a healthy export market for tamarack until disease hit the region's stands in 1878, and the International's locomotives consumed firewood until 1884, as well as providing access to the region's urban fuel market.[64] Finally, a number of small, steam-driven mills sprang up alongside the rail lines, breaking Clark's river-based monopoly over the marketing of saw logs.[65] Perhaps the opportunity to supply these mills explains why the unusually sharp dip in the conception curve for the normally fecund month of June is apparent only for the pre-1870 period (see Figure 5.2). Presumably, during the 1860s French-Canadian farmers were forced to seek outside sources of income between the seeding and haying seasons.

The summer conception pattern displays a striking rise in the curve during July, with high levels in August and September, months when heavy farm labour traditionally reduced conceptions within European peasant societies.[66] Mid-summer conceptions were also high in eighteenth-century French Canada, however, leading Henripin to conclude that "l'intensité du travail des mois d'été n'était pas un frein à l'ardeur sexuelle de cette population."[67] Given that the most arduous labour in St Romain would be required with the hay crop in July and August, one must still explain the decline in conceptions during

September and October.[68] The district's Catholic schools' inspector provided the likely answer in 1877 when he reported: "A considerable number of farmers in these townships, especially in the more recently-settled ones, were in the habit every year of spending a portion of their time in the neighbouring American States, where they received wages during the harvesting season. With the money thus earned in a comparatively short space of time, these people were able to meet their engagements, pay their taxes, etc., while the products of their farms supplied their families with the means of subsistance."[69] The inspector claimed that "since the beginning of the crisis this state of things is completely altered," with "the farmers who used to go and work in the United States or in the cities of the Dominion" spending more time in clearing land and sowing crops, but Figure 5.2 shows that any such interruption was not reflected by a flattening out of the fall conception curve during the 1870s.

No comparable analysis of seasonality can be made for the Scots because of the nature of their baptismal records, but evidence suggests that it was the mature sons and not the fathers who engaged in seasonal migration. A Scots visitor noted in 1870 that "many of the young men leave this district in winter and go into the United States, where they readily find employment, and can earn high wages, which they save and return to their own location when the crops require their attention."[70] Much later, a son of one of the Stornoway merchants recalled that "as the families grew up the young men and young women made it a practice to seek employment in the United States where money was more plentiful and wages were higher, and with the assistance given the people at home in this way their farms were well stocked and many of them became prosperous farmers."[71]

The changing labour strategies of the French Canadians, and the contrasting pattern for local Scots, suggest a complexity of economic life not hitherto suspected for the marginal colonization zones of Quebec. The off-farm dimension to the family economy explains how the Winslow settlers were able to maintain a rough balance between labour power and land supply without expanding and contracting the size of the farm, as in Russia, or hiring and dismissing servants, as in Austria.[72] The colonists clearly had to be resourceful in order to survive on their farms, and strategies were influenced by cultural background more than has been suggested by most historians in Canada and the United States.

In pointing out the apparently overwhelming impact of the environment on the rural economy of immigrant groups in the United States, Kathleen Conzen states: "The physical and economic context of farming was so different, the impact of American example so strong, that historians examining numerous groups in a variety of different settings have found few major differences attributable to ethnicity in farming practices, tenure, or persistence and success rates."[73] Conzen argues that to escape the misleading Turnerian stereotype of cultural simplification and individualism on the frontier, social scientists need to concentrate less on the agricultural economy and more on the family as a social and cultural institution. Focusing on the church, rather than the family, Robert Ostergren's study of a pioneer Swedish community in Minnesota found that "the evidence for a transplantation of the old way of life in the area of economic activity is as weak as the evidence for a transplantation of the social organization is strong."[74]

The fact remains, however, that the social and cultural aspects of the family as an institution are strongly influenced by its fundamental economic role. A contemporary observer listing the visible differences between the two ethnic communities in Winslow would not have had to refer only to kitchen gardens, hearths, houses, and implements, as suggested by Graeme Wynn for Atlantic Canada.[75] The essentially household-oriented economy permitted survival of certain culturally related agricultural practices, such as the high production of barley and wool among the Highlanders and the cultivation of flax, rye, and tobacco by the French Canadians.[76] Even the greater concentration by the Scots on raising cattle was consistent with the nature of the pre-migration economies of the two cultural groups as was the greater reliance of the French Canadians on the products of the forest.[77]

The two groups nevertheless shared a dependence on non-agricultural sources of income, a characteristic that again parallels their pre-migration experiences. Thus the crofters had been semi-independent kelp gatherers as well as wage labourers in the herring fishery and harvests of northeast Scotland,[78] while the Lauzon habitants had worked in the timber operations of the Caldwells and, quite likely, in the shipyards of Thomas Davies and others. Fundamentally, however, the aim of both groups – before and after migration to Winslow – was to remain as economically independent as possible.

Thus the Highlanders' agrarian base remained crucial long after the mid-century famine, and contemporaries frequently remarked on their contemptuous attitude toward wage labour.[79] In 1851, Sir John McNeill observed how Lewismen "regard the exaction of labour for wages as oppression." He added: "Many of these very men are bold and adventurous fishermen, who, on a coast singularly destitute of safe creeks, as is the district of Ness, prosecute the winter cod and ling fishery in open row boats at a distance from the land that renders it invisible, unless in clear weather; and in a sea open to the Atlantic and the northern oceans, with no land beyond it nearer than Iceland or America. They cheerfully encounter the perils and hardships of such a life, and tug for hours at an oar, or sit drenched in their coats without complaint, but to labour with a pick or a spade is to them most distasteful."[80] This independent attitude appears to have been carried by emigrants well beyond the upper St Francis district, for in 1871 Canada's population of Scots origin was the most inclined to be farmers, and the least inclined to be labourers, of all the major eth-nocultural groups.[81]

While French Canadians were not disproportionately drawn to farming as of 1871, they had only a slightly higher ratio than the total population in labouring and semi-skilled occupations.[82] This evidence runs counter to the claims by social scientists, reacting against Quebec's clerico-nationalist agrarian myth, that the French Canadians were more drawn to wage labour than to agriculture.[83] But the fact remains that farms remained the basis of the labour market in the lumber industry until well into the twentieth century.[84]

Finally, while the French-Canadian and Scots families pursued semi-agricultural/semi-labouring economies before and after their arrival in Winslow, their contrasting cultural backgrounds ensured that they would develop different family strategies to do so. The Scots might have appeared to the casual visitor to have been engaged in a more exclusively agricultural economy, but further inquiry would have revealed heavy dependence on the wages of mature offspring in the United States.[85] Such a system would remain viable only as long as these sons and daughters resisted the individualistic North American norms of their working environment.[86] The necessity for heads of French-Canadian households to seek employment off their farms even in late spring and in autumn must have seriously impeded their agricultural pursuits, though the breaking of the local lumber monopoly during the 1870s appears to have at least enabled them to remain at home in June. Certainly, the French Canadians' exploitation of local forest products was the more appropriate strategy for long-term survival in the upper St Francis district.

As Bouchard and his colleagues have found for the rural Saguenay region, so too did Winslow's economy fail to conform to either a strict market logic or to a strict Malthusian one.[87] Cultural and social psychological factors played a role in Winslow despite, or perhaps because of, the limited economic options the township offered. Before attempting to gain some insight into those factors by examining community-based institutions, we shall continue to explore the nature of the links between local production and the market by turning to the economic careers of the local agents of capitalism – the millers and the merchants.

CHAPTER SIX

Local Capital

If most of Winslow's agricultural production was consumed on the farm, and most of its timber taken by an outside lumber company, there nevertheless remained a role to play for local, small-scale millers and merchants. The primitive hand mills traditionally used to grind grain for home use in the Hebrides quickly gave way in Winslow to water-driven grist mills, saw mills sprang up to serve local lumber requirements, and carding mills refined wool for the domestic manufacture of cloth.[1] Even though much of this production was consumed by farm families themselves, some of it had to be marketed in order to pay for the factory-produced necessities and small luxuries they purchased each year from local merchants. The most obvious "cash crop" was lumber, yet, as we shall see, control by the timber lease holder rendered local saw mills less viable enterprises than grist and carding mills despite the latters' more limited resource bases. Under these conditions the petite bourgeoisie could not develop the links between Winslow's economy and that of the outside world that would have made local farm families less dependent on seasonal labour in that world.

Perhaps the first manufacturing entreprise in the township was a rather large saw mill and grist mill built near what would become the village of St Romain (on rang II NW, lot 8 – see Map 8) prior to the entrenchment of C.S. Clark and Co. in the district. The 1852 census enumerator recorded that Pierre Gagné dit Bellavance's saw mill was thirty feet long by twenty-two feet wide, with two saws capable (when well supplied with water) of producing 3,000 feet of boards in twenty-four hours. With the grist mill, half-owned by a local farmer, construction costs for the whole had been $1,200. The lumbering side of the business soon declined in relative importance: a new two-storey grist mill was erected in 1858, a carding mill added by 1861, and an agreement signed in 1863 stating that the saw mill would operate only when surplus water power was available.[2] By 1871 the saw mill was processing only 700 logs, worth $160, even though it had had no competitor in Winslow North for most of the year, while the grist mill ground 8,600 bushels of grain valued at $4,300. The son who inherited the grist mill expanded or rebuilt it once again to forty feet by thirty feet in 1877, while the son who took over the saw mill fails to appear in the 1881 census.[3]

If the Gagné family managed to survive as millers in Winslow North, in part by operating a large farm at the same time, the Therriens were less fortunate.[4] In 1856 François Therrien of St François de Beauce paid $400 to his brother for a mill site adjacent to Lake St Francis, at the northern boundary of the township (rang VIII NE, lot 19). Three years later he mortgaged this property and a mill site in Beauce for $400, and in 1861 he transferred the Winslow property to the British American Land Co. for only $141.20, though the census reported the same year that the company was leasing out a saw mill worth $1,400, as well as a grist mill of unspecified value.[5] By 1862 Therrien had shifted operations a little further east to a lot (rang III NW, lot 8) neighbouring that of Pierre Gagné, on which he mortgaged a saw mill and grist mill for $320.[6] Before he lost this property as well to the British American Land Co. in 1865, his father sold him yet another mill site further down stream (rang VIII NE, lot 27) for $60, but a month later his seventeen-year-old son sold it with a saw mill for $292. The money was then transferred to a Lambton merchant, presumably to repay a debt.[7]

Therrien's struggle to start a milling business did not end there, for in 1868 François Jr, who would soon marry, purchased a crown lot (rang II NW, lot 21) on another stream entering Lake St Francis. He agreed to support his father for the rest of his life in return for assistance in constructing the saw mill, and he formed a partnership with a local farmer in order to build a grist mill.[8] The farmer would contribute $300 in cash or labour, as well as half the lumber required, but François Jr then became seriously ill, drafting a will in August. He subsequently sold his half-interest in the property for only $125 to the Lambton doctor and merchant Pantaléon Cadieux. Therrien had the right to repurchase it in a year at 15-per-cent interest but failed to do so, signing an agreement to build the mill instead in return for $10 in cash and $90 in produce from Cadieux and $100 in labour on the mill from his former partner.[9] Cadieux soon purchased the other half-interest in the property for $400, but he had problems with the machinists; when the enumerator visited two years later, in the spring of 1871, the grist mill had been in operation only for a month and the saw mill was still under construction.[10] An 1891

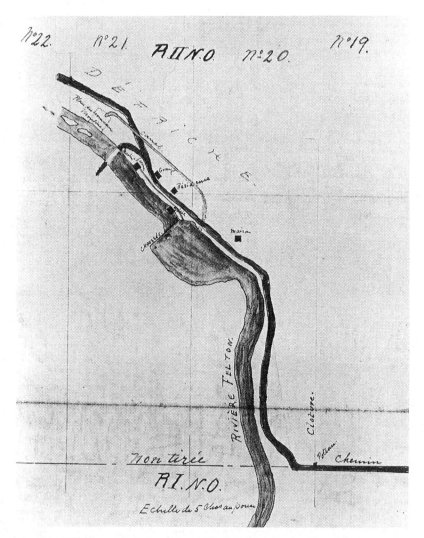

Map 14   Mill Site on the Felton River, 1891 (J.G. Bignell, a.p., Plans Démontrant la Position du Pouvoir d'Eau situé sur le lot no. 21 du 2eme R. N.O. de Winslow, Quebec, 6 mai 1891, Ministère d'Énergie et Ressources, Service arpentage)

surveyor's map (Map 14) illustrates a dam, a saw mill, and a grist mill, fed by by a small canal, with a larger canal under construction to a new mill site a little further downstream. Meanwhile, in 1874, the younger Therrien had signed an agreement with his brother to operate a grist mill and saw mill in neighbouring Stratford, where he continued to be hounded by debt.[11]

Pierre Pelchat, who acquired the Therriens' third saw mill (rang VIII NE, lot 27) in 1864, appears to have concentrated instead on a carding mill that he built on a crown mill site adjoining that of Pierre Gagné dit Bellavance. Pelchat is not listed as a saw mill owner by the 1871 census, and his grist mill had operated only for a month (processing $300 in grain), but his carding mill had combed $1,800 in wool. With four workers – a man, a woman, and two girls – the carding mill was the largest single industrial employer in the township, though the level of production suggests that the employment was part-time. Pelchat's debts accumulated to the point that in 1879 he and two local farmers mortgaged their properties jointly to Rufus Pope, son of the county's powerful MP, for $593.96. Neighbour Octave Gagné dit Bellavance mortgaged his grist mill and other properties to Pope the same year, but both men were still present and presumably active as of the 1881 census.[12]

Finally, yet another mill was established in 1880 when Benoit Bouffard paid $200 for a lot (rang VIII NE, lot 18) bordering Lake St Francis. Bouffard is listed as a "meunier" in the 1881 census. Given his location, he was probably operating a saw mill, but its history lies beyond the time-frame of this study. In short, Winslow North's economy prior to 1881 supported a successful grist mill and carding mill, but the saw mill industry was more marginal (at least before construction of Cadieux's mill in 1871), even though it was able to attract more investors.

The pattern was similar in Winslow South, although, as we saw in the previous chapter, more lumber was milled there than in the northern half of the township. The first store, saw mill, and grist mill were established at Stornoway (or Bruceville as it was officially called) by a Scot from Lingwick, but he sold them in 1855 to a Sherbrooke merchant for $2,000.[13] This individual in turn sold the property in 1858 to the English-born Richard Pallister, who formed a partnership with another Anglican named Henry Layfield.[14] They apparently never operated a store, but in 1861 they reported an investment of $2,500 in the mills, with one labourer employed at $20 per month, 1,000 spruce and pine logs converted into 12,000 boards, and 800 bushels of grain refined, for a total production value of $1,000.

The business was apparently not active enough to support both families, for in 1866 Pallister sold his share plus three lots to Layfield for $2,600.[15] The grist mill subsequently became the most important part of the business: in 1871 Layfield reported a fixed capital of $3,000 in it, but only $500 in the saw mill. The grist mill employed two hands and ground 8,000 bushels of grain valued at $4,000, while the saw mill employed one man and processed only 700 logs worth $175. By 1877 Layfield felt secure enough to pay $3,000 for a second saw mill and grist mill property located in Lingwick. When he died in 1881, he had achieved a material status far beyond that of the district's farmers, with the Stornoway property valued at $5,150, the Lingwick mills at $4,840, various other lots at $500, and household goods at $643. Layfield had avoided mortgage loans, and his total debt in 1881 was only $290.[16]

Despite his success in milling, Layfield had also continued to operate a farm throughout his career. In the spring of 1871 there were fifty acres in cultivation producing twenty tons of hay, 300 bushels of potatoes, and 200 bushels of oats. The Layfields also kept a horse, two oxen, six cows yielding 500 pounds of butter, two other cattle, fourteen sheep, and twenty-eight pigs. Their farm production was well beyond the range of most of their rural neighbours, yet Isabella Layfield and her fifteen-year-old daughter wove seventy yards of homespun in 1871. Ten years later, the Layfields had more cattle, but fewer sheep and pigs, and the inventory listed instead of a spinning wheel or loom, a $30 sewing machine. The only cloth in the house was thirty-six yards of flannel, eleven yards of "etoffe," and ten yards of Canadian linen – presumably acquired as payment from customers. Layfield's younger daughter may not have had to learn to spin like her older sister, but the family economy did continue to depend heavily on the labour of the three sons, who in 1881 were each credited with $700 in wages since coming of age. It appears, then, that business success in the difficult economic environment of Winslow and area required a certain amount of capital to start with, a cautious approach to expansion, a farm to fall back on in hard times, and a relatively large family to help operate it.

Judging from the list of Layfield's debtors at the time of his death in 1881, few of his customers were French Canadians. Of 165 separate entries, many of them for residents beyond Winslow's borders, only fourteen had French names. Most francophones in Winslow South obviously took their milling business to the Legendres, the only French-speaking family in Stornoway prior to 1880, when a French-Canadian blacksmith moved in. With the help of a $354 loan from the curé of Stratford, Ferdinand Legendre purchased mill site no. 2 (see Map 15) and erected a saw mill and grist mill in 1862.[17] In 1865 Ferdinand sold the property for $1,418 to his brother, Télésphore, but soon afterward their father was suing the two men for the $665 that he had advanced over the previous five years.[18] How the matter was settled is not clear, but Ferdinand left the district for a few years,

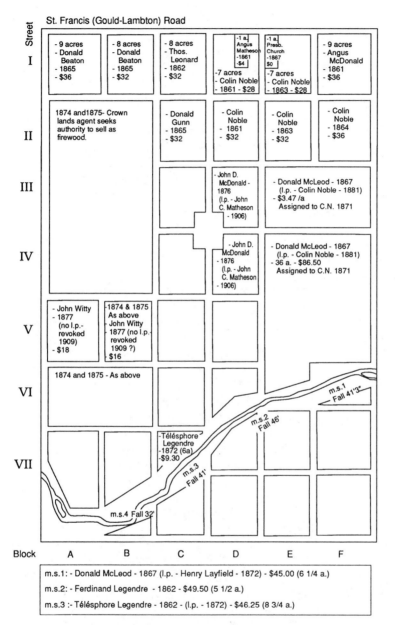

St. Francis (Gould-Lambton) Road

Street

I

- 9 acres
- Donald Beaton
- 1865
- $36

- 8 acres
- Donald Beaton
- 1865
- $32

- 8 acres
- Thos. Leonard
- 1862
- $32

-1 a.
Angus Matheson
-1861
-$4

-7 acres
- Colin Noble
- 1861 - $28

-1 a.
Presb. Church
-1867
$0

-7 acres
- Colin Noble
- 1863 - $28

- 9 acres
- Angus McDonald
- 1861
- $36

II

1874 and 1875- Crown lands agent seeks authority to sell as firewood.

- Donald Gunn
- 1865
- $32

- Colin Noble
- 1861
- $32

- Colin Noble
- 1863
- $32

- Colin Noble
- 1864
- $36

III

- John D. McDonald - 1876 (l.p. - John C. Matheson - 1906)

- Donald McLeod - 1867 (l.p. - Colin Noble - 1881) - $3.47 /a Assigned to C.N. 1871

IV

- John D. McDonald - 1876 (l.p. - John C. Matheson - 1906)

- Donald McLeod - 1867 (l.p. - Colin Noble - 1881) - 36 a. - $86.50 Assigned to C.N. 1871

V

- John Witty
- 1877 (no l.p.- revoked 1909)
- $18

-1874 & 1875 As above
- John Witty
- 1877 (no l.p.- revoked 1909 ?)
- $16

VI

1874 and 1875 - As above

m.s.1
Fall 41'3"

VII

-Télésphore Legendre
-1872 (6a)
-$9.30

m.s.2 Fall 46'

m.s.3 Fall 41'

m.s.4 Fall 32'

Block   A   B   C   D   E   F

m.s.1: - Donald McLeod - 1867 (l.p. - Henry Layfield - 1872) - $45.00 (6 1/4 a.)

m.s.2: - Ferdinand Legendre - 1862 - $49.50 (5 1/2 a.)

m.s.3 :- Télésphore Legendre - 1862 - (l.p. - 1872) - $46.25 (8 3/4 a.)

Map 15   Crown Land Purchases in Stornoway to 1880   (J. Bignell, PLS, Plan of the Central Village Reserve of Bruceville, October 1854, Québec, Ministère d'Énergie et Ressources, Service arpentage; Sherbrooke and Cookshire Registry Offices, Land Registers)

and in 1871 the thirty-two-year-old Télésphore was still unmarried and living in his father's household.

Télésphore had added a wool carding mill at a cost of $770 in 1868, and in 1870 he expanded the mill property by 150 acres.[19] According to the 1871 census, the saw mill employed two labourers and sawed 1,000 logs to produce $600 in lumber, and the grist mill employed one labourer and ground 12,000 bushels of grain worth $6,000. Both mills were therefore more productive than those operated by Layfield. The Legendre carding mill combed 15,000 pounds of wool valued at $4,500, even though Scots descendants still vividly recall home carding bees.[20] After subtracting the value of the raw material and wages, returns for the saw, grist, and carding mills were $150, $450, and $500, respectively.

The Legendres' financial difficulties appeared to be over by 1871, but only a year later Télésphore mortgaged the property for $1,000 to a retired Sherbrooke hotel keeper. The burden was eventually shared by the prodigal son, Ferdinand, who in 1874 was given mill site no. 3 by his father in return for assuming $300 of the mortgage. The agreement also stipulated that within a decade Ferdinand was to establish one plant to manufacture furniture, doors, frames, or carriages and another for shingles.[21] In 1878 Télésphore expanded operations to Lake Megantic by erecting the first saw mill in the future railway centre, a large building measuring sixty feet by forty feet. Perhaps his debts had become too burdensome, however, for within two years he had sold the Lake Megantic mill to an American company and the Stornoway operations to his three younger unmarried brothers.[22]

Although on a smaller scale than the Layfield family, the Legendres also operated a farm in addition to the milling business. In 1871, when two of the sons in the parental household were listed as millers, and three were attending school, the father reported twenty acres improved, nearly half of which was in pasture and half in hay. The only other crops were 200 bushels of potatoes and six bushels of corn, but the family also had one horse, two cows, two sheep, and nine pigs. Esther Legendre and her seventeen-year-old daughter must have had little time to spare from feeding and caring for the six males in the family in 1871, but they did produce 100 pounds of butter and twenty yards of homespun. If there were serious tensions within the Legendre family, they obviously did not prevent most of the members from working closely together over an extended period of time, subordinating individual ambition to an extended-family strategy. That strategy appears to have paid off economically, for the

Legendre brothers' company remained in business until well into the twentieth century.[23]

In Winslow South as in Winslow North, then, the milling industry was strongly family- and agrarian-based, with saw mills bringing lower returns than grist mills and carding mills even in this lumber-producing district. While the small saw mill operators of early-nineteenth-century New Brunswick could obtain cutting licences from the crown to ensure their own supply of timber, Clark simply monopolized all the crown lots in Winslow and district.[24] Furthermore, Table 6.1 demonstrates the smaller scale of saw mill production in Winslow North, even though the farmers there were more dependent on the forest economy than were their counterparts to the south.

Perhaps Clark and Co. guarded its timber supply in Winslow North more carefully, and harvested it more rapidly, because of its closer proximity to Lake St Francis. The monopoly would be broken partially through government sales of wood lots after Confederation, but primarily through poaching after the Quebec Central and the International railways ended the district's dependence on the St Francis River as the only route to the lumber market. Unfortunately for Winslow, however, it lay between the paths of these two lines, as well as the steam-powered saw mills that sprang up alongside. As a result, the villages of Stornoway and St Romain would atrophy while the boom town of Lake Megantic emerged on the eastern settlement frontier.

As producers mostly for the local market, Winslow's mill owners were somewhat isolated from contacts with outside capital, aside from seeking the occasional mortgage loan. As in the rest of the region, they must have operated on a cashless basis with their clientele, taking payment for services with a portion of the finished product.[25] In contrast to the upper St John Valley, no owner of a local mill lived outside the district, and none combined milling with the operation of a store.[26] Village merchants, rather than millers, acted as local agents for the forces of commercial capitalism. Unfortunately for those merchants, their services were not needed by the lumber monopoly, and the physical environment strictly limited any agricultural surplus that could be produced for market.

While transactions important enough to be recorded in the notary records were generally measured by the monetary standard, farmers could clearly by-pass merchants and the need for cash by bartering among themselves. Because of its very nature, such a hidden economy is impossible to measure, but there are references to it even in

Table 6.1

Mill Production and Returns (Dollars) in Winslow North and Winslow South, 1871

	Processed Material	−	Raw Material	−	Wages	=	Return
WINSLOW NORTH							
Saw mills (2)	328		164		18		146
Grist mills (3)	5,330		4,800		250		280
Carding mills (1)	2,040		1,800		218		22
Totals	7,698		6,764		486		448
WINSLOW SOUTH							
Saw mills (2)	1,020		425		280		315
Grist mills (2)	11,000		10,000		375		625
Carding mills (1)	5,200		4,500		200		500
Totals	17,220		14,925		855		1,440

notarized documents. In 1864, for example, Gabriel Audet dit Lapointe sold Joseph Dion a mare for 1,500 bundles (twelve tons) of first-quality hay, to be delivered at the rate of 300 bundles per winter.[27] Parcels of land were not infrequently traded among farmers, and occasionally they were even exchanged for an annual payment in produce. Thus, in 1863, Joseph Goulet transferred a partial lot with no buildings to Narcisse Rosa of Aylmer Township in return for pasturing ten ewes for two years and supplying six quintals (600 pounds) of "gaudriole" (a mixture of oats and peas) per year.[28] Finally, in situations where barter was impractical, promissory notes could be drafted. Thus, when Jean Guay mortgaged lot 20, rang VII NE, to Jean-Baptiste Cameron, his first payment was in the form of a $56 debt acknowledged by Narcisse Richard.[29] While such notes obviously represent a major step toward actual currency, they were commonly paid off in kind and created a local network of mutual obligation.

The annual store purchases made by French-speaking farmers can be gauged to some extent from the "rentes viagères" established to support ageing parents when they transferred their farms to the succeeding generation. An example of the stipulations made by a relatively well-established couple is to be found in the agreement reached in 1879 between Michel and Marie Audet dit Lapointe with their son Joseph.[30] For footware each year, Michel was to be given two pairs of red leather boots, and Marie one pair of red shoes; Marie was to get as well a pair of "bottines" every three years. Michel's clothing would all be made of wool and "grosse étoffe," but Marie would receive each year a skirt, shirt, and blouse of "flanelle du pays," a cotton handkerchief and apron, and a "blouse d'indienne" (presumably a cotton print). Finally, as an unusual indulgence, she could also choose once only a coat or collar, and every five years a dress of black Cobourg with a hat "à son goût."[31] Not every woman in Winslow could expect so much; when the twenty-six-year-old Camille Richard died, for example, she left only two dresses of Indian cloth, the traditional homespun "capot," two blouses, an old petticoat, a skirt of drugget, and a hood – all valued at $4.96.[32]

As for food, the extensive list compiled for Michel and Marie Audet dit Lapointe specified only a small number of items, and in small quantities, that would have to be purchased at a store – twenty-five pounds of green cod, six salted eels, twelve pounds of rice, one gallon of red wine, one gallon of gin, two pounds of green tea, one pound of green coffee, one minot of salt, one pound of pepper, and one gallon of coal oil for lighting. Clearly the retired couple expected to be fed with essentially what the land produced.[33]

By the early 1870s, the tiny village of St Romain could boast two grist mills, a carding mill, and a small saw mill, in addition to supporting two or three carpenters, a blacksmith, and several other tradesmen, but no retail business of significant size or longevity emerged during our study period.[34] Pierre Boucher established the first store in 1866 but sold the property to cancel his debts only two years later.[35] More successful was Flavien Marceau, who purchased a village lot in 1872. Although he had to mortgage his property to a Lévis merchant for a $1,000 loan in 1877, he was still operating as a merchant in St Romain in 1881, according to the spring census enumeration.[36] Finally, the farmer Raymond Richard was identifying himself as a merchant by 1877, and he too was still present in 1881.[37] The businesses of both these men must have been limited in volume, however, for it was only outside merchants who acquired mortgages on the land of local farmers. Yet even the merchants in the nearby district centre of St Vital de Lambton held only $308 in mortgages on Winslow farms.

In South Winslow, Stornoway's favourable location at a cross-roads near several mill sites allowed it to serve the same central functions for the surrounding Scots communities as did St Vital for the French Canadians to the north. There was therefore a stronger merchant presence in Stornoway than in St Romain, but again with only limited operations. Furthermore, Winslow's Lewis Scots did not produce a single successful miller or merchant during our study period.

One of the first attempts to operate a store in Stornoway was made by Donald Gunn during the early 1860s. He was backed by another Lewis-born merchant, Lewis McIver of Bury, but by 1867 he had mortgaged his business to ten wholesale firms for $3,615.[38] Gunn appears to have underestimated the poverty of his clients, for he confessed to McIver: "I have committed such errors in my first carrear [sic] in business that I now find myself in such position as to be unable to overcome. I have battled against this misfortune untill [sic] my peace of mind is destroyed. I cannot get my due & in consequence I cannot pay. These dues can be collected but not hasty it is utterly impossible for these people to pay at once."[39]

A year later, when the Montreal merchants agreed to settle for 50 per cent, McIver paid them the $300 outstanding on that amount, as well as $450 for a new order from a Montreal firm. In return, Gunn renewed his mortgage to McIver, specifying that the debt to him would be repaid in full.[40] Gunn had been granted a little breathing space, but it left him strictly dependent upon payments from his farmer clients. In February 1868, two months after the new arrangement with McIver, Gunn wrote that so far he had received "no more than $50 worth of grain alltogether." It would appear, then, that Winslow merchants still engaged in commodity exchange, though it was generally dying out elsewhere in the country.[41]

If the Scots had been active in logging or sugar-making, Gunn might have expected an influx of cash in the early spring, but he could only suggest that half the local farmers would be so "hard up" by May that they would have to begin buying provisions once again. The catch in this strategy, as Gunn had to admit, was how these already indebted farmers would pay for their new purchases. The fact that fellow merchant Colin Noble could still offer credit was already making it difficult for Gunn to compete.[42]

The beleagured merchant was able to win some additional time in the fall of 1868 by mortgaging his seventy-acre farm to McIver for the deficit in the first year's instalment, but his debt had grown to $2,000 by the spring of 1870. McIver offered to settle for $1,400, but Gunn presumably could not pay, for two months later he was successfully sued for $1,100 in back payments he had failed to meet. He was finally forced to declare insolvency in the fall of 1871, transferring all his property to McIver the following spring.[43]

Gunn's property eventually fell into the hands of the Leonard family, whose experience as local entrepreneurs proved much happier.[44] Thomas Leonard had left Inniskillen, Ireland, in 1844, first settling on a farm in Bury, then moving briefly to Lingwick, and finally establishing a business in Stornoway around 1860.[45] As with Edouard Legendre, he had a number of sons who would soon be old enough to help him diversify activities. The family eventually operated a store, hotel, stage-coach service, and farm. The proportional impor-

Table 6.2
Categories of Merchandise (Ratio to Total Value in Parentheses) in
Inventory, Leonard's Store, Stornoway, 1871

Alcohol	$114.15 (17%)	Tools/implements/	
Medicinal	$28.23 (4%)	equipment	$61.22 (9%)
Other consumable	$68.62 (10%)	Clothing	$127.43 (19%)
Dyes	$37.15 (6%)	Cloth and	
Household		thread	$93.27 (14%)
miscellaneous	$131.51 (20%)	School supplies	$11.51 (2%)

tance of each enterprise is difficult to judge, but the inventory
drafted when Leonard's wife died in the spring of 1871 reveals that
the store stock was worth only $673 of $11,411 for all movable property and business assets.[46] By way of contrast, Claude Pronovost has
found that the average stock value for thirteen rural merchants operating north of Montreal in the early nineteenth century was $2,351,
which represented about 45 per cent of their movable property.[47]

While his stock may have been somewhat depleted at this pre-
harvest point in the seasonal cycle, Leonard's June inventory indicates
the sort of commercial products purchased by local farmers (see
Table 6.2). Food items totalled only $60.72 in value, and the main
one was 226 pounds of sugar ($15.82), which would be sold to the
many Scots who did not produce their own supply of maple sugar
(as we saw in chapter 5). The only other foods were a barrel of
crackers ($5.00), 100 pounds of rice ($4.00), ten pounds of butter
($1.50), and five pounds of dried apples ($0.50). Related items
included twenty-nine pounds of tea ($16.40), ten pounds of coffee
($1.70), sixteen pounds of tobacco ($6.40), five and a half bushels of
salt ($3.30), fifteen pounds of saltpetre ($1.50) which was commonly
used for preserving meat, and a variety of spices. The stock of goods
for medicinal or health purposes for this community with no doctor
was more impressive, including thirty gallons of cod liver oil ($20.75),
one case of castor oil ($3.00), seventy pounds of alum ($2.10), twelve
pounds of epsom salts ($0.48), a pound of senna leaves ($0.20), and
an ounce of camphor ($0.20).[48] There were also a few dozen sets of
dishes and utensils, and thirty pounds of candles, but the total value
of all the foregoing household items was only $131.51. Leonard's
stock of tools and implements was valued even lower, at $53.12, and
included nothing more expensive than two forks at $1.50 each.

The selection of clothing was also limited, totalling $127.43 and
consisting primarily of collars, straw hats, caps, and a few pairs of

boots and shoes. There were no women's dresses or skirts or men's shirts or trousers (apart from two suits valued at $23.50). A more impressive stock of various kinds of cloth, primarily cottons, was valued at $87.11, but, at 14 per cent, its relative value in the toal inventory was considerably lower than that generally found for cloth in Quebec's village stores during the late eighteenth and early nineteenth centuries. The persistence of homespun is reflected in the large quantities of various dyes in the store – fifty pounds of venetian red ($1.50), forty pounds of copperas ($0.80), thirty-two pounds of logwood ($3.20), eight pounds of cochineal ($8.00), one barrel of madder ($23.00). and sixty-five cents worth of spruce yellow and sulphur, presumably yellow dyes. The Scots' clothing would not be entirely drab, despite their church's fulminations against the vanity of colours.[49] While the dyes were commercial items, their presence also draws attention to the fact that Winslow did not have a fulling or dyeing mill, though these had long been associated with carding mills elsewhere in the region.[50]

Leonard's store inventory noted a considerable volume of spirits, including more than five cases of gin ($34.50), three cases of brandy ($18.00), one case of flask Scotch whiskey ($6.00), thirty gallons of whiskey ($19.50), two gallons of old rye ($10.00), and eighteen and a half gallons of wine ($26.15). Some of this liquor was perhaps destined to supply the hotel bar, which did not appear in the inventory, but historians have found that merchants in the seigneuries at the turn of the nineteenth century held stocks of a similar magnitude.[51] They, however, carried imported rum, where Leonard favoured gin and whiskey, which could be distilled from home-grown barley and rye. They would therefore be less effective as a "battering-ram" to break into the self-sufficient household economy.[52]

Volumes of the items in Leonard's inventory may have fluctuated throughout the year, and from year to year, but the merchandise listed above strongly suggests a frugal and self-sustaining population. The store's clientele extended well beyond the limits of Winslow Township, for its inventory records a total of 432 debtors. Leonard may not have been one of the merchants referred to in the bitter lines by a Gaelic bard who had arrived in the early 1860s, but his ledger too could have appropriately been called "the legion":

There were two merchants beside me in this corner of the world
A man from Lingwick and a man who was raised in Winslow
Remember if you go they will have you in their claws
Like a plucked chicken you would be left to waste

There was no escape from them
Except joining the Legion.[53]

Numerous as Leonard's debtors were, however, the sums they owed were relatively small, even for such an impoverished environment. If we except the atypically high entry of $249.49 for Major William McMinn, a local gadfly of independent means who spent a good deal of time at Leonard's hotel, the value of the average debt was $9.33.[54] As Catholics, the trilingual Leonards had contacts with the local French Canadians through their church in Stratford, but only seventy-four of the names in the inventory were French, with an average debt of $6.31 each.

While the settlers of Winslow clearly engaged in commercial exchange the numerous credits in Leonard's ledger reflected the lack of specie in the community. These debts could be cancelled with the sale of a small agricultural surplus in the fall or winter, but people who failed to meet the annual payment would eventually have to sign promissory notes, which would in turn force them to aim for a larger marketable surplus.[55] But Leonard clearly did not allow debts to accumulate beyond a certain level: even though some individuals had signed more than one note, only six were dated from more than two years earlier. The 160 notes listed in the inventory (six were for French Canadians) averaged only $25.33 each – at interest rates of 6 to 12 per cent – or the equivalent of 29 per cent of the total debts owed to the store.[56] Scots farmers' indebtedness increased steadily after this inventory was drafted in 1871, as we shall see, but the Leonards apparently continued to refuse extension of credit beyond two or three years' purchases. Certainly, no properties were mortgaged to the Leonard family during our study period.[57]

Perhaps not surprising, few luxury items were listed in the Leonards' household inventory. A large part of the durable goods, valued at $769 (including $185 for beds and bedding), was related to the hotel and stage-coach business (see Table 6.3). When such items are removed, the family's possessions were valued no higher than those of the smallest Quebec City merchants during the 1820s.[58] Thomas Leonard also owned land within, and close to, the village reserve estimated optimistically at $2,375. He had managed to acquire 230 acres of these lots directly from the crown and to purchase the remaining 152 acres from third parties as low-priced unpatented claims.[59] These seemingly strategic acquisitions never acquired a high value because the village failed to develop beyond a rather rudimentary service centre. Indeed, Leonard's sons still owned the total acre-

Table 6.3
Value (Dollars) of Durable Goods by Category in
Household Inventory, Leonard Family, Stornoway,
1871

Furniture, bedding	251.40
Dishes, cutlery	7.55
Household miscell.	24.26
Heating, light	29.85
Transportation	336.75
Shed, outdoors miscell.	118.80
Total	768.61

age in 1881. Not unexpectedly, they had acquired little additional
real estate during the 1870s: only 362 acres (including the property
of failed merchant Donald Gunn) costing $930 and a 103–acre mort-
gaged farm at a sheriff's auction for only $15.[60]

The Leonards valued land for its productive capacities rather than
as a source of speculative income. As early as 1861, they had
improved fifty-six acres, producing ten tons of hay, 500 bushels of
potatoes and turnips, and 160 bushels of grain, while feeding two
cows, two steers or heifers, two horses, and four pigs. By 1871, they
had 100 acres under improvement, presumally to feed themselves
and the coach horses. According to the census, their hay production
was three times that of a decade earlier, but the grain and root harvest was essentially the same, and livestock was limited to one cow
and five horses.[61]

The land owned by Thomas Leonard may have been of limited
value, and a large proportion of the liquid assets may have been in
credits to a poor population ($13,786), but as of 1871 he owed only
$2,004 to six Montreal firms and $295 to one in Stanstead. Like
Henry Palliser, but on a more generous scale, Leonard could afford
to pay his oldest sons a cash settlement for the labour they had contributed since reaching the age of twenty-one: $1,700 went to the
twenty-three-year-old Hugh, who was listed as a store clerk in the
census, and $500 to twenty-one-year-old Thomas Jr, who drove the
stage-coach.[62] Including $430 cash in hand, the net value of Leon-
ard's movable assets after these deductions was only $537, but his
wealth was on an entirely different scale than that of his farmer
clients. After little more than a decade in Stornoway, the cautious and
astute Irishman had established a solidly successful business, which

would remain in the hands of his elder sons long after his death in 1872.[63]

Stornoway's location at the crossing of the two most important roads in the district did attract competitors, but only one would prevail. With assets worth only $850 and liabilities of $1,475, Angus McDonald was forced to close the doors of his hotel in 1872, leaving merchant Colin Noble as the Leonards' chief rival in business as well as in politics.[64] Born in Inverness, Scotland, Noble had arrived in the Eastern Townships with his parents in 1838, when he was ten years old. During the 1840s, his father purchased a farm and saw mill in Gould, and Colin later joined his brother in operating a saw mill and furniture shop in Massachusetts. In 1852 he returned to purchase a log-built store in Stornoway.[65] R.G. Dun's local credit assessor reported in 1857 that Noble was the "son of a Farmer in that neighbourhood who is in very good circumstances, commenced about 2 years ago, has a cap. of say $1000, & is doing a sm. safe bus., good for a sm. amt." Within a few months the tone had changed to "doubtful, not much means, & not too honest," but by 1859 he was said to be "improving in means." From then until the last entry in 1862 reports were favourable, but with caveats such as "not much bottom" and "trading in a hard region to grow."[66]

The 1861 census records that Noble had invested $6,000 in his business, with $1,000 as the "annual product." He still owned only a six-acre village lot, but within three years he would purchase from the government thirty-nine acres of the best-situated land in the village reserve (see Map 15, above). As with Thomas Leonard, the speculation would prove disappointing. Noble made only a couple of small sales prior to his retirement from the village in 1892, when he finally sold most of the lots as a block for $2,000. This transaction may have represented a sizeable net profit on paper, but Noble had made an investment in his store and farm and waited thirty-two years for this return on his original land purchase.

Noble was more fortunate with the few rural properties he acquired in Winslow South during the early 1860s, making a quick 275 per cent profit on three lots he sold for $400 in 1864. But, once the expansionary settlement phase had ended, land speculation ceased to be profitable. As an example, six rural properties that Noble purchased throughout his career in Winslow South would finally be sold to his son-in-law in 1899 for $555 less than he paid for them. Most of the lots accumulated by Noble had already been mortgaged to him, but these too failed to bring him a net gain. He lost over $500 in straight sales of his rural properties in Winslow South by the time he had rid himself of most of them, thus demonstrating the Leonards' wisdom in avoiding mortgages. In addition to the forty-four purchases Noble made in Stornoway and rural Winslow South throughout his career, he also acquired eight properties in Whitton, three in Marston, and three in Hampden, realizing somewhat less than a thousand dollars of profit in total.

Noble allowed debts to accumulate into mortgages, perhaps because he depended more than the Leonards on retail trade, for his only other occupation was that of village postmaster. Noble's position would have been stronger in another province because English-Canadian property law decreed that a mortgage was effectively a temporary property transfer, with the mortgager entitled to seize the bonded property in default of payment. In Quebec, however, one issued not a mortgage per se (though the words "obligation and mortgage" were used in the English-language documents), but a hypothec, which did not transfer title to the bonded property. Instead, the hypothec was non-specific, covering a debtor's entire landed property and requiring a sheriff's auction in order to recover a debt in default. If the auction failed to bring the full sum specified in the contract, the creditor(s) would simply be out of pocket for the difference.[67]

Thus, even though Noble could have acquired his debtors' farms at lower prices through sheriff's sales, there was no financial incentive for him to do so. Rather than launch legal suits which would have alienated the local community, he consistently paid slightly more for his farms than the sums specified in his hypothecs.[68] Conversely, it was in the debtor's interests to sell to Noble rather than face an auction which would almost certainly have provided no surplus cash beyond the value of the hypothec.[69]

While Noble was clearly under considerable pressure to purchase the farms of customers who failed to meet their payments, his losses from the subsequent resales were probably more than balanced by wood cut on at least some of these lots. Even if the struggling original owners had taken most of the merchantable logs before selling their farms, by the 1880s new-growth spruce and fir could be sold to the pulp mills which were springing up on the lower St Francis. Also, Noble may have collected as much as $3,000 in interest on the $8,000 invested in mortgages throughout his career, but only in the highly unlikely case that instalments were paid faithfully while the principal of each loan was not reduced until the date of amortization.

Noble's family was no less dependent than other village merchants and millers on its own agricultural production. In the spring of 1861, when they were assisted by two young women servants and a man, the Nobles kept three cows, three sheep, seven pigs, and a horse.[70]

There was no outside help listed ten years later, when the eldest son was still only six years of age, but the two teenaged daughters no doubt churned most of the 100 pounds of butter yielded by the five cows. They did not weave any cloth, however, nor was there any grain or many potatoes harvested on the farm, though the Nobles did cut ten tons of hay to feed their cattle, three pigs, and three horses. In 1892, at the ages of sixty-four and fifty-nine, respectively, Colin and Maria Noble retired to a large and modern brick house on twelve acres in the county seat of Cookshire, but it cost them $325 more than they received for their farm and store in Stornoway.[71] When Maria died in 1903, the only surviving son received the Cookshire property and 150 acres in Winslow in return for his father's keep and a dollar per week in spending money. Apart from the $300 promised to a married daughter,[72] Colin Noble appears to have had few other assets, for no will could be found in the local registry office.

There is a striking contrast between Noble's financial career and that of fellow merchants Rémi Hudon of Hébertville and Jacques Picard of Wotton, who also operated in rather marginal colonization zones during the latter half of the nineteenth century. Between 1865 and 1899 Hudon, succeeded by his widow, negotiated 100 hypothecs totalling $18,127 in value. He also gained more than $7,000 in profit from land sales, realizing between 40-per-cent and 50-per-cent profit on each transaction.[73] Jacques Picard's situation was closer to that of Noble, because the price of land in Wotton Township appears not to have increased much faster than it did in Winslow.[74] Nevertheless, between 1856 and 1905 Picard would sign 109 hypothecs totalling $30,123, from which he appears to have more than doubled his investment.[75]

The marked contrast in the business careers of Noble and Picard requires some explanation, given that each of them became dominant figures in townships opened to colonization by the same government-sponsored project at mid-century. As a long-time MLA, Picard held political sway over Wotton's settlers, but Noble was himself the most powerful figure in Winslow South. He was the first mayor, member of the municipal council and school commission for many years, justice of the peace for more than thirty-five years, commissioner of the Magistrate's Court for thirty years, postmaster for forty years, and major in the 58th Battalion of militia.[76] Most important, he was also chief political agent among the Scots settlers for John Henry Pope, the county's all-powerful MP. Noble's alliance to the Pope clan was formalized by the marriage of his daughter to Pope's only son in 1877.[77]

Picard did operate in a somewhat more promising township than did Noble, and he undoubtedly exercised more direct political power, but the explanation for the contrast in their financial careers must be sought elsewhere. Perhaps Noble was simply less content than Picard to collect annual interest on each hypothec without the principal being reduced, for long term, wide-scale client indebtedness was certainly part of Picard's financial and political strategy.[78] Given the losses Noble frequently took on his land sales, however, it is unlikely that he would have exerted a great deal of pressure on clients who were meeting their interest payments. By a process of elimination, then, it would appear that the farmer clients of the two merchants must have responded differently to bonded debt. Bitter experience presumably instilled in the Highlanders a traditional suspicion toward contracts that might limit property rights. It was said of the habitants, however, that they would not hesitate to mortgage their farms to a local merchant of property who could afford to see them through the years of deficit.[79] Perhaps this precaution explains why none of the farms in Winslow North was mortgaged to the struggling merchants in the local hamlet of St Romain.

Table 6.4 shows that the mortgages of the Winslow Scots were generally close to the value of their farms, particularly during the 1860s. Prior to 1881, the mean value of the thirty-eight Scots transactions was $260, for a total of $9,889. The reason for drafting the hypothec was not often specified in the contract, but some of the earlier ones represented loans to finance farm improvements or expansion. Thus Table 6.5 suggests that the mortgagees of the 1860s were somewhat more progressive farmers than the Scots population as a whole. They were more likely to have settled as early as 1852, and, as of 1861, they had improved 40 per cent more land, kept 40 per cent more cattle, and owned movable and immovable property valued at 25 per cent more than that of the general Scots farm population. Finally, slightly more of them had older sons who would provide extra labour, as well as requiring extra land. Perhaps some of these farmers were attempting to take advantage of the market created by the US Civil War, as suggested in the previous chapter, but seven of the twelve mortgages were signed by Colin Noble during the later 1860s, when the American market was in decline. Five ended in sales within a few years. The low farm values and oats yields of Noble's mortgagees, and the small, uneven sums in their contracts (such as $166.33 and $261.20), all suggest consolidation of accumulated debts.

The number of Scots mortgages climbed significantly during the 1870s, but not as a result of loans for farm expansion and improve-

Table 6.4
Mean Value (Dollars) of French-Canadian and Scots Farm Mortgages and
Sales (Value per Acre in Parentheses), Winslow, 1850–80*

	French Canadians		Scots	
	Hypothecs	Sales	Hypothecs	Sales
1850–60	52 (0.94)	199 (4.11)	–	–
1861–70	110 (1.92)	265 (4.35)	283 (2.90)	283 (3.59)
1871–80	147 (2.17)	245 (4.39)	247 (2.91)	361 (5.06)
1850–80	123 (1.99)	246 (4.34)	260 (2.90)	333 (4.51)

*Sales "à faculté de réméré" (i.e. those subject to cancellation on repayment of
principal) are considered to be mortgages, and hypothecs that represented security
on land purchases (i.e. primary mortgages) and appointments to public office are
excluded.

Table 6.5
Socioeconomic Profile of Scots Mortgagees, Winslow, 1860–80

	No.	Age	Sons 13+	Farm Size	Improved (Acres)	Cattle	Yield	Farm Value
1860–69							(Oats)	
Mortgagees	9*	48	1.1	103	35	9.6	24	$744
To Colin Noble	5	52	1.2	100	28	9.2	16	$580
All farmers	113	46	0.8	107	25	6.9	22	$563
1870–80							(Potatoes)	
Mortgagees	21†	43	0.9	122	38	7.0	104	
To Colin Noble	13	45	0.8	119	38	8.2	108	
All farmers	120	48	1.1	114	40	7.7	112	

*Three other mortgagees were not present in 1861.
†Three other mortgagees were not present in 1871.

ment. Colin Noble dominated the scene still more strongly than during the 1860s, with fifteen of twenty-four mortgages, and seven of
his clients sold out to him within a five year period. In contrast to
the 1860s, mortgagees were slightly younger and owned fewer cattle
than the Scots farmers as a whole, but otherwise there was nothing
unique about their profile. Certainly, they do not appear to have been
among the more successful farmers.

The brief spurt in Scots mortage-taking during the late 1870s
suggests economic difficulties, with the impact of the 1873–8 recession at its peak. Also, extension of railways into the district brought

Winslow all the disadvantages of external competition on the limited district market, with none of the advantages of a rail link within the township itself.[80] In the face of a steadily declining Scots population, and the apparent reluctance of French Canadians to take over their farms, capitalists became hesitant to negotiate mortgages in Winslow South after 1880. Colin Noble signed only five, and a preliminary study ending in 1900 reveals marked decline in mortgage activity by farmers along the main St Francis Road.[81] The Scots community would therefore never experience what was arguably the chief force behind agricultural commercialization in North America – rising land values.[82]

If the Scots preferred to make a new start elsewhere after their local agricultural options became restricted by a sizeable mortgage, many of their French-Canadian neighbours followed the strategy of Picard's Wotton clients. Indeed, they had still less reason than the Wotton debtors to move because the value of the average French-Canadian hypothec in Winslow was considerably less than those negotiated by Picard. Registry-office and notary records reveal that during the period 1850–80, Winslow's French Canadians negotiated seventy-one mortgages valued at $8,749, for an average of only $123 each, exactly half the average Scots transaction (see Table 6.4).

In contrast to the Scots, the French Canadians commonly mortgaged their farms for much less than their value. Their lower level of concern toward bonded debt presumably reflects their greater familiarity with the less onerous terms of the hypothec as compared with an English mortgage. They did not allow a hypothec on a property to stand in the way of further loans, or even further hypothecs on the same property, each without reference to previous ones that still remained in effect. It was not easy for a mortgager to trace the encumbrances on a property: prior to codification of the civil law in 1866, there was no legal obligation to register hypothecs.[83] Many of Winslow's notarized property contracts from the later period as well were not recorded at the county registry office. It was obviously in the interests of the creditors to see that their loans were legally secured, and most of the bourgeois money lenders did so, but local farmers who held mortgages apparently sometimes felt that it was not worth their effort to travel to the registry office in Sherbrooke or, later, in Cookshire. Also, most of these contracts were drafted by notaries in the village of St Vital de Lambton, whose official ties were with the Beauce County registry office in St Joseph. Given the obvious difficulty of tracing every claim on a mortgaged property, creditors would probably hesitate before forcing a sheriff's auction.

Table 6.6
Mean Value of French-Canadian Mortgages According to Source (Number
of Cases in Parentheses), Winslow, 1850–80

Local Merchants/ Bourgeois	Local Farmers/ Rentiers	External Merchants/ Bourgeois	External Farmers/ Rentiers
$94 (4)	$93 (20)	$140 (30)	$103 (11)

There was no equivalent capitalist to Colin Noble or Jacques Picard
in Winslow North. Over half the French-Canadian hypothecs were
from outside merchants or self-styled bourgeois (see Table 6.6), some
of whom lived in the seigneurial parishes whence Winslow North's
settlers had originated.[84] The most active individuals on the local
mortgage market were the widow Rosalie Genest and her son Charles
A. Collet, a "négociant" of St Henri de Lauzon. They advanced
$1,825 in ten transactions, while $1,105 came from six other non-
rural sources on the South Shore, $557 from three non-farmers in
Ste Marie de Beauce, and $400 from two English-speaking sources
in Eaton Township.

Hypothecs from such distances were probably loans, though the
contracts do not always specify purpose, while those from merchants
closer to home were more likely to represent accumulated debts. Table
6.6 shows that the average size of mortgages advanced by outside
merchants was considerably larger than those in the other categories.
In contrast to the Scots, there were few hypothecs from local merchants – $308 from two such individuals in neighbouring Lambton
and $104 in two contracts with Colin Noble. The Winslow miller,
Pierre Pelchat, held a hypothec for $72, and a local "bourgeois" one
for $200, but all the other local mortgagers were farmers or (less
commonly) "rentiers."

The most important local figure among the French Canadians was
Jean-Baptiste Cameron, a farmer who had become a village rentier
by 1877. Cameron advanced $827 in nine hypothecs, while six other
local farmer/rentiers held eleven hypothecs, generally for purchases
rather than for loans per se. The same can be said for the hypothecs
held by outside farmers – one from Lauzon and the other ten from
neighbouring parishes. Though most contracts stated only that the
debt was for value received, one specified a pair of oxen, and seven
others (including four from outside merchants) referred to the purchase of a horse. In these cases, at least, the "loans" probably encouraged integration into the seasonal lumbering economy rather than

into the agricultural market. Even though we have no farmers' account books from which to examine the nature and volume of their exchanges, these hypothecs testify to the importance of the trading network among farmers themselves as opposed to that between farmers and local merchants.

As a result, only twelve of thirty-seven mortgages taken out by French Canadians during the 1860s ended as sales prior to 1881. The rate would probably have been no higher for the 1870s, when the French-Canadian population began expanding once again, but research on sales beyond 1880 would be needed to verify our supposition. Given careful controls over crown land grants, and failure of land prices to increase significantly, there was little scope for speculation in Winslow. Only a few of the local French Canadians bought and sold land for profit, primarily in connection with St Romain's development during the 1870s. An exception was the farmer-merchant Raymond Richard who paid $800 for three farms in 1872, the same year that his father gave him another farm in return for a life pension. Richard quickly made a profit of $165 on the sale of two of these properties, but his only other investment during our study period was $6.41 paid for a farm at a tax auction. The major opportunity for speculation in Winslow was not in agricultural land or even in village lots, but in timber lots purchased from the crown. As we saw in chapter 2, however, this activity was confined largely to English-speaking capitalists from outside.[85]

Until quite recently, local merchants and millers played an important role in rural communities throughout North America, and Winslow Township was no exception. They sawed logs, ground grain, and carded wool, as well as shipping surpluses to the outside market and selling factory-produced goods and imports locally. As Richard Judd has noted, the elaborate system of credit and exchange that revolved around local merchants provided the economic basis for the development of agriculture.[86] Because of their control over the local market, "surplus values" tended to flow toward the members of this local élite. Stornoway boasted two successful milling families and two modestly affluent merchants, but much of the township's limited wealth floated down the streams that flowed into the headwaters of the St Francis River, thereby escaping the grasp of the local petite bourgeoisie.

Thus, if some farmers from Winslow North travelled as far as the parish of St Henri de Lauzon in order to borrow enough money to purchase a horse, it must have been at least partly because of lack of capital in their own district. Colin Noble acquired a number of

Scots farms after they had been mortgaged to him, but they failed to bring him substantial profits. While increased rural debt is generally associated with growing agricultural consolidation and commercialization, the Scots either rejected the loss of economic independence implied by increased reliance on the market or, more likely, were unable to compete on that market. Local capital was certainly not a powerful force for socioeconomic transformation. It appears to have had little effect on the French Canadians, and, in the guise of credit, it did little more than delay Scots emigration by a few additional years.

In 1870 a Scots visitor recorded a conversation with James Ross, the Compton MLA and Lingwick merchant. Ross stated that he was anxious to attract settlers from the more agriculturally advanced parts of Scotland, "who might, by a better practical example of skill and industry, stimulate the Highlanders to further improvement." In Ross's opinion too many of his fellow Highlanders were "ready to rest satisfied as soon as they have attained to a comfortable subsistence, and live on in the log house rather than labour more to get a better dwelling, or otherwise to add to their wealth."[87] We saw in the previous chapter that agriculture in Winslow was indeed subsistence-oriented, but Ross apparently failed to appreciate the constraining forces of the physical and political environment. As traditional values slowly began to be altered by contact with more "progressive" outsiders, and by dealings with merchants like himself, local Scots would simply begin to move in search of more promising economic opportunities. In the following two chapters we shall attempt to gain some insight into the role of formal community-based institutions in accelerating or retarding the integration of Scots and French Canadians into the increasingly capitalist-oriented North American society.

CHAPTER SEVEN

Religion and
Public Morality

Most of the evidence presented in the foregoing chapters, with their focus on the family as an institution, is of a quantitative nature. This is the case even for the brief section on the psychology of the family, based on Lawrence Stone's model, but Stone himself claims that studies of this nature "offer a thin and watery gruel to those who wish to penetrate deeper into the rich psychological content of family life."[1] Stone also admits, however, that the more descriptive documents that relate to the "bottom" 90 per cent of society are tainted by the middle-class prejudices of the observers who produced most of them.

For the Winslow area, we do not even have extensive or intimate reports by members of the bourgeoisie, but we can gain more direct insight into the settlers' cultural values or "mentalités" by expanding our focus from the family level to that of the community. A broader scope can help us assess the family's role as a social institution, and the strictly cultural component of a society is more visible at the level of secondary institutions. Winslow's settlers did not have to be fluently literate to be more active and decisive in local churches, schools, and municipal governments than the dominant "social control" interpretation would lead us to expect. Their role can be adequately examined, however, only by incorporating where possible the type of quantitative data that Stone so readily dismisses.

THE FREE CHURCH

Nowhere was the religious reform movement and revival that produced a permanent schism in the Church of Scotland in 1843 more powerful than on the Isle of Lewis. There the influence of the establishment ministers was rather weak in most communities largely because there were only four of them to serve the island prior to 1828, and six thereafter. Even after the parish of Cross was separated from Barvas, the latter still covered eighty-four square miles of territory where travel was largely by foot and small boat. In 1833 the minister of Stornoway reported that his church was twelve miles from the farm of Tolsta, and half that distance was pathless and rugged moor. Travelling conditions were of little relevance, because there were no church seats available for the 1,253 crofters living between the manse and Tolsta.[2] To make matters worse, most of the ministers came from the upper ranks of society and preached above the heads of their flocks. With stipends of £150, plus local collections, they became identified in the popular mind with the society and interests of the landlords.[3]

As Alexander MacLeod learned when he was appointed to Uig in 1824, the people's knowledge of the Bible and church doctrine was far from profound: "There were but few among them that could tell me the names of our first parents, of Noah, or of any of the patriarchs and prophets, and but few could tell the nature of our Lord's mission, and the names of His disciples and their history ... when I enquired their hope of salvation as to its grounds and foundation, good conduct and doing the best we could was the answer."[4] But Uig and Barvas had already experienced a frenzied revival two years earlier,[5] and the religious outlook of the crofters throughout the northwest Highlands and Islands was changing radically because of the evangelical movement that MacLeod himself helped to initiate.

The ground was prepared by the Gaelic School Society of Edinburgh, founded in 1811. In 1820 it had eight schools in Lewis, with 642 students enrolled, and by 1838 there were 446 students in the parish of Barvas alone. The sole official purpose of these schools was to teach Highlanders to read the Bible, recently translated into their native tongue. This task was fulfilled quite efficiently by having the teachers move from district to district on a regular basis.[6] Inevitably, the zealous Gaelic schoolmasters ignored their instructions not to preach and therefore clashed with the moderate ministers. The Stornoway incumbent complained in 1832, for example, that the teacher at Back had "alienated the people from me in a great measure, so that on the Sundays I preached they would in droves pass me on the road."[7] The Edinburgh patrons of the School Society were clearly not opposed to such interference, for their annual report of 1840 linked the Gaelic schools and "the wonderful revivals of vital godliness in the districts of Skye and Lewis."[8]

Serving a more explicitly evangelistic purpose was an unofficial order of devout laymen simply known as the Men. The first leaders of any sort to emerge from the crofters' own ranks, their semi-official function was to take charge of the fellowship meetings held on the Friday of a Highland communion celebration, but they did not hesitate to interpret matters of doctrine and theology, and they did not confine their activities to communion week. The Men were known for their "fervent piety, personal experience of religion and second sight," and they roamed widely throughout the Highlands, where they were recognized by "their long hair, black cloaks and spotted handkerchiefs."[9] Integral to their creed were "visions of heaven or hell, prophetic utterances, [and] intensely personal conflicts with the devil and his angels."[10] If a parish minister did not measure up to their lofty evangelical standards, the Men simply did not attend his services or partake of the sacraments he dispensed.[11]

According to Gordon MacDermid, it was largely because of the influence of the Men that the established church lost almost all its adherents in Lewis with the disruption of 1843. They had nevertheless emerged relatively late on the island, being instituted only in 1824 with the arrival of the first evangelical minister, Alexander MacLeod of Uig. MacLeod stirred up an emotional religious awakening, reporting proudly that "a considerable number are so affected that it is with difficulty that I can go on sometimes with the sermon."[12] His influence spread rapidly: one observer noted that "men and women traveled from Ness, Back, Knock, distances of from twenty to forty miles, to Uig Ferry from Saturday till Sabbath to overtake the boats for church, which often required to leave very early on account of headwinds, and the distance travelled by sea, which cannot be less than ten or twelve miles."[13] In 1828 no less than 9,000 people were estimated to have attended one communion service at Uig. Before such enthusiasm could wane, evangelical ministers were appointed to Cross (1829), Lochs (1831), and Knock (1831). Consequently, four of the six ministers in Lewis left the established church in 1843, while only one-third of the ministers in the northwest Highlands as a whole did so.[14]

The evangelicals taught that only the sensation of personal assurance guaranteed a person that he or she had saving faith, and they witheld the sacraments from those judged not to have highly developed spiritual and moral faculties. Despite the growing attendance at his communion celebrations in Uig, MacLeod slashed the role of full participants from between 800 and 1000 to six. Parishioners who wished to follow the Highland custom of baptizing their infants as soon as possible after birth had to take the long journey to Harris, but such evasive action soon came to an end as people grew obsessively introspective and pessimistic about their spiritual worthiness.[15]

In MacDermid's words, "the belief that the Sacraments could be duly administered only by a special kind of minister and only to a special kind of Christian ... became a most durable characteristic of northwest Highland Christianity."[16]

The evangelical movement, with its strict moral code and comprehensive schedule of spiritual exercises, was inimical to much of traditional Highland culture.[17] Hunter argues, however, that its origins actually lay in the social and psychological consequences of that culture's destruction in the eighteenth century. Because the ecclesiastical "disruption" challenged the landlords' control of church patronage, Hunter sees in it elements of a class conflict, with "the line between the small tenantry on the one hand and sheep farmers, factors and proprietors on the other."[18] Given the support of Mrs Stewart MacKenzie of Seaforth for the evangelical ministers, however, it is questionable that in 1843 the Lewis crofters perceived themselves to be standing up to their landlord, to use Hunter's phrase. One informant assured Mrs MacKenzie in 1837 that "I may say of those poor people who have sincere religion in this Island that they are the most forward in all the duties required of them, the most submissive and persevering in the Island; I wish they were all religious, they would be much easier managed in every respect."[19] Still, Hunter is on solid ground in asserting that the crofters had forged a new group consciousness and sense of moral purpose by the time of the large-scale emigration.

The emigration movement may have stimulated the evangelical fervour of the dissenting ministers by providing the opportunity to spread the Gospel further afield. Referring to the initial migration of 1838, the *Inverness Herald* reported that "many Bibles were given to the emigrants, at reduced prices, from the depot of the Gaelic School Society, in Stornoway."[20] In 1842, after reporting that the majority from Brenish in Uig planned to emigrate, Alexander MacLeod asked that the Gaelic School Society open its "gospel treasures, with an especial alacrity, in those districts where the tide of emigration has recently set in, so that the people, when they go abroad, may be instrumental in resuscitating those dying embers, instead of throwing upon them a mass which shall only tend to hasten their extinction."[21]

The Canadian embers were far from extinct by the time that the first Scots families settled in Winslow, for the ecclesiastical disruption in their homeland was followed a year later by a similar division in the Presbyterian Church of Canada. Here, the Free Church had the same hallmarks as its counterpart in Scotland, including "a remarkable missionary zeal and vitality, theological orthodoxy, and a concern

for the ordering of society according to biblical precepts."[22] Author-
itarian as it may have been, the Free Church nevertheless continued
the Presbyterian principle and structure of local control through the
kirk session, in which the minister had no more power than the lay
elders. The elders were ordained for life, but not before their
appointments were approved by all the communicants in the congregation, as was that of the minister or "preaching elder." Each year
the minister and one of the lay elders would represent their congregation at the meeting of the presbytery and the synod. Final appeals
on all matters could be made to the general assembly, which met only
to perform specific duties. It consisted of one-sixth of the ministers
and an equal number of elders.[23] The structure and the spirit of the
Presbyterian church contained forces for social unity as well as dis-
harmony within the local community, as we shall see.

There would be no opposition to the secession from the Church
of Scotland among the first Highland settlers in the upper St Francis
district. Five years after the arrival of the first settlers in Lingwick
and Bury, they were still without a minister, but in 1843 they finally
came to the attention of the evangelical Edinburgh Ladies' Society in
Aid to Colonial Missions. Credited by Laurie Stanley with single-
handedly forging Cape Breton Presbyterianism, the Ladies' Society
provided £10 each to two Lingwick settlers who were serving as part-
time catechist and teacher.[24] It would be another two and a half years,
however, before the first missionary visited the isolated settlements.[25]

The Reverend John Fraser met an enthusiastic reception when he
arrived in January 1846: "My visit to the Salmon River will never be
forgotten by me ... There is a good work going on there."[26] Fraser
had discovered the same emotional response that characterized evangelical gatherings in the Highlands: "All the meetings were well
attended – indeed crowded to excess ... The sense they often have
of the Redeemer's love is so over-powering that they cannot contain
themselves, and they break forth into exclamations of wonder and
gratitude. One woman was carried off from the meeting-house by
her friends, literally "sick of love;" she had fainted away while we
were singing the first few verses of the 65th Psalm, and for many
hours she had no strength – her heart was melted like the wax. She
was one of those who accompanied me for several miles, on my departure from the settlement."[27] Not everyone was caught up in the fervour, however: "others are still in great distress – walking in darkness,
and having no light."[28]

The religious revival had apparently begun some time earlier, for
when the Reverend Daniel Clark visited the settlements soon afterward, in the spring of 1846, he was informed that some eighteen

months previous "a very great and manifest change to the better took place upon the people. Previous to that period many used to indulge in intemperance and fighting, both at home and in the neighouring villages, and were very irregular in their attendance upon the meetings held by the catechist and the elders." Clark himself met with a reception similar to that of Fraser: "Very many seemed to be deeply impressed, men and women, and young persons were seen to tremble, to sob, and to weep, while they endeavoured to conceal their feelings from each other. There was no crying out or other manifestations on the part of any one to be distinguished. Their conduct soon made it apparent that very many had undergone a real change."[29]

The local catechist had obviously been effective: Clark found that the large number who presented their children for baptism "possessed a competent knowledge of the fundamental doctrines of Christianity, and also a considerable measure of Christian experience." Of the six whose names were rejected by the catechist and elders, the offences of only two "were of such a nature as to require a public profession of penitence, and a rebuke before all." By the end of his ten-day visit, Clark had baptized ninety-nine children and one adult, an American Unitarian.[30]

The revival appears to have continued unabated with the visit several months later of a third Gaelic-speaking missionary, the Reverend McLauchlan. On the Sabbath he preached three times in Gaelic to large congregations, and once in English to the few Irish and American settlers. The following day he held a three-and-a-half-hour prayer meeting, during which "numbers appeared very much overcome." When the missionary left the settlement "we were meeting [settlers] on the road for miles," eager to converse "about the state of their souls."[31] Two years later, McLauchlan would write of his visit that "this distant spot became like a fair and fertile oasis in a great desert."[32]

The nearby American-settled townships had experienced a similarly profound Millerite revival in 1842, but the failure of its apocalyptic prophecy had caused disillusionment to set in a year or two later.[33] The revival in Bury and Lingwick therefore appears to have had spontaneous origins, insofar as it erupted without the presence of a missionary, but the influence of the Free Church was clearly strong enough to ward off the pessimistic post-millenarianism that characterized not only the Millerites but also the Highland followers of Donald McDonald in Prince Edward Island during the 1840s.[34] The revival in Bury and Lingwick was therefore not the product of "frontier conditions of social life," to use S.D. Clark's phrase, but rather the continuation of a pattern already established in the homeland.[35]

While the Scots of Lingwick and Bury considered themselves members of the Free Church, they had no official status as a congregation. McLauchlan reported in 1846 that they were preparing a memorial to the presbytery of Montreal asking to be received into the protesting (i.e. Free Church) synod. Considerable outside assistance was needed to build a proper church; even though the settlers had hewn timbers and raised £40 among themselves, the estimated cost was £200. In the mean time, their meeting house was built of rough logs roofed with bark and reportedly on the verge of crumbling into ruins.[36] By 1848 the Ladies' Colonial Association had again come to the rescue with a £50 contribution for the erection of the church at Lingwick, £50 per year for the support of two catechists and a teacher, and several boxes of Bibles and "instructive" books.[37] The catechists convened prayer meetings every Thursday and Sunday, and one visiting minister reported that "they seem to be judicious and devoted men, and to be useful among their brethern."[38] These lay preachers were following in the Highland tradition of the Men, though, in sharp contrast to Cape Breton Island, there is no reference to this title in the documents relating to the local Scots.[39]

Hopes for the appointment of a minister were high, for the British American Land Co. had promised an annual stipend of £50 over a five-year period. The evangelistic fervour of the revival ensured that the Scots would not slip into religious indifference, but it also heightened the danger of factionalism. In 1851, the wife of the first appointee, Daniel Gordon, reported that despite the good work of their "devoted catechist (now deceased) ... some differences had arisen between some of them, and the heartburnings and jealousies arising out of them were soon extended to the rest, so that the settlement was divided into two factions."[40]

On learning that there was no serious cause for dissension, the Reverend Gordon simply declined to hear the statements of either party and convinced the leaders to promise publicly "henceforth to live together as brethern." According to Mrs Gordon, "a powerful work of grace was manifest from that time ... The people are remarkably regular and attentive, affectionate and united."[41] They had built a manse and a new church with a seating capacity of 600, and very little debt attached.[42] The tranquillity would not last, however, nor would future quarrels be so easily resolved.

Perhaps inevitably, once the enthusiasm of the revival had subsided, the question of who would gain access to full church privileges became a divisive issue. From the approximately 300 families there was an average attendance of 350 individuals at the church services, 100 at the two weekly prayer meetings, and fifty at the week-day lecture. As in Lewis, however, the standards for admission to communion were strict, and only eighty-eight individuals held the status of official "members" of the congregation.[43] As early as 1852 five "adherents" inquired if Gordon had the right to refuse baptism to their children "on the ground that they are not in full communion with the Church." They were informed by a delegation from the presbytery that he did.[44]

A more contentious issue to be considered by the delegation was the merchant James Ross's objection to suspension by the Lingwick kirk session because of a conflict arising from the general election. The delegates reported that Ross (a future Conservative MLA) had claimed without grounds that the Reverend Gordon favoured John Henry Pope's candidacy and that he "entertains feelings of undue irritation towards Mr Donald MacKay, a member of the Kirk Session, and has employed towards him harsh and opprobrious language." Ross was also warned that the "opening of a house for drinking ardent spirits and the attendance on excited convivial entertainments are not in any case, safe or suitable for a professing Christian." Since he had not been charged with committing "any act of dissipation," however, the delegation asked the kirk session to consider lifting its suspension once Ross had apologized to MacKay.[45] Richard Vaudry claims that discipline was exercised with a minimum of difficulty throughout the presbytery, but Ross would not be the last individual to file a complaint against a local kirk session.[46]

The 1852 delegation to Lingwick considered as well the call from Winslow for the services of Ewen McLean. As we saw in chapter 1, McLean had accompanied the 1851 emigration, but he had initially decided to stay with the minority who remained in Brompton. The presbytery did not feel that Lingwick and Winslow were ready to support two ministers, and so in 1853 it encouraged Gordon to accept his call to Glengarry and instructed McLean to serve both stations from Lingwick.[47] By 1854 the shift in population from the British American Land Co. lots to the government's free grants had reduced the Lingwick congregation drastically, to sixty families, with only thirty-five members of the church. As a result, McLean was instructed to devote two-thirds of his time to Winslow, with its 160 families and twenty-five members.[48] In response to a petition from the families of Lingwick, they were granted the services of a "probationer" in the fall of 1855, but the elders then asked to be reunited

Table 7.1

Contributions (Dollars) to the Free Church, Winslow, Selected Years, 1854–80

Year	Families	Stipend	Paid	Arrears	Congregational Purposes	Various Funds	Paid per Family
1854	160	?	320	?	83	6	2.58
1867	210	650	420	850	250	–	3.19
1868	210	520	380	990	70	22	2.25
1869	225	520	400	740	42	37	2.13
1872	?	400	400	500	13	78	?
1874	?	300	200	250	25	706*	?
1876	67	430	288	500	380†	13	10.16
1880	90	500	500	–	170	41	7.90

Sources: Ecclesiastical and Missionary Record, 1854; The Home and Foreign Record of the Canada Presbyterian Church, 1867–74; Acts and Proceedings of the General Assembly of the Presbyterian Church in Canada, 1876, 1880.
*$650 to college building fund.
†$300 spent on church, $16 on manse.

with Winslow. This motion was rejected by Winslow, and the temporary minister assigned elsewhere, leaving Lingwick worse off than ever. It would not receive another minister until the fall of 1858.[49]

Winslow meanwhile was experiencing its own problems. McLean was enthusiastic in 1854, when he reported that the Sunday service was regularly attended by 480 people, and the weekly prayer meeting by 300, but by 1858 he was complaining that his congregation was "in a most unsatisfactory position in many respects socially and religiously." The presbytery therefore assigned the Reverend Gordon to visit Winslow, where he was "to intimate to the people that unless the minister and the ordinances were better supplied, the Presbytery would require to remove Mr McLean."[50] McLean had reported in 1854 that he had collected, in addition to his subsidy from the Home Mission Fund, a stipend of £80 ($320). The presbytery average was much higher, at £150, but, with the other collections included, the average family in this exceptionally poor community had contributed $2.58 to the church (see Table 7.1). Two years later, in 1856, the stipend had not increased, even though the prescribed amount had been raised to £150, but other collections did reach approximately £86.[51]

McLean had also complained of religious indifference, but it soon became obvious that the Winslow Scots were anything but indifferent when it came to church matters, and especially to McLean himself. In the spring of 1858 the presbytery received a petition from Winslow with "grave statements of improper and immortal [sic] conduct" against their minister.[52] The first charge concerned the school and a lot once intended as the site for the church. The commission of inquiry exonerated McLean on this matter, finding the accusers to have been "inconsiderate and rash." As for the second charge, the commisioners admonished a widow "to be more careful and circumspect in her future conduct and conversation." Finally, the third case was dismissed on the grounds that the complainant's only witness was his wife and that he was moved by "malice and uncharitableness," being under the censure of the church at the time.[53] The nature of the latter two accusations was not disclosed in the minutes of the presbytery, but future developments suggest that they concerned sexual impropriety.

Little was heard from Winslow during the following three years, aside from a complaint about the administration of baptism, but internal dissensions culminated in an open rift during the summer of 1861.[54] The precipitating issue was amalgamation of the Free Church, known as the Presbyterian Church of Canada, with the more strictly voluntarist United Presbyterian Church to form the Canada Presbyterian Church. McLean reported that because they had been led to believe that the union represented a break with the Free Kirk of Scotland, some of the Winslow congregation had formed a separate congregation under the leadership of one of the elders. He laid the blame at the door of the Reverend Gordon, who had been assisting at the Lingwick communion.[55] The case against Gordon was dismissed after he presented letters from Winslow denying that he had caused the separation from McLean, but written disapproval was registered against the terms Gordon had used "towards his brethern." Displeased with the admonition, Gordon appealed to the synod on the grounds that McLean had publicly accused him of "going about carrying from place to place a foam, or froth, of lies and that his black physic of lies was operating before him in both places – here and in the Upper Province."[56]

Before this matter could be settled, the presbytery received the report of the minister it had sent to investigate the schism in the Winslow congregation. He pointed to failure to provide the settlers with the requested information on church union and concluded that suspension of the elders and deacons involved was "wholly indefensible."[57] But doctrinal matters were not the only divisive issue. The manner in which the minutes of the kirk session were drafted required the presbytery's attention (a special committee later found serious irregularities), and, most disturbing of all, "certain accusations of lewd and immoral character had been made by certain parties office-bearers and members of the Church at Winslow" against the Reverend McLean. One married woman accused him of acting "in a lewd manner" and taking "improper liberties" in the front parlour of the manse during the summer of 1855, and a second married woman alleged that much the same had taken place with her in the chapel. The third accuser was a widow with the same last name as one of the the women involved in the unspecified charges of 1858, but her accusation now referred to a later period, the winter of 1859–60. It was also more serious than the charges of the other two women, for she claimed that McLean had attempted to commit adultery with her in a bedroom of the manse.

Based on the testimony of six men and eleven women (including McLean's wife, daughter, and servant) that the accusers had spoken well of their minister since the alleged acts, the investigating minister decided that the case should be dropped. McLean, however, should leave Winslow "both for your own sake and for that of the people."[58] The presbytery decided otherwise. After declaring that the Winslow kirk session's suspension against the elder and two deacons was irregular and of no force, and after postponing the question of separate congregational status for the dissidents, the presbytery moved that a process of libel should be heard against McLean at the next synod meeting.[59] The charges of the aggrieved were recorded in graphic detail at the August synod, and each woman suggested a considerable degree of force on the minister's part. After a number of witnesses were heard, and McLean entered a plea of not guilty, the hearing was transferred to Winslow.[60] The evidence gathered here was considered at the October synod, where twelve members voted that the widow's charges of attempted adultery were "not proven," two voted more decisively that McLean was "not guilty," and six voted that the case was proven. Of the less serious charges made by the two other women, McLean was cleared by only two votes in one case and found guilty by three votes in the other. No one voted "not guilty" in either case, but McLean's punishment was surprisingly lenient, considering the nature of the alleged offences and the puritanical doctrine of the church. He was simply given a six month's suspension and warned to be "more watchful and circumspect in his conduct in the future."[61]

The decision to leave McLean in Winslow would have serious repercussions, for it ensured that his supporters and opponents would continue their contentious debate. To start with, Reverend Milloy of Lingwick was physically prevented from following his instructions to serve Winslow during McLean's suspension, and in December four elders submitted a petition which the presbytery declared to contain "accusations of caluminous [sic] kind" against Milloy and the investigating minister who had uncovered the hornet's nest. Yet another delegate was sent to learn who had closed the church door against Milloy and to demand that they, along with the recalcitrant elders, deacons, and trustees, explain their actions at the next meeting of presbytery. In a conciliatory gesture toward the McLean loyalists, the Winslow settlers were also to be told that the presbytery would recognize only one congregation and one kirk session and that McLean would not be recalled. Finally, sermons in church were to warn against "giving place to the unholy feelings of malice, emnity or uncharitableness, or against doing ought that would grieve the Spirit of God, disturb the Unity of the Church and its peace or hinder the progress of the Kingdom of Christ in the district."[62]

The warning had little effect, for divisions within the congregation became increasingly irreconcilable. A charge brought against one elder was dismissed as "vexatious" by the next presbytery, though a dissenting voice did claim that he should be censured for the "practice of promiscuous sleeping on the floor." Here, it would appear, was a last vestige of the communal sleeping arrangements found in the Highland black houses. The six elders submitted their resignations, as requested, in order to facilitate reconciliation within the community, but none of them obeyed the summons to appear before the presbytery, and three withdrew from the Canada Presbyterian Church. The Reverend McLean did likewise, boldly requesting a certificate of standing to enable him to minister to the dissident flock. The response of the presbytery was again to send a delegate to Winslow in order to bring the congregation "to a right state of mind," but the dissidents remained adamant.[63] They would return to the fold only if recognized as a separate congregation with McLean as their minister. McLean obviously maintained a firm grip within a large segment of the community, for 189 heads of families signed a call for his services. They finally accepted his assignment to Argenteuil County, however, in return for the dismissal of the case against the former elders.[64]

The role played by local congregations in the choice of their minister is illustrated by the induction of McLean's successor in February 1864. As was customary, John McDonald was tested publicly in Greek, Latin, Hebrew, church history, theology, and "practical religion." He then delivered a homily, a lecture, and a sermon, each based on a different verse from the Bible. Once the examiners and the congregation had expressed satisfaction with McDonald's performance, and he was ordained, the moderator preached in Gaelic from a rather pointed text, Jeremiah 8: 12: "Were they ashamed when they had committed abomination? nay, they were not at all ashamed, neither could they blush: therefore shall they fall among them that fall: in the time of their visitation they shall be cast down, saith the Lord."[65]

Little more was heard from Winslow during the first five years of McDonald's tenure, and local lore suggests that he was a highly respected pastor.[66] Identifying him as "the poor man's friend," Angus MacKay sang the praises of McDonald in six stanzas of his ode to the Megantic Outlaw, two of which follow:

Lamented, good, and holy man,
    We little prized his worth,
Until the summons quickly came
    That called him forth from earth.
Alack the day, the woeful day,
    That laid him in his shroud;
He was a bright and shining light,
    Of whom we all were proud.

Regardless of emolument
    He journeyed night and day,
Relieving pain and sickness
    That he met upon the way;
He ever was attentive to
    The poor man's needy cry,
Where'er he moved he ever proved
    His broad humanity.[67]

McDonald's Glasgow medical training clearly stood him in good stead in a community with no doctor, but even he could not heal the rift within the Winslow congregation. Because of this division, and because the congregation fell behind with his stipend payments, McDonald submitted his resignation in 1869. According to the reports submitted to the *Home and Foreign Record*, McDonald's stipend was supposed to be $650 in 1867 and $520 in 1868 and 1869, but payments had remained at the $400 level. McDonald claimed that, as a result, his arrears had reached $850 by the fall of 1869 (see Table 7.1).[68]

Summoned to explain this state of affairs, the chairman-secretary of the trustees sent a letter attributing it to "the incessant conflict of two parties in the Congregation, the discouragement of the weak, and the indifference of the careless."[69] The presbytery appointed a committee of four with presbyterial powers to investigate the situation, but McDonald withdrew his resignation before it could proceed. A deputation of two ministers and an elder nevertheless did visit the settlement, only to find one faction in favour of McDonald's resignation and another opposed. The congregation was instructed that the arrears would have to be paid before any further steps would be taken concerning McDonald's removal and that it should resort to the Home Mission Fund in order to supply him with an assistant.[70]

It appears that a portion of the community, including three members of the kirk session, was no longer taking an active part in the congregation. These men were informed by the presbytery "that there has been, and can have been, in the circumstances, no sentence of excommunication against them." Having failed to fulfil their duties for nearly one and a half years, however, they could no longer be considered to be office holders.[71] Meanwhile, McDonald left the question of his resignation in the hands of the next meeting of presbytery. Letters were sent by Whitton asking that it be accepted, but he was persuaded to stay by a petition of 399 names submitted in his favour. Recognizing that there was no hope for reconciliation between the two parties, the presbytery resolved that the dissidents should form a missionary station at Lake Megantic, Hampden Township, or some other central locality.

The split in the Winslow congregation appears at least in part a geographic one, with the younger settlements pitted against the township of Winslow. The issue is confused by the fact that the Presbyterian church did not have a parish system with strict geographic boundaries, but at least two of the three elders pressing for McDonald's replacement do not appear to have resided in Winslow itself, and the eighty family heads who expressed a desire to separate were concentrated in the local district known as Dell, where the boundaries of Winslow, Whitton, Hampden, and Lingwick meet.[72] A third congregation was formed at Lake Megantic in 1874.[73] Nowhere do the presbytery minutes suggest that the issue was as simple as a dispute over access to church services, but divisions stemming from McLean's tenure were probably exacerbated by expansion of the population eastward toward the Lake Megantic frontier.

Whatever the underlying cause of the rancour, formal division of the congregation did not entirely solve the problem, because the new group claimed a material interest in Winslow's manse and glebe and demanded access to the church every second Sunday. John McDonald, however, claimed that the new congregation owed him $257.85 in arrears. The presbytery's resolution was to deny this group any share of the church property and to declare that its members were morally responsible for their debts to McDonald – however, "it would not be for edification to press that claim."[74] This decision did nothing to win over the independent-minded congregation, which proceeded to make its own arrangements with a minister from the Presbyterian church in Australia who had acquired an extensive tract of land in the Hampden area. The presbytery grumbled that its rules had been contravened, but it appears to have accepted the newcomer as a probationer during the following two years.[75]

In 1875, after the Canada Presbyterian Church had joined forces with the Church of Scotland and two other branches to become the Presbyterian Church in Canada, a delegation of three was sent to investigate the troubled Scots congregations in Compton County. It found that the families who had seceded from Winslow were now themselves divided "over matters of what appeared to be of a trivial nature." Unfortunately for him, the man from Australia who had agreed to supply them "with preaching" had involved himself in their disputes, with the result that one faction "strongly insisted on his removal."[76] The presbytery responded by attaching the Dell congregation to Scotstown, the saw mill town recently founded near the junction of the Hampden-Lingwick-Bury boundaries, but this union lasted only a year.[77] Still more troublesome for the presbytery, the question of shared responsibility for the debt to McDonald had surfaced once again. The inability of the central body to solve this issue for close to three more years, as we shall see, is a good indication of how weak its authority actually was.

Responding to the Winslow request that the second congregation contribute $261 to the $500 still owing, the presbytery resolved that this group's share from the sale of a church property in Sherbrooke should be appropriated for that purpose.[78] When the Dell settlers rejected this resolution on the grounds that the debt was owed by a few individuals rather than the congregation as a whole, the presbytery switched courses by asking McDonald to hand over Dell's share of the sale money. His claim would now have to await separate adjudication by the presbytery. It was McDonald's turn to resist, with the result that the beleagured presbytery reversed itself once again in September, allowing McDonald to retain the financial grant until the new congregation paid its share of the arrears. Finally, in December, it was decided that the matter should be submitted for arbitration by the presbytery.

After the passage of more than a year, the arbitrators reported that they had reached an impasse. A motion was then passed in presbytery by the narrow margin of five to four to divide the money equally between the second congregation and McDonald.[79] Unwilling to compromise in any way, the second congregation then appealed to the synod of Montreal and Ottawa, whence the case moved to the general assembly. There, the new concern was raised that McDonald had not disposed of the Sherbrooke sale money as he had been instructed to in 1874. Exactly what he had done is unclear, but it is probably more than a coincidence that he reported a $650 contribution by the Winslow congregation to the synod's college building fund in 1874 (see Table 7.1). Was this meant to be a loan? If not, why the assumption that McDonald still had the grant money to distribute in 1878?

When McDonald expressed unwillingness "to yield to the supreme court in this matter," it was moved "with a view not to push matters to an extremity at this stage," that no action be taken until the next meeting of presbytery.[80] McDonald was persuaded within the year to pay the second congregation its full share of the grant, and its account with the minister was finally settled to the satisfaction of Winslow in 1880.[81] In the mean time, however, the sheriff had seized the debt-ridden McDonald's livestock and other personal possessions in the fall of 1879. Having failed to pay the $516 mortgage he had had negotiated with J.H. Pope, McDonald finally lost his twenty-two wood lots (no. 71–92, rang 1 SE) at a sheriff's auction a year later.[82]

The strong sense of identity, self-denial, and independence that were fostered by the Free Church no doubt helps to explain why the Scots took root for several generations in a district shunned by other British-origin people.[83] But the record of internal dissension that unfolded after the fires of revival had dimmed reveals how destabilizing a strict puritanical code could be when combined with decentralization of authority.[84] The problem was perhaps less accentuated in towns and longer-established, more prosperous rural communities. There the bourgeoisie and wealthier farmers would be able to influence the kirk session sufficiently for their common class interests and identity with the minister to act as a brake against popular enthusiasms and local feuds.[85]

In a relatively egalitarian and impoverished township such as Winslow, however, wealth could not constitute an important prerequisite for ordination as an elder, particularly when each member of the kirk session was chosen to supervise his own "district" within the territory covered by the congregation. The name of Colin Noble, who had married an Anglican, never appears in connection with church affairs, even though he was the dominant figure in the Scots community in most other respects. For Winslow and the surrounding congregations, the moderating influence of the middle class was limited to the presbytery, whose vacillating stands only undermined its conciliatory goals.

It is not hard to imagine the potential for community tensions created by a structure in which certain individuals decided who of their neighbours and relatives would enjoy access to the privileges of the church to which they belonged and contributed. Laurie Stanley suggests that the session records she has examined from Cape Breton Island reveal a milder form of discipline than had been exercised in Scotland, but Duff Crerar notes a renewed moral rigour in those Bathurst Synod congregations that split from the established church in 1843.[86]

Certainly there is evidence to suggest that Winslow's kirk session applied strict moral and spiritual standards. In 1867 there were only seventy-nine individuals on the Communion role in a congregation of 210 families. In 1868 the ratio was only slightly higher, at eighty-six of 210; in 1869 it was ninety-five of 225.[87] Considering that the average family would have included at least three potential communicants, the ratio of the select must have been less than the 20 per cent. Even after the Dell dissidents had hived themselves off, the fraction of the Winslow congregation who were communicants remained quite small, though it did climb from twenty-five individuals out of sixty-seven families in 1876 to fifty-five out of ninety (perhaps a third of those who were eligible) in 1880.[88]

Crerar also found references to "public rebuke and confession" in several of the Upper Canadian congregations he examined. Unfortunately, no session records for Winslow have survived prior to 1878, but, for the final three years of our study period, they are concerned largely with the election of elders (presumably because of accelerating emigration from the township) and preparations for the annual outdoor communion services. Perhaps enforcement of the moral code was modified smewhat after reunion with the Church of Scotland in 1875 and after members of the Canadian-born generation began to come of age.[89] The absence of any hint of internal divisiveness in the session records, as well as in the presbytery minutes for the late 1870s, suggests that the Winslow congregation itself had come of age after a rather turbulent adolescence.

Based on her study of early-nineteenth-century Presbyterianism on Cape Breton Island, Laurie Stanley has written of evangelical religion that "it softened the sharp discontinuities of experience, it glossed over painfully-felt deficiencies, it validated emigrant status, and it restored a stabilizing sense of identity and solidarity."[90] Certainly, the revivals that took place in the early years of Scots settlement in the upper St Francis district conformed to a pattern that had developed as an integral part of the crofter identity in Lewis, and they must have strengthened emotional bonds among settlers in a strange and difficult new environment.

Those bonds would continue to be reinforced by the traditional outdoor communion festivals which brought the members of several congregations together for five days each year. Angus MacKay describes the truly "communal" nature of these events in the following idyllic terms:

The ministers are now arrived –
　All wend their way to church;
The day is clear, they seek the shades
　Of maple, beach [sic] and birch;
And there beneath yon lofty dome,
　The blue ethereal skies,
Sweet songs of love, to God above,
　In grand hosannahs rise.

...

How sweet it is for Christian souls
　Thus yearly to commune!
When with the sacred rites performed
　All Nature seems in tune
A sense of deep conviction falls,
　Like blessings from on high,
When anthems of eternal love
　Are wafted to the sky.[91]

While the ongoing religions squabbles disrupted the harmony of the Scots community, there was no long-term break of any group from the Free Church, nor does the census reveal any individual apostates. Not only was the evangelical branch of the Presbyterian church an integral part of the local Scots' cultural identity, but the unusually homogeneous (by Canadian standards) nature of their community meant that there were no other Protestant, or even Presbyterian, churches in the vicinity to tempt the disgruntled to switch allegiances. Joining the Catholic church would have been out of the question, even if it had not been identified locally with an entirely different culture.

From another perspective, even though pioneer families uprooted themselves only after much of the religious dissension had ended, the church-related feuds reveal an ongoing religious dogmatism that may have encouraged back-sliders and the liberal-minded to leave the district. Their numbers could only grow as youths became exposed to the more relaxed standards of the outside communities where they worked on a seasonal basis. Furthermore, while being surrounded by French-speaking Catholics may well have heightened the Scots' sense of group identity and religious purpose, it also hastened their flight once the dreaded papists began to make inroads into their immediate neighbourhoods.

The disappearance of the kirk session records for most of our period makes it impossible to know the preoccupations and standards of the Winslow elders. Crerar found considerable variety in the congregations he examined, but he notes that the outstanding issues in the Scots communities were related to the abuse of alcohol, sexual misconduct, and absenteeism, as well as incidents of quarelling, business infractions, and petty crime.[92]

Peter Ward has assumed that Presbyterian sanctions against premarital sexual relations were stricter than those of the other churches,[93] but in Lewis the evangelical revival made little impact on the custom known as bundling – the sharing of a common bed by a courting couple supposedly without engaging in sexual intercourse. Anderson Smith painted a vivid picture in 1875: "Most of the unmarried young men pass the winter nights with their sweethearts. The want of light in most dwellings, and the general habit among the people of throwing themselves down on the straw, simply divested of their outer garment, gives every facility for courtship in the Hebridean fashion."[94] There was also ample opportunity during the summer months for the young men of Lewis to spend the night with girls who were tending cattle on the hillside shielings, albeit under the watchful eye of older women.[95] Such supervison appears to have been effective, for illegitimacy rates in the Western Isles were among the lowest in Europe, generally remaining around 2 per cent of births in Lewis between 1880 and 1900.[96]

But what of Winslow, where separate pastures and bedrooms presumably ended community courtship rituals, but the custom of delaying both marriage and permanent departure from the parental household survived?[97] One might expect at least some of the young men and women who worked seasonally in the United States to have rejected the traditional constraints on premarital sexual activity. Unfortunately, the nature of the Presbyterian registers prevents us from calculating illegitimacy rates with any accuracy, but there are enough scattered pieces of evidence to give us some idea of the Scots' response to the moral strictures of their church.[98]

Winslow's ministers identified only one child as illegitimate at baptism, but they probably followed the Scottish custom of recognizing the legitimacy of any offspring born to couples who subsequently married.[99] Less direct evidence can be found in the 1871 manuscript census, where at least three Scots families are listed with children of the same last name who were too young to have been conceived by the married female of the household. In the first case, Margaret was sixty years old, Henry was five, the next oldest family member was fifteen, and the unmarried Christy was twenty-eight. Christy was still single and living in the same household a decade later, as was a fifteen-year-old boy named Donald – presumably the Henry of 1871. In the second such case, Christy was seventy-one, unmarried daughter Christy was thirty, and there were two boys aged twelve and five. The younger Christy had also been enumerated in the household in 1861, when the older boy was three and the next oldest member of the family was twenty-one. In the third household, the widow Margeret was sixty-two, Annabelle was three, and unmarried daughters Effie and Catherine were thirty and twenty-eight, respectively. Effie married eight years later, but Catherine was still living with her mother and the thirteen-year-old girl in 1881. It would appear, then, that the second daughter was the natural mother of the child.

While the ongoing single status of the three young women suggests that pregnancy out of wedlock jeopardized their chances to marry, it appears that premarital sexual intercourse between betrothed partners was not uncommon. We saw above that only one Winslow child was declared illegitimate at the time of baptism, but, of the fifteen cases where marriage date and birth date of the first offspring are known, one child was born only three and a half months after the wedding, and two were actually born out of wedlock. The marriage followed eight months later in one case, and nearly three years later in the other. Both children were baptized only after these weddings.

Presumably, the practice of late baptism removed some of the ecclesiastical pressure to marry prior to the first conception, and even for some time after the first birth in a few cases. While Crerar's study discovers considerable concern with sexual transgressions in the Scots communities of Ontario, it also notes a sharp distinction between fornication and adultery. In the strictest of the Free Church congregations, those charged with the former offence were usually questioned and restored to church privileges in private, while adulterers received public rebuke.[100]

It would appear, as well, that the young adults of Winslow were not simply reacting to declining opportunities to marry and establish themselves locally or to lack of family supervision in their seasonal places of employment. While Flinn states that he could find no references to regular cohabitation outside marriage in the Highlands,[101] the Lewis crofters practiced a betrothal custom that seems to have been in effect a popularly sanctioned marriage. In 1875 Anderson Smith described such a ceremony in which the couple simply joined hands in the presence of friends and promised to be man and wife. After the friends had drunk to their health, outsiders were allowed to enter "and help to pass the evening merrily." The couple would ultimately visit the parish church on a day fixed to suit the minister.[102] Local historian Donald Macdonald describes as well the all-night festivities which, even in the twentieth century, preceded the official "kirking" by a few days.[103] While we have found no references to this secular ceremony in the upper St Francis district, it survived as late as the 1920s in parts of Cape Breton Island, and it appears that the traditional, rather relaxed approach to the church sanction of marriage did persist among at least a minority of the Winslow settlers.[104]

Perhaps a more serious problem in the minds of the Winslow elders was the consumption of alcohol, though temperence supporters did not prevent the Catholic Leonards from renewing their liquor permit annually until 1892.[105] The Highland crofters remained an exceptionally law-abiding people despite their tradition of consuming large quantities of locally distilled spirits. There was no prison in Lewis, where the only crimes noted for the 1832–8 period were "petty theft from poverty" in Barvas and a few cases of sheep stealing in the parish of Stornoway (see Appendix A).[106] Likewise, the few criminal court records to have survived for the Winslow area reveal no widespread instances of law-breaking during our period, though there were a couple of cases involving collective violence against merchants outside Winslow.[107] With the arrival of the International Railway in 1879, the boom-town of Lake Megantic acted as a magnet for rowdy Scots from the neighbouring communities, but the only charge uncovered against a Winslow resident prior to 1880 concerned a Scot's assault against the local miller, Henry Layfield, for which he was fined $10.

Though they begin only in 1882, Sherbrooke's surviving prison records confirm the image of the Compton County Scots as a law-abiding people, but one in which community standards of justice and loyalty sometimes clashed with outside authority. Most of those jailed from the district prior to 1891 were labourers residing in the young towns of Scotstown and Lake Megantic, many of them of Irish origin. As for the Winslow Scots, in 1883 one old farmer was incarcerated for a few days charged with debt, and five years later a thirty-seven-year-old labourer spent a day in prison because of insanity. These cases were hardly signs of a turbulent community.

However, serious trouble erupted in 1889 after a main street shoot-out in which Donald Morrison killed the American who had been deputized to arrest him. Morrison had been harassing the new

French-speaking owners of the homestead that his father had lost to a creditor even though the young man had been sending money home during his seven years of work in the prairies. The following lines from Angus MacKay's ode to the "Megantic Outlaw" capture the Scots' sentiment after the provincial government declared martial law and the law enforcement agencies clamped down on district Scots for granting refuge to the famous fugitive:

Though mothers with their children weep,
  The ruthless monsters come
To tear brave fathers, brothers, sons,
  At midnight from their home;
Old men of marked benevolence
  Were also captive led,
Because 'twas thought each humble cot
  Had sheltered Donald's head.[108]

Four of those imprisoned and charged with accessory to murder after the fact were from Winslow, and three of them escaped from jail five days later. The cases were presumably dropped with Morrison's arrest shortly thereafter, but deep-seated community resentment was slow to dissipate.

Once again, Angus MacKay describes the hostile attitude toward legal authority that followed the Morrison affair:

'Tis said we must respect the law,
But how can mortal claim
Respect for law when deeds so vile
  Are practiced in its name?
If judges swayed by prejudice
  A jury may control,
Then Justice fled may hide its head
  And Purity sing dole![109]

Within six months of Morrison's capture, a fifty-year-old Scots farmer from Winslow was jailed for "shooting with intent," but local rebelliousness appears to have died quickly, for there would be no more Winslow names entered in the Sherbrooke prison register from late 1889 until at least the end of 1891.[110]

While the Morrison saga had undoubtedly tightened the communal bonds of the Scots, it may also have hastened their exodus by intensifying their sense of alienation in an increasingly French-speaking district and a hostile political environment.[111]

THE CATHOLIC CHURCH

Religious revivalism was not confined to the Protestants during the 1840s, for the Catholic church in French Canada was experiencing its own spiritual renewal with the rise of the ultramontane movement, which fostered the widespread organization of religious processions, pilgrimages, retreats, temperance societies, and devotion to relics.[112] While the first French-Canadian settlers in the upper St Francis district did not experience the emotional upheaval of the Scots, they must have been inspired by the religio-nationalist message of the Association des Townships which had fostered their colonization project. But that association failed to provide more than one priest for the widely scattered settlements on the colonization roads, and, as we saw in chapter 2, Winslow North was officially cut off from the services of nearby Lambton's curé in 1856 because the two townships lay in different dioceses.[113] The lack of a resident curé until 1863 lay at the root of most of the religious controversies, as we shall see. Similar problems faced by the Scots beyond the eastern border of Winslow had resulted in internally directed quarrels, but the hierarchical structure of the Catholic church helped to ensure that the French Canadians' conflicts would be with ecclesiastical authorities.

The first open strains between hierarchy and settlers emerged in February 1856, when Mgr Thomas Cooke of Trois-Rivières decreed that a chapel should be built near the centre of the township. Winslow's centre was completely uninhabitable, and the site arbitrarily pinpointed on a map proved to be in a swamp.[114] Father Duhaut of Wotton made two alternative suggestions for sites on the main road, but he was too late to prevent the settlers from voicing their own preferences. Many of them wanted the chapel to be built on what was known as the Grande Ligne, closer to where most of them actually lived, rather than in the projected centre of any future population.

The long and involved struggle that ensued was typical of those in many communities where a new church site was being chosen, for the local village almost invariably grew around the church, thereby enhancing the value of nearby property. The bishops were anxious that a central location be chosen in order to avoid inconveniencing later colonists, or having to switch sites in the future, but their judgments depended on the reports of the far-from-infallible emissaries sent to investigate each area. Fortunately, the hierarchy tended to be flexible in these matters, so that in some cases the colonists managed to win their point.[115]

In the Winslow affair, however, Bishop Cooke stuck by the judgment of his agent. Suspecting that the real preference of Winslow

North's settlers was to be reattached to Lambton, Father Duhaut suggested that Cooke take punitive measures in order to make them
more co-operative. They clearly could not be expected to travel to
far-off Wotton, where Duhaut was technically responsible for them,
but they might be placed under the charge of a new appointee in
Stratford and receive his services only once every three months until
they built the chapel.[116] Consequently, the following year a curé was
assigned to centrally located Stratford, with instructions to serve the
neighbouring townships of Weedon, Garthby, and Winslow.[117] But
the bishop did not follow Duhaut's advice that Winslow be officially
reprimanded, asking him instead to find a church site that would
satisfy the colonists while making it clear that "ils doivent se montrer
dociles et ne pas prétendre nous faire la loi."[118]

Duhaut nevertheless continued to insist on a site that displeased
the majority. The frustrated priest complained that the curé of Lambton was working against him in order to annex Winslow to his parish
and suggested that Winslow's settlers be cut off from Lambton's services at once: "si les habitants de St Romain n'avaient plus accès à
Lambton, tout s'arrangerait à merveille."[119] The parishioners of
Lambton responded to the charges against their priest by giving their
southern neighbours six months to join the diocese of Quebec or
cease attending mass at their church. Bishop Cooke was therefore
left with little choice but to take a tougher stand. He ordered Winslow
to start building immediately. If the opponents persisted, there would
be no chapel whatsoever, and the Winslow colonists would have to
travel to Stratford for religious services.[120]

The warning was to no avail, for two and a half months later some
Winslow parishioners sent Cooke a petition threatening, in his words,
"des mesures d'opposition sérieuses suivant eux, mais réellement fri-
voles."[121] The petition claimed that Duhaut's church site was near land
that could never be cultivated, but the bishop responded with a pastoral letter that stated that there would be no mass or confession at
Winslow until the chapel was completed. In the mean time, settlers
would have to attend church at Stratford, still served by Duhaut from
Wotton, but the Lambton curé would be available for confessions,
burials, marriages, and at Easter.[122] Baptisms were not mentioned,
but the small number of Winslow entries in the Wotton and Stratford
registers indicates that most baptisms continued to be performed at
Lambton until 1858.

When the Winslow settlers remained unmoved, Duhaut felt com-
pelled to justify his own obduracy to the bishop. He argued, first,
that the site he had chosen would become central in the future
because neighbouring lands were being purchased. Second, it was an
excellent property in its own right, with good lumber, all eight acres

under cultivation, and fifty more acres readily available. Third, the cemetery was already blessed, and the frame of the building had been completed. Fourth, the number of workers on the church was growing; and, fifth, it would be impossible to reconcile opposing factions within the near future. Duhaut closed by stating that, should the bishop finally decide against this site, he wanted nothing to do with finding an alternative.[123]

Neither side budged until November, when a large group of settlers took the extraordinary step of commencing a chapel on the site of their own choosing. Mgr Cooke angrily authorized Duhaut to tell them that "quand ils voudront construire une chapelle, ils devront m'adresser une requête en forme et signée de la majorité, comme celle qu'ils ont bien su faire et présenter en opposition; que puisqu'ils veulent prendre les formalités légales, qu'on désirait leur épargner, on y tiendra à l'avenir, et que ne refera [?] à l'amiable mais tout strictement et selon la loi."[124] Even if the settlers had followed the legal formalities, however, the bishop probably would have rejected their site. With little choice but to succumb, the inhabitants of Winslow North within nine months began to build a chapel on the lot chosen by Duhaut.[125]

The building was finished by the spring of 1858, when Bishop Cooke wrote optimistically to the curé of St Gabriel de Stratford, whose charge Winslow was now under: "Les gens de St Romain, finiront par se faire aimer et leur zèle leur méritera une desserte mieux suivie, avec St Gabriel."[126] But, whether partly as punishment or not, Winslow North would remain a mission station for another five years, and the colonists' discontent did continue to manifest itself openly on occasion. In 1861 Mgr Cooke chastized the parish for the scandal caused by a man, presumably speaking for more people than himself, who had openly denounced the priest in church. Punitive measures were threatened, but the indiscretion was forgiven after the guilty party was persuaded to make a public request for pardon.[127]

The following year, the people of St Romain bitterly criticized Father Bouchard for choosing to remain in the smaller parish of Stratford. To settle the issue without losing face, Cooke offered Bouchard another posting. When the priest still declined to move, the St Romain colonists again threatened to join Lambton and the Quebec diocese, even though it was clearly not in their power to do so.[128] Faced with such open insubordination, the bishop had little choice but to rebuke the three leaders who had sent the petition: "Croyez que ce n'est pas comme cela que l'on écrit à un Évêque et que si l'on veut obtenir une faveur ce n'est pas par des menaces. Vous gâtez votre cause." The letter added that Bouchard was free to choose the place of residence he wished and that the best policy was to try to win him to Winslow through persuasion, not threats.[129] Cooke nevertheless did intervene on behalf of the colonists. He admonished Bouchard for not choosing to live in the wealthier community of St Romain and ordered him to spend six months of every year there in future. The matter was finally settled in 1863, when Bouchard was replaced and the new priest was instructed to reside in St Romain full time.[130]

Having at last received their wish, the colonists of Winslow North engaged in no further serious disputes with the clergy.[131] Their behaviour may have reflected the weakness of ecclesiastical authority on the frontier, but the settlers' aims were simply to replicate the familiar parish institutional structure as closely as possible. Ironically, one of the chief obstacles to this goal had been the rather arbitrary border-line imposed between them and Lambton in 1852. Though Normand Séguin has stated that township boundaries were essentially irrelevant to the geographic definition of parishes in the Lac St Jean district,[132] this was certainly not so in the Eastern Townships, where parish and township boundaries coincided wherever possible. In the case of Winslow, the small number of Catholics in the south did remain within the parish of St Gabriel de Stratford, but those in the north may not have been reattached to Lambton, as they wished, in order to prevent one township from being divided between two dioceses. In addition, the Compton–Beauce county line, defined in 1853, runs between Winslow and Lambton.

Most French-Canadian parishes never again experienced disruptions as serious as those associated with the choice of a church site, but a perennial bone of contention between priest and parishioners remained collection of tithes and other ecclesiastical taxes. Because potatoes and hay were relatively more important in the Eastern Townships than in the cereal-growing seigneuries, Catholic farmers in this region commonly promised their priests a supplement to the grain tithe during the earlier years of settlement. Thus the colonists of Winslow North offered to pay an unspecified supplement in 1862, when they were attempting to attract a curé to their community.[133] Five years later Bishop Laflèche of Trois-Rivières asked them to contribute for one more year their voluntary supplement of potatoes, hay, and sugar, after which St Romain would become an official parish.

Implicit in Laflèche's promise must have been the belief that the grain tithe would increase in volume once St Romain was canonically recognized, even though clerico-nationalist legal experts claimed that church taxes were also legally enforceable in unincorporated missions.[134] The problem of supporting curés with the grain tithe in an

Table 7.2
The Curé's Revenue (Dollars) in St Romain, Selected Years, 1873–81*

	1873	1878	1879	1880	1881
Population	866	977	1,025	848	850
Families	–	149	168	132	137
Tithe	250	311	377	295	278
Other income	190	100	100	100	100

Source: Registre de Fabrique, St Romain Presbytery (SRP).
*Includes Whitton until 1880.

economy based on livestock and the forest finally ended in 1874 when
the bishop of the newly created diocese of Sherbrooke decreed that
all future taxes would be based on the municipal evaluation rolls.[135]
Whether such a levy had the same legal status as the tithe is not clear,
but in 1869 the archbishop of Quebec had rejected a provincial bill
to this effect on the grounds that it would raise a storm of protest.[136]
In the final analysis, the church probably did not wish to push the
question of its state-sanctioned coercive powers too far, preferring to
rely on its authority to refuse Easter communion to anyone who had
not made his or her annual contribution.[137]

St Romain's first official parish report to the bishop appears not to
have been submitted until 1873, when the curé reported a tithe worth
$250, plus $190 in revenue from other sources. Most of this supplementary income came from the "fabrique" or vestry, for it had agreed
to pay a $100 supplement as long as the tithe remained below $400,
which it did consistently into the 1880s.[138] With a total revenue varying from $400 to $500 (see Table 7.2), Father Brassard was not a
great deal poorer than the average country curé in 1900, whose
income was only $600.[139] Brassard's reports also suggest that he took
the economic hardships of his parishioners into account, for he generally expressed satisfaction with their contributions.

Official parish status gave unquestioned legal authority to the levies
imposed by the elected vestry for administration of church property,
but major expenditures such as construction or expansion of church
buildings were supposed to be sanctioned by the parish assembly.[140]
In fact, the vote to raise $3,000 for construction of St Romain's new
church and presbytery took place shortly before the parish was officially recognized.[141] The levy on each family was no less legally bind-
ing, however, for the curé apparently held a promissory note from
each family to cover construction costs. Thus, in 1871, when the
municipal council decided to devote its $400 grant from the seig-

Table 7.3

Vestry Accounts (Dollars), St Romain, 1870–80

	Forwarded	Pew	"Casuel"*	Collections	Other	Borrowed	Total	Balance
1870	53.00	179.57	57.45	2.40	–	–	292.42	+20.20
1871	110.32†	199.91	52.04	36.65	12.30	–	411.22	−269.55
1872	55.45	196.44	40.27	34.41	3.72	–	330.29	−135.26
1873	89.74	196.46	54.98	33.93	21.90	–	397.01	−165.12
1874	55.88	202.34	135.32	37.11	128.95†	200.00	759.60	−669.56
1875	105.44	221.46	85.13	44.72	16.75	50.54	524.04	−550.54
1876	–	260.61	24.05	31.56	–	88.65	404.87	−558.47
1877	–	239.53	16.70	35.28	–	300.00	591.51	−498.35
1878	1.65	209.34	20.90	41.51	20.50	300.00	593.90	−794.08
1879	5.92	226.94	46.05	40.94	–	232.90	552.75	−903.70
1880	–	230.89	41.55	31.20	–	295.48	599.12	−950.00

Source: Registre de Fabrique, SRP.
*Masses, burials, special services.
†Includes $90.12 identified as "balance de l'argent de l'église."
‡Includes $124.00 from sale of a lot.

neurial indemnity fund to local road improvements, it directed all the workers' earnings toward notes held by Father Vanasse "en faveur de notre Église."[142]

Distinctions between the realms of church and state were rather blurred in St Romain, but the vestry did depend upon more orthodox sources for its regular annual income of approximately $275. Some two-thirds of that sum came from the rental of pews, which were to be held for life, and paid for bi-annually on 1 January and 29 June.[143] Most of the remaining revenue was produced by fees for burials, high masses, and other religious services (see Table 7.3). Which building expenses should be assumed directly by the parishioners as opposed to the vestry was far from clear in St Romain. Thus, in 1871, after the general assembly had submitted somewhat reluctantly to Father Brassard's request for $450 toward renovation of the presbytery, he suggested lightening the load by having the vestry contribute $50 per year, with another $50 coming from the annual "quête de l'Enfant Jésus." The curé himself would compensate the difference should this collection fall short, which it invariably did by significant amounts.[144]

Before the debt for renovation of the presbytery could be paid off, the bishop instructed St Romain to complete construction of its church.[145] In 1874 the vestry agreed to pay $500 for an expansion from seventy-four to 103 pews. After negotiating a $200 loan with a priest from outside the parish, the vestry's total debt was increased to $670.[146] In order to make its full annual payments for the church, the vestry also fell into debt to the local curé – by $50.54 in 1875 and another $88.56 in 1876. In 1877 Father Brassard received his arrears, plus the year's full $100 supplement, but only after a second $300 loan was contracted with yet another priest.

The parish, which now owed $500 to two outside clerics in addition to the amount remaining to the contractor, borrowed another $300 from a local villager the following year. The additional debt was assumed directly by the parishioners, however, to be directed toward completion of the church vault. The curé had admitted in 1873 that the vault would normally be the responsibility of the vestry, but noted that it was burdened with the supplement traditionally paid directly by parishioners. He reasoned that they would rather finance the vault than assume the burden of the curé's supplement.[147] Parishioners had also "donated" the altar at a cost of $500 advanced by the curé. He was to be recompensed with the delivery by each family of seventy-five bundles of hay per year over a ten-year period. Indeed, Father Brassard claimed in 1875 that of the $3,000 spent to complete the interior of the church, the vestry would assume responsibilty for only $600 and the individual parishioners the rest.[148] Furthermore, the municipal council voted in 1875 to make an even more direct contribution to the church than it had four years earlier. This time it donated $400 from its seigneurial indemnity fund grant of $443 toward the church interior and "ornement."[149]

Building expenses aside, by 1878 the people of St Romain were beginning to fall behind in their payments for the religious services associated with burials, anniversaries, and so on. Whereas only six individuals were in arrears by a total $11.60 in 1875, three years later the number had expanded to fifty-four, owing $70.54. Most of the amounts outstanding dated only from 1878, evidence of the impact of loss of outside income caused by the depression. In 1879 fewer delinquent names were entered, but their debts had accumulated to $75.81, in addition to the full $300 still owing on the vault. The vestry continued to borrow from priests in order to meet its obligations to the contractor. An additional $100 came from one of the clerics who had already advanced a loan, and $104 was credited to Father Brassard – presumably his supplement for the year.[150]

With the parishioners of St Romain individually in arrears by $376, and through the vestry by $904, the bishop finally decided that it was time to curb expenditures. During his pastoral visit in 1879 Mgr Racine congratulated the parish for its zeal and generosity "pour l'établissement de la maison de Dieu" but added that further outlays should be avoided until the dangerously high debt was reduced.[151]

The economy began to improve during the winter of 1879–80, but St Romain's financial situation would be injured by the separation of fifty-four families living in Whitton.[152] In 1880, despite the bishop's earlier advice, another $150 was added to the parishioners' debt for work on the vault, bringing their arrears to $497. The vestry again borrowed $250 from a priest after failing to pay Brassard $45 of his supplement, pushing its total debt to $950. By the end of our study period, arrears to the church represented an average of $10.96 per family, a not insignificant sum when added to the annual church, municipal, and school taxes, as we shall see. According to a parish history published in 1892, $3,800 was spent on the church and presbytery between 1871 and 1877 alone, bringing total investment in church buildings to $6,800, or about $45 per family, in a single decade.[153]

Normand Séguin's study of a parish in the upper Saguenay region emphasizes the material basis of clerical control in rural Quebec, but we have seen that the curé of St Romain relied principally on the general assembly of the parish, not the vestry, for funds for his church buildings. While the curé in the community studied by Séguin was able to become an important financial power locally because of his annual income of $1,125 to $1,450, Father Brassard collected only one-third to one-half that amount in St Romain.[154] Apart from the $354 loan made by the Stratford curé to assist Ferdinand Legendre in launching his milling business at Stornoway, there is no record of a priest advancing money to any individual in Winslow during our study period. The Legendre loan may well have been inspired largely by the desire to gain a French-Canadian foothold in a Protestant stronghold. And, while the two priests who made substantial advances to the St Romain vestry did collect 6 per cent in annual interest, they could point to an obvious religious justification for their loans.

The curé of St Romain did, however, exercise considerable financial clout less directly, through his influence over the municipal council, as we have seen, as well as his control over provincial colonization road grants. Parish priests had considerable say about which roads would be designated for such grants and often oversaw construction. Thus, in 1868, shortly after Father Vanasse petitioned for funds to build a road from his church eastward through North Whitton to the Chaudière, he was placed in charge of the project. This assignment gave him control of a $500 grant for the first year, $1,200 the second, and $1000 the third, while he distributed an additional $500 as overseer for the Stratford and Weedon Road in 1868.[155] In 1871 Vanasse was succeeded as overseer of the Winslow-Whitton Road by the new curé, Father Brassard. The budget was $300 that year, and

$400 in 1872. Grants appear to have been sporadic thereafter, but Brassard was still in charge of the road when it received $400 in 1880.[156]

No protests appear in the departmental correspondence concerning the St Romain curés' distribution of this grant money, but one can assume that recalcitrant tithe payers would not be high on their list of potential road workers. In 1880, the Whitton colonists did charge that three years earlier Brassard had rejected a grant of $3,000 for their road. The assistant commissioner of public works wrote to assure them that this was not so, that the entire budget for the county had not reached this level since 1877, and that it was only because of Brassard's persistent demands that the grants were as high as they had been. To ensure that the colonists felt sufficiently contrite, this letter was deposited in the parish papers by order of the bishop, "comme marque de l'ingratitude des colons de la Mission de Ste Cecile de Whitton à l'égard de leur Curé."[157] The curé was to be considered the conduit to a vital source of local income, yet one who was above the unseemly political competition for what was, after all, the ruling party's largest source of patronage.

While support of the ecclesiastical structure imposed a heavy burden on the families of St Romain, that burden was clearly the product less of the church's legal and financial powers, per se, than of its political and moral hegemony. No expenditures could be made on church property without approval of at least the vestry, if not a public meeting, but the extent of Father Brassard's personal authority over the wardens can be deduced from the fact that no minutes of meetings were kept, and no votes recorded, except to state that they were unanimous.[158] The curé could not rule through a small clique, however, because each warden's term of office was limited, and those in St Romain did not sit for consecutive terms. Control by village notables was further prevented after 1875, with the declaration that wardens were to be elected from each range or sub-district, much like the kirk elders of the neighbouring Scots.[159] The bishops had earlier in the century come to accept the admission of all rate-payers to meetings held to elect wardens and inspect accounts.[160] Father Brassard's note-book contains references to this effect throughout the 1870s. One might question who was effectively in charge of the accounts, given that the curé wrote them up each year for the senior warden who was usually illiterate. However, the vestry presumably controlled collections and expenditures throughout the year, for Brassard reported to the bishop in the spring of 1873 that he had not yet received the parish accounts.[161]

Table 7.4
Easter Communion and Annual Confession at St Romain, Selected Years,
1872–81

	1872	1873	1878	1879	1880	1881
Communicants	495	514	586	621	529	533
Easter communion	488	507	582	617	525	532
Not confessing	4	?	4	4	4	1

Sources: Registre du Curé, 1873, 4–5, SRP; Rapports sur les missions et paroisses,
St. Romain, Archives de l'archevêché de Sherbrooke.

The colonists achieved at least some independence after the new
church was completed in 1869 by deciding at a public meeting, that
the pews would be rented for life.[162] Trivial as this principle might
appear, it had been firmly resisted by the bishops at the turn of the
century.[163] The St Romain parishioners lost ground in 1876 when
delinquent payments led the church wardens to declare that all pews
returning to the vestry would henceforth be auctioned for one year
at a time, with half the rent payable in advance.[164]

While the Catholic church's moral authority was heavily inter-
twined with its coercive powers, some perspective can be gained by
comparison with the financial outlay of the Winslow Presbyterians.
Even though the Scots did not build the elaborate structures that
drove St Romain into debt, and even though their contributions were
entirely voluntary, their church-related contributions were of a similar magnitude to those of the French Canadians. Thus, in 1880 (see
Table 7.1), ninety Scots families paid their minister (who had a wife
and children to support) a $500 salary and donated $211 for other
religious purposes, representing an average contribution of $7.90 per
family. That same year, the 132 families of St Romain delivered $395
to their curé and $320 to their vestry, in addition to falling another
$233 into debt, for an average contribution of $7.18 per family.

If the high expenditures of the 1870s are a debatable indicator of
popular commitment to the church in St Romain, a more direct (and
voluntary) index is the proportion of parishioners who partook of
Easter communion after their annual confession, a basic requirement
to maintain membership in good standing.[165] In the Mauricie, while
few failed to make their annual confession, a significant proportion
of the communicants were still working in the woods at Easter.[166] We
have already seen that the conception curve suggests that such was
not the case in St Romain. Also, the six surviving reports to the bishop
between 1872 and 1881 do reveal almost universal conformity (see

Table 7.4). The curé of St Romain felt he that had to remind those who were planning to make sugar about their Easter duty, but he was flexible enough to offer communion throughout the fourth week of Lent "pour ceux qui se disposent à partir p. le sucre."[167] The annual reports suggest that the few individuals who missed communion were also non-confessants.

Perhaps the delinquents included the two or three habitual drunkards occasionally mentioned in the annual reports of the 1870s and 1880s. In 1868 the curé noted pointedly in his "cahier d'annonces" that he would ask for prayers on behalf of "un petit ivrogne sans religion et sans coeur qu'on a ramassé dans le chemin la semaine dernière."[168] By dint of constant vigilance, however, Father Brassard generally managed to prevent the municipal council from granting a licence for the sale of alcohol in St Romain.[169] As for other categories of moral outcasts, the curé made no mention of concubines, and only in 1881 did he report five "pécheurs scandaleux." The transgressions most commonly mentioned were drinking, dancing, and youthful insubordination, all seemingly interrelated in the curé's mind. His sermon notes make frequent references to these so-called public disorders, and in 1880 he ordered those who had participated in dances on a Sunday and Monday to atone for the scandal by repeating five Paters and Aves in honour of the Sacred Heart.[170]

In contrast to the parishes of the Mauricie, St Romain's annual reports made no mention of swearing during the 1870s and 1880s, and a taste for luxury items was referred to only twice, although both subjects were occasionally the topics of weekly sermons.[171] Since only one local resident made a significant number of loans, as we saw in the last chapter, usury was rarely mentioned in the sermon notes, and never in the annual reports. And even though rentier Jean-Baptiste Cameron charged only 7 per cent interest, he took the precaution of donating a statue of the Virgin Mary to the local church.[172] On the whole, then, the curé of St Romain was obviously satisfied with the behaviour of his parishioners. In 1874 he wrote to the bishop: "Ma paroisse est une paroisse modèle; elle est composée en entier de canadiens-français venant des paroisses qui avoisinent Québec, et cette population se fait remarquer par son union et sa soumission."[173]

Had systematic examination of court records been possible, it might have provided clearer insight into the church's role as an agency of social control. René Hardy has recently demonstrated the surprisingly close links between civil and ecclesiastical authority in the St Maurice region, where certain curés effectively assumed the role of local police officers, and others reported to the justice of the peace such "crimes" as blasphemy and failure to attend mass.[174]

The only court case discovered that involved French Canadians from Winslow took place early in the history of the township and may have been related to the contentious Dion land claim discussed in chapter 2. In October 1852 indictments were issued against eight men involved in the escape from local custody of four of their number. Three of these men were found guilty of the reduced charge of simple assault, and three of the full "rescue and escape" charge. The escapee in the second case was sentenced to one month at hard labour, while the others avoided arrest for more than two years. Constables were sent to Winslow on four different occasions, but the fugitives were "always on the watch."

Early in 1855, the curé of Lambton headed the list of a 186–name petition pleading the case of five of these men. They were said to be "des gens honnêtes, paisibles, et de pauvres pères de famille" who were innocent of the charges. An attached affidavit stated that Pierre Dion had not returned the $22 paid him by two of the accused, even though he had promised to do so if he failed to have the lawyers drop the charges. Whether some sort of arrangement was reached with the parties in question is not known, but the attorney-general did note in the spring of 1856 that they had surrendered and undergone sentencing.[175] At least three of them remained in Winslow until they died, a fourth disappeared from the local records in 1874, and two others were still in the township in 1881.

Any further tendency to frontier lawlessness was probably discouraged by the anxiety that this case must have caused. The Sherbrooke prison register suggests that by the 1880s, at least, the local French Canadians were considerably more quiescent than the Scots. The only two Winslow francophones to be incarcerated were a fifty-year-old clerk who served a three-month sentence after being arrested a third time for the illicit sale of alcohol, and a fifty-four-year-old farmer who spent a day in jail for drunkenness.[176] The fragmentary civil records therefore corroborate evidence provided by the curé that St Romain was a peaceful and law-abiding community.

More significant than the incidence of law-breaking, in terms of assessing the church's role as an agency of social control, is the nature of sexual morality among its charges. In contrast to the Scots, there is only one French-Canadian family listed in the 1871 census with a child who appears to have been the illegitimate offspring of a resident daughter. At sixty years of age, the female head of household could possibly have given birth to the four-year-old girl, but there is a fourteen-year gap between her and the next oldest child, and a twenty-three-year-old daughter is also listed in the household. One other French-Canadian child is identified as a "batarde" in the 1871 census, and her last name identifies her as the daughter of a sixteen-year-old adopted girl. Aside from this infant, recorded inaccurately at baptism as an "enfant trouvé," there were two other foundlings listed in the St Romain registry during our study period. One died at the age of five days in the home of a thirty-eight-year-old widow who had a fifteen-year-old daughter. Finally, the annual reports for 1878 to 1881 mention only one extra-marital birth, said to be from another parish. At the rate of only four births per thousand, illegitimacy recorded in the St Romain baptismal register was lower than in the province as a whole, where it varied from eleven per thousand in 1851–60 to seventeen per thousand in 1861–70.[177]

Given only three infants identified as born out of wedlock in St Romain, and all said to be foundlings even when the mother of at least one of them must have been known, it is clear that powerful moral sanctions existed in the parish. Indeed, while Laslett claims that a high proportion of all spouses at all times and in all places had engaged in sexual intercourse with each other before they married, it appears that French Canadians traditionally had a very low rate of premarital conceptions.[178] The evidence certainly suggests that the women of St Romain rarely became pregnant out of wedlock. Of the thirty-nine couples whose marriage and first conception dates are known, only one gave birth within eight months of the wedding. Even in this particular case, the interval in question was seven months and six days, so the marriage must have taken place prior to the pregnancy being confirmed. One reason for the sharp contrast with the pattern already noted for the local Scots was presumably the Catholic church's attitude toward premarital engagements. Bishop Saint-Vallier's *Rituel* of 1703 accepted such arrangements only on condition that they not lead to what he called abuses and that they be celebrated "avec modestie."[179] Perhaps the desire to avoid morally dangerous delays explains why so many of St Romain's betrothed couples were able to gain dispensation from at least one of their marriage banns.[180]

It is considerably easier to gauge the level of public religious observance, as well as the social role of the church, than it is to grasp the intensity of religious belief within the population. Normand Séguin claims, for example, that even though only a few individuals missed Easter communion in Hébertville, the curé was constantly frustrated by his parishioners' readiness to stay home during the harvest season or when snowstorms made travel difficult. Sometimes they simply went visiting or fishing.[181] The same concerns do not appear in the St Romain curé's "cahier d'annonces." While it does note a few Sundays each year when no one appeared in church because of the cold weather, only once does it mention him chastizing the congregation for poor attendance.[182]

Public decorum during church services was a matter of greater concern in St Romain. The curés asked people not go outside during mass, not to argue or hold meetings at the church door, and not to take books into their pews. Women were to cover their shoulders, children were to be kept off the railings, and the pews were to be washed at least once a year.[183]

But the one issue that appears to have aroused the most anger in any of St Romain's three curés was the seemingly trivial matter of the church choir. Shortly before Christmas in 1879, Father Brassard was inspired by this subject to write the only detailed notes to appear in the "cahier d'annonces" during our study period. Apparently the parishioners had been grumbling not only about the cost of the organ (which was recorded in the accounts as a gift), but about the added length that music and singing brought to the service, the presence of girls in the choir, the quality of the singing, and the hurt feelings of one who had apparently not been asked to sing at vespers. Brassard did not mince words:

C'est le démon qui est jaloux de la splendeur que la
    chante [sic] donne au culte ...
Ceux qui trouvent les offices trop longs, montrent le
    peu de dévotion etc
Ceux qui disent que le chant n'est pas beau, sont
    des envieux ou des gens qui n'ont pas de goût.

...

Si on est si scandalisé, qu'on achète des bancs en
    bas ...
Petit nombre de ceux qui n'aiment pas le chant et la
    musique, je les plains, car ils vont s'ennuyer
    fort s'ils ont le bonheur d'aller au Ciel ...

Petty as the issue may appear, it possibly provided an outlet for growing concern about the curé's ambition to acquire all the accoutrements of the long-established parishes in the St Lawrence Valley. The various vessels and furnishings in the church were valued at $1,031 as early as 1873.[184] Some French Canadians may have taken note of the austere example set by the neighbouring Scots, who stubbornly adhered to their precentor until the church doors were closed forever in 1923.[185] Certainly, the curé hinted in his diatribe that he discerned a somewhat troubling puritanical impulse among his charges.

Nevertheless, if the settlers of Winslow North did not protest more loudly against the increasing debt their church was imposing on them, it was presumably because the ultramontane-inspired program of stimulating popular piety was having some effect. The retreats conducted by charismatic preachers apparently came close to matching the emotional fervour of a Protestant revival. During the 1840s and 1850s, priests such as Forbin-Janson and Chiniquy imprinted the Catholic temperance movement with the same sense of religious fervour as that found in the contemporaneous Presbyterian crusade against alcohol.[186] No temperance society appears to have been founded in St Romain during our period, but we have already seen the curés' obsession with the issue.

As for retreats, Father Brassard reported to the bishop that a five-day event on the occasion of the papal jubilee in 1875 had been a complete success, producing the greatest effect on his parishioners' consciences.[187] The following year saw the introduction of the three-day pre-Easter Devotion of the Forty Hours. Neighbouring curés participated in this ritual, celebrating high mass and vespers each day, parading the holy sacrament twice, and holding two nightly vigils. Brassard congratulated his charges for their enthusiastic attendance in 1877 and reported that 533 of 586 communicants took part in 1878. A year later, enthusiasm had apparently not dwindled, for 544 of the 621 communicants again participated in the devotion, a level that left Brassard "très content."[188]

An integral part of the nineteenth-century ultramontane resurgence was promotion of certain practices and institutions associated with popular piety which had once been suppressed in Europe as manifestations of local secular control and pre-Christian tradition.[189] In addition to acquiring statues of Mary and Joseph, and relics of St Clement, Ste Justine, Ste Anne, and St Romain, all between 1875 and 1877, the curé of St Romain established a "chemin de croix" and inducted sixty members into the Confraternity of the Very Blessed and Immaculate Heart of Mary in 1870, established two "dizaines" of the Society for the Propagation of the Faith in 1873, and introduced the Confraternity of the Holy Scapular in 1875.[190] Missing from his notes, however, is any reference to the pilgrimages so central to the local religious programs of the diocese of Trois-Rivières.[191] The only shrine in the upper St Francis district, established by the repatriation agent at Notre-Dame-des-Bois in 1876, was not promoted by the bishop as a pilgrimage site until 1883.[192]

Several other quantitative indicators suggest that the ultramontane movement made a deep impression on the settlers of St Romain. In contrast to the diocese of Trois-Rivières, Sherbrooke did not include a question concerning fasting or abstinence on the form it printed for the annual parish reports, but the large quantities of fish specified in many of the "pensions alimentaires" suggests that meat was avoided on Fridays and during Lent. Also, the curé of St Romain did state in 1873 that these obligations were "assez fidèlement observés."[193] Figure 5.1, above, makes it clear that sexual continence was not widespread within married couples during Lent and Advent, but it is questionable whether the church made this a requirement in French Canada.[194]

More concrete evidence of popular piety is to be found in the timing of baptisms, which the Catholic church decreed should take place as soon as possible after birth. In St Romain, 72 per cent of all christenings after 1858 took place within the first three days of life, another 11 per cent before the first week had elapsed, and another 15 per cent within the month. After 1865, when St Romain acquired a resident curé, all baptisms were performed before the infants passed two weeks of age.[195]

The church's campaign to have infants given saints' names was also highly successful in St Romain.[196] The influence of the curé is unmistakable in the case of the name Amédé(e), for example, since it first appears in the register in 1864 when it was given to no less than six boys before quickly fading from popularity. The use of compound names, such as the admittedly atypical Marie-Anne Henriette Flavienne Juliette, made it possible to acknowledge saints as well as relatives and godparents. Such a wide variety of obscure saints were honoured (for example, Zélia, Zéria, and Zorila) that 193 female baptisms between 1858 and 1870 produced eighty-three different names in various combinations. For the 217 infant boys baptized during the same period there were ninety-four distinct names. Furthermore, 159 girls (83 per cent) received Marie as one of their names, but only eighteen of them (9 per cent) were given the next most popular name, Philomène. As for the boys, only sixty-eight (31 per cent) were baptized Joseph, and following in popularity was the secular Napoléon, adopted in twenty-four cases (11 per cent), but most of their names were those of saints.[197]

All indicators suggest deep religious faith among the settlers of Winslow, but a final question remains concerning the nature of that faith. It would appear that, to a considerable degree, the Scots perceived God as a being to fear and propitiate. In Lewis, public thanks was given in good years so that people might retain the deity's favour, and public fasting and humiliation were practised in poor years to avoid greater punishment.[198]

God may have been seen as playing a more benign role in the Catholic world; certainly sermon notes from St Romain make no mention of crop failures as acts of divine retribution.[199] The curés nevertheless did assume an intermediary role between God and the forces of nature.[200] In St Romain, special high masses were sung for "les biens de la terre" of each range during the spring, and early in the summers of 1874 and 1875 prayers were offered to prevent frost. The following year, and in 1878, there were processions to stop the advance of grasshoppers. In 1876 a special ceremony was held for Ste Anne in the hope of ending an outbreak of smallpox ("la picotte").[201] Quebec's priests may have encouraged the tradition of such semi-supernatural intercessions, but they nevertheless had deep historical roots in the persistent demands of a somewhat desperate peasantry.[202]

The cult of Purgatory was another tradition with popular roots, for it offered the promise to the living that they could intercede directly on behalf of departed loved ones, particularly by participating in the rituals of religious confraternities. Thus, in 1877, the parishioners of St Romain were promised forty days' indulgence for each time they attended the "offices de triduum" being held to raise money for the church at Ste Anne de Beaupré.[203] We also saw in chapter 4 that wills and deeds in gift commonly requested special masses to speed the souls of the departed to Heaven.[204] Occasionally popular religious enthusiasm had to be reined in, as in 1877, when a six-year-old girl from a township near Winslow claimed that she had seen the Holy Virgin. Bishop Racine hastened to decree that her parents were not to collect any money for the spring water she distributed nor allow her to wash the sick with this water.[205]

The dualistic concept of clerically imposed social control overwhelming a deeply-entrenched popular culture has little relevance for French Canada, where Tridentine Catholicism was planted on essentially virgin soil.[206] And, even though the evidence for mass conformity to orthodox Catholic rites and morality is overwhelming in St Romain, resistance to clerical dictate was persistent enough in the early years to demonstrate that the church depended heavily on popular consent. In this respect there was little to distinguish the township's French Canadians from its Highland Scots, with their strictly voluntarist and decentralized ecclesiastical structure. In each community the church's authority rested essentially on the spiritual needs and fears that it had fostered in the settlers.

CHAPTER EIGHT

Education and
Local Government

If the argument that the church served as an instrument of social control is self-evident yet incomplete, there remains the question of public schooling, particularly with the rise of the educational reform movement in the 1840s. The establishment of the modern school system has been largely overlooked by Quebec's historians, but certainly not by their Ontario counterparts, most of whom have adhered to the social control model. Given that Upper and Lower Canada were united as one province in 1841, one assumes that the state had a similar agenda for both areas, albeit modified in French Canada by the prominent role of the Catholic church.

In this chapter I shall argue again, however, that more attention needs to be paid to the responses and initiatives emerging from the local level of society. The same applies to the institution of municipal government, a topic sorely neglected for all sections of the country. The final result of the movements for educational and municipal reform may have been to strengthen the centralized power structure, but only at the cost of establishing locally elected institutions with important taxing and spending powers. Even in a "backwater" township such as Winslow, school commissions and municipal councils appear to have filled a number of self-perceived needs; certainly the evidence suggests that both the Scots and the French Canadians supported them to the best of their rather limited abilities.

Proponents of the social control thesis have argued that school promoters of the 1840s and 1850s were driven by concerns about what they perceived to be dangerous influences in the community. They conceived of the school essentially as a protective environment.[1] However, the main thrust of school reform and centralization took place when the province of Canada was still a well-ordered rural society. The 1840s witnessed the turbulence of large-scale immigration from Britain, but not of the fractious, urban-bound masses that historians have traditionally assumed.[2]

Furthermore, the social control theory cannot explain why school reform became widely accepted after mid-century without presupposing the pliable population that it claims the reform movement was designed to create. Thus Alison Prentice is reduced to tautological reasoning: "Because there were schools and more and more children went to them, on a regular basis, people gradually became convinced that all children ought to go regularly to school."[3] Prentice's more recent book, written with Susan Houston, considerably modifies the social control thesis, but it claims that only by the 1870s were "the sensibilities of rural women and men ... becoming attuned to the need for schooling in the new industrializing economy."[4] The suggestion remains, therefore, that the publicly supported educational system was foisted on them during the previous three decades: the education department had quite simply done "a gigantic job of salesmanship."[5]

While Jean-Pierre Charland avoids the social control thesis in his analysis of educational reform in Canada East, he also implies that all the pressures for the expansion of schooling came from the official élite.[6] From radically different perspectives, Bruce Curtis and R.D. Gidney (with co-authors) have shown considerable sensitivity to the local dimension, but their focus remains on the creation of an educational bureaucracy.[7] Consequently, Wendie Nelson's recently completed thesis on the violent resistance to school reform legislation in one Lower Canadian community stands out as a demonstration of the complex forces at work at the local level.[8] One element of that complexity, as far as Winslow was concerned, was the sharply contrasting cultural and religious backgrounds of the two main resident groups.

SCHOOLS

The strongest incentive for the Highlanders to become literate in the early nineteenth century was their desire to read and discuss the Bible. In 1827 the minister of Stornoway wrote: "O fan the flame. Without schools I can do little. Curiosity may be excited, and people may admire what they do not understand; but without schools, they cannot understand the word preached."[9] According to statistics published six years later, there were 6,888 individuals above the age of six in Lewis (population 14,451) who could read neither Gaelic or English. The minister of Lochs reported in 1833 that, while half his parishioners between the ages of twelve and twenty-four could read Gaelic, only twelve individuals of any age could write.[10] The focus on reading literacy clearly resulted from the fact that about half the schools on the island during the 1830s and 1840s were taught by the twelve to fourteen peripatetic teachers sponsored by the Gaelic Schools' Society of Edinburgh. The minister of Barvas in 1826 reported that forty-five students in one school read the Bible, fifteen the testament, seven the Guide, six the first books, and two the Extracts.[11]

The Gaelic schools were unique in their narrowly defined subject-matter, their language of instruction, and their migratory nature, and they did not consider old age a barrier to instruction. Indeed, the society was especially concerned with adults. A teacher at Barvas informed his community in 1829 "that the object of the Society, in sending me amongst them at present, was not so much for the purpose of teaching their children, as themselves; and that if they would now promise to attend School two days a week, besides every Sabbath morning and evening, I would be most willing to remain amongst them. As they were anxious to secure a Teacher for their children, they of course promised to comply with this request."[12]

According to the local minister, William McRae, students were "of all ages and stages of progress, from the great-grandmother to the child of five years of age."[13] In one of the Barvas schools, 120 of the 222 students enrolled in 1826 were above the age of twenty, many of them reportedly nearing sixty. McRae wrote that "it is agreeably amusing to see one pretty numerous class of *ancients* of both sexes, attending the School, provided with spectacles, struggling through the Elementary Books, and some of them already reading the New Testament."[14] The sexes were quite evenly balanced: in the eleven schools on the island providing such statistics in 1826, 384 students were males and 441 were females. Husbands and wives were said to have gone to classes together, and mothers repeated their lessons with infants in their arms. Adults unable to attend were apparently instructed by their children or grandchildren.[15]

The teachers and ministers no doubt exaggerated the popular enthusiasm for Gaelic schools, designed as their reports were to loosen the purse strings of pious readers, but public petitions testify to a strong desire for education. In 1835, for example, the residents of a largely illiterate community in Barvas promised "the regular and constant attendance of from 40 to 50 children, besides many adults of both sexes." They had been "contributing their mite" toward support of the society during the previous few years, and they were willing to furnish accommodation for a teacher.[16] In 1844 the society boasted that it had taught upward of 90,000 people to read the Bible in their native tongue.[17]

The ability to read Gaelic would be of little practical use in North America, but itinerant teachers helped plant a new religious-based group consciousness among the crofters. The primary emphasis on religious and moral precepts may not have ruled out development of a genuine interest in knowledge, as the following description from "desolate Tolsta" in 1840 suggests:

Having no intention to put intricate questions to them, the first part of the intellectual category was simple; but from the ready answers returned, it was necessary to adopt a more difficult mode, lest the Highland pupil continue to boast, "Cha do chuir e ceist orm nach do dh'fhuasgail mi." (He did not put a question to me which I was unable to answer.) The apparently most concealed subjects were proposed as questions, yet these were answered readily except two ... This stage of the examination attracted the particular attention of the parents; their eyes beamed with pleasure, the smile of satisfaction played upon their lips, and those who sat for three hours apparently listless, when the lessons were read, (waiting for baptism), rose and cocked their ears, eager to catch the questions and answers, particularly the answers.[18]

Widespread familiarity with schooling may have been relatively recent in Lewis, but the strong desire for literacy continued among the Scots settlers of Winslow. As in the Highlands, the schools of Lower Canada were supported largely by voluntary subscription for many years, but major centralizing reforms were implemented shortly before Winslow's settlement. The government-supported system instituted in 1841 proved ineffectual in most parishes because it made no provision for enforcement of local taxes. Only in 1846 did the state introduce a law that included a compulsory tax provision.[19] The result was the protracted and occasionally violent period of popular resistance known as the Guerre des Éteignoirs (the Candle-Snuffers' War). Wendie Nelson has demonstrated for one of the main centres of hostility – St Grégoire in Nicolet County – that the habitants were far from indifferent to education. What they chiefly objected to – influenced greatly by the landed gentry – was compulsory school taxation during an era of general economic crisis.[20]

After suppression of the riots in St Grégoire and elsewhere in 1850, Lower Canada's habitants appear to have responded positively to the school reforms. Studies of literacy reveal a marked increase in the ability to sign official documents during the latter half of the nineteenth century. Thus Michel Verrette claims that signatures on French-Canadian marriage registers increased from 23 per cent during the 1840s to 47 per cent during the 1870s, and 68 per cent during the 1890s.[21] Allan Greer's analysis of the 1891 census suggests greatest advances among those of school age during the 1840s and 1850s.[22]

Greer notes also that literacy in the younger parishes was generally lower than average, and Gérard Bouchard has found that only 8 per cent of those married in the Saguenay signed the registers during the 1850s, increasing to 25 per cent the following decade.[23] The situation in St Romain was similar, with only 3 per cent (two individuals out of sixty-two) signing the marriage register between 1860 and 1869, but 40 per cent doing so between 1870 and 1880. As elsewhere in French Quebec, women were more likely to sign than men, but the margin between the sexes was only 7 per cent in the province as a whole during the 1870s, as compared with nearly 20 per cent in St Romain.[24] The St Romain margin increases further if we eliminate non-farmers and all partners non-resident before marriage, for the ratio of grooms who signed their names in the 1870s becomes only 12 per cent (four of thirty-three). The baptismal records suggest that the gap between male and female literacy was growing. The ratio of resident godfathers who signed the register doubled from 13 per cent in 1871 to 26 per cent in 1880, but that of godmothers climbed from 17 per cent to 48 per cent.

A more comprehensive index of literacy is to be found in the literacy schedules of the census reports, but, judging by the parish registers, these are considerably inflated. Thus, in 1861, 28 per cent of French-speaking family heads declared that they could either read or write; ten years later, 57 per cent said they could read and 46 per cent that they could write. The discrepancy between the census data and the lower values from the parish register is no doubt affected by the fact that the former source does not measure actual performance, while the latter does.[25] Research on the Saguenay region in this era none the less reveals that up to half the grooms who failed to sign their marriage register subsequently signed other parish documents.[26] But even if data from marriage registers and census reports fail to provide precise measures of literacy, they at least indicate a high rate of French-Canadian illiteracy in Winslow, though one that was declining markedly over time.

The declared illiteracy of the Scots was much lower – 1861 only 5 per cent of family heads admitted that they could neither read nor write. Given their educational background, however, many would have been able to read only in Gaelic and not write in any language. Even a decade later, when only 2 per cent of family heads claimed that they could not read, 53 per cent were reported unable to write – a ratio almost identical to that of the township's French Canadians. Literacy data are unfortunately not available from the 1881 census, but the Scots marriage registers suggest considerable progress in the ability to write. Between 1864 and 1877, 73 per cent of those who married in Winslow (57 of 78) signed the marriage register, virtually the same ratio as the non-Montreal, British-origin Quebecers as a whole during the 1870s.[27] In contrast to French Canadians, though not to the norm elsewhere, more Scots grooms than brides were able to sign their names – 79 per cent versus 67 per cent.[28] The similarity of ratios, however, in light of the relatively small size of the study group, suggests relatively equal opportunities for boys and girls to acquire a basic education.

This impression is reinforced by census statistics on school enrolment. In the spring of 1852 neither Scots nor French Canadians reported any children in school, but in 1861 there were 175 Scots enrolled, representing 78 per cent of the boys and 72 per cent of the girls aged five to sixteen. Ten and twenty years later, the ratio of the boys in school was slightly lower, while that of the girls remained stable (see Table 8.1). In 1861, enrolment was considerably higher for Scots there than for prosperous Peel County, where it was only 60 per cent.[29] Further, most Scots children did not start school until age seven. Eliminating the five-and-six-year-olds from our calculations would add 21 per cent to the enrolment ratio in 1861, and 13 per cent in 1881.

As for the French Canadians, only seventeen of their children were reported in school in 1861, but a decade later their ratio was close to that of the Scots, at 62 per cent. As with the Scots again, the two sexes were quite evenly balanced in 1871. By 1881, however, the proportion of boys enrolled had dropped to 53 per cent, while that of girls had increased, producing a 14-per-cent gap between males and females.[30] Clearly, then, the signatures on the Catholic parish registers accurately reflect the divergent schooling trends for French-Canadian boys and girls.

A closer look at the age levels in 1881 (see Figure 8.1) reveals that the French-Canadian male enrolment ratio began to decline as early as the age of ten. By the age of fifteen, only 7 per cent of the males were recorded as students, whereas the enrolment ratio for French-Canadian girls and Scots boys dropped only after thirteen (the former more rapidly than the latter), and nearly all Scots girls attended classes until the age of fifteen. Thereafter, the Scots gender balance tipped the other way, as a few boys continued to enrol until the age of seventeen while the girls virtually disappeared from school. The Scots enrolment statistics may appear somewhat surprising, given the general assumption that most children in nineteenth-century Canada quit school by the age of thirteen or fourteen, but Michael Katz found

Table 8.1
School Enrolment according to Sex (Ratio to Total Aged 5–16 in Parentheses), in Winslow, 1861, 1871, 1881

| | Scots | | French Canadians | |
Years	Males	Females	Males	Females
1861	99 (78%)	76 (72%)	9 (6%)	8 (6%)
1871	101 (69%)	71 (72%)	92 (61%)	95 (63%)
1881	64 (70%)	62 (74%)	95 (53%)	145 (67%)

Sources: Canada, manuscript census, 1861–81, Winslow Township.

that the religious group with the highest enrolment ratio in mid-nineteenth-century Hamilton was the Free Church Presbyterians.[31] The experience of their parents and grandparents in the family-oriented Gaelic schools might help to explain this phenomenon.

Enrolment statistics do not necessarily reflect the amount of time spent in school, for attendance in the nineteenth century tended to be sporadic at best.[32] Christie MacArthur, who was born near Winslow in 1888, recalled that during her youth families could scarcely afford to allow their children, especially the boys, to remain in school once they were able "to plough, or harrow, or fix stones, or cut wood."[33] The fact that some Scots boys did go to school for longer than their sisters, even though their overall enrolment was slightly lower, suggests that they had not spent as much time there when they were younger.[34] Nevertheless, they clearly gained more schooling than their French-Canadian counterparts, no doubt in part because they had greater opportunity. We have seen that French-Canadian family heads were inclined to work off the farm for part of the year, particularly during the 1870s, when enrolment of their sons dropped significantly. Many school-age Scots boys, in contrast, had older brothers who were resident at least part of the year, when they could presumably take charge of the more time-consuming chores.

Scots settlers demonstrated a strong desire to provide their children with an education soon after their arrival in Winslow. They were hindered at first by the inability or unwillingness of the district inspector, Marcus Child, to travel through the "uncleared swamps" to their settlement.[35] Schools were operating by the spring of 1855, however, when the Reverend McLean reported as secretary-treasurer that the commissioners were "highly gratified at the progress of the Scholars."[36] The Scots schools apparently remained ineligible for the

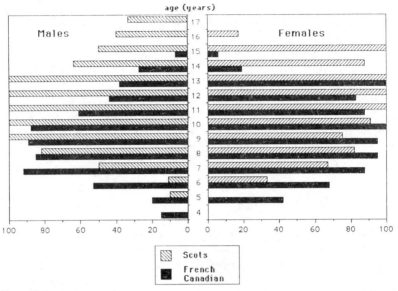

Figure 8.1
Ratio of Children Enrolled in School by Age, Sex, and Ethnicity, 1881

government grant, for McLean drafted a petition in the fall complaining that they could not be established "agreeably to the Act, for want of men in office to enforce said Act." The petition asked that four settlers be appointed as legal officers and concluded that "if we are neglected in this respect as we are in many others we will grow up a set of ignorant & boorish men that will give trouble to the public laws in other respects." The government replied that a justice of the peace could be appointed at once but that a commissioners' court required the certified signatures of at least one hundred proprietors in the township.[37]

The government did begin in the fall of 1855 to provide a grant of $50 per term for each of three schools, and inspector Child finally submitted a report in 1857.[38] Enrolment was recorded as 166, and assessments as $207, including $50 for construction of schools and $48 in monthly fees.[39] Child clearly admired the efforts of the recently settled families:

The settlers do all they can to support them [the schools], and send their children to school regularly. But there is much to be done to lay a good foundation for their schools, which are literally in the forest. The commissioners manage and apply their slender funds to the best interests of the schools, and, by the special aid liberally sent to them, all arrears for teachers' wages are to be paid off, and a small balance remains in the treasurers' hands. Their school-houses are built of logs, hewn, and covered with long shingles on the roof and gables, forming but a poor shelter for the groups of healthy but ragged children which assemble in them. Such destitution I never saw before; but even here I found some of the children making good progress in grammar, and most of them read quite well in easy lessons of the "National Series."[40]

Child concluded: "Their minister has taken an active interest in their education, and much of their progress has depended and will depend upon his influence and labour." Unfortunately, as we saw in the previous chapter, McLean's influence in the township would soon be anything but positive.

A clear sign of trouble was the drop in school taxes in 1858, from $227 to $128, which forced fees to increase from $48 to $118 (see Table 8.2). When inspector Child visited in January of that year, he found no schools open. He was unable to settle difficulties with the accounts because the secretary-treasurer was not at home.[41] After two men from Lingwick complied with the invitation to examine the books publicly in February, an impromptu decision was taken to elect another board at once in order to reopen two schools for the remaining two months of the term. The new secretary-treasurer, merchant Colin Noble, admitted that proper notice had not been given for the election, but claimed that a sizeable number of voters were present. Not only were his fellow commissioners "quite Inteligent [sic] young men, all of whom can speak good English, can read and write also," but a regular election would be held in July for the next school year.[42]

Members of the original board objected strenuously, not simply on the technical grounds of an irregular election, but on a more personal level as well. They complained that one new member had been hired to teach in his own district, in contravention of the schools act, and that Colin Noble "has made a Breach of the Laws of God & man that is, he is the father of more than one child which he dont own or support either the Childs or the Mothers. Besides other things which we do not think proper to mention here as we are a people that were Brougt [sic] up or reared under the pure Gospel in our former Country." Finally, another commissioner was said to be "a man that Neither regards God or man Neigher [sic] ask a Blessing at his meals or dont Keep a family worship as god ordained in his word."[43]

Asked to investigate the matter, Child noted that "the contestation is violent" but concluded simply that neither party had followed proper procedures, and therefore no properly constituted board existed.[44] This was certainly a safe course to take, since the July elec-

Table 8.2
School Finances (Dollars) in Winslow South, Most Years, 1856–81

	Grant	Supplement	Assessment	Fees	Construction	Total
1856	100.63	–	157.16	48.00	50.00	355.79
1857	100.63	40.00	226.80	48.00	48.00	463.43
1858	100.63	–	128.00	118.40	–	347.03
1859	100.63	45.00	308.63	100.00	600.00	1,154.26
1860	100.63	32.00	499.37	161.32	–	793.32
1861	100.63	34.00	500.00	83.20	–	717.83
1862	78.34	–	194.00	40.00	–	312.34
1863	78.34	29.00	190.00	100.00	–	397.34
1864	102.18	26.00	205.06	39.00	–	372.24
1865	102.18	–	205.00	60.00	–	367.18
1867	102.18	–	214.50	120.40	–	437.08
1868	102.18	22.00	227.77	142.80	–	494.75
1869	102.18	36.00	295.48	229.37	–	663.03
1869–70	102.18	46.00	813.23	128.70	135.00	1,225.11
1870–71	102.18	46.00	874.93	95.20	515.00	1,633.31
1871–72	118.65	46.00	734.98	59.60	490.42	1,449.65
1874–75	126.63	20.00	572.61	147.25	–	866.49
1875–76	126.63	–	500.00	153.20	–	779.83
1876–77	126.63	20.00	399.99	118.80	–	665.42
1878–79	126.63	20.00	550.00	163.80	–	860.43
1879–80	126.63	12.02	585.00	94.40	–	818.05
1880–81	126.63	12.02	506.00	107.40	–	752.05

Sources: Distribution to poor municipalities, 1870–81, Art. 58, E13, Archives nationales du Québec à Québec; Reports of Superintendent of Education (or Minister of Public Instruction), in Province of Canada, *Journals of the Legislative Assembly*, 1857–9; Canada, *Sessional Papers*, 1860–6; and Quebec, *Sessional Papers*, 1869–82.

tion was to be held the day Child finally submitted his report. Unfortunately, it did not solve the dispute. Daniel McIver, the secretary-treasurer whom Noble had replaced, complained that on the day of the July vote the ratepayers were searching for someone lost in the woods. Noble, who "intends to rule this Municipality," had nevertheless proceeded with two or three others to hold the election. Opponents had therefore decided to take another vote in a week's time, but McIver was informed by the superintendent's office that the law courts alone had jurisdiction over contested elections.[45]

Defeated for the time being, McIver and five others who signed with crosses complained the following December that their teachers were incompetent and that "as you did not give us justice we have written to an advocate in Sherbrooke."[46] McIver was not heard from again until 1860, when he protested that residents of his immediate district were required to pay full taxes, even though the lack of a stove in their school had necessitated its closure every winter but one since it was built six years earlier.[47] As with the religious disputes, then, moral charges appear to have disguised localized struggles over distribution of limited resources and services. Unfortunately for McIver and his neighbours, the law dictated that all property owners must contribute to the municipality's schools whether one was open in their own district or not. We shall see that the French Canadians were, nevertheless, successful in bending that law.

Despite McIver's ongoing complaints, the new inspector, Henry Hubbard, reported in 1859 that the disputes that had closed Winslow's four schools were subsiding. A year later he wrote in his characteristically patronizing manner: "The School Commissioners are endeavouring, though rather ignorantly, to do the best they are able for the School."[48] Having fallen to $128 in 1858, school taxes increased dramatically to $309 in 1859 and to $499 in 1860, or about $5.30 per family when fees are included. An additional $600 was invested in building schools, presumably from the special levy that the commissioners were allowed to impose "on account of poverty" (see Table 8.2). The irony of this phrase appears to have escaped the government, which provided no funds to school commissions for construction purposes.[49] Map 16, drawn by the census enumerator in 1861, reveals that the Scots had six evenly distributed school-houses, while the French Canadians had none, but Hubbard was not impressed with the results in Winslow South. In 1862 he wrote that "affairs are yet in a very crude state. The school houses which are built, are of the roughest kind, having a few apologies for seats and writing desks."[50]

The Scots settlers were clearly feeling the financial burden of their schools, for the commissioners reported in 1859 that there were twenty-five to sixty-three children aged five to sixteen in each of seven districts, yet only four schools could be kept open. They complained that the number of potential students had tripled since the survey was taken on which was based the annual $100 grant – an amount that failed to increase substantially throughout our study period (see Table 8.2).[51] By 1861 the Scots were finding it so difficult to pay their teachers for the full eight months required to receive the government grant that they decided to opt out of the provincial system. They refused to elect replacements for the two commissioners retiring in July, but the inspector informed them that because the

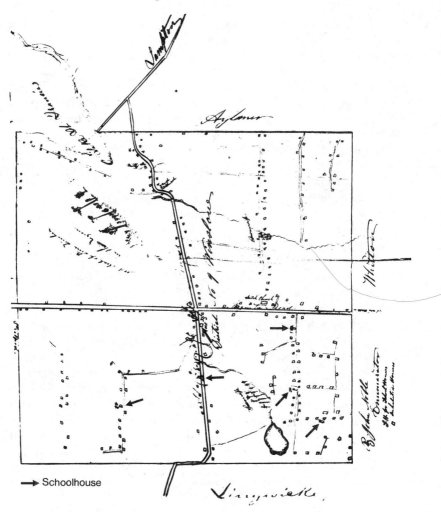

➤ Schoolhouse

Map 16   Census Enumerator's Winslow, 1861

commission still had a quorum it had to proceed with its duties. If its members refused to do so, "they must be made to act." The superintendent supported Hubbard by stating that he would appoint two commissioners as soon as their names were forwarded.[52]

The four schools reopened in the fall, but the commissioners proved less than eager to follow the regulations of the public system.

They failed to obtain receipts from their teachers, two of whom subsequently left the region, or to submit a report at the end of the
spring term in 1862. When the board finally decided to apply for
government funds after all, the superintendent agreed to consider
the case, but his office had mistakenly sent the spring grant to the
newly established board in Winslow North. The French-speaking
commissioners in turn refused to reimburse the $39.17 on the
grounds that it had already been spent.

The comedy of errors continued when the superintendent's office
mistakenly sent Winslow South the supplement of $34 that Winslow
North was entitled to as a poor municipality. It was the Scots' turn
to refuse to hand the money over. The education office then decided
to allow each commission to keep the money it had received, which
appeared fair enough, except that Winslow South lost its own supplementary grant in the process.

In addition, the county treasurer had mistakenly informed the
government that Winslow North's population outnumbered that of
Winslow South by three to two, and so the former municipality
received a grant of $104.46, while the latter's dropped to $78.34. A
census taken a year later revealed that the south actually outnumbered the north by 848 to 670.[53] A number of ratepayers in the south
were French Canadians who effectively remained outside the school
system, but the secretary-treasurer nevertheless had reason to be discouraged: "It seems that we are reduced if not wholly neglected by
the Education Office whatever [sic] when North Winslow are
favoured by a much more share of the Grant and also of supplementary aid in one respect we are to blame ourselves. But that is on
account of poverty which prevails on our people."[54]

The schools of Winslow South needed all the assistance they could
obtain because the tax collection dropped drastically from $500 in
1861 to $194 in 1862, remaining below its former level until the end
of the decade. Whatever the initial cause, the situation was exacerbated by internal feuding. In the fall of 1863 eighteen families of
district 2 decided to form a dissenting school, electing three trustees
and paying a teacher for five months through voluntary contributions. Once again the expressed motivation combined local self-inter-
est with moral indignation. After complaining that the board had
failed to open another school in their district to replace the first
building, which had burned to the ground in 1861, the dissidents
added that one commissioner was a tavern keeper and two others
"partake in strong Liquors." They concluded darkly that "by deeper
examination more could be said of them." Unfortunately for their

cause, "dissentient" schools could be established only on religious grounds. The superintendent's office therefore refused to interfere with the legal action launched by the board to collect back taxes.[55]

Divisions apparently persisted, for student enrolment declined from 133 in 1861, according to the education report (or 175 according to the provincial census), to 96 in 1864. By 1865, however, the inspector saw hopeful signs: "Old difficulties have been somewhat overcome, and although others have arisen, still matters are, on the whole, in a much more hopeful state. Some four schools have been kept, though with considerable interruption, and some progress has, I trust, been made."[56] His optimism was well founded, for finances began to improve (see Table 8.2), and enrolment had jumped to 208 by 1867, remaining somewhat higher than that level for the next several years (see Table 8.4, below).

Meanwhile, another dissenting school in Winslow South would have the support of the authorities because it served the French-speaking minority. According to Hubbard in 1864, the Catholics had been ignored by the school commissioners, "they having neither allowed them a school nor collected assessments from them."[57] He was not being entirely fair, for the Catholics themselves admitted that the commissioners had encouraged them to establish a school, but the problem was the nature of its relationship with the Scots-controlled board.

The Irish-born Peter Henry petitioned with twenty-four French Canadians for a school under the authority of the commissioners, while a counter-petition with twenty-six French names asked permission to establish a dissenting school managed by three "syndics." The latter group claimed that among those who signed the English petition were a number of youths with no property, while others had signed under the impression that it requested exemption from taxes, and still others had simply changed their minds since the previous year "par esprit de parti." The French Canadians' attempt to elect one of themselves to Winslow South's school commission had failed, "et le different langage entre eux et nous nous laisse dans l'impossibilité de rien connaitre des affaires d'Ecole." Finally, if they were to build a school under the authority of the commissioners, settlers would have to resort to taxation rather than voluntary labour. All the taxes they could raise were needed for the teacher's salary.[58]

The French-speaking minority apparently managed to open a school in 1864, but continuing internal divisions closed it the following year. Finally, in February 1866, the Catholic minority officially declared itself a dissenting body. When the Scots commissioners expressed concern about the distribution of assessments and collection of arrears, the authorities declared that dissent in no way changed the commission's relationship with the Catholic ratepayers; it simply relieved that body of the responsibility for managing the Catholic school.[59] The Catholics were nevertheless soon managing their own assessments, even though the government continued to deliver the annual grant to Winslow South in one lump sum.

This arrangement appears to have functioned smoothly, though factionalism among the French Canadians closed their school in 1876. When this was finally brought to the attention of the superintendent two years later, he responded quickly by threatening to end the Catholics' dissentient status, leaving them liable to pay two years of back taxes to the Protestant commission. Given the political climate of Quebec, this was clearly an empty threat. Furthermore, it would have had little effect: a group of French-Canadian families living near Stornoway openly stated that it would renounce dissentient status if a school were not opened in their neighbourhood. The provincial office subsequently revised its tactic by threatening the syndics with legal action if they did not open the second school.[60] Whether the syndics did so is not clear, but Stornoway miller Ferdinand Legendre continued to send his children to the Protestant school. When he was pressed by the syndics on a yearly basis to pay taxes to the Catholic system, he received no support from the superintendent's office, which told him incorrectly in 1881 that he was breaking the law. Two months later, however, the syndics were finally informed that no one had to pay taxes toward their schools unless he or she expressly declared himself or herself to be a dissentient.[61]

There was never a question of the French Canadians in Winslow North contributing to the same school commission as the Scots, because the first schools in the north were not opened until 1862, four years after the township had been divided into two municipalities. As we have seen, Winslow South's grant was reduced as a result, even though there had been no legal or practical connection between it and Winslow North. The northern ratepayers not only gained the temporary advantage of larger grant with a smaller population, but an apparent bureaucratic error gave them a double subsidy in 1863 (see Table 8.3).[62] They invested $700 in their four schools over the next two years, and in 1865 Hubbard could report that the buildings were "tolerably fair." The teachers had also given "pretty good satisfaction," the arrears in assessments from the previous year had been mostly collected, and teachers' salaries were not far behind. The

Table 8.3
School Finances (Dollars) in Winslow North, Most Years, 1862–81

	Grant	Supplement	Assessment	Fees	Construction	Total
1862	104.46	30.00	182.40	–	–	316.86
1863	104.46	29.00	182.40	–	–	315.86
(St. Rom.	82.14	–	280.00	–	300.00	662.14)
1864	80.62	26.00	388.00	16.00	400.00	910.62
1865	80.62	–	300.00	52.00	19.00	451.62
1867	80.62	–	312.00	105.20	–	497.82
1868	80.62	22.00	312.00	124.00	–	538.62
1869	80.62	25.00	269.00	134.22	–	508.84
1869–70	80.62	30.00	282.40	130.00	–	523.02
1870–71	80.62	30.00	283.00	164.00	–	557.62
1871–72	85.43	–	283.00	116.00	–	484.43
1874–75	91.18	30.00	294.00	52.00	–	467.18
1878–79	91.18	25.00	250.00	86.00	400.00	852.18
1879–80	91.18	–	286.24	79.60	330.00	787.02
1880–81	91.18	–	369.56	177.00	40.00	677.74

Sources: As for Table 8.2.

inspector was not exaggerating when he declared: "Considering the poverty of the people, this municipality has, I think, so far done well."[63]

By 1868 the Catholics of the region had their own inspector, W.T. Stenson, who commented on the poor spring weather of the previous two years but nevertheless felt hopeful about the advances made in teaching and the eageness of the colonists to support their schools. In the first division of St Romain, spelling and writing were good, and note-books remarkably neat, but progress had been delayed in the other two schools by childhood fevers. There were also two poorly attended independent schools in the most distant parts of the municipality, where ratepayers planned to join the provincial system as soon as there were more school-age children in their neighbourhoods.[64]

The only unique features of these schools were that they did not operate for two full four-month terms, and they did not employ certified teachers. In contrast to the commissioners of Winslow South, therefore, those of St Romain tolerated the loss of a tax base in the districts where they could not afford to operate schools. The assumption tended to be that each "arrondissement" was essentially responsible for its own school: in 1866 the commissioners actually attempted to levy extra taxes on each family in the more thinly populated districts.[65] Again, in 1879, a farmer complained that the more populous districts had so much money that their families did not pay fees, while he paid a dollar per child each month, and families who lived in districts too poor to support their own schools had paid no taxes whatsoever in three years.[66] Inspector Stenson denied the charges, and the curé had made it known that no arrondissement could be exempt from taxation, but the custom was apparently for less populous districts to save their tax money for two or three years so that they could operate a local school for one year. The portion of the government grant they were entitled to was supposed to be deposited in a chartered bank during the interim.[67]

In a lengthy report written in 1876, inspector Stenson declared that "the advantages derived from the establishment in any locality of a greater number of schools than the Corporation can afford to maintain on a good footing are *nil*." He played down the problem of accessibilty by arguing that wherever a good school was established many children "come on foot from long distances to learn lessons which they afterwards turn to advantage."[68] But such travel would have been particularly difficult in the harsh environment of Winslow North, and neither the inspector nor the superintendent attempted to interfere with its localized tax distribution system.

One could argue, in fact, that the alternative options – operating a school for a shorter term outside the official system or on a rotating basis within it – represented creative solutions to poverty and government under-funding. Indeed, the French Canadians had effectively adopted the decentralized system which operated in Ontario into the twentieth century. Gidney and Lawr claim that eliminating this system in that province "would in one stroke equalize assessment, provide better and more uniform facilities, support better-qualified teachers in the poorer sections, enable all schools to open the full year, and allow parents to send their children to the nearest school."[69] For Winslow North, however, subdistrict autonomy appears to have ensured that more remote families did not have to pay taxes for schools that their children could not reach. The greater flexibility of the subdistrict system also made it easier to annex portions of adjoining parishes for school purposes. Thus in 1880 ten lots in the first range of Aylmer and one lot in Lambton were joined to rang 1 SE of Winslow North to make it possible to build and operate a local school.[70]

If difficulty in funding sufficient schools remained characteristic of St Romain during the 1870s, poverty also kept attendance low. Inspector Stenson reported that parents "cannot in certain cases clothe their children comfortably to protect them against the rigor of the seasons, and in others they cannot send them in vehicles to the school, which is often situated at a great distance from their domiciles."[71] In 1876 he noted general improvement in attendance, as well as in school quality and teachers' salaries, but the international commercial crisis finally began to make an impact the following year.

As we saw in chapter 5, farmers accustomed to working on the American harvest were instead expanding their own clearings. Because the result was increased demand for family labour in planting crops, older children were less able to attend school regularly. While in 1872 Winslow North had supported four schools under provincial regulation, and three that were independent, in 1877 Stenson reported only three of the former and one of the latter. He feared that debt might close all of them: partial salaries were still owed to two teachers, and ratepayers had been assessed $1,300 for the year's railway tax, as well as facing a bill of $600 from their church's contractor. As the inhabitants had no means to earn cash, Stenson asked that their grant be issued even if they failed to pay the teachers by the end of the school year. He also supported their request to hire young local people without diplomas for the coming year only. Quebec complied with both requests.[72]

The following year, in 1879, the Catholic inspector again commented on the reduced attendance in his district resulting from the "monetary crisis," but he expressed admiration for the sacrifices made by families "in order to maintain schools as well as they do." He added:

The fact is that it is impossible for anyone who is not familiar with the position of a settler now-a-days, to form an exact idea of the obstacles which he has to overcome and the sacrifices he has to make, not only to meet the expenses required for the working of the schools, but even to enable his children to attend them.

In the first place, it is very difficult for a settler to procure the needed money, no matter how little it may be, to pay the school assessments and monthly contributions; then there is the necessity of clothing the children a little better, in order to send them to school, than is necessary when they remain at home. These two obstacles being overcome, there arises another quite as serious; he has to deprive himself of those services which settlers' children of fifteen years of age may render to their parents; to this we must add that the greater number of the children reside at a considerable distance from the schools and, that during certain portions of the year, they are unable to attend either on account of the roads or of the inclement weather peculiar to the climate.[73]

Even when economic conditions improved in 1880, attendance continued to decline, because many farmers went to work in American factories in order to pay off debts accumulated during the recession. With local labour scarce, children were withdrawn from school in order to help with the farm work, "and particularly in picking potato bugs."[74] Some progress was finally reported again in 1881, despite the epidemic reported to be afflicting the district's children.[75] As we saw above (Table 8.1), however, the census taken that same spring suggests that the enrolment of Winslow's French-Canadian boys had far from recovered.

Difficult as conditions obviously were during the 1870s, the Protestant inspector's reports did not dwell on the economic crisis, and there is no evidence of declining school attendance among the Scots. Hubbard was still complaining in 1870 about the quality of the school-houses in Winslow South, the slow progress of the pupils, and the difficulty of hiring teachers with diplomas, but his statistics reveal that taxes had increased dramatically in one year, from $295 to $813, and that a significant sum had been invested in buildings for the first time in a decade.[76] That investment would reach $1,140 by 1873, when the new inspector, William Thompson, reported that the commissioners of Winslow South had built two "splendid" school-houses in districts 3 and 4, were planning another one for district 1, and wished to establish a model school in district 2. He also noted that accounts continued to be well kept and the teachers punctually paid.[77] The Scots were apparently not entirely immune from the effects of the recession, however, for no more money was invested in construction during the remainder of the decade, and they did not employ a teacher qualified for a model school until 1880.[78] Assessments had also declined notably by 1874–5, reaching the nadir of $400 in 1876–7.

Small budgets made it difficult for commissioners to keep a qualified teacher for more than a single term. Hubbard complained several times about the constant changing of teachers throughout his territory. He did add in 1865, however, that the problem was minimized by the turn-over of pupils from winter to summer, since older children who generally attended during the December–April term required the more "efficient" male teachers, while females, in his opinion, were more suited to teaching the younger children, who enrolled for June to October.[79] The Catholic inspector, Stenson, displayed the same bias when he claimed that female teachers might be qualified to teach young students, but they did not know how to interest the older ones, who consequently stopped attending school.[80]

Women dominated rural teaching early in French Canada, particularly in parishes where the agri-forestry economy attracted men to the woods during the winter school term. Once the public school system was introduced, ratepayers' resistance to higher taxes provided added incentive to employ women throughout Canada. This pressure was somewhat offset in English-speaking communities by the influx of immigrant men in need of cash.[81] Winslow South's commissioners continued to employ a few males during our study period. The two who were teaching in 1861 earned $100 and $150, while the four females earned only $100 each. Sexual discrimination had apparently ended by 1867, when salaries for men as well as women varied from $100 to $125.[82]

In Winslow North, in contrast, all the teachers were female, and only in 1869–70 did one of them earn more than $100 per term. In 1880, when each of the four teachers in the Protestant schools was paid between $130 and $180, the seven French Canadians received a mere $40 to $60 each. Because most of these women were married to local residents or still living with their parents, they would not even be given their board.[83] The manuscript census of 1881 reveals, for example, that four of the teachers in St Romain were young unmarried sisters living with their widowed mother and five younger siblings. We shall see below, however, that in at least one case a French-Canadian teacher and her husband were living in the school building, presumably rent-free.

Not only were teachers poorly paid, but they sometimes had to wait long periods before receiving their salaries. In 1864 Marie-de-Lime Roy complained near the end of one term that she had still not been paid for the previous one: "on abuse de ma bonté."[84] In a similar case in 1877, the school commissioners were warned by superintendent Gédéon Ouimet that he would act "avec rigueur" against municipalities that did not pay their teachers promptly. When his threats were ignored, Ouimet wrote that he personally was taking the commissioners to court, but two months later he was counselling the aggrieved teacher to wait for her remaining $41.[85]

The superintendent's interventions on behalf of teachers were not limited to salary cases, for on at least one occasion he coerced the commissioners of St Romain into rehiring a teacher. In 1871 Marie McKenzie was informed that her contract would not be renewed because she was too strict, but the curé expressed his strong support for her, based on personal observation in his official capacity as school visitor. As a result, the superintendent warned the commissioners that because their reasons for dismissing Miss McKenzie were insufficient, they might either lose their grant or have to pay her an indemnity.[86]

It is doubtful that such a threat was enforceable, given that this was not a dismissal case, for teachers in some rural municipalities were not rehired as a matter of course until well into the twentieth century.[87]

Because their moral standards were supposed to be exemplary, teachers were vulnerable as well to rumours spread by ill-disposed persons.[88] Only one case from Winslow came to the superintendent's attention prior to 1881, but it does demonstrate how petty local grievances against teachers could be. In 1879 a farmer named Laurent Gagné complained about the married teacher in his district, who, he noted in an accusatory tone, was five months pregnant and who could be seen knitting, sewing, and carrying water during school hours. Worse still, his thirteen-year-old son had followed her into the upstairs living quarters, where her husband "la tenait par le cou et lui tappait les fesses, par dessus ses hardes." Another witness informed the inspector that when he had brought his children to school before 8 a.m. the couple was still in bed. As the teacher went upstairs in her night-shirt "j'y ai vu les jambes jusqu'au Corps." The teacher replied that this family had arrived at seven o'clock and that she had done the children a favour by not forcing them to wait outside in the cold while she dressed herself. As for the younger Gagné, if he saw her and her husband as he said he had, he must have lifted the trap door to the living quarters, which he had no right to do. She did admit to knitting (but not sewing) while listening to the lessons of the youngest children but said she did so only because she knew the text by heart. Finally, witnesses testified that she carried water only for the use of the students. Inspector Stenson abstained from comment in his report, but superintendent Ouimet wrote to Gagné that if there was scandal in the school, he had caused it.[89]

The exceptional nature of these cases suggests that the commissioners generally had a free hand in managing their teaching personnel. Apparently the same was true of the curriculum during much of this period, for there was no official program of study in Quebec until 1873.[90] Even though catechism (not mentioned in the annual reports) was apparently an important part of the Catholic school program,[91] St Romain managed to offer a more ambitious curriculum of secular subjects than did the Scots schools. In 1864 nineteen of the 129 French-speaking students were studying grammar, and ten history, though only ten were being taught arithmetic and four geography. Two years later, nearly half the students (eighty) were learning simple arithmetic, and twenty-four were studying geography, while the enrolment in grammar and history had climbed to forty-seven and thirty-nine, respectively.

The pattern for the Catholic school in Winslow South was similar, but the Scots began to study history only in 1872–3, and Table 8.4 reveals that the ratio of French-Canadian students taking all the aforementioned courses remained consistently higher than that of the Scots. The Catholic school inspector was not greatly impressed, however, for he questioned the value of much of the education outside "reading, spelling, writing, arithmetic, and mental calculation." Stenson reported in 1875 that about one-fifth of the students in the elementary schools within his jurisdiction were taught grammar, but he doubted that many realized any benefit because books were simply forgotten after students left school. For the same reason, young men who could read "passably well" when in class after a few years "are puzzled to read any kind of a document or to sign their names." One contributing factor was that the text books were beyond the comprehension of young children, preventing them from learning to read "with pleasure and interest."[92]

Stenson's comments are consistent with the surprisingly high ratio of St Romain grooms who did not sign the marriage register during the 1870s, as we have seen, but by 1877 he was expressing satisfaction with the recently introduced Montpetit readers: "The avidity with which the chidren take possession of them makes me hope that I did not exaggerate the great advantages which would result from their introduction into our schools." He hoped, as well, that the government would encourage the opening of parish libraries.[93]

Table 8.4 reveals that in 1864 only 40 per cent of the St Romain's students were reported to be learning to read but that within three years all were said to be studying at one of three reading levels. Indeed, 36 per cent were apparently functioning at the highest level, as compared to only 16 per cent of the Scots, though the margin had disappeared by 1870 and was reversed by 1873. If the Scots students were somewhat more advanced than the French Canadians in their ability to read, the same does not appear to have applied to writing. After 1864 the Scots consistently had a lower ratio learning this skill, which can be explained once again by their emphasis on biblical literacy. If a higher proportion of Scots could sign the marriage register, it was presumably because the large number of French-speaking boys who stopped attending classes around the age of eleven would have little opportunity to practise their literacy skills before marrying more than a decade later.

Popular belief in the English-speaking community of the Eastern Townships, not least among those of Hebridean origin, has been that its population declined in numbers in part because of the emphasis placed on education. Sons and daughters are said to have become

Table 8.4
Curricula (%) in the Protestant and Catholic Schools of Winslow, Selected Years, 1861–73

	No. of Schls	No. of Stud.	Percentage Distribution									
			Read ABC	Read Fluently	Read Well	Learn Write	Simp. Arith	Comp. Arith	Geog.	Gram.	Parse	Hist.
WINSLOW SOUTH – PROTESTANT												
1861	5 *	133	18	56	16	30	19	7	4	–	–	–
1864	4	96†	26	75	37	48	37	7	2	2	–	–
1867	6	208	29	48	16	23	15	8	2	7	–	–
1870	6	225	11	62	27	44	33	18	13	13	7	–
1873	5	226	30	35	35	37	29	9	13	15	10	15
WINSLOW NORTH												
1864	4	129	16	20	5	23	8	–	3	15	–	8
1867	5	170	21	43	36	52	47	–	14	28	–	23
1870	6‡	191	26	48	26	62	50	4	16	28	–	23
1873	7§	170	21	59	20	49	28	17	8	18	–	22
WINSLOW SOUTH – CATHOLIC												
1867	1	29	19	58	23	42	39	–	31	23	–	8
1873	1	39	17	61	22	69	47	22	11	28	–	25

* Includes one independent school with 13 students.
† The ratio said to be reading totals more than 100%. It seems likely that an error was made in recording the total number of students.
‡ Includes three independent schools with 46 students.
§ Includes three independent schools with 51 students, filed mistakenly with "Oxford."

Sources: Grand Statistical Tables, Reports of the Superintendent of Education, Canada, *Sessional Papers*; Minister of Public Instruction, Quebec, *Sessional Papers*.

overqualified for the difficult life of a farmer in this region, a life that French Canadians were more willing to embrace because of the poorer quality of their schooling.[94] Geographically and temporally restricted as our comparative study may be, it does suggest that this belief is actually a myth: it contains elements of truth but also elements of fundamental distortion.

Winslow's Scots certainly opened their schools earlier than did the French Canadians, as well as paying higher taxes, apparently hiring better-qualified teachers during the winter term and sending their male children to classes until an older age. The inspectors, however, failed to distinguish sharply the efforts of the two communities and the results attained in their schools. We also saw above that the Scots enjoyed certain advantages in schooling, at least during the 1870s, when French-Canadian householders' greater involvement in a semi-agricultural economy left their families vulnerable to the prolonged recession. The Scots appear also to have been motivated by a genuine religious impulse, not the secularized version known as the Protestant ethic.[95] Such an impulse was hardly designed to motivate students to rise far above their current social status. No doubt, a few professionals and businessmen emerged from the upper St Francis district, but the one-room school-houses were essentially institutions of assimilation into the English North American milieu. That assimilation would include not only language, but greater knowledge of North American geography, and perhaps even a taste of the discipline needed to become cogs in the modern industrial machine.

It is doubtful, however, that students learned to adjust their lives to a strictly mechanical rhythm rather than a seasonal one when attendance was sporadic at best and the school terms and class levels were scheduled according to the agricultural calendar. The products of such schools continued to resist becoming full-time members of the proletariat by adjusting their annual labouring schedules to a seasonal cycle. Much the same could be said for the French-Canadian schools, except that they taught the language of Quebec, not that of the United States and western Canada, where so many of the Scots would migrate.[96] Of course many francophones went to New England mill towns where they could speak their own tongue, at least for a time, but their cultural identity was certainly a stronger impediment to emigration than was that of the British Canadians in the Eastern Townships.

We have seen little evidence from Winslow Township that the public school system was imposed on an unwilling population. Stenson did write in 1879 that "if I advocate the cause of the settlers, permit me to assure you that I allow no opportunity to pass of convincing these good people that they must increase their zeal for the education of their children ..., while in the case of those who are indifferent or stingy, and unfortunately there are a good many of them, I employ all the authority at my disposal to compel them to carry out the laws which govern our system of education."[97] That authority was limited, however, as he complained two years later: "The inspector should have the power of ordering peremptorily the improvements which now he can only ask for."

Threats to withold the annual grant were effective, in Stenson's words, only three times out of ten, clearly because it covered only a fraction of the annual expences.[98] The departmental correspondence to Winslow reveals, furthermore, that such threats rarely emanated from the provincial education office. As for the inspector's reports, Stenson himself admitted that they invariably expressed admiration for the sacrifices made by the impoverished settlers to educate their children. Even though all the inspectors bemoaned low attendance at one time or another, none of them suggested (in writing at least) that Quebec should follow Ontario's example by introducing compulsory education.

The French Canadians operated several schools outside the state system, but only because they could not afford to keep all their schools open for a long enough term to qualify for the provincial grant. This two-tiered system of schools, whereby submunicipal districts flouted official regulations by effectively controlling their own tax revenues, nicely illustrates the limits of state authority at the local level. If the government had provided sufficient funds for schools to operate everywhere they were needed, Stenson and his colleagues would have found their authority considerably augmented. The chief obstacle to educational progress in communities such as Winslow was material impoverishment, not cultural resistance to change. This the inspectors clearly realized, even if their reports could not openly criticize their employer by demanding more generous public grants.

If the inspectors' relationship with the school commissioners of Winslow was less coercive than the general analysis of Curtis and Corrigan might have led us to expect, was it perhaps because the commission was dominated by a local élite imposing its values and its authority on the general populace?[99] Wendie Nelson has shown how educational reform was embraced in St Grégoire by the village "notables" as a means of enhancing their own status, and Normand Séguin claims that "l'école est par excellence le terrain de l'alliance du clergé et de la petite bourgeoisie dans la paroisse rurale du xixe siècle."[100]

Michel Monette has nevertheless found that farmers continued to hold most of the positions on the school commissions of the two nineteenth-century parishes he studied. He suggests that these farmers were of the agricultural élite, but his data reveal that the great majority owned only fifty to two hundred arpents.[101] The superintendent of education, Jean-Baptiste Meilleur, had criticized the £250 property qualification at the time it was imposed,[102] and he and his successors may simply have ignored it as unenforceable. If the full letter of the law had been applied in Winslow Township, where the average farm was valued at only $500 in 1861, the great majority of family heads would have been disqualified from election.

The correspondence of the education office lists only once the names of all Winslow North's school commissioners, in the spring of 1872, but there is no reason to believe that this was not a typical year. The five elected commissioners were all farmers, two of whom had held office for three years, one for two years, and two for one year. The secretary-treasurer, also a farmer, had held his appointed post for seven years, testifying to the shortage of literate candidates for the position.[103] With an average property-holding of only seventy-five acres each, according to the 1871 census, these men were below the local French-Canadian mean of eighty-seven acres. The more important statistic is the amount of land they had improved, which was seventeen acres more than the French-Canadian average (fifty-four acres to thirty-seven acres), but they were relatively mature men. Whereas the average age of French-speaking family heads was forty-two in 1871, only one of this group was in his thirties, and the others were in the forty-six to fifty range. The chief qualification for the post of school commissioner in St Romain appears to have been maturity rather than wealth.

Since Stornoway was a larger centre than St Romain, villagers played a greater role in Winslow's Protestant school commission. Thus Colin Noble acted as chair in 1871, and the Reverend McDonald followed in 1872. During the three years for which all names are available, however, local farmers held four of the six positions, including that of secretary-treasurer.[104] The minister was a permanent fixture, while Noble was replaced by Henry Layfield, who in turn was replaced by the Catholic Hugh Leonard. The village's merchants and millers held only one seat apparently because representation was as localized as possible, with each submunicipal district ideally having its own school commissioner. The minister would presumably be considered a community-wide representative.

There are too many Scots homonyms to identify where each commissioner lived, but the French-Canadian commissioners were widely distributed throughout the parish of St Romain in 1872. This sharply decentralized pattern of control is consistent with the pressure by ratepayers to ensure that their tax dollars were spent on their particular schools. Indeed, each French-Canadian board member appears to have been in charge of hiring the teacher for the district he represented.[105] Such a pattern may not have been foreseen by the school legislation, but a model for the Scots did exist in the Presbyterian system of choosing elders from local subdistricts. Despite the more centralized authority of the Catholic church, we saw in the previous chapter that the St Romain wardens began to be elected on the basis of subdistrict representation. It remains to be seen whether this centrifugal force proved as persistent in municipal government.

MUNICIPAL COUNCILS

The municipal records of Winslow South have unfortunately not survived, making it impossible to determine whether each councillor generally represented a specific locality, as with church and school. The village of Stornoway monopolized the mayor's seat, however, for Colin Noble was elected to the office first in 1855, holding it until 1857, again from 1864 to 1866, and finally from 1868 to 1872. Of the six other mayors prior to 1875, Thomas Leonard and Henry Layfield were also businessmen; Hugh Leonard then held the post for twenty-three consecutive years.[106] The fact that Leonard was a Catholic member of the Scots community who could speak the three local languages no doubt stood him in good stead. There was no such village domination in St Romain. Between 1870 (when minutes were first recorded) and 1881, eight individuals, all farmers, held the office of mayor. When the secretary-treasurer, who was also a farmer, had to leave the township "pour gagner le soutien de ma famille," the council had to hire a non-resident as his replacement.[107]

Not only were there few members of the petite bourgeoisie living in Winslow North, but it is unlikely that the mayor's chair held much prestige in an era when municipal budgets were similar in size to those of the school commission and church vestry. Public charity was managed informally through the curé, as in 1867, when Father Vanasse announced that "ceux qui ont de la fleur à vendre, doivent par charité la vendre aux plus indigents. Inutile d'attendre un plus haut prix, elle est déjà assez chère ce me semble."[108] During the spring of the same year, he asked the parish to help seed the ground of a farmer who had been injured, and on New Year's day 1873 a wood-chopping bee was organized for a widow whose supply of fuel had been exhausted. Throughout the following years there were regular requests made for assistance to two widows in particular. On several occasions the curé even urged the men to commence work after the Sunday service. In this respect, at least, the strict sabbatarian Scots would not have followed the example of their Catholic neighbours.[109] In addition, St Romain's roads were maintained by statute labour as late as 1872, with the result that municipal taxes that year totalled a mere $80.[110] Even when the council decreed that all future road work was to be at the expense of the municipality, the budget for the winter of 1872–3 was only $250, while that for the following summer was $600. As Tables 7.3 and 8.3 show, vestry and school revenues were generally in the range of $500.[111]

The secretary-treasurer's minutes fail to identify the councillors for certain years, but there is no evidence of a tightly knit local élite. Clearly, low property value and illiteracy did not constitute significant bars to office in the region, given the consistent position taken by the government that all contested elections had to be decided by the courts.[112] Thus five members of the 1870 council reported owning only fifty acres to the census enumerator of 1871, the sixth claimed seventy acres, and the seventh one hundred acres. Like the school commissioners of 1872, they also represented a reasonably dispersed geographical area, coming from five different ranges. It is likely that few farmers escaped playing at least a minor role in local affairs, for by 1876 St Romain had eleven roads inspectors, two fence viewers, three agricultural inspectors, three property assessors, and an auditor. Louis Fortier held three of these positions, but no one else had more than one, and the roads inspectors were dutifully rotated every year.

As with the school system, again, local neighbourhoods maintained a good deal of control over their tax contributions. While statute labour had been dropped for Eastern Townships counties by the Municipal and Road Act of 1860,[113] Winslow North's farmers continued to be responsible for maintaining the roads on their own ranges until 1872. In addition, the $400 grant from the seigneurial indemnity fund was distributed in 1871 according to the assessment of each subdistrict.[114] The same principle was followed after assessments technically replaced corvées – perhaps not surprising, given that ratepayers could continue to commute their road taxes by statute labour. Thus, during the summer of 1873, each proprietor was able to fulfil his obligations by working in his own arrondissement at the rate of a dollar per day for a ten-hour day.[115] Only in 1876 did council begin to transfer revenues between arrondissements. It was made clear, moreover, that the money (or its equivalent in labour) did not come from a general pool but was being paid by one specific subdistrict to another specific subdistrict. Thus, during the summer of 1877, Paul Roy's subdistrict was to receive $15 from that of Georges Cameron, $6 from that of Pierre Bolduc, $4 from that of Louis Fortier, and $2 from that of Honoré Coulombe, while Féréol Roy's subdistrict would gain $4 from Louis Fortier and $2 from Laurent Gagné.[116] In this manner, the municipal system remained localized and personalized, and obligations were clearly established for the future.

While road work appears to have been largely a matter for individual councillors and their neighbours to regulate, railways were a contentious issue, of vital concern to all the municipalities of Compton County throughout the 1870s. In 1870 J.H. Pope convinced the county council to provide his projected Lennoxville–Lake Megantic line with a $250,000 subsidy, but it was rejected by the voters in a majority of the local municipalities. St Romain was among that majority, even though Pope had promised to construct a branch line through Winslow to the Lévis-Kennebec Railway and had plied local residents with whiskey on voting day. The parish voted the same way again several months later when Pope managed to win a narrow eight-to-seven victory in the county. Winslow North's property owners were therefore legally bound to pay a sizeable tax for a railway that would not come within many miles of their community.[117]

We saw in chapter 5 that Winslow's French Canadians took advantage of railway construction by cutting large quantities of tamarack, but the municipal debt remained burdensome. With the recession at its peak by 1876, and threats emanating from the Eastern Townships Bank, St Romain's council began to threaten delinquent ratepayers with legal action. Early in 1877 six local residents had to sign promissory notes for the $1,050 interest owed by the parish municipality on the county's railway debentures. A special levy was imposed to raise this money, but the six individuals remained liable to the bank two years later.[118] The local council had even made the futile gesture of appointing three delegates to remind Pope of his promise to purchase the stock that his regulation had imposed on the impoverished parish.[119] Consequently, in March 1879, St Romain borrowed $1,500 from the Eastern Townships Bank at 10 per cent in order to cover the previous three years' interest and cancel the promissory notes. It then moved to raise $1,100 in taxes, authorizing the secretary-treasurer to enforce payment through the courts. The council backtracked in May by voting that ratepayers would be given a chance to ratify the loan at a public meeting, but it changed its mind once again two weeks later.[120]

The March loan failed to buy much time. With July came more letters from the bank's lawyers threatening all municipalities in arrears. St Romain's council responded by serving notices on everyone who had not paid railway taxes during the previous two years. The result was clearly disappointing, however, for in August the mayor was given authorization to sue delinquents. The council's hand was being forced by three of the men who had signed the promissory notes in 1877. At a public meeting called to consider the issue, twenty-nine ratepayers voted to reach a settlement, while sixteen voted against it.[121]

St Romain's arrears on the railway debentures were finally reduced to a manageable level in 1880, when, as we have seen, the school inspector noted an economic improvement in the district. The $550 payment made in 1880, and the $500 in 1881, were a lot of money for a municipality that raised only $370 in taxes for its schools during the 1880–1 school year.[122] As for Winslow South, in 1880 its council was still imposing a railway tax of eight mills on the dollar, or the equivalent of about five dollars for every resident family, but the majority could not complain that they were being forced to contribute to a subsidy that they had voted against.[123]

The negative railway vote in St Romain did not necessarily mean that residents were less attuned to "progress" than the Scots to the south – they were simply further from the International station at Milan. Even though the county was already committed to subsidizing Pope's line in 1873, St Romain had made overtures that year to the rival Sherbrooke and Kennebec Railway by voting a conditional subsidy of $5,000. The conditions were that the track cross the municipal boundaries and that a station be built within those boundaries, but what became known as the Quebec Central Railway passed some twenty miles north-west, on the opposite side of the St Francis River.[124] To gain access to the nearest station at the village of Disraeli, 139 residents of Winslow North petitioned, with others from Lambton, Price, Stratford, and Aylmer, for ten miles of new road across Price and Stratford.[125] The estimated cost was $3,000 for the road and $2,000 for bridges, but the government's commitment to the so-called colonization railways left it without funds for the very colonists who wished to gain access to them.

Some idea of the internal dissension caused by the railway issue can be gained from regulations passed by Winslow North's council to maintain order in its meetings. As early as 1870 it was not only decreed that members of the audience were to refrain from smoking and not to talk unless requested to do so, on pain of a two-dollar fine, but they were to pay a dollar simply for attendance and two dollars if they wished to bring forward a proposal.[126] It is doubtful that these rather undemocratic restrictions were enforceable, for in 1876 the councillors resolved that people would be allowed to speak, presumably free of charge, but only so long as they did so politely and with permission.[127] Prior to construction of railways through the district, accountability had been guaranteed by simply having each councillor manage the roads in his own arrondissement, but by 1878 council decreed that all future votes were to be recorded.[128] If the International taught a lesson in community-wide government, however, it also demonstrated how that government could be used as an unwilling agent of forces that were virtually unaccountable to local citizens.

This study is focused on the township/parish because that is the level at or for which official records have traditionally been organized. Township boundaries were arbitrary lines drawn on a map often long before the first settlers had arrived and should not be allowed to exaggerate or to limit our conception of community.[129] The geographical area enclosed by those boundaries was nevertheless originally meant to be developed by a township "leader" and his group of "associates," and presumably to adopt the New England model of local self-government. Town meetings were not encouraged by British officials, but each township did have its own justice of the peace, captain of militia, and eventually its own school commission and municipal council. Furthermore, parish boundaries tended to conform to those of the township. These local institutions would inevitably create a certain sense of community at the township level, and Winslow's unusual division into two municipalities in 1858 simply recognized the geographic and cultural barriers that separated north from south. But the two official communities remained to some extent artificial constructs, with forces pulling at them from several directions.

Winslow North was in part an extension of Lambton Township, because it failed to develop a significant service centre of its own and because its main access to the outside world led in that direction. The marriage patterns illustrated in Map 17 reveal an orientation toward the parishes further north, but a strong internal cohesiveness as well.[130] Evidence of that cohesiveness is still more marked in the baptismal records, for in 1869–71 only 13 per cent (twenty-eight of 224) of godparents were non-residents, with a slight increase to 17 per cent (twenty-eight of 164) in 1878–80. In Winslow South the small French-Canadian settlement was obviously a continuation of the one in Stratford Township, and it remained part of that same parish. Its Scots neighbours were a more self-contained community, however, because of the slow development of the parent settlement in neighbouring Lingwick and because Stornoway's cross-roads location and

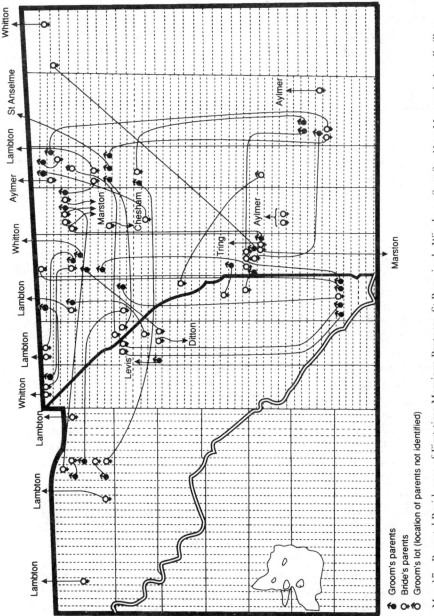

Map 17 Parental Residences of First-time Marriage Partners, St Romain de Winslow, 1850–80. *Note*: Map excludes all village marriages except those to farmers' sons or daughters outside the village.

Legend:

- **f⊙** Groom's parents
- **O** Bride's parents
- **O⋅f⊙** Groom's lot (location of parents not identified)

Labels on map: Whitton, St Anselme, Lambton, Aylmer, Whitton, Lambton, Whitton, Lambton, Whitton, Lambton, Lambton, Lambton, Marston, Chesham, Aylmer, Aylmer, Tring, Ditton, Levis

water-power attracted a number of merchants, millers, and hotel-keepers. Indeed, Stornoway's status meant that Winslow South had its own extension in the frontier settlement of southeastern Whitton.

While social ties extended beyond township boundaries to some degree, there were also localized communities within the various townships. More properly, for the Scots, township boundaries were irrelevant to most of these subcommunities, which consisted of local districts overseen by the church elders. The Scots generally identified themselves as from a certain district rather than a township, and each district had its own cemetery, suggesting that the sense of community implied communion with the dead as well as with the living.[131] With most of the old farm buildings and many of the Protestant churches in the upper St Francis district now demolished, these carefully maintained cemeteries are the last testimony to the Scots presence in this region. The French Canadians too had their "arrondissements," generally equivalent to the different ranges of a township, and, as in the seigneuries, it was at this very localized level that many fundamental activities of community life took place.[132] Thus we saw that Winslow North's road and school taxes (or the equivalent in labour or goods) were collected and put to use by the municipal councillors and school commissioners, who informally represented each local area.

Local districts may have had varied boundaries for church, school, or municipal government, but they were nevertheless socially cohesive neighbourhoods. The settlement pattern in the older American-settled townships further south was widely dispersed, with roads running in all directions, but the roads of Winslow and area were laid out according to the orderly mind of the government surveyor, and lots were defined at a much smaller scale than elsewhere in the region. As a result, families in both the Scots and French-Canadian communities lived in densely settled pockets, isolated from each other by swamps and large outcroppings of rock. One small enclave was so far removed that it was popularly known as "California."[133]

An understanding of social dynamics at the township/parish level therefore requires some appreciation of at least two other community levels, that of the local subdistrict and that of the subregion, in this case the upper St Francis district. However, it is more important to recognize the varying levels of social, economic, and political organization than to identify the single most significant one. Each level of analysis, including that of the family, offers its own insights, and each is enriched by an understanding of the dynamics within the other levels.[134]

Conclusion

Social scientists have frequently commented on the need to put theories of community development to the test with local studies and just as frequently lamented the failure of local historians to place their studies in a broader theoretical context.[1] In this volume the various aspects of Winslow's development have been examined from a comparative perspective where possible, but there has been no attempt to apply a particular theory of settler societies because none appears to exist that would suit our purposes in this study. This brief conclusion will nevertheless examine the degree to which several general concepts help to illuminate the analysis undertaken in the preceding chapters.

The writings of Frederick Jackson Turner have ensured that no study of settlement communities in North America can ignore the impact of the frontier. Louis Hartz attempted to shift the balance in the other direction by stressing the importance of the European background, but most historical geographers retain their environmental biases. Thus James Lemon argues that the traditional sense of community broke down on the frontier, while Graeme Wynn writes more cautiously that "the fine edge of tradition was blunted and meaning rubbed off in the act of relocation."[2]

Cole Harris has recently acknowledged that "the fragmented, discontinuous human geography" of British North America fostered "distinctive local cultures for generations,"[3] but his own theory of settlement stresses the common elements of European settler societies. Thus, Harris argues that the western European institutional framework was stripped to its bare essentials on the settlement frontier, with the result that "a society in which people knew their place within a finely graded hierarchy had given way to a far more atomistic society built around the nuclear family in possession of the means to provide its subsistence."[4] The debt to Turner is obvious, but Harris claims further that the frontier's impact was not permanent because the old structures of class inequality re-emerged as land became less available and markets more accessible. Lower Canada had reached this stage early in the nineteenth century, and so "land values rose, the young were forced into non-agricultural activities, and society in the older *côtes* became more stratified."[5]

What, then, of society on the marginally arable frontier of the mid-nineteenth century and beyond? The image Harris paints of the exploited French-Canadian settlers in Petite Nation is very different from his rather idyllic description of their self-sufficient and inde-pendent forbears in the St Lawrence Valley.[6] Harris's theory was con-ceived for national societies in their early formative years, not for small districts settled long after the North American frontier had swept westward; nevertheless, the Winslow of our study period shared the basic frontier conditions of cheap land and isolation from markets that Harris describes. In addition, its social structures were similar to those he attributes to the earlier frontier experience. An exami-nation of how the "simplification" model fits and does not fit Winslow may be a poor test of its general validity, but it should at least help us to appreciate how and why the "typical" North American coloni-zation experience was altered at this time, in this place.

Winslow's Scots represent a better test case for Harris's theory than the Irish Protestant settlers he studied in early-nineteenth-century Mono Township, because rural Ulster had already evolved in an essentially individualistic direction prior to migration.[7] On the Isle of Lewis, in contrast, one minister reported as late as 1833 that his parishioners lived in "detached villages, having a population varying from 40 families downwards."[8] Here there were no long-term leases encouraging family-based independence as in Ulster, the beach-front crofts were designed for the quasi-communal activities of fishing and kelp-gathering, and the livestock was herded together during the summer on the hill-side shielings.

Francis Thompson describes the organization of labour in the crofting township: "A working unit of four men was deemed the minimum to ease the progress of, say, the work of digging at a rate which would be quicker than four men working on their own and in isolation. They could also combine to form a Gaelic farm-team for planting, harvesting and dipping sheep. Similarily, a boat-team of four men was needed to haul a boat above the water-line or to pull on the oars when at sea."[9]

Thompson also notes that each crofting community had one or more persons regarded as tradition-bearers. Gatherings known as "ceilidhs" were occasions "when memories were revived, when the lineage of the folk of the township was re-stated, when the bards and singers were given the chance to freshen up old songs and poetry with yet another airing, and when the young were gradually made aware of their responsibilities to their families and to the community at large."[10]

As already noted, however, much of the traditional Gaelic culture had been undermined by military conquest, evangelical religion, and the crofting system itself. In contrast to the communal basis of traditional peasant land-holding and agriculture, each croft was leased and supposedly exploited by a single family. The family therefore had to keep a careful accounting of its income in order to make the annual rent payment to the island's proprietor. After their migration to Winslow, the Lewis crofters settled on fifty-acre lots strung along straight roads and farmed their individual homesteads without becoming deeply involved in the local forest-based economy. These farms were expanded somewhat over the years but ultimately passed on to a single son rather than being subdivided or even mortgaged to compensate other offspring.

As with the several settler populations that Harris has studied, the frontier experience of the upper St Francis district clearly strengthened the Scots nuclear family as a social structure. But that family was rather unique at its mature stage, when it included offspring who would have long since flown the nest in most other Western societies. Young men in particular became seasonal labourers who had no means of establishing families of their own in the area and whose wages, in true Highland fashion, helped to support the parental family on its subsistence-oriented farm. If the Scots settlers remained remarkably persistent under such conditions, it must have been largely because of their attachment to kin and community, as well as a strong desire to resist permanent proletarianization.

Harris's model takes into account the obsession with family-based economic independence, but it assumes that the land provided a sufficient livelihood, and it fails to explain the high degree of cultural retention or even the early establishment of churches and schools. The incessant religious feuding may have been a symptom of frontier dislocation, but it appears to have been a fundamental characteristic of the Presbyterian church in long-established communities as well. Certainly, religion lost little of its influence in the transatlantic crossing, and many similar chords are struck by Robert Ostergren's revealing study of Swedish settlements in Minnesota, with its emphasis on the church as the key agency of cultural transfer.[11] A recent study suggests further that the pull of the Lutheran church in Minnesota and Wisconsin was the main reason that the Norwegians who had settled near Winslow uprooted themselves during the 1850s.[12] Schools, unlike the church, were an instrument of assimilation to the norms of North American society, but their success among the Scots cannot be explained without reference to the educational revolution already taking place in Lewis.

Harris's thesis stresses also the egalitarian nature of society during the settlement phase of development, when land was plentiful and markets scarce. Aside perhaps from the Civil War era, agricultural markets were not readily available to the Winslow farmers, and, as in New France, land was worth little more than the annual labour invested in it, even if it was in short supply. Material conditions therefore failed to favour an agricultural élite, and it is not surprising that the Winslow Scots community remained socially unstratified. This aspect of Harris's thesis therefore appears to fit nicely at first glance, but there remains the question of the European background. Harris interprets the frontier's impact on Old World class structure to be considerably more radical than on the family, for in the former case a historical process was temporarily reversed, while in the latter it was simply accelerated. As we saw in chapter 1, however, crofter society in Lewis was itself basically egalitarian. Thus there was actually little change on the Winslow frontier. Their crofter background may not be the basic reason that a social hierarchy failed to develop among the Scots in Winslow, but it does help to explain why they would remain in a district that provided little scope for such an option.

As with the Scots, more needs to be known about the background of the French Canadians who moved to Winslow before we can assess the full social impact of frontier conditions. The habitants of Lauzon clearly had a less egalitarian socioeconomic structure than the Highland crofters, but without the extremes of wealth and poverty found in most European peasant societies. And characteristic as the nuclear family structure was for Winslow's French Canadians, they too clearly transferred kin and community ties from their home parishes.

Finally, this research on Winslow does not support Christian Morissonneau's argument that there were "deux mondes religieux ruraux québécois," one in the St Lawrence Valley and one in the Laurentian-Appalachian plateau.[13] The initial rebelliousness over the location of St Romain's church site was typical of the old parishes as well whenever population pressures forced their subdivision. Once a resident curé was finally appointed, his authority became strong enough to prevent the bitter feuds that divided the Scots community for many years. Indeed, the curé's dominant status may have enabled him to undermine popular customs on the frontier,[14] but this process was also taking place in the older parishes, as in the Highlands. Certainly, the contrasting ecclesiastical structures of Winslow's two ethnic groups did affect settlers' daily lives.

Without studies on the progress of the schools and municipal government systems in the older seigneurial communities after mid-century, it is impossible to judge whether those of St Romain were significantly slower to develop. To the extent that they were, it is likely that poverty played a greater role than did frontier conditions per se. Cultural values were also of considerable importance, for if the Scots placed more emphasis on educating their children than did the French Canadians, that impulse appears to have originated with their Bible-centred evangelicalism. Also, the cultural predisposition for Scots sons to remain at home for at least part of the year until they were well into their twenties may explain why their younger brothers could remain in school considerably longer than their French-Canadian counterparts. The fact that the French Canadians took fuller advantage of the forest resource than did the Scots is another indicator of the key role played by cultural background. To emphasize the importance of culture in the broadest sense is not therefore to suggest that one group was more innately "progressive" than the other, nor to resort to all too convenient generalizations about the Protestant ethic.

Harris's version of the frontier thesis is, in the final analysis, not particularly useful for our purposes, in part because it presupposes a stratified home society. Lewis and Lauzon obviously each had a middle class and a growing working class, but, outside the centres of Stornoway and Lévis, the great majority had long been subsistence-oriented farmers relying on supplementary income from seasonal labour in the kelping and lumbering industries, respectively. That delicate balance was upset when kelp lost its commercial value, the timber frontier moved beyond Lauzon, and the wheat and potato crops failed repeatedly. For many of those pushed out as a result, the upper St Francis district offered one of the few remaining opportunities to preserve the limited independence they had clung to in the home parishes. Thus we have an explanation for the successful transfer of community-based institutions such as the church, a transfer that does not conform to Harris's model.

As already noted, that model was devised for earlier settler societies, and the late timing of Winslow's settlement was crucial to the rapid appearance of its secondary social institutions. School commissions and municipal councils were, for example, imposed by a state bureaucracy that first extended its tentacles to the local level during the 1840s. Indeed, Winslow was, to a degree, the product of bureaucratic design. The state sanctioned the province-wide campaign that drew settlers' attention to the upper St Francis district, financed the colonization roads that brought them there, surveyed the small fifty-acre grants that retarded their agricultural expansion, and leased most of the land to an externally based lumber company which stripped the area of its most valuable natural resource. In some respects, then, Winslow's colonization is less representative of the westward-moving wave of European-origin settlement than it is of capitalist exploitation of the so-called Third World.[15] From this point of view, the inhabitants of Winslow would have to be seen not only as colonists, but, paradoxically, as the colonized as well.

It was from precisely this perspective that Normand Séguin applied to Quebec's northern colonization frontier the development-of-underdevelopment theory originally conceived by scholars studying Latin America. Séguin argues that large-scale forest companies favoured, or at least tolerated, settlement in the more remote districts of the province, such as the Saguenay, because it provided them with a captive source of seasonal labour and agricultural produce. Agricultural development was in turn retarded by the necessity felt by settlers to work for these companies during the winter in order to offset the low prices offered for their produce.[16] I suggested in an earlier study that the agri-forestry model is not entirely appropriate for the upper St Francis district because there was no strong tie between the economy of the settlers and the lumber monopoly's operations, which could not begin to support the labour and agricultural market needs of the local population.[17] The additional research described in chapter 5 of this study only confirms my position, for we see that the Scots depended on wages earned by older offspring working outside the district, while French-Canadian heads of household sought external employment as well.

Part of Séguin's analysis is predicated on the domination of outside capitalist interests through the agency of the local petite bourgeoisie, but more relevant to the situation in Winslow is Bouchard's hypothesis that in situations of disarticulation between market economy and local society the petite bourgeoisie itself becomes marginalized.[18] Thus our examination of the local religious, educational, and municipal structures failed to uncover a true political élite in either of Winslow's communities.

Outside domination was more direct in Winslow, for John Henry Pope did not need the local council when he could manipulate the county level of government into forcing residents to subsidize his International Railway. Furthermore, Pope did not rely heavily on the support of the local clergy, for the district's priests helped to organize

the petitions against the lumber monoply with which he was intimately involved, and we saw that he did not hesitate to risk votes by
seizing the property of the popular Reverend McDonald in 1878.
Indeed, if the local petite bourgeoisie had been less marginalized, it
might have organized more effective political opposition to Pope's
exploitation of the district through the lumber monopoly and the
railway tax.

The failure of the settlers to develop their own oppositionist movement – or even to desert Pope's political party in large numbers –
may reflect the success of church and school in promoting a submissive attitude toward constituted authority. This study has not
attempted to deny that such was a principal aim of these two institutions or that they succeeded to a certain extent. Winslow, however,
was part of a recently settled, culturally divided district, where mere
economic survival was a priority and where political patronage could
be distributed to considerable effect. Furthermore, French-Canadian
farmers did sign petitions protesting against the lumber monopoly
and the railway tax; those of both communities did squat on crown
land, trespass on company timber berths, and reject clerical authority
on more than one occasion; and the Scots did repudiate the forces
of law and order by sheltering the fugitive Donald Morrison for close
to a year. Under these circumstances it would seem less accurate to
speak of "social" control than of basic economic and political domination by the forces of industrial capitalism. The very persistence of
a population engaged in subsistence-oriented agriculture represents
a partially successful resistance to the forces of proletarianization. Of
course such resistance could be tolerated, even encouraged, because
it also benefited those industries that relied on a seasonal labour force
as well as precluding the need for social welfare support during periods of economic recession.

The physical environment of Winslow and area would have dictated
a subsistence-oriented, quasi-agrarian livelihood under the best of
political-economic circumstances, but such a mixed, peasant-style
economy could have resulted in something other than impoverishment had the colonists been encouraged to become full participants
in the lumber industry. Because of the strength of the agrarian and
capitalist ideologies in Quebec (and North America), the nationalist
promoters of colonization failed even to consider granting larger
areas of crown land to individual settlers so that they might pursue
the true agri-forestry economy of their counterparts on the frontier
of Finland and northern Sweden.[19]

It would be foolhardy to offer a general theory of settlement developed from a situation as distinctive as that of Winslow and the upper

St Francis district, where the cultural values carried by the colonists were clearly more resistant to change than on North American frontiers that were less isolated from market forces. But the fact that Canada never had a continuous expansive frontier such as lay across much of the United States suggests that the Winslow experience might not be entirely uncharacteristic of that in much of the rest of the country. Only more studies which examine comprehensively the social institutions of settler societies will reveal whether or not this is so.[20]

While the theme of ethnicity is never absent from the preceding chapters, the approach used is not that of the cultural anthropologist: little attempt is made to examine the extent to which specific customs and other elements of folk culture survived the process of migration and historical change. Rather than focusing on the degree to which the crofters in particular became "assimilated" in the new environment, the important point for this study has been the nature of the collective response made by both communities to that environment.[21] In rejecting Turner, therefore, this study does not embrace Hartz, with his emphasis on cultural fragments frozen in time.

Neither is the response of the two communities measured in terms of the progress either one made toward some abstract concept of "modernization." Each group adapted in its own way to the exigencies of a harsh physical and economic environment. If the strategy of the Scots contributed to the eventual disappearance of their community, it does not follow that they were either more or less "successful" than the French Canadians. The question of success depends on the standards one chooses to measure by. As for "progress," the Scots may have more fully entered the North American mainstream by leaving the upper St Francis district, but the nature of their family and community structures makes it hard to argue that while living there they were more individualistic and materialistic than their French-speaking neighbours.

In order to apply general historical and social concepts to the study of any settler society, it is important to understand the nature of the cultural values in the homeland, why and how the colonists migrated, the limitations imposed by the new physical environment, and the nature of the political-economic structures imposed on the community. One should then examine as many facets of that community as possible. If society represents more than the sum of all its parts, then an exclusive focus on one or even several of those parts not only precludes a vision of the whole, it also produces a distorted view of the very parts that are being examined.

Appendixes

Conditions in Lewis, 1836–37

Parish	Population	Arable	Occupiers Employing Labourers, 1831	Occupiers not Employing Labourers, 1831
Barvas	3,326	1,468	5	610
Lochs	3,400	2,500	18	538
Stornoway	6,990	2,700	6	636
Uig	3,400	2,840	33	592
Totals	17,116	9,508	62	2,376

Parish	Other Males 20 yrs +, 1831	Manufactures	Persons on Relief	Needing Assistance
Barvas	92	None	30	All
Lochs	127	50 tons kelp	116	600 families
Stornoway	509	1 rope	200	2,000
Uig	51	Home spinning, 226 tons kelp	50	(no data)
Totals	779		396	

Parish	Advantages of Parish	Crimes since 1832	Disposition to Emigrate
Barvas	Fuel and peaceable character of people	Petty theft from poverty	At least ⅓ if means provided
Lochs	–	None	Yes, young men and women
Stornoway	–	Sheep stealing, a few cases	Cottars and labourers disposed
Uig	Good fishing, plenty of fuel	–	Not disposed

Source: Fullarton and Baird, Remarks, 105, 107, 109, 122–3, 125, 128–9, 131.

APPENDIX B

Conditions in Lewis, 1847

Abstract of Answers to Some of the Queries of the Free Church Committee respecting the Lews (1847)

	1.	7.	6.	12.
	Population	Has the Potato Crop this year failed, and are there now any remaining?	How many Families have regular Employment affording subsistence throughout the year, including the usual produce of the soil they cultivate?	Do you know of any Families, exclusively of ordinary and legal Pauperism, now destitute of Food? If so, state their number.
Stornoway, civil parish	6,500	It has been a complete failure.		Fully 100 families
Knock, or Eye	*1,741	It has failed this year.	All the able-bodied men in the parish have employment; but it is doubtful that this, along with the produce of the soil, will afford them subsistence throughout the year. Wages low, and the price of food high.	12 families

	19.	18.	20.	22.
	Has any remunerative Employment been provided this season? and to what extent?	Do you know any able-bodied Men unemployed who would accept remunerative labour at a distance, if procured for them, and means of transport provided?	Can you suggest any means by which some return might be made by Families now destitute of food, as a remedy against the evils of gratuitous distribution?	Has Sickness been more prevalent than usual since the month of August, and is it on the increase or decrease?
Stornoway, civil parish	Employment is extensively given by the proprietor, which, in ordinary years, would be remunerative; but, owing to the high prices of provisions this year, is inadequate to support a family.	Able-bodied men are generally employed.	We are aware of no means at present.	Sickness has doubtless been more general; but not on the increase.
Knock, or Eye	The proprietor has provided employment for many; others have fishing; but since wages are low, it is likely most of the people, when the tilling of the ground comes on, will require assistance.	None. All the able-bodied men are either employed in fishing, or by the proprietor.	None	Sickness has been more prevalent this season than it has been for some time past. It is on the decrease. The want of food was not the cause of it.

	1.	6.	7.	12.
	Population	How many Families have regular Employment affording subsistence throughout the year, including the usual produce of the soil they cultivate?	Has the Potato Crop this year failed, and are there now any remaining?	Do you know of any Families, exclusively of ordinary and legal Pauperism, now destitute of Food? If so, state their number.
Back	*1,571	One-third.	Completely; but some individuals have tried to keep a few barrels for seed.	26 families
Barvas	2,038	None	Failed much; but about 34 families use them hitherto as food.	23 families now destitute, and 38 families more will be destitute a month hence.

	18. Do you know any able-bodied Men unemployed who would accept remunerative labour at a distance, if procured for them, and means of transport provided?	19. Has any remunerative Employment been provided this season? and to what extent?	20. Can you suggest any means by which some might be made by Families now destitute of food, as a remedy against the evils of gratuitous distribution?	22. Has Sickness been more prevalent than usual since the month of August, and is it on the increase or decrease?
Back	None	There is employment provided, to a certain extent, by the proprietor.	None	Sickness is more prevalent this season than usual. The cause I am not able to describe. The nature is British cholera and measles; the former on the increase, and the latter on the decrease.
Barvas	There are able-bodied men unemployed; but the prospect offered a free passage to such as might be inclined to go south to procure remunerative labour.	There is no employment at present; but there is a prospect of some employment.	None	Measles have been prevalent this season; but no sickness hitherto which might be ascribed to the scarcity of food.

	1.	7.	6.	12.
	Population	Has the Potato Crop this year failed, and are there now any remaining?	How many Families have regular Employment affording subsistence throughout the year, including the usual produce of the soil they cultivate?	Do you know of any Families, exclusively of ordinary and legal Pauperism, now destitute of Food? If so, state their number.
Ness	1,809	It has failed chiefly in half the district. In the other end, towards the Butt, there are some remaining, and used as ordinary food.	The utmost will be 60 or 70 families; but not so many unless the fishing prosper, or the time be good.	40 families. Almost the whole lands on the west side of the Lews being occupied by small tenantry, the population have far more food of *their own growth* (not withstanding the great failure in the potato crop) than the system followed elsewhere in the Highlands and Islands can ever produce.
Carloway	2,000	Almost a complete failure. None used as food; but a few kept for seed.	Almost the whole who are able to work have been always making a livelihood between labour, fishing, and the produce of the soil; but in such a season as this few or none can support their families.	Upwards of 200 persons.

	19. Has any remunerative Employment been provided this season? and to what extent?	18. Do you know any able-bodied Men unemployed who would accept remunerative labour at a distance, if procured for them, and means of transport provided?	20. Can you suggest any means by which some return might be made by Families now destitute of food, as a remedy against the evils of gratuitous distribution?	22. Has Sickness been more prevalent than usual since the month of August, and is it on the increase or decrease?
Ness	Some employment given by the proprietor, and more in prospect. Rate from 10d. to 1s. 2d. per day – too little, the price of food being so high.	The able-bodied men are regular and enterprising fishermen, though often ill remunerated. Last year's fish in still unpaid.	Some females can spin hemp and wool.	Far more prevalent, and on the increase; 42 have died since August, mostly children. Measles (frequently by relapse after it, from too much exposure to cold), acute croup, and British cholera, have been the general type of the sickness.
Carloway	There are a number employed at roads, fishing, &c.; but as the season advances, employment will become more general.	I do not know of any.	Of the destitute, there are very few who could give anything at all.	I cannot ascribe the amount of disease to the want of food; but diseases have been very general – such at typhus fever, influenza, meazles, croup, bloody flux, &c.

	1.	7.	6.	12.
	Population	Has the Potato Crop this year failed, and are there now any remaining?	How many Families have regular Employment affording subsistence throughout the year, including the usual produce of the soil they cultivate?	Do you know of any Families, exclusively of ordinary and legal Pauperism, now destitute of Food? If so, state their number.
Lochs	—	Nearly all failed. Hardly any used as food.	In winter no regular employment; for the rest of the year the people can have regular employ; but it will not this year afford subsistence to themselves and families.	All the ordinary pauper families in the parish are thought to be actually destitute of food, and to be placed in a worse condition under the operation of the late statutory enactment.
Uig	3,500	It has failed entirely. There are no families now using them as ordinary food; and they endeavour to preserve what they have left for seed.	Six tacksmen are comfortably off; and there are, besides, about 100 families that in former years made a livelihood between their fishing and land, but very few this season; the rest eke out a miserable existence.	A considerable number of families, exclusive of paupers, are in want, chiefly from their other crops, besides the potato, having been destroyed by the sea-spray in a storm in July.

* These two form part of the above 6,500.

Source: SRO, HD 6/2, *Uncorrected Correspondence from February to September 1847 Relating to the Measures Adopted for the Relief of Distress in Scotland, 2nd Part.* (London: W. Clowes & Sons, 1847), 143–4.

Note by the Proprietor. – The returns from which the above answers are taken, appear to have been drawn up between the end of December 1846, and the middle of January, 1847; and the Proprietor is indebted to the Convener of the Free Church Committee for having kindly communicated them. At that period the number of labourers employed was 1270, at wages averaging about 50*ol*. per week; but as the season has advanced, and the weather become more favourable, the numbers have been considerably increased, so as to meet, as far as possible, the exigences of every locality throughout the island. The meal distributed up to the early part of March is as follows: –

Meal distributed in the Island of Lews by the Proprietor.

In exchange for labour	2,574	bolls.
In advance for labour, &c.	900	"
For cash	1,807	"
	5,281	
Meal on hand	5,199	
Indian corn, pease, oats, and beans on hand, estimated to meal	3,400	8,599
Total provided bolls		13,890

James Matheson

	19. Has any remunerative Employment been provided this season? and to what extent?	18. Do you know any able-bodied Men unemployed who would accept remunerative labour at a distance, if procured for them, and means of transport provided?	20. Can you suggest any means by which some return might be made by Families now destitute of food, as a remedy against the evils of gratuitous distribution?	22. Has Sickness been more prevalent than usual since the month of August, and is it on the increase or decrease?
Lochs	There is remunerative labour in prospect, but the remuneration is not such as would be necessary to support themselves and families.	There are a great many able-bodied men unemployed; but whether they would accept remunerative labour at a distance, cannot be properly ascertained until the visiting members are come.	I do not know any means by which some return might be made.	The number of deaths has been more than ordinary; but there is no sickness that can as yet be traced to the want of food.
Uig	Nearly 200 persons are employed on a road, and there will be more by and by. Wages too small – 1s. a day the highest.	A goodly number of able young men are willing to be employed anywhere.	There are three modes: – First, on roads from the main road to their own farms or hamlets. Secondly, the women might spin, and the old men might make nets. Thirdly, a great many might be profitably employed in the fishing.	There are several cases of sickness believed to arise from want; but sickness, as yet, is not very general. No medical man in the parish.

APPENDIX C
Vital Statistics, St Romain de Winslow, 1858–82

Year	Ms Census	Parish Reports	Births	Marriages	Deaths	Natural Increase
1858			26	6	5	21
1859			35	3	7	28
1860			35	2	2	33
1861	644*		27	4	10	17
1862			32	3	6	26
1863			29	1	17	12
1864			47	4	16	31
1865			33	5	8	25
1866			31	3	11	20
1867			31	2	3	28
1868			33	2	11	22
1869			40	6	22	18
1870			31	6	18	13
1871	699	690	47	5	11	36
1872		857	28	3	14	14
1873			33	5	15	18
1874			38	5	18	20
1875			46	4	18	28
1876			36	9	7	29
1877		831	28	4	14	14
1878		†	36	13	11	25
1879		818	32	7	12	20
1880		850	36	6	27	9
1881	867	829	33	7	16	17
1882		787	44	7	13	31

* The mixed-up order of the families enumerated makes it impossible to determine exactly how many French Canadians to subtract as residents of Winslow South. The locations of most families could be identified, however.

† The figure of 1,025 given for this year appears to include Whitton Township, also served by the curé of St Romain.

Abbreviations

AAS	Archives de l'archevêché de Sherbrooke
AETR	Archives de l'évêché de Trois-Rivières
ANQQ	Archives nationales du Québec à Québec
ANQS	Archives nationales du Québec à Sherbrooke
CGQ	*Cahiers de Géographie Québécois*
CHA	Canadian Historical Association
CHR	*Canadian Historical Review*
CO	Colonial Office
CPRH	*Canadian Papers in Rural History*
EMR	*Ecclesiastical and Missionary Record*
ETHS	Eastern Townships Historical Society, Sherbrooke
HFMRFCS	*Home and Foreign Missionary Record of the Free Church of Scotland*
Hs-SH	*Histoire sociale – Social History*
JEH	*Journal of Economic History*
JFH	*Journal of Family History*
JIH	*Journal of Interdisciplinary History*
JLAC	Canada, Province of, *Journals of the Legislative Assembly*
JLALC	Lower Canada, Province of, *Journals of the Legislative Assembly*
MHB	*Material History Bulletin*
MTF	Ministère des Terres et Forêts
NA	National Archives of Canada, Ottawa
NCL	New College Library, Edinburgh
NLS	National Library of Scotland, Edinburgh
NMC	National Map Collection, Ottawa
PP	*British Parliamentary Papers*
PP, IUP	*British Parliamentary Papers*, Irish University Press
RHAF	*Revue d'histoire de l'Amérique française*
RL	Registre de Lettres

RS	*Recherches sociographiques*
SCHEC	Société canadienne d'histoire de l'Église catholique
SPC	Canada, *Sessional Papers*
SPQ	Quebec, *Sessional Papers*
SRO	Scottish Record Office, Edinburgh
SRP	St Romain Presbytery
UCCA	United Church of Canada Archives, Victoria College, Toronto (unless Bishop's University is mentioned)
WMQ	*William and Mary Quarterly*

Notes

1 Robert Gagnon, "La colonisation"; Blanchard, *Le centre*, 101, 107; Morin et al., "Des Cantons-de-l'Est," 252–4.

2 *SPQ*, VII (1873–4), 29; VIII (1874–5), 98; X (1876), 29; XIII (1879), no. 5, 54. The enumerator in 1852 also commented on the early fall frosts and the late spring. See the manuscript census for Winslow Township. On the climate in nearby Maine, see David C. Smith et al., "Climate Fluctuation," 185.

3 Ramsay, *John Ramsay*, 63–87. For a description of the physical geography of the upper St Francis watershed, see Little, *Nationalism*, 15–16.

4 Manuscript census, Winslow Township, 1852.

5 MacLeod, *Settlement*, 5.

6 M.N. MacDonald, *Family Tree*, 15.

7 See Little, *Nationalism*, chapter 4.

8 This is how Willigan and Lynch (*Sources and Methods*, 434–5) define the approach of the French "Annalistes."

9 Katz, *People*; Gagan, *Hopeful Travellers*.

10 On mobility in the Saguenay region, see Bouchard, "L'histoire," and Bouchard and Lavoie, "Le projet."

11 MacFarlane, *Reconstituting Historical Communities*, 35.

12 On the lack of integration between the "demographic" and "sentiments" approaches to the history of the family, see Anderson, *Approaches*, and D.B. Smith, "The Study of the Family," 22.

13 Little, *Nationalism*.

14 The term "peasant" is not entirely appropriate for Winslow's colonists because it implies that they did not own their land. More suitable is the term "yeoman" as defined by Allan Kulikoff in his "Transition to Capitalism" (p. 141): "petty producers who owned the means of production

(as absolute owners) and participated in commodity markets in order to sustain family autonomy and local exchange."

15 One notable exception is Rosemary Ommer, though she too studies marginal areas of Highland Scots settlement. See, for example, her "Primitive Accumulation."

16 Gagan, *Hopeful Travellers*, 163–6.

17 A similar approach is described in Gaffield, *Language*, 191–2.

18 For a brief description of the various files related to land grants in the former Ministry of Lands and Forests of Quebec, see Séguin, *La conquête*, 273–5.

CHAPTER ONE

1 Devine, The *Great Highland Famine*, 212.

2 James Hunter (*The Making of the Crofting Community*) emphasizes the psychological transformation among the landlords after 1745, while Eric Richards (*A History of the Highland Clearances*) stresses the influence of market incentives.

3 Hunter, *Crofting Community*, 12. For a useful brief account of the changing agricultural landscape, see Fenton, *Scottish Country Life*, 1–26. A good general account of the Highland transformation is Youngson, *After the Forty-Five*.

4 See Richards, *Highland Clearances*, 191–3.

5 Macdonald, *Lewis*, 160, 165.

6 Gray, *Highland Economy*, 125, 136–7.

7 Hunter, *Crofting Community*, 18; Gray, *Highland Economy*, 129, 133–4.

8 Gray, *Highland Economy*, 198.

9 On the "potato economy," see Devine, *Famine*, 12–18.

10 Hunter, *Crofting Community*, 30.

11 Alex. Stewart to Seaforth, Stornoway, 21 Feb. 1833; Stewart to Mrs Stewart Mackenzie, Stornoway, 25 June 1833, Seaforth Muniments, GD 46/1/530, SRO.

12 Gray, *Highland Economy*, 155–8; Hunter, *Crofting Community*, 35.

13 Cited in Hunter, *Crofting Community*, 45.

14 Ibid., 46; D. Macdonald, *Lewis*, 97, 127, 160–2. According to Macdonald (*Lewis*, 160) the island's number of summonses for removal increased from a total of approximately 500 between 1780 and 1813 to over 2,300 between 1818 and 1832.

15 *New Statistical Account of Scotland*, Island of Lewis, 121.

16 Hunter, *Crofting Community*, 38.

17 Ibid., 111–13; D. Macdonald, *Lewis*, 57ff, 74, 81–2; V. Macdonald, "On the Agriculture," 164–5; *New Statistical Account*, Lewis, 128–9.

18 Gray, *Highland Economy*, 123–7, 215–19.

19 Cited in Hunter, *Crofting Community*, 37.

20 See Cameron, "Changing Role," 77–87.

21 Hunter, *Crofting Community*, 41, 43.

22 Richards, *Highland Clearances*, 365; D. Macdonald, *Lewis*, 166; Hornsby, "Migration and Settlement," 18.

23 D. Macdonald, Lewis, 166; Murdo McLeod to Mrs Tolme, Glasgow, 26 June 1838, Mackenzie Papers, SRO, GD 403/63/31.

24 Quoted in Epps, "Immigrant File," 5.

25 Macdonald, *Lewis*, 161; PP, IUP, Emigration Series, III (1841), First Report from the Select Committee Emigration, Scotland, 124–5, 174; XX (1839–41), Buchanan's Annual Report for 1838, 39–44; Epps, "Immigrant File."

26 Lawson, "Emigrants," 133–4. Three hundred thirty-four of these families are listed in Lawson, *Register of Emigrant Families*.

27 Lawson, "Emigrants," 129.

28 For details see Little, *Nationalism*, 53–5.

29 *PP*, IUP, Emigration Series, XXII (1843–53), 10; Smout and Levitt, *State*, 243. Lawson *(Register)* identifies only ten families as having arrived in 1842 and fourteen in 1843. In both years nearly all were from Barvas.

30 Smout and Levitt *(State*, 239, 248) state that most systematic attempts to encourage Hebridean emigration in 1839–42 originated with the landlord of North Uist and part of Skye, in co-operation with the trustees of the fund established for the relief of Highland destitution in 1836–7.

31 Seaforth to Hugh Cameron, Colombo, Ceylon, 31 Oct. 1839, Seaforth Muniments, 9/6, GD 46, SRO. Seaforth did cling, however, to the unrealistic hope that someone would advance him £150,000 to enable him to consolidate his debts. Seaforth to Wm. Murray, Esq., Colombo, 15 Oct. 1839, ibid., 109.

32 Greenberg, *British Trade*, xi, 170, 201, 213.

33 *PP*, IUP, Emigration Series, XXII, 423; MG 11, CO 384/75, 155; CO 384/76, 40; CO 384/77, 239; CO 384/81, 185; CO 384/83, 146, NA.

34 Hunter, *Crofting Community*, 52.

35 Ibid., 53.

36 Quoted in D. Macdonald, *Lewis*, 126.

37 Robert Graham to Sir, Stornoway, 14 April 1837, Highland Destitution Records, 1783–1851, HD 7/9, 103–6, SRO; D. Macdonald, *Lewis*, 126.

38 D. Macdonald, *Lewis*, 127. There is no evidence of a sharp increase in Highland mortality in 1836–7. Flinn, *Scottish Population*, 36.

39 Macdonald, *Lewis*, 127; Flinn, *Scottish Population*, 431–2; Flinn, "Malthus, Emigration, and Potatoes," 56; Hunter, *Crofting Community*, 54; Devine, *Famine*, 57–63.

40 Ibid., 33–40, 151–61, 301–2, 307.

41 Ibid., 57–63. Flinn *(Scottish Population*, 524) speculates that the high child mortality in Lewis was caused by reduced resistance to disease,

but there were no epidemics in the worst-hit parish of Uig from 1846 to 1850. Devine, *Famine*, 312.

42 For details on the provision of relief, see Devine, *Famine*, 111–45.

43 D. Macdonald, *Lewis*, 42; J. Macdonald, "Agriculture," 157; *PP*, XXVI (1851), Report to the Board of Supervision by Sir John M'Neill, G.C.B., on the Western Highlands and Islands (hereafter McNeill Report), 917–18; Highland Destitution Reports. Edinburgh Section. Private Papers, 14, NLS.

44 Macdonald, "Agriculture," 157.

45 Highland Destitution Reports, Glasgow sect. 1848–50, 8th Report, App. 9, 61, Stornoway, 27 July 1848, NLS.

46 McMichael, "Potato Famine," Appendix F.

47 Highland Destitution Reports, Glasgow sect. 1848–50, 8th Report, App. 9, 56; 10th Report, App. 4, 10, Glasgow, 14 Nov. 1848; 11th Report, Report on Outer Hebrides, Aug. 1849, 15–16, NLS; Devine, *Famine*, 100–2. D. Macdonald (*Lewis*, 40) and J. Macdonald ("Agriculture," 157) both claim that Matheson borrowed only £30,000.

48 Matheson's expenditure is calculated on the basis of the cost of clearing the new lots in addition to the £412 his factor claimed was spent on the old crofts up to 31 March 1851. See McNeill Report, 1042–6. According to Devine (*Famine*, 89), Matheson spent £30,000 on meal and seed for crofters between 1846 and 1851 and £259,248 on improvements and emigration during the 1840s and 1850s. Smout (*Century*, 70) states that Matheson spent a total of £384,000 on Lewis before his death in 1878.

49 Highland Destitution Reports, Glasgow sect., 1848–50, 8th Report, App. 9, 56, 11th Report, 11; Report on Outer Hebrides, Aug. 1849, 15–16, NLS.

50 Devine, *Famine*, 329.

51 McMichael, "Potato Famine," Appendix F.

52 Devine, *Famine*, 212.

53 D. Macdonald (*Lewis*, 41) says that the Caithness herring fishery came to the rescue, but Devine (*Famine*, 164–5) suggests that it did not recover until 1852.

54 Hunter, *Crofting Community*, 73–5.

55 Ibid., 86–7; HD4/5, 151, Highland and Island Emigration Society List of Emigrants, SRO.

56 Hunter, *Crofting Community*, 76–7; Flinn, "Malthus," 57; Flinn, *Scottish Population*, 437.

57 HD 4/5, 151; C.E. Trevelyan to Sir J. Matheson, 3 July 1855, Highland Emigration Society Letterbook no. 4, 29, HD 4/4, SRO.

58 Hornsby, "Migration," 19; Morgan, "Poverty," 92. A few settlers moved from Cape Breton to the upper St Francis district. For example, the forty-five-year-old wife (unnamed) of Donald McIver, "lately from Cape Briton," was buried at Lingwick in 1852. Lingwick Register, Presbyterian Church and Church of Scotland, 1849–53, ANQS.

59 McNeill Report, 919. For other examples of landlords' enticements to emigrate see Richards, *Highland Clearances*, chap. 20.

60 A.C. Buchanan to Sir, Que., 26 Nov. 1851, *PP*, 1852, xxxiii, 566–8; Hunter, *Crofting Community*, 81; Hutchinson, "Emigration," 19–20.

61 Devine, *Famine*, 213–18. Eviction notices, which had dropped from 382 in 1849 to 141 in 1850, jumped again to 657 in 1851; ibid., 329.

62 For details on the removal of several communities, see D. Macdonald, *The Tolsta Townships*, 17–19, 137–8; D. Macdonald, *Lewis*, 162; Hunter, *Crofting Community*, 80.

63 Smout, *Century*, 70.

64 *PP*, 1852, xxxiii, 568; 1852–3, lxviii, 475; 1857, Session 2, xxviii, 156; D. Macdonald, *Lewis*, 41–2; J. Macdonald, "Agriculture," 157; Devine, *Famine*, 206, 213, 325. Mackenzie (*Highland Clearances*, 147) claims that 2,231 left for Canada between 1851 and 1863 at a cost to Matheson of £11,855.

65 A.C. Buchanan to Sir, Que., 26 Nov. 1851, *PP*, 1852, xxxiii, 568. Buchanan later stated that 600 of the immigrants went to the Eastern Townships; A.C. Buchanan to A.N. Morin, Que., 12 Feb. 1852, Civil Secretary's Correspondence (Incoming), Vol. 308, no. 298, rg 4c1, na. According to Devine (*Famine*, 219), 855 emigrants left Lewis aboard three ships in May and June.

66 James Matheson to A.C. Buchanan, Stornoway, Island of Lewis, 10 Oct. 1851, *PP*, 1852, xxxiii, 568.

67 Devine (*Famine*, 220) claims that they were maintained by Scottish charities in Hamilton before eventually finding work on railways. Construction on the Great Western had begun the previous year; McCalla, *Trade*, 63. The names of the Lewis emigrants are scattered throughout Whyte's *Dictionary*. These families settled too late to be included in the 1851–2 census, but the 1861 enumerator for subdistrict 2 of Huron Township identified many of the residents as Lewis-born. Only the local county or the outside country of origin was recorded for the other three subdistricts.

68 Clarke and MacLeod, "Concentration," 107–13.

69 Memorial of J.G. Robertson et al., Sherbrooke, 30 Jan. 1852; A.C Buchanan to A.N. Morin, Que., 12 Feb. 1852; S.M. Taylor to A.C. Buchanan, Melbourne, 24 Feb. 1852, rg 4c1, na.

70 Unidentified newspaper clipping attached to 4 Feb. 1852 minutes, Minute Book, Montreal St Andrew's Society.

71 Devine, *Famine*, 220; *Home and Foreign Record of the Free Church of Scotland* (Edinburgh), July 1852, ucca. Only sixty-three of the 828 railway labourers enumerated in the spring of 1852 were Scots, while 674 were from Ireland. For an analysis based largely on this census, see Kesteman, "Les travailleurs."

72 Seccareccia, "Immigration," 136.

73 Gray, *Fishing Industries*, 85–7, 110, 115–17; Hunter, *Crofting Community*, 87, 125; Devine, *Famine*, 206, 222–3.

74 Devine, *Famine*, 206; Memorial of Inhabitants of Winslow and Whitton to Joseph Cauchon, Winslow Manse, 3 Sept. 1855, RG 4C1, 1855, no. 2508, NA.

75 Presbyterian Church of Canada (Free Church), Presbytery of Montreal, Minutes, Vol. 1, 23 Jan. 1856, UCCA.

76 Donald Campbell to Dr M'Lauclan, Winslow, 9 May 1872, in *The Free Church of Scotland Monthly Record* (Edinburgh [no date]), 211, UCCA.

77 This account was written by Mary's grand-nephew, John Patterson, and published in the *Stornoway Gazette* (Lewis), 7 May 1963. John lived in Barvas but had worked in Scotstown, Quebec, for several years. See McLeod, *The Milan Story*, 84–7.

78 Devine, *Famine*, 47.

79 Lawson, "Emigrants," 129. On estimated emigration from the two parishes, see Devine, *Famine*, 69–70, 79–80.

80 Cited in Devine, *Famine*, 220. On the Barvas emigrants see Lawson, "Emigrants," 129.

81 Cited in Devine, *Famine*, 214.

82 For a more comprehensive picture, see Table 1.8.

83 Bennett-Knight, "Folkways," 51.

84 Rosemary Ommer ("Highland Scots") has traced Scots kinship in Cape Breton Island and Newfoundland through Gaelic patronymics, but there is no written record of these for the Lewis settlers in Quebec.

85 Blake, "Distribution," 156–8.

86 For a revisionist interpretation of the nature of clan ties and the role of names in the Highlands, see Dodgshon, "Pretence."

87 Molloy, "No Inclination," 240

88 Elliott, *Irish Migrants*, 6.

89 Gray, *Highland Economy*, 144. See also his "Famine," 361–2.

90 *PP*, IUP, Emigration Series, III, 174.

91 McNeill Report, 917; Gray, *Highland Economy*, 204–5. Devine (*Famine*, 4–9) stresses the socioeconomic differentiation not only between crofters and cotters but also within the crofter class, but he admits that the kelping areas were quite homogeneous in this respect.

92 Fullarton and Baird, *Remarks*, 68; Cooper, *Road*, 74.

93 Allan Greer ("Fur-Trade Labour") reaches a similar conclusion concerning the impact of the fur-trading companies on the habitants of the Sorel area of Lower Canada. For a brief analysis of the various forms the development-of-underdevelopment thesis has taken, see Goodman and Redclift, *From Peasant to Proletarian*, 29–43.

94 This is also the thesis of recent works on the earlier, more voluntary emigration. See McLean, "Peopling Glengarry County" and "Achd an Righ," and Bumsted, "Scottish Emigration," 79.

95 Richards, *Highland Clearances*, 11.
96 See, for example, F. Ouellet, *Lower Canada*, and Paquet and Wallot, "Crise agricole." For a critical summary of the debate see LeGoff, "Agricultural Crisis." For the more recent interpretation, see McInnis, "Reconsideration," and Courville, "La crise."
97 Armstrong, *Structure and Change*, 72–4.
98 See S. Gagnon, *Quebec and Its Historians*, chapter 5.
99 See Kelly, "Wheat Farming," and McCallum, *Unequal Beginnings*, chapters 2 and 3.
100 A recent summary of their position can be found in Wallot, "L'impact du marché." For brief surveys of the timber industry's history see Armstrong, *Structure and Change*, 115–22; and Garon, "Le Bas-Canada," 295–7, 115–22.
101 Courville, "Villages and Agriculture," 145–6, "L'habitant canadien," 185–6, and "Un monde rural."
102 Paquet and Wallot, *Lower Canada*, 19. See also Paquet and Wallot, "Structures sociales," and Gadoury, "Les stocks."
103 Louise Dechêne ("Observations," 198) feels that few potatoes were cultivated in the Quebec district before 1816.
104 Courville, "La Crise," 204. Oats production more than doubled, to 7,239,000 minots, while barley production tripled. Parker, "Revolution," 190.
105 Lower, *Assault*, 96–7, 105–8; Garon, "La mise," 351.
106 McCalla, "The Wheat Staple," 190.
107 Jones, "French-Canadian Agriculture," 119.
108 RG 1E1, Executive Council, Minute Books (State Matters), 1764–1867, D, 608, 16 Oct. 1845, NA; RG 7, G14, Governor General's Corresp., Vol. 17 & 18, 9,721–9,968, NA; *JLAC*, V (1846), Appendix J, Agricultural Societies.
109 No petitions were discovered in Province of Canada *Journals of the Legislative Assembly* (*JLAC*), between 1844 and 1849, but the Executive Council's minute books refer to one from the inhabitants of Bonaventure County in 1848 (rejected) and two from Robert Christie, MPP, in 1849 and 1852. One thousand pounds was voted for seed in 1849, but nothing was offered in 1852, despite Christie's claim that families would starve. According to a petition from the potato contractor for the Quebec jail, the Quebec area too had been hit by a crop failure in 1852. RG 1E1, Minute Books, Vol. 1, 355, 6 Dec. 1848; J, 73, 81–2, 5 May 1849; L, 590, 20 Feb. 1852; M, 100, 31 March 1852, NA.
110 Garon, "La mise," 351; Ouellet, Hamelin, and Chabot, "Les prix," 98, 100.
111 Courville, "La crise," 221.
112 Ibid., 197.

113 *JLAC*, VIII (1849), Appendix no. 2, Report of Select Committee on Emigration to the United States (Chauveau Report).

114 R.L. Jones, "French-Canadian Agriculture," 125–6.

115 Courville, "La crise," 197.

116 O'Bready, *Histoire*, 71; Hare, Lafrance, and Ruddel, *Histoire*, 187; *Annuaire de Séminaire Saint-Charles Borromée* (Sherbrooke), 1887–8, no. 13, 290; 1889–90, no. 15, 487; *Le Journal de Québec*, 14 Nov. 1848, 18 Nov. 1848; Canada, manuscript census, 1851–2, Stratford and Garthby Townships.

117 P. Brassard to Mgr Racine, Saint-Romain de Winslow, 27 Nov. 1874, Papiers des Paroisses, Saint-Romain, Correspondance, folio 3; N. Bélanger to Mgr Signay, Bécancour, 28 March 1849, Papiers des Paroisses, Saint-Roman, Hist., folio 7, AAS. The Acadians had colonized St Grégoire in the eighteenth century, after the Seven Years' War, but they were still identified as a distinct group. Thus crown lands agent Arcand wrote in 1848 that rang II SW, lots 15–50, of Winslow had been "pris par les Acadiens." Rapport Général et Statistique de l'État des Chemins et Établissements sous la Surintendance de J.O. Arcand, 24 Dec. 1848, Vieux dossiers, Correspondance, no. 5226, MTF. See also *Stornoway 1858/1983*, 62. On the Acadians in St Grégoire, see Nelson, "La guerre."

118 Pouyez and Lavoie, *Les Saguenayens*, 137–9; Gauvreau and Bourque, "Mouvements migratoires," 185–8.

119 On the construction of this road, see Little, *Nationalism*, chap. 3.

120 My thanks to the Société de généalogie des Cantons de l'Est for identifying these twenty-three birth places. Many of Lambton's pioneer settlers originated from St Henri de Lauzon and from St Charles and St Michel de Bellechasse. Lapointe, *Historique*, 30, 33, 47.

121 The same pattern of prospective marriage partners seeking spouses in their communities of origin has been observed for Bonavista Bay, Newfoundland; Macpherson, "A Model Sequence," 128.

122 Bouchette, *British Dominions*, I, "Lauzon."

123 J.E. Roy, *Histoire*, I, 36–42, 45, 77.

124 Ibid., II, 21, 116.

125 Ibid., 38, 124–5, 130, 355, 373–5, 380–1, 429; IV, 105; V, 207; Caya, "Henry Caldwell," 130–1; Ruddell, *Quebec City*, 119. For comparisons with other seigneurial practices, see Greer, *Peasant, Lord, and Merchant*, 122–33; Noël, "La gestion," 577; and Baribeau, *La seigneurie*, 66–7.

126 J.E. Roy, *Histoire*, III, 136–7, 188–9. On the survival of the aristocratic ethos among the British merchants of Lower Canada, see Couture, "La conquête," 386.

127 J.E. Roy, *Histoire*, III, 270, chap. 4, 5, 23, 32; V, 187. There was also some resistance in the parish of St Henri to the muster of 1807. Ibid., III, 410–12.

128 Noël, "La gestion," 579–81. Compare also the entrepreneurial career of Bathélemy Joliette described in Robert, "Un seigneur."

129 Roy, *Histoire*, III, 427–9; IV, 94–100, 107–8; Héroux, "Sir John Caldwell."

130 Roy, *Histoire*, IV, 298, 377, 389, 393; V, 477, 521–2; Héroux, "Caldwell."

131 Roy, *Histoire*, V, 148–9, 462; *JLAC*, VIII (1849), Appendix YYYY, Seigneury of Lauzon.

132 Roy, *Histoire*, V, 197, 201.

133 The great majority of the rentes in the Bellechasse seigneuries were uniform, at only 1s. 8d, no matter what the size of the roture. Courville, "Rente déclarée," 45, 59–60; Lower Canada, manuscript census, 1831, Bellechasse.

134 On the seigneur's role in opening the back country to settlement, see Jarnoux, "La colonisation," 173–5, and Greer, *Peasant*, 83.

135 Bouchette, *British Dominions*, "Lauzon"; Courville, "Rente déclarée," 206–8.

136 *JLAC*, VIII (1849), Appendix YYYY, Seigneury of Lauzon; Roy, *Histoire*, V, 150–1. Françoise Noël ("La gestion," 572–7) stresses the difficulty of collecting rentes in Christie's upper Richelieu seigneuries.

137 The 1844 census identifies a small part of St Joseph as in Bellechasse County.

138 This is the practice followed by Marvin McInnis in his recent work on Lower Canadian agriculture; see his "Reconsideration," 25. Courville ("Villages and Agriculture," 131–4) follows the much more painstaking method of identifying villages and subtracting their populations from the total but admits that not all those living outside those villages were necessarily farmers.

139 On farm sizes between 1807–12 and 1830–5, see Paquet and Wallot, "Les habitants," 104, and "Stratégie foncière," 568–70.

140 All crops were destroyed by inclement weather in 1833, reducing much of the seigneurie to indigence and necessitating a government grant of £300 for seed. Roy, *Histoire*, V, 357–9.

141 Greer, *Peasant*, 34–6, 206.

142 Héroux ("Caldwell") claims that Caldwell's censitaires supplied most of his lumber from ungranted land on the seigneurie.

143 Bouchard, "L'étude," 568–70; Bouchard, "Les systèmes," 35–60; Greer, *Peasant*, 21, 225–6.

144 Paquet and Wallot, *Lower Canada*, 19, and "Stratégie foncière," 573–4.

145 Dépatie, "La structure."

146 Dessureault, "L'égalitarisme," 389, 399–406.

147 This problem is recognized for the Montreal area in Gadoury, "Les stocks," 141–2.

148 Dessureault, "L'égalitarisme," 393–5.

149 Ibid., 382.

150 See Ruddel, *Quebec City*, 85–9, and "The Domestic Textile Industry," 95–6, 101–2, 108–9, 113.

151 Courville suggests that ties between village workers and agriculturists were becoming more and more tenuous by mid-century. Courville, "Croissances villageoises," 215.

152 *Le Journal de Québec*, 15 July 1848.

153 *JLAC*, VIII (1849), Appendix no. 2, Chauveau Report.

154 Faucher, "Decline," 199.

155 The 1852 manuscript census reveals that most of the Garthby settlers had themselves been born outside Quebec, in Beauport, Ile d'Orléans, Kamouraska, Rivière-du-Loup, and other areas east of the city.

156 The Saguenay region, too, was colonized largely by young families. See St-Hilaire, "Origines," 14, and Bouchard and Larouche, "La dynamique," 383.

157 La Société généalogique, *Les Mariages*, 29; St Romain de Winslow, Parish Registers, Baptism of Vitaline Roy, 8 April 1860.

158 By way of contrast, Adams and Kasakoff ("Migration," 32) suggest that in colonial New England it was rare for people to join extended kin who had moved beyond the sphere of easy geographical interaction.

159 The Irish who settled in Upper Canada's Euphrasia Township generally had to wait until their children were older; Norris, "Migration," 132–3.

160 *JLAC*, VIII (1849), Appendix YYYY.

161 The negative impact of the seigneurs on the agricultural economy is stressed in Greer, *Peasant*, chap. 5; F. Ouellet, "Libéré;" and Courville, "La crise," part 2. Interpretations concerning the seigneurs' impact on early industrial development have been more positive. See, for example, Schulze, "Rural Manufacture"; Noël, "Chambly Mills"; Courville, "Croissance villageoise"; and Robert, "Un seigneur."

CHAPTER TWO

1 Winslow, no. 3, 59501–18, 96817–25, Lower Canada Land Petitions, RG 1 L3L, NA. For a brief description of how the leaders and associates system operated in Lower Canada see McGuigan, "Administration."

2 Winslow, no. 2, 27245–7, 44455, 95118–20, RG 1L3L, NA.

3 Winslow, no. 1, 33752, 73807–9, ibid.

4 See Langelier, *Liste*.

5 For details, see Little, *Nationalism*, chap. 2.

6 The following details are from ibid., chap. 3, which contains more information on the history of the Lambton Road.

7 The following section summarizes ibid., chap. 4, which gives more detailed source references.

8 Report of A.N. Morin, Commissioner of Crown Lands, B7/54, British American Land Company, 54, Upper Canada Land Petitions, RG 1 L3, NA.

9 *JLAC*, VIII (1849), Appendix 2.

10 On the absentee problem in the Eastern Townships, see Little, "Imperialism" and "Colonization."

11 Report on present condition of the roads opened under the direction of J.O. Arcand, Garthby, 12 Oct. 1850, no. 1453, 1850, Vieux Dossiers, Correspondance, MTF.

12 Ibid.

13 Winslow Township, Canada, manuscript census, 1852.

14 Arcand to Jean Langevin, Lac Aylmer, 12 April 1852, no. 544, 1852, Vieux Dossiers, Correspondance, MTF; François Bégin to Mgr. Turgeon, 11 April 1852, cited in *Annuaire de Seminaire Saint-Charles Borromée* (Sherbrooke, 1889–90), no. 15, 500–1.

15 *Stanstead Journal*, 6 May 1852.

16 Memorial of J.G. Robertson, George N. Brooks, and William Brooks, Sherbrooke, 30 Jan. 1852, no. 298, vol. 308, RG 4C1, NA.

17 F.N. Primrose to A.N. Morin, Que., 11 Feb. 1852, no. 298, vol. 308, no. 298, RG 4C1, NA.

18 Montreal, St Andrew's Society, Minutes, vol. 1, 4 Feb. 1852. For a vivid description of the assistance campaign in Fredericton and Saint John for Welsh immigrants in 1819, see Thomas, *Strangers*, 156–71.

19 A.C. Buchanan to A.N. Morin, Que., 12 Feb. 1852, no. 298, vol. 308, RG 4C1, NA; Civil Sec. to J.S. Sanborn, MLA, 14 Feb. 1852, 96, Civil Secretary's Correspondence (Outgoing), RG 4C2, NA. The 1852 enumerator for Brompton Gore reported "very poor" Presbyterian Scots who had settled during the previous two years. Canada, manuscript census, Brompton Gore, 1852.

20 Report of Executive Council Committee, 13 Feb. 1852, no. 298, vol. 308, RG 4C1, NA.

21 S.M. Taylor to A.C. Buchanan, Chief Emigration Agent, Melbourne, 24 Feb. 1852; Buchanan to Morin, Que., 1 March 1852, no. 298, vol. 308, RG 4C1, NA.

22 See an account of his speech to the Sherbrooke meeting in the unidentified newspaper clipping located in Montreal, St Andrew's Society, Minutes, Vol. 1, 4 Feb. 1852.

23 *The Home and Foreign Record of the Free Church of Scotland* (Edinburgh), July 1852, 412, UCCA.

24 Taylor to Buchanan, Montreal, 14 May 1852, no. 298, vol. 308, RG 4C1, NA.

25 The remaining £20 was distributed as seed grain by the Sherbrooke relief committee; ibid.

26 See the comments of the enumerator for Bury in the 1852 manuscript census, as well as Mrs C.M. Day, *History of the Eastern Townships*, 407.

27 Canada, *Census Reports*, 1851–2, 1860–1.

28 Winslow Township, Canada, manuscript census, 1851–2.

29 J.O. Arcand to Jean Langevin, Lac Aylmer, 21 May 1852, no. 807, 1852, Vieux Dossiers, Correspondance, MTF.

30 McIlwraith, "Adequacy."

31 Petition of inhabitants of Winslow and Whitton to Commissioner of Crown Lands, Winslow, 19 July 1853, no. 4430/895, 1852, Vieux Dossiers, Correspondance, NA.

32 Minute Books (1841–67), State Book N, 342, 2 July 1853, RG 1E1, NA.

33 Andrew Russell to A.N. Morin, Quebec, 20 May 1854, [no number], Vieux Dossiers, Correspondance, NA.

34 Channell, *History of Compton*, 121.

35 Memorial of Inhabitants of Winslow and Whitton to Joseph Cauchon, Commissioner of Crown Lands, Winslow Manse, 3 Sept. 1855, no. 2508, 1855, RG 4C1, NA.

36 Ewen McLean to J. Cauchon, Winslow Manse, 12 Sept. 1855; Draft letter to Rev. Ewen McLean, Que., 20 Sept. 1855, ibid.

37 Between 1852 and 1860, location tickets for lots on which settlement conditions were not fulfilled, or full payment made, could be cancelled only by order-in-council. Thereafter, cancellations could simply be ratified by the minister in charge. Bouffard, *Le traité du domaine*, 20, 25.

38 J.O. Arcand to T. Bouthillier, St Olivier du Lac Aylmer, Mal-Maison, 21 March 1850, no. 502, 1850, Vieux Dossiers, Correspondance, MTF.

39 J.O. Arcand to T. Bouthillier, Malmaison, Garthby, 18 May 1849, ibid.

40 Memorial of Inhabitants of Winslow and Whitton to Joseph Cauchon, Commissioner of Crown Lands, Winslow Manse, 3 Sept. 1855, no. 2508, 1855, RG 4C1, NA.

41 J.T. Lebel to E.A. Généreux, Wotton, 8 March 1861, adj. 186, MTF.

42 Report on application for free grants, 30 Jan. 1860; 15 Feb. 1860, adj. 89, MTF.

43 J.T. LeBel to Andrew Russell, Garthby, 30 March 1858, adj. 1431, MTF.

44 J. Bte Bernier to Jean Langevin, St Anselme, 11 May 1853, 3024/623; Petition of inhabitants of Lambton and area, St Vital, 15 May 1853, 3692/378; Hector L. Langevin to Commissioner of Crown Lands, 12 July 1853, 4020/1807; W.L. Felton to Sir, Sherbrooke, 5 Aug. 1853; Jos. Laverrière to Monsieur, Lambton, 25 Oct. 1853, 4517/908, Vieux Dossiers, Correspondance, MTF.

45 Laverrière to Monsieur, Lambton, 25 Oct. 1853, 4517/908, ibid.

46 Petition to the Commissioner of Crown Lands, 10 June 1853, 3583/725, ibid.

47 Cyprien Blanchet to Jean Langevin, Québec, 11 May 1853; Petition of inhabitants of Lambton and area, St Vital, 15 May 1853, 3692/738, ibid. See also Précis of affidavits, etc., in favour of the Dions [n.d.], 3583/ 725, ibid.

48 Winslow, 6 Dec. 1853, 7525/1475, ibid.

49 Winslow Township, vol. 219, no. 31(a)-31(e), RG 1L3, NA. The associates were Joseph Pennoyer, Joseph Gibb Robertson, and Thomas Wiley. At the end of the copper boom in 1866, the association's lands were resold to the parent company. Skelton, *Life and Times*, 14.

50 B7/54, British American Land Company, 54(a)-54(f), RG 1L3, NA; Hector Langevin to A.N. Morin, Quebec, 6 March 1854, no. 1612, 1854, Vieux Dossiers, Correspondance, MTF.

51 R.W. Heneker to L.V. Sicotte, Toronto, 11 May 1858, no. 5061/653, 1858; J.T. LeBel to Commissioner of Crown Lands, Malmaison, Lac Aylmer, 25 Jan. 1856, no. 12703/1593, 1856, Vieux Dossiers, Correspondance, MTF.

52 Jean Dion to LeBel, Winslow, 6 Oct. 1858, no. 12703/1593; R.W. Heneker to A. Russell, Sherbrooke, 31 Dec. 1860, no. 43/11, 1861, ibid. The Dions ultimately acquired the location ticket to only half of a fifty-acre lot. Terrier, Winslow, rang III NW, lot 1, MTF.

53 The prices received by the squatters are not recorded in the crown lands or registry records, but the Chaudière crown lands agent claimed that the association had paid $700 to $1,200 each for several fifty-acre lots on the Lambton side of the boundary. The government itself charged $825 for the 132 acres adjoining the lake where the Quebec and Megantic Land Co. had chosen its projected town site. Sale no. 1238, Jan. 1854, Recettes, Branche Est; O.C. 538, 25 Jan. 1854, Orders-in-Council, Branche Est, MTF. According to one local historian, the land company invested $75,000 in 1863 in a Ham North gold mine which never operated; Gravel, *Mélanges historiques no. 5*, 2.

54 Hunter, *Crofting Community*, 156–9; Macdonald, *The Tolsta Townships*, 138–9.

55 Petition of inhabitants of Winslow and Whitton to the Commissioner of Crown Lands, Winslow, 19 July 1853, no. 4430/895, 1853, Vieux Dossiers, Correspondance, MTF.

56 Alexander McLeod et al. to Sir, Lingwick, 2 Oct. 1851, no. 5843/1185, 1853; Murdoch McLeod to A. Russell, Stornoway, 9 Jan. 1860, no. 658/ 47, 1860; Murdoch McLeod to A. Russell, Winslow, 16 March 1860, no. 3930/311, 1860, Vieux Dossiers, Correspondance, MTF; Terrier, Winslow, rang I SE., SW 1/2 lots 61, 62, and 66, MTF.

57 Alexander McLeod, Elder, to Jean Langevin, Winslow, 6 Sept. 1853, no. 5843/1185, 1853; Andrew Russell to A.N. Morin, Quebec, 20 May 1854

[no no.], Vieux Dossiers, Correspondance, MTF; Terrier, Winslow, rang I SE., lots 63 and 65, MTF.

58 Alexander McLeod, Elder, to Jean Langevin, Winslow, 6 Sept. 1853, no. 5843/1185, 1853, Vieux Dossiers, Correspondance, MTF.

59 Andrew Russell to A.N. Morin, Quebec, 20 May 1854 [no no.], ibid.

60 For their letters, see no. 1495, 18 June 1852; no. 2308, 18 Dec. 1853; no. 471/4434, 9 April 1857; no. 1019/479, 20 April 1857; no. 882/97, 21 Jan. 1858; no. 1188/126, 3 June 1859, ibid.

61 Christopher Dunkin to Vankoughnet, Acton Vale, 23 Feb. 1861, no. 2657/159, 1861, ibid.

62 Petition of inhabitants of Winslow to F. Evanturel, 29 Sept. 1862, no. 14928/1180, 1862, ibid.

63 W. Farwell to Andrew Russell, Robinson, 22 Nov. 1861, adj. 214, MTF.

64 Macpherson, "An Old Highland Parish Register," 108.

65 Bennett-Knight, "Folkways," 46–7.

66 Farwell to Russell, adj. 214, MTF.

67 W. Farwell to G.A. Bourgeois, Robinson, 27 Feb. 1869, adj. 4040, MTF.

68 B. Lupien to John Rolph, Garthby, 14 April 1853, no. 5102/1185, 1853, Vieux Dossiers, Correspondance, MTF.

69 Rod. McLennan to A. Russell, Winslow, 18 June 1859, no. 8507/1352, 1859; 3 Oct. 1859, no. 14235/2837, 1859, ibid.

70 Dépatie, "La structure," 82; Noël, "Seigneurial Survey," 170.

71 MacKay, *Scotland Farewell*, 206; Ommer, "Highland Scots," 221–4.

72 Béatrice Craig notes that the first Acadian settlers in the upper St John Valley marked empty lots as reserves for their offspring. Craig, "Early French Migrations," 236, and "Économie," 123–4.

73 Marc St-Hilaire ("La structuration," 143) notes a similar strategy for the settlers of St Fulgence in the Saguenay region.

74 Séguin, *La conquête*, 182.

75 Léon Gérin wrote, late in the nineteenth century, that the habitants of St Justin in the Trois-Rivières district commonly held two or three pieces of geographically separated land as a permanent part of the family domain. One such lot would produce hay, while another might supply wood. Gérin, "L'habitant," 62–3.

76 Here the definition of a squatter's claim does not include those lots on which the claimant himself ultimately took out a location ticket, for most settlers appear to have occupied their lots before actually registering them.

77 Terrier, Winslow, rang I NW, lot 100; rang I SE, lot 100; rang I NW, lot 79; rang II NW, lot 79, MTF.

78 Daniel Larouche ("Le mouvement," 169) has noted the same phenomenon for the township of Laterrière in the upper Saguenay district.

79 On the "faux colon" phenomenon, see Lower, *Settlement*, 29, 52, 64, 66; and Hamelin, *Les premières années*, 238–9.

80 Hamelin and Roby, *Histoire économique*, 175; Séguin, *La conquête*, 76.

81 J.T. LeBel to Joseph Cauchon, Malmaison, Lac Aylmer, 9 Feb. 1856, no. 1420/226, 1856, Vieux Dossiers, Correspondance, MTF.

82 Because location tickets were not always issued for free grants before assignment of letters patent, there is a slight margin of error in estimating time lapses.

83 In sharp contrast to Winslow, 42 per cent of Laterrière's settlers patented lots within four years of receiving location tickets, though one-third had still not received full title after thirty years. See Larouche, "Le mouvement," 173–4. However, Larouche does not separate settlers from timber operators and other absentees.

84 Lockwood, "Irish Immigrants," 173.

85 Hamelin and Roby, *Histoire économique*, 178.

86 Report of Charles Patton, 23 Jan. 1884, adj. 5120, MTF.

87 Two lots in Patton's first list and one in his second appear to have been included by mistake, for they had already been patented. Statement of Inspection of Lands Unsold, or Sold but not Patented, May 1885, E21, ANQQ.

88 *Weekly Examiner* (Sherbrooke), 17 Oct. 1879, clipping found in Hon. J.H. Pope vs A. McMaster, no. 36, Queen's Bench, St Francis, ANQS.

89 Séguin, *La conquête*, 135–6. Larouche ("Le mouvement," 169, 179) notes that such crown land auctions were common in the upper Saguenay region after 1871.

90 See Little, "Public Policy," 17–18.

CHAPTER THREE

1 N. Godbout to Mgr. Cooke, 8 Sept. 1857, Papiers des Paroisses, Saint-Romain, AAS.

2 Canada, Manuscript Census, Winslow Township, 1861, 1871, 1881. The 1871 and 1881 figures are in close agreement with those in the published census, but 1861 *Census Reports* mistakenly records a population of 749 French Canadians.

3 Strictly material motivations for mobility/persistence are implied by historians such as Heller and Moore in their "Continuity," 240.

4 By 1891 the Scots population had dropped to approximately 500, and the French Canadians to 980. Ethnic origins were not recorded in the published census but can be calculated from religious affiliation.

5 Gravel, *Les Cantons de l'Est*, 204. This theory is usually applied to the region's Anglo-Protestant population as a whole. See, for example, O'Bready, *De Ktiné à Sherbrooke*, 40.

6 Enumeration is said to have missed as many as 20 per cent of census year's deaths in Canada. Emery, "Ontario's Civil Registration," 480–6,

491. There has apparently never been any requirement that a curé record the cause of death. See Bouchard and LaRose, "La réglementation," 82–3.

7 In contrast to the Catholics, few Protestant congregations in the Eastern Townships obeyed the law that required that duplicates of registers be presented annually to civil authorities. For the French Canadians this study used the St Romain duplicates, now found at ANQS, whereas the Winslow Presbyterian registry consulted was in private hands. A microfilmed copy of surviving records has since been deposited at ANQS.

8 W.A. Smith, *Lewsiana*, 96–7; MacDermid, "Religious and Ecclesiastical Life," 207; Devine, *Famine*, 57.

9 David Levine uses a similar approach in a study that compares baptisms in an English parish with names listed in the 1851 census. Levine, "Reliability."

10 A family is considered resident during the year of the birth if it is recorded in the preceding census report or if the baptismal record of the preceding child indicates a Winslow residence. Births identified in the burial records but not in the baptismal records are not considered to have been missed by the curé.

11 Hélène Laforce (*Histoire*, 54–6, 62) has found that women in the Quebec region sometimes gave birth at the home of a close relative, particularly that of their parents.

12 Because the registers fail to identify the parents' domicile in these cases, non-residence had to be inferred from failure to appear in other records.

13 On this problem, see Pouyez and Lavoie, *Les Saguenayens*, 51, and Gautier and Henry, *La population*, 170.

14 In St Romain, of 283 deaths recorded between 1858 and 1880, forty-six were on the day of birth. No more than thirteen of these were reported to be still births, but an additional fourteen were not recorded as having been "ondoyé" (sprinkled) by a secular attendant, as was the custom when death threatened in the absence of a priest to perform the baptism. Of the fourteen St Romain cases in question, four simply recorded that their graves were blessed, and ten more had no ceremony mentioned whatsoever. If these fourteen cases were all still births, as seems likely, they raise the ratio of still births to total deaths from 4.6 per cent to 9.5 per cent. Further, Laforce (*Histoire*, 35) notes that "ondoiements" were commonly performed during the birth process, which suggests that the ratio of still births may have been still higher than we have calculated.

15 Bouchard and Bergeron, "Les rapports annuels." The 1873 report for St Romain stated that the Catholic population was 866 that year, but 690 at the last pastoral visit, a figure very close to the 699 of the domin-

ion census for 1871. The 1881 and 1882 reports for St Romain recorded the population at 850 and 829, respectively, while the census total for 1881 is 867.

16 Gautier and Henry, *La population*. The family-reconstitution method was adapted to England by E.A. Wrigley; see his "Family Reconstitution."

17 On the criticisms that have arisen from this aspect of European family reconstitution, see Dupâquier, *Pour la démographie historique*, 101–9; and Bouchard, "L'histoire démographique," 23–4.

18 See Gaffield, "Theory and Method," 125–6; Bouchard, "L'histoire démographique."

19 The birth intervals in a twentieth-century Gaspé parish were actually shorter than those for St Romain throughout each rank, but the St Romain study group is not restricted to women with larger families and therefore presumably shorter birth intervals. See Charbonneau, "Les régimes," 481–4, and Henripin, *La population*, 85. William Marr ("Family-Size Limitation," 278) has also found relatively uniform spacing between all births for women in the 1852 census of Canada West.

20 On decline of fertility with age, see Gautier and Henry, *La population*, 141–9; Wrigley, *Population and History*, 92–3; and Marcy, "Factors," 311. For eighteenth-century Canada, births per wives' age cohort were: 15–19: 2.5; 20–4: 2.5; 25–9: 2.5; 30–4: 2.4; 35–9: 2.1; 40–4: 1.2; 45–9: 0.2. Averages for the seventeenth century were similar; Charbonneau, "Les régimes," 450. See also the less uniform figures recorded in Henripin, *La population*, 60.

21 Charbonneau, "Les régimes," 462–3. Women in the Hebrides appear to have given birth at a later age than did those elsewhere in Scotland. See Flinn, ed., *Scottish Population*, 343–5.

22 Byers, "Fertility Transition"; Gee, "Early Canadian Fertility Transition," 29; and Marr, "Family-Size Limitation," 279. In the Connecticut Valley at the turn of the nineteenth century, however, the onset of fertility control was reflected by increasing intervals between all births. Temkin-Greener and Swedlund, "Fertility Transition," 36–41.

23 Marr ("Family-Size Limitation," 280) suggests that Presbyterians and Scots-born were more likely than other groups in the Canada West of 1852 to have limited family sizes.

24 Gagan (*Hopeful Travellers*) finds much the same for younger cohorts in Peel County. What he rather confusingly calls a decline in marital fertility on p. 73 he identifies as the product of later marriages on p. 77. The standard index of fertility is the number of children under five years of age per thousand married women aged twenty to forty-nine (Hareven and Vinovskis, "Patterns," 92), but Table 3.5 here follows Gagan's format.

25 Modell and Hareven, "Transitions," 252.

26 See, for example, the essays in Tilley, ed., *Historical Studies*.
27 Pouyez and Lavoie (*Les Saguenayens*, 298) have discovered a similar ratio for the first twelve months in the Saguenay, as has Jean-Claude Robert ("City," 29) for Montreal between 1821 and 1846.
28 Gadoury, Landry, and Charbonneau, "Démographie différentielle," 376; R.E. Jones, "Infant Mortality," 305.
29 Sorg and Craig, "Patterns," 104.
30 Lithell, "Breast-Feeding Habits," 184.
31 Gérin, "L'habitant," 101.
32 Shorter, *The Making of the Modern Family*, 170–1.
33 Sorg and Craig, "Patterns." See also Dinet, "Statistique," 221–2; and Greven, *Four Generations*, 187–8.
34 Cahier d'annonces pour St Romain et St Gabriel, SRP. "La picotte" might be translated as chicken pox, but this disease would rarely be fatal to children, and the school inspector reported in 1859 that "that fatal and filthy disease Small Pox" was in every house throughout Stratford, Garthby, Weedon, Wolfestown, Ham South, and Winslow North. Lettres reçues, no. 417, 1859, Éducation, E13, ANQQ.
35 For an analysis of similar mortality crises in the Saguenay, see Pouyez and Lavoie, *Les Saguenayens*, 201–32.
36 Leridon, *Human Fertility*, 146. See also Marcy, "Factors," 314–6; Knodel and Van de Walle, "Breast Feeding," 112–14, 129–31; Mesnick, "Demographic Impact"; Treckel, "Breastfeeding," 39; and Short, "Breast Feeding."
37 See also Henripin, *La population*, 86.
38 Flandrin, *Families*, 206, 208; Greer, *Peasant*, 69–70.
39 Bernier, *La médecine*, 132.
40 Short, "Breast Feeding," 41.
41 Compare Flandrin's findings in *Families*, 208–9.
42 See also Charbonneau et al., *Naissance*, 99, 102.
43 Bennett-Knight, "Folkways," 57, 84. Henripin ("La fécondité," 84) has estimated that the highly fecund women of eighteenth-century Canada breast-fed for approximately fourteen months.
44 See Hareven and Vinovskis, "Patterns," 90.
45 Flandrin, *Families*, 202–3.
46 See Sorg and Craig, "Patterns," 107, 110–1; Knodel and van de Walle, "Breast Feeding," 130.
47 Robert, "City," 32.
48 See, for example, Easterlin, "Human Fertility"; Leet, "Human Fertility"; Laidig, Schutjer, and Stokes, "Agricultural Variation"; McInnis, "Childbearing"; and Atack and Bateman, *To Their Own Soil*, 55–70. For a critique of attempts to define availability of farms, see Vinovskis, "Recent Trends," 615–18.

49 Tilley, "Historical Study," 65–7; Charbonneau, "Les régimes," 452–60; and several other essays in Léridon and Menken, eds., *Natural Fertility*.

50 Gagan, *Hopeful Travellers*, 76–7, and "Land," 308–10. Greven (*Four Generations*, 200–1) also emphasizes the demographic impact of delayed marriages but reports only a two-year increase in female age at wedlock for his study group – enough, he states, to reduce completed family size from 8.3 to 7.6 offspring.

51 Tepperman, "Ethnic Variations," 331–2, 338–9. Ellen Gee ("Early Canadian Fertility Transition," 29) also claims that the threshold year for deliberate marital fertility control within Canada as a whole was 1871.

52 Fullarton and Baird, *Remarks*, 24; W.A. Smith, *Lewsiana*, 16–17; Flinn, ed., *Scottish Population*, 32, 38, 307, 328, 330–1, 342–5.

53 Tepperman, "Ethnic Variations," 331–2.

54 Hajnal, "European Marriage Patterns," 108. Ages are not recorded in the marriage registers (though seven of the sixteen French-Canadian marriage contracts listed the bride as a minor) but ascertained through linkage with census and birth records. During the eighteenth century, the average French-Canadian woman not previously married was wed at twenty-two years of age. Henripin, *La population*, 96.

55 See the tables in Pouyez and Lavoie, *Les Saguenayens*, 266–7; and Bouchard, "Family Structures," 359.

56 On this theme see Gossage, "Family Formation."

57 A. MacKay, *By Trench*, 89, 140.

58 Flinn, *Scottish Population*, 37–8, 342–5; D. Campbell and R.A. McLean, *Beyond the Atlantic Roar*, 186–7.

59 Gagan, *Hopeful Travellers*, 72. For data on completed family size in other North American communities see Brookes, "The Golden Age," 63. In 1836 the average number of children per family in the parish of Stornoway, Lewis, *of Scotland*, was reported to be five, and, in Barvas, four. *New Statistical Account*, Lewis, 127, 146.

60 Bouchard and de Pourbaix, "Individual," 235. Not included in my calculations were families in which the father died before the mother reached forty-five or in which one spouse had remarried. Twins were counted as single births.

61 Bouchard, "Family Structures," 351, 363,

62 St-Hilaire, "La structuration," 140. See also his "Origines," 20–2.

63 Bouchard's formula ("Family Structures," 362–4) for measuring population turn-over is of little use here because it fails to account for single emigrants and assumes that emigrant families were of the same size as the township mean. In Winslow they tended to be younger and smaller than the average. In- and out-migration can be measured quite accurately from family reconstitution records, but only for a larger geographical area than a single parish. See Gauvreau, Jetté, and Bourque, "Migration."

64 Mays, "A Place to Stand," 196.

65 Gaffield, *Language*, 51.

66 See, for example, Adams and Kasakoff, "Migration," 28–9; Lockridge, *A New England Town*, 63–4; Pouyez, Roy, and Bouchard, "La mobilité"; and Mathieu et al., "Peuplement," 133. But contrast the findings in Norris, "Household," 414; and Conzen, *Frontier Farming*, 48–50.

67 Of fifty-nine families considered persistent for at least twenty years prior to 1881, nineteen represented a succeeding generation, and of the twenty-five persistent since 1852, only sixteen were headed by the same individual. Pouyez and Bergeron ("L'étude," 30) make the same argument.

68 Only seven of the forty-four "new" household heads were positively identified as sons of the township, but an additional seventeen had local names and were under thirty-five years of age in 1881. The eight doubtful cases were all older than thirty-five and had probably formed a family elsewhere before moving to Winslow in the 1870s.

69 Similar patterns have been described for pre-1850 New England (Adams and Kasakoff, "Migration," 33–5), nineteenth-century Toronto Gore Township (Mays, "A Place to Stand," 198), and the Saguenay region (Bouchard, "Sur la reproduction," 242). For a detailed analysis of how one family expanded on its home rang in Wotton Township, see Sevigny, "Le capitalisme," 72–5.

70 See, for example, Maisonneuve, "Structure," 238; Ostergren, "Land," 405; Heller and Moore, "Continuity," 238; and Adams and Kasakoff, "Migration," 29–30. But note the contradictory evidence once again in Conzen, *Frontier Farming*, 128–30.

71 Craig, "Économie," 129.

72 On application of this method elsewhere, see Ramirez and Lamarre, "Du Québec."

73 See Little, *Nationalism*, chap. 6 and 8.

74 Report for 1872, Register, 5, SRP.

75 No. 1019, 23 April 1869, F.S.A. Bélanger, n.p., Palais de Justice, St Joseph de Beauce.

76 See Molloy, "No Inclination"; Ommer, "Highland Scots"; Brookes, "The Golden Age"; Ramirez and Lamarre, "Du Québec"; and Elliott, *Irish Migrants*, chap. 7. Adams and Kasakoff ("Migration," 33), in contrast, have found a relatively dispersed pattern for brothers in colonial New England.

77 MacLeod, *Settlement*, 7.

78 The descendants of the three McIver brothers who settled in Lingwick in 1841 were considerably more persistent, but two members of the second generation moved to Lowell, Mass., and two to Pennsylvania and Montana. Members of the third generation located in Worcester, Hart-

ford, Chicago, Duluth, Indiana, and Granby (Quebec). Sherman, *History*, 64–71.

79 Elliott, *Irish Migrants*, 190.

80 MacKay, *By Trench*, 116–17.

81 Ibid., 130–1.

82 Comparable persistence rates for the Ontario Irish are recorded in Lockwood, "Irish Immigrants," 11, and Norris, "Migration," 146.

CHAPTER FOUR

1 See, for example, Berkner, "Use and Misuse." For helpful brief review of recent literature on this question, see Anderson, *Approaches*, 22–33.

2 On the influence of LePlay and his disciples on French Canada, see Falardeau, "Présentation," and P. Trépanier, "Les influences."

3 Bouchard, "L'étude," 555–60.

4 Waters, "Family," 68.

5 This possibility tends to be dismissed by Vinovskis, "Household Size."

6 The definition of a two-family household employed here includes a married couple living with a widowed parent and one or more unmarried siblings, which is more commonly considered to be the structure of a single extended family. For a brief summary of the different types of household structure, see Katz, *People*, 215–16.

7 The provincial average for simple-family households in 1871 was only 69 per cent, which suggests that Winslow did not conform to Darroch and Ornstein's generalization that complex households were associated with marginal rural economies; "Family," 165, 173–4.

8 Bennett-Knight, "Folkways," 95.

9 Gérin, "L'habitant," 83.

10 For examples of seasonal migration taking place within family and local community networks, see Darroch, "Migrants," 260–3, and Norris, "Household," 414.

11 Gagan, *Hopeful Travellers*, 64–6.

12 Ibid., 65.

13 Hareven and Vinovskis, "Introduction," 19.

14 Alan Brookes ("The Golden Age," 64) comments on the development of a similar phenomenon in Nova Scotia, but he does not provide household statistics. Chad Gaffield (*Language*, 50) does provide data for Alfred Township during the 1860s, claiming that male and female offspring left parental households at about age twenty and seventeen, respectively, though he appears to have confused ages at the time of the 1861 census with ages at departure.

15 John Macdonald, *General View of the Agriculture of the Highlands* (Edinburgh, 1811), quoted in Youngson, *After the Forty-Five*, 183.

16 Quoted in Gagan, "Enumerator's Instructions," 363. See also Darroch, "Class." 57.

17 Youngson, *After the Forty-Five*, 180. See also Hunter, *Crofting Community*, 31.

18 Morel, *Les Limites*, 52; Lavallée, "La transmission," 344–8.

19 See, for example, Bouchard, "Les systèmes;"; Bouchard, "Sur la reproduction"; Henretta, "Families," 21–9; Friedberger, "The Farm Family," 1, 8; Ostergren, "Land and Family," 405–6; and Elliott, *Irish Migrants*, 314–15. Gagan claims that in Peel County all the extra land acquired as a family matured was usually transferred with the homestead to a single son, but his analysis is confined to wills even though the family estate was generally transferred while at least one of the parents was still alive. Gagan, "Indivisibilty," 135; Elliott, *Irish Migrants*, 210–12, and "Sources of Bias," 131.

20 Bouchard and de Pourbaix, "Individual," 228–30.

21 Easterlin, "Population Change." Allan Bogue's critique which follows Easterlin on pp. 79–80 reveals that he is not entirely convinced by Easterlin's data.

22 Dépatie, "Les pratiques," 36–7.

23 Bouchard, "Sur la reproduction," 245.

24 Eighty-five per cent of the sons established as farmers in the Saguenay region of the nineteenth century lived in the same parish as their parents, but only 57 per cent of the established daughters did so. Bouchard and Larouche, "Paramètres sociaux," 135–6.

25 For definitions of the various types of "donations" see Santerre, "La sécurité," 3–4.

26 K.N. Conzen, "Peasant Pioneers," 272–5. Greven (*Four Generations*, 136) also stresses the mutually exclusive nature of these two types of intergenerational transfer.

27 Séguin, *La conquête*, 185–6.

28 After the death of Paul Jr's second wife in 1874, his only assets were listed as tools and furniture valued at $17.33, and his debts outweighed his credits by $117.22 to $25.10. E.M. Mackenzie, n.p., no. 759, 13 Oct. 1872, ANQS; F.S.A. Bélanger, n.p., no. 1734, 24 July 1875, Palais de Justice, St Joseph de Beauce.

29 Greer (*Peasant*, 74) found a similar pattern for the French Canadians of the lower Richelieu, as did Elliott (*Irish Migrants*, 201–3) for the Irish Protestants of the Ottawa Valley. Even in the four Saguenay townships studied by Bouchard, only 25 per cent of non-established offspring were compensated by the deed in gift between 1870 and 1900, a ratio that dropped to 3 per cent between 1900 and 1940. Bouchard, "La donation," 6, 27. See also Girard, "Familles et patrimoines," 151, and contrast the findings of Gagan in "Indivisibility," 132, and "Land," 305.

30 S.A. Brodeur, n.p., no. 117, 7 Aug. 1875; no. 128, 14 Sept. 1875; no. 175, 28 Jan. 1876, Palais de Justice, Valleyfield.

31 Keyssar, "Widowhood," 103. The situation in colonial Chesapeake Bay was closer to that of Winslow. Carr and Walsh, "The Planter's Wife," 569–70.

32 See Le Collectif Clio, L'histoire, 82.

33 E.M. Mackenzie, n.p., no. 754, 30 July 1872, ANQS.

34 See N. Davis, "Patriarchy"; Cohen, Women's Work, 49–51; Elliott, Irish Migrants, 198–201; Gagan, "Indivisibility," 134–5; and Keyssar, "Widowhood," 106.

35 E.M. Mackenzie, n.p., no. 154, 20 Aug. 1865; no. 295, 6 Nov. 1866, ANQS.

36 See Macklam, "Patterns," 6; Craig, "La transmission," 16–17; and Santerre, "La sécurité," 10.

37 On the moral authority of peasant women in nineteenth-century France, see Segalen, Love and Power.

38 Castelli, "Le douaire," 315–20.

39 On this theme, see Ward, Courtship, 42–3.

40 Le Collectif Clio, L'histoire, 82–5, 150–2.

41 The average delays in early-eighteenth-century Canada were 25.5 months for widowers and 38.4 months for widows; Greer, Peasant, 52.

42 See also Gérin, "L'habitant," 72, and Cohen, Women's Work, 55–6. Bouchard ("Les systèmes," 38) claims that transfer of the patrimony through deed in gift was not always the last step in the process of property transmission. Movable goods were sometimes divided on the death of a father or mother to indemnify sons who had remained at home to work on the farm or daughters who failed to marry. If such a practice was followed in Winslow, however, the items were not of sufficient value to require a notarial contract.

43 Quoted in Bennett-Knight, "Folkways," 58.

44 Elliott (Irish Migrants, 208) makes the same observation of the Tipperary Protestants in Ontario.

45 Reg. B, vol. 4, no. 2118, Cookshire Registry Office.

46 Paul Craven ("Law," 177) points out that in Ontario the labour an unmarried woman provided on the property of a male relative gave her neither a claim on the property nor a claim to a wage. There is no evidence to suggest that unmarried men living with parents or brothers in Winslow could expect any different treatment. Indeed, Scots families appear to have been reliant on off-farm wages earned by their sons, with no apparent guarantee of material recompense to those sons.

47 For a good description of common specifications in the Montreal and Quebec areas, see Vermette, "Les donations," 508–12.

48 This point is made in Greer, Peasant, 79–80.

49 Stone, "Family History," 69–70; Lemon, "Early Americans," 121. On the latter point see Elliott, *Irish Migrants*, 199–200; Santerre, "La sécurité," and Segalen, *Love and Power*, 68–71.

50 D. Campbell and R.A. MacLean (*Beyond the Atlantic Roar*, 186–7) make the same point for the Highlanders of Cape Breton Island.

51 Shorter, *Making*, 32.

52 Marc St-Hilaire ("La structuration," 141–2) suggests a retirement age of about fifty in St Fulgence during this period, but Béatrice Craig ("La transmission," 14) states that the average French-Canadian farmer in the upper St John Valley transferred the homestead at age sixty-two, and Gérard Bouchard ("La donation," 17) has found that two-thirds of the donors in his Saguenay sample for 1871–1940 were over sixty.

53 For both the French Canadians and the Scots, these averages include the ages of several sons involved in partible transfers.

54 German farmers in Minnesota had to retire early in order to entice their sons to take over their farms; Conzen, "Peasant Pioneers," 281–4. On this point, see also Greven, *Four Generations*, 229–30, 241–2; and Anderson, *Family Structure*, 93.

55 E.M. Mackenzie, n.p., no. 109, 28 Oct. 1861; no. 45, 30 June 1864; no. 89, 3 Dec. 1864; no. 107, 21 Jan. 1865; no. 173, 18 Oct. 1865, ANQS.

56 Reg. B, vol. 8, no. 672–6, Cookshire Registry Office; F.S.A. Bélanger, n.p., no. 2637, 23 Aug. 1880, Palais de Justice, St Joseph de Beauce.

57 Research by Luce Vermette ("Les donations," 508) shows that restrictions to the successor's control over the farm were considerably more common in the Montreal area than in the less arable Quebec area.

58 Contrast the earlier situation of the Tipperary Protestants in the Ottawa Valley, where more than half the sons received farms from their fathers, and only 10 percent migrated from the region without obtaining land. Elliott, *Irish Migrants*, 238.

59 See Lockridge, "Land."

60 Berkner and Mendels, "Inheritance," 212–13.

61 Stone, "Family History," 73–4.

62 In order to determine when all of the St Romain successors were married, one would have to research the registers of the surrounding parishes, but most of those who married in St Romain did so within a year or so of the transfer. See also Bouchard, "Le donation," 3, 5; Santerre, "La sécurité," 11; Dépatie, "Les pratiques," 14; and Mathieu, "Mobilité," 219.

63 A. MacKay, "A Leap-Year Ball," in A. MacKay, *By Trench*, 88. Peter Ward's "Courtship" stresses the lack of restrictions felt by rural bachelors, as well as the independence of young rural women. The concerns of St Romain's curé are dealt with in more detail in chapter 7.

64 Major Haliday to Mr Trevelyan, Portree, 11 April 1847, 184, *Uncorrected Correspondence from February to September 1847 Relating to the Measures Adopted for the Relief of Distress in Scotland*, Second Report (London: Wm. Clewes & Sons, 1847), SRO.

65 Report on Outer Hebrides, Aug. 1849, Highland Destitution Reports, Glasgow sect., 14, NLS. See also *New Statistical Account*, Lewis, 131, and Macdonald, *Lewis*, 75–6.

66 Quoted in Epps, "Immigrant File." On Howe, see Campbell and MacLean, *Beyond*, 152.

67 On this point, see Flandrin, *Families*, 112–15.

68 Robert, "City," 29.

69 Gauldrée-Boileau, "Paysan," 23–4.

70 See Gagnon, *Mourir*, 22.

71 Johnston, *Religion in Life*, 150.

72 Ibid.

73 Shorter, *Making*, 172.

74 A similar interpretation can be found in Lemieux and Mercier, *Les Femmes*, 202–3, 335–9.

75 Anderson, *Family Structure*, 8, 42, 62. For similar interpretations, see Shorter, *Making*, 5, 26; and Hareven, "Les grands thèmes," 206–7.

76 D.S. Smith, "Parental Power," 425.

77 See Falardeau, "Religion populaire," 289, and J. Roy, "Religion," 416.

78 N.Z. Davis, "Ghosts," 92–4.

79 Ibid., 96.

80 Bennett-Knight, "Folkways," 103–6.

81 On the Quebec context see Genest, "Réflexion," 341–2.

82 Segalen, *Love and Power*, 49.

83 Statement of Inspection of Lands unsold, or sold but not patented, in the township of Winslow, Chas Patton, May 1885, E21, Terres et Fôrets, Art. 940, ANQQ.

84 On the rural dwelling in two of Quebec's colonization zones, see Verdon, *Anthropologie*, 27–32; and Lafleur, *La vie*, 53–63.

85 On this theme, see S. Gagnon, "Amours interdits," 316–18, and N.Z. Davis, "Ghosts," 101–5.

86 St Romain's baptismal registers of the 1870s note the godparents who were married to each other.

87 Roy, Landry, and Charbonneau, "Quelques comportements," 70. These ratios are lowered by the fact that the authors considered hyphenated names such as Marie-Catherine, Marie-Anne, and even Marie to be mutually distinct. Hyphens were rarely used in the St Romain registers.

88 Molloy, "No Inclination," 240.

89 Cited in Dunkly, "Studies," 34–8.

90 See Harris, "Extension."

91 Flandrin, "Histoire de la famille," 142.

CHAPTER FIVE

1 For a historiographical summary, see the recent contribution by Allan Kulikoff, "The Transition to Capitalism," which sees early American society as in a transitional phase between the two orientations.

2 Allan Greer's *Peasant, Lord and Merchant* marks a new departure for French-Canadian historiography in arguing that family-oriented self-sufficency was a rational economic strategy. For a similar perspective on Upper Canada, see Johnson, "New Thoughts."

3 Report on Outer Hebrides, Aug. 1849, 17, Highland Destitution Reports, Glasgow Sect., 1848–50, NLS.

4 This theme is stressed in Courville and Séguin, *Rural Life.*

5 Gauldrée-Boileau, "Paysan," 30.

6 Some farms may have extended across township boundaries, but registry records reveal that residents purchased little land outside Winslow, and it appears that, as of 1871, census enumerators reported all of each farmer's acreage no matter where it was located. See Fortier, "Les recensements," 274–7.

7 Lemon, "Early Americans," 118–22.

8 For a revealing study of the influence that soil types had on agricultural practices in a culturally mixed township, see Casteran, "Les stratégies."

9 Similarily, in the upper St John Valley of 1833, and the seigneurie of Petite Nation in 1842, only 5 per cent of the farmers were commercial producers, but on a larger scale than in Winslow. See Craig, "Agriculture," 135, and Baribeau, *La seigneurie,* 91.

10 French-language census forms were used for Winslow North in 1852 and 1871. Individual crop areas do not always add up to the total area declared to be in crop in by each farmer in 1852, but indiscrepancies roughly cancel each other out. Thus the "en culture" column is 254 ½ acres while the areas in wheat, barley, and so on add up to 258 ¼. Régis Thibeault ("Les limites," 226–7) reveals a similar situation in the Saguenay region. See also Fortier, "Les recensements," 271–3; and McInnis, "Pitfalls," 1851–52 224–8.

11 Special Meeting of the Municipal Council of the United Townships of Whitton, Marston, and Hampden, 20 May 1862; Petition of the Municipal Council of Whitton, 20 May 1862, no. 1517, vol. 516, RG 4C1, NA.

12 See Atack and Bateman, *To Their Own Soil,* 170. The 1861 Winslow enumerator reported rust damage in one Scots section.

13 Canada, manuscript census, 1861, Newport and Wotton Townships. The word "Newport" is not recorded in the county's agricultural schedule,

but it can be identified by linkage of farmer names to the personal schedule.

14 Baron and Bridges, "Making Hay," 166, 170, 177–80.

15 Fenton, *Scottish Country Life*, 136. The hay and cereal grain yields of the Saguenay region during this period were similar to those of Winslow. See Bouchard, "L'agriculture," 368.

16 Bennett-Knight, "Folkways," 69–70.

17 See Ball, "Technology," 258–60.

18 Oats grew poorly in the Hebrides, where a primitive form of barley known as bere was sometimes used as bread grain. See Smout and Levitt, *The State*, 23–4, and Fenton, *Scottish Country Life*, 166–8. On the Lewis diet specifically, see Macdonald, *Lewis*, 54–6.

19 The idealist nature of the "pensions" is suggested by oral testimony from the Beauce district. Vermette, "Les donations," 512. For a criticism of the use of similar documents by American historians, see Pruitt, "Self-Sufficiency," 335–45.

20 McInnis, "Marketable Surpluses," 43.

21 Greer (*Peasant*, 206) states that the typical "pension" for an individual in the lower Richelieu parishes of the 1830s specified seventy-five pounds of salt pork, twenty pounds of beef, seven-and-a-half minots of potatoes, seven-and-a-half minots of wheat, three-quarter minots of peas, and certain quantities of garden vegetables. For various American estimates, see Atack and Bateman, *To Their Own Soil*, 209.

22 The adult equivalent ratio was calculated as follows: males aged fifteen plus – 100 per cent; females aged fifteen plus – 90 per cent; child eleven to fourteen – 90 per cent; child seven to ten – 75 per cent; child four to six – 40 per cent; child under four – 15 per cent. See Atack and Bateman, *To Their Own Soil*, 294, n. 37.

23 Ibid., 214; Baribeau, *La Seigneurie*, 86.

24 See Table 12.4 in Atack and Bateman, *To Their Own Soil*, 210; they appear to equate one bushel of corn with 0.86 bushels of oats (see their p. 213). Lewis and McInnis ("Agricultural Output," A-19, A-21) adopt considerably higher fodder estimates based on recommended levels rather than contemporary observations.

25 Atack and Bateman, *To Their Own Soil*, 294, n. 54.

26 Lewis and McInnis, "Agricultural Output," A-19.

27 See ibid., A-3–4.

28 Life of John Leonard, 25 Jan. 1931, Fonds Famille John Leonard (1855–1935), P98–4, Documents Divers, ETHS. During the 1870s Eastern Townships beef producers would benefit temporarily from increased demand on the British and French markets, but a large-scale meat-canning plant in Sherbrooke would close its doors permanently in 1876. The major beef breeders in Compton County began to shift operations

to the western foothills after 1880. Kesteman, "Une bourgeoisie," 720; Breen, *The Canadian Prairie West*, 11–12.

29 Judd, "Lumbering," 66–7.

30 For Quebec and the Eastern Townships, respectively, see N. Perron, "Genèse," and Little, "The Peaceable Conquest," 223–5.

31 Atack and Bateman, *To Their Own Soil*, 159–60; Lewis and McInnis, "Agricultural Output," A-10. Bateman has estimated per-capita consumption in the northern United States of 1861 to be twenty-five pounds of butter and five to six pounds of cheese. Bateman, "Marketable Surplus," 354.

32 McInnis, "Marketable Surpluses," 46–8.

33 Ibid., 55.

34 On the farm lease, see E.P. Felton, n.p., 3 March 1859, no. 41; 26 Aug. 1859, no. 149; 18 Nov. 1865, no. 170, ANQS. The company owed $1,593 to the two merchants by 1879. See ibid., 7 Feb. 1879, no. 141.

35 Smith et al., *History*, 221, 225.

36 8th Report, App. 9, 55–6, 58–9; 10th Report, App. 4, 9, Highland Destitution Reports, Glasgow sect., 1848–50, NLS; John Scobie to James Matheson, Stornoway, 1 March 1847, 140; James Smith to James Matheson, Glasgow, 26 April 1847, 140; Arch. Cameron to Hugh M'Pherson, Stornoway, 15 March 1847, 142, *Uncorrected Correspondence from February to September 1847 Relating to the Measures Adopted for the Relief of Distress in Scotland*, 2nd Report (London: W. Clowes & Sons, 1847), SRO.

37 On provincial production averages, see Grant and Inwood, "How Urban?" 4.

38 Roelens and Inwood ("Labouring," 226) find that weaving families in Leeds County in 1871 had more women aged sixteen and above than did non-weaving families.

39 Perron, *Un grand éducateur*, 26–7; Kesteman, "Une bourgeoisie," 213–14.

40 Grant and Inwood, "Gender and Organization," 27. See also Cohen, *Women's Work*, 76–9.

41 The 1861 Newport enumerator stated that cotton cloth was considered cheaper than linen.

42 Kesteman, "Une bourgeoisie," 573–4.

43 Atack and Bateman (*To Their Own Soil*, 141–2) admit that few families reported implements of this value. Also Richard Bushman ("Family Security," 240–2) points out that during the pre-industrial era most American farms lacked basic items, such as essential tools. They generally compensated for such deficiencies through exchanges of labour.

44 Bouchard ("L'agriculture," 369) claims that changes in agricultural technology were minor, if not negligible, in the Saguenay region prior to the

1880s. On farm mechanization in the province as a whole, see Blouin, "La mécanisation."

45 Wynn, *Timber Colony*, 21.

46 S.A. Brodeur, n.p., 7 Aug. 1875, no. 117, Palais de Justice, Valleyfield. At the auction held the following month, however, the mare brought only $60.00 and the other livestock $83.15. Ibid., 14 Sept. 1875, no. 128.

47 McInnis ("Marketable Surpluses," 52) claims that horses may have been the most profitable commodity available to mid-nineteenth-century farmers, but Table 5.8 reveals that in 1871 the French Canadians in Winslow had only enough animals, including colts, to represent one team per farm.

48 See Traill, *The Canadian Settler's Guide*, 142–50; Beattie, *A New Life in Canada*, 46; and Cohen, *Women's Work*, 88.

49 N. Bélanger to Archbishop of Quebec, Bécancour, 28 March 1849, Parish Papers, Saint-Romain, AAS.

50 In 1861, $350 in pearlash was manufactured in Stratford, $728 in Aylmer, and $1,200 (forty barrels) in Weedon. In 1871, Weedon produced 4.9 tons of pearlash and potash; Lambton, 8.3 tons of potash. One Lingwick merchant was said to have manufactured pearlash for trade to Montreal. Channell, *History of Compton*, 258.

51 See Little, *Nationalism*, chap. 5.

52 Report of George Lanigan, 15–18 Feb. 1866, RG 171, Canada, Department of Agriculture, Correspondence, no. 2055, NA.

53 According to Gentilcore ("Agricultural Background," 396), the Highland settlers of Antigonish, N.S., engaged in lumbering at the expense of farming, even though they were poor woodsmen.

54 E.M. McKenzie, n.p., 10 Dec. 1860, no. 110, ANQS.

55 Judd, "Lumbering," 60–3.

56 Return of Timber cut by C.S. Clark & Co. during the season of 1857–8, ANQQ, MTF, Correspondance Générale.

57 In 1874 Morin became the first inhabitant of the future town of Lake Megantic (originally called Morinville), where he oversaw the local operations of the G.B. Hall Co. of Montmorency Falls. Jones, "History of Lake Megantic." If any subcontractors had lived in Winslow, notarized contracts would presumably have been discovered as in the Mauricie, particularly considering that it was a common practice to mortgage land as a guarantee. See Gauthier, "La sous-traitance."

58 Baribeau, *La Seigneurie*, 48–53. The pattern for Petite Nation is not inconsistent with that found by Gaffield (*Language*, 85–7) for conceptions in nearby Prescott County in 1871 and 1881. Note also the sharp drop in eighteenth-century Canada's conception curve from February

to April, again suggesting periods of winter absenteeism. Henripin, *La population*, 42–3.

59 The rise in the conception curve for March suggests, however, that local married men did not play an active role in the drive, as does the fact that the mortality curve dipped that month while peaking in Petite Nation. Baribeau, *La Seigneurie*, 52–3.

60 Roach, "Farm Woodlots," 205–6.

61 C. Curtis, "Shanty Life," 46.

62 Hosie, *Native Trees*, 56.

63 This estimate is based on a volume of thirty-four cubic feet per tree, which is that assumed by the government for non-pine timber during this period. Gaudreau, *L'exploitation*, 23.

64 Booth, "Changing Forest Utilization," 116; Kesteman, *Histoire*, 51. In 1871 neither Scots nor French Canadians had cut more firewood than the twenty-five cords said to be the minimum needed for home consumption. Gérin, "L'habitant," 60; Wynn, *Timber Colony*, 19.

65 Saw mills also proliferated in the Mauricie when the rail network was extended through that district during the late 1870s. Hardy, Lanthier, and Séguin, "Les Industries," 242. For more on French-Canadian settlers as independent lumber producers, see Gaudreau, "Le rapport," 77–8, and Hardy and Séguin, *Forêt*, 152–6, 166–70.

66 See Gautier and Henry, *La population*, 63.

67 Henripin, *La population*, 43.

68 The haying season in the Saguenay region and Maine during the nineteenth century was mid-July to mid-August. Bouchard, "L'agriculture," 362; Baron and Bridges, "Making Hay," 172.

69 *SPQ*, XI, 1877–8, no. 2, 232.

70 Ramsay, *John Ramsay*, 65.

71 Typewritten address by Mr Leonard, n.d., Fonds Affaire Morrison, P153, ETHS.

72 Berkner, "The Stem Family," 415.

73 Conzen, "Peasant Pioneers," 265.

74 Ostergren, "A Community Transplanted," 208. Another study of Scandinavian settlement in Minnesota reaches essentially the same conclusion: Rice, "Role." See also Graeme Wynn's comments on the recent literature in his "Settler Societies," 356–7, 363–4.

75 Wynn, "Ethnic Migrations," 10–11.

76 Baltensperger ("Agricultural Change," 181, 186–7) has found that, among immigrants to Nebraska, Old World crop preferences reasserted themselves after several years of absence during the pioneering process.

77 On the cattle economy in Lewis, see Macdonald, *Lewis*, 81–4.

78 Devine, *Famine*, 47–8, 151, 154–5. Lewis was also an important source of labour for the Hudson's Bay Co. Goldring, "Lewis."

79 The concept of proto-industrialization does not apply to Lewis, at least prior to the migration, because it refers to the mass production of handicrafts on a year-round basis. See Medick, "Proto-Industrial," 297.

80 McNeill Report, 918–19. For a fuller description of the labour involved in the Lewis fishery, see Macdonald, *Lewis*, 94–5. On the crofters' attachment to the land, see Smout, *Century*, 67, and Flinn, *Scottish Population History*, 67.

81 Darroch and Ornstein, "Ethnicity," 311–15.

82 Ibid., 311.

83 See, for example, Beauchamp, "Milieu rural," 222–3.

84 See Fortin, "Socio-Cultural Changes."

85 As other historians have begun to find for the Highlanders of Nova Scotia, this examination of Winslow suggests that their reputation as poor farmers is not deserved. For examples of the traditional view, see Campbell and MacLean, *Beyond the Atlantic Roar*, 56–7, 63–4, 86–91, 182–4; and Pentland, *Labour and Capital*, 94. For revisionist interpretations, see MacNeil, "Cultural Stereotypes"; DeVries and MacNab-DeVries, *They Farmed*; and Bittermann, "Hierarchy."

86 On the integration of wage labour into the farm family economy, and its implications for young single men, see Gaffield, "Children," 3, 8. McCann's "Living" discusses the deeply entrenched tradition of occupational pluralism in the Maritimes.

87 Bouchard et al., "Croissance," 100.

CHAPTER SIX

1 There is no reference to the use of hand grist mills in Winslow, but they were made by the first group of settlers who moved to the shores of Lake Megantic in 1856. MacLeod, *Settlement*, 3–4. For a reference to their continued use in Lewis, see Smith, *Lewsiana*, 75.

2 The personal schedule of the 1852 census mentions only that Gagné was part owner of the grist mill, but an "acte de société" signed in 1863 states that the farmer, Louis Bouffard, and Gagné's son had built the two-storey grist mill together; E.M. Mackenzie, n.p., 6 April 1863, no. 32, ANQS. Seven months later Bouffard sold his interest to an Aylmer farmer for $650; Reg. B, vol. 6, no. 2893, Cookshire Registry Office. The 1861 census refers to "Peter Belliveau" as the owner, but his age proves that it was actually Pierre Gagné dit Bellavance.

3 Reg. B, vol. 10, no. 5953, Sherbrooke Registry Office; S.A. Brodeur, n.p., 18 June 1877, no. 455, Palais de Justice, Valleyfield; F.S.A. Bélanger, n.p., 24 Nov. 1877, no. 2109, Palais de Justice, St Joseph de Beauce.

4 The 1871 agricultural schedules list Octave Gagné, the grist mill operator, with fifty-four acres in crop, eight head of cattle, ten sheep, eight pigs, and eighty-seven yards of homespun.

5 Therrien had a year to repay the company, plus interest and costs, but he formally forfeited this right in 1865. Reg. B, vol. 13, no. 293; vol. 14, no. 386; vol. 14, no. 436; vol. 18, no. 164–5, Sherbrooke Registry Office; E.M. Mackenzie, n.p., 3 Sept. 1861, no. 98, ANQS.

6 Reg. B, vol. 14, no. 436, Sherbrooke Registry Office.

7 E.M. Mackenzie, n.p., 6 Sept. 1864, no. 64; 8 Oct. 1864, no. 77; 17 Oct. 1864, no. 79, ANQS.

8 Ibid., 29 April 1868, no. 450; 17 Feb. 1869, no. 491–2; 13 July 1869, no. 504–5.

9 Ibid., 31 Aug. 1868, no. 470; 1 Sept. 1868, no. 471; 13 July 1869, no. 503; Reg. B, vol. 21, no. 458, Sherbrooke Registry Office.

10 E.M. Mackenzie, n.p., 24 Dec. 1869, no. 527; 31 Dec. 1869, no. 528; 7 June 1870, no. 552; 12 Aug. 1870, no. 568; 1 April 1871, no. 615, ANQS.

11 F.S.A. Bélanger, n.p., 13 June 1874, no. 1591, Palais de Justice, St Joseph de Beauce; S.A. Brodeur, n.p., 23 March 1875, no. 86, Palais de Justice, Valleyfield.

12 The hypothecs were not discharged until 1889 and 1899, suggesting that the mills remained in the hands of their original owners, at least until those dates. Reg. B, vol. 8, no. 4806; vol. 10, no. 5954, Cookshire Registry Office.

13 Reg. B, vol. 9, no. 323, Sherbrooke Registry Office. The lot was actually just outside the village reserve, on rang 1 NW, lot 68.

14 I found no record of the sale or of the partnership agreement, but the 1858 transfer is noted in the crown land records, and in 1859 Pallister and Layfield jointly sold the property for $686, with the right to repurchase in a year; ibid., vol. 9, no. 3.

15 E.M. Mackenzie, n.p., 17 Oct. 1866, no. 281, ANQS.

16 Reg. B, vol. 6, no. 3515; vol. 11, no. 6262, Cookshire Registry Office.

17 Legendre remortgaged the mill site to the Lévis mechanic who installed the machinery. Reg. B, vol. 14, no. 314; vol. 17, no. 8, Sherbrooke Registry Office. For a description of the grist mill's operation, see Bennett-Knight, "Folkways," 68.

18 Reg. B, vol. 17, no. 382, Sherbrooke Registry Office; Edouard Legendre, pltf, vs Ferd. Legendre, dft, and Tel. Legendre, garnishee, Queen's Bench, Sherbrooke, no. 986, fyled [sic] 3 Dec. 1866, ANQS.

19 Reg. B, vol. 20, no. 545, Sherbrooke Registry Office; Reg. B, vol. 2, no. 930, Cookshire Registry Office.

20 Bennett-Knight, "Folkways," 73. For a description of the Legendre carding mill, rebuilt in 1897, see ibid., 73–4. At $700, the output (value of

total product less raw materials) was 10 per cent higher than the provincial average for carding mills in 1871. Grant and Inwood, "Gender," Table 2.

21 Reg. B, vol. 2, no. 966; vol. 4, no. 2155, Cookshire Registry Office.

22 Kesteman, *Histoire*, 57. Presumably to help finance construction, Legendre had remortgaged his Stornoway property in 1878 to the Smith-Elkins foundry of Sherbrooke. Both hypothecs were recorded as discharged in 1880. Reg. B, vol. 7, no. 4169; vol. 9, no. 5387, Cookshire Registry Office.

23 *Stornoway 1858/1983*, 30–1.

24 Wynn, *Timber Colony*, 97–9, 111, 116–17.

25 Kesteman, "Une bourgeoisie," 302–4.

26 Craig, "Agriculture," 132–3. Milling and merchandizing were also carried on as joint efforts in Aroostook County, Maine. Judd, "Lumbering," 62–3.

27 E.M. McKenzie, n.p., 4 Dec. 1864, no. 94, ANQS.

28 Ibid., 29 Aug. 1863, no. 59.

29 Reg. B, vol. 7, no. 4052, Cookshire Registry Office; F.S.A. Bélanger, n.p., 29 Oct. 1877, no. 2092–3, Palais de Justice, St Joseph de Beauce. Michael Merrill ("Cash," 56) claims that in the early-nineteenth-century United States these notes were rarely circulated to a third party.

30 Reg. B, vol. 9, no. 5126, Cookshire Registry Office. The 150–acre farm had been settled by the family some thirty years earlier. According to the 1871 census, it had thirty acres cleared, a horse and colt, a pair of oxen, two cows, four other cattle, ten sheep, and three pigs.

31 Compare the very detailed clothing budget presented by Gauldrée-Boileau ("Paysan," 54–7) for the Gauthiers in 1861–2. Items this family purchased in the store (which included woollens and "bottes sauvages") cost about $88 per year, while those produced at home were worth about $51 and the purchase of homespun items came to $10.

32 F.S.A. Bélanger, n.p., 24 July 1875, no. 1734, Palais de Justice, St Joseph de Beauce.

33 Camil Girard ("La dynamique," 132) has found that the store purchases of one Saguenay farmer over a fifty-year period in the nineteenth century were similar in nature to those of the Audet family.

34 Joachim Cameron had established himself as a hotel-keeper in St Romain in 1866 but appears to have gone out of business in 1870, presumably because of the curé's successful lobbying against a liquor permit in the parish (see chap. 7). Reg. B, vol. 19, no. 137, Sherbrooke Registry Office; F.S.A. Bélanger, n.p., Sale by Joachim Cameron to Thomas Cameron, 5 July 1870, Palais de Justice, St Joseph de Beauce. On the problems of identifying rural merchants, see Pronovost and St-Georges, "L'identification."

35 E.M. Mackenzie, n.p., 25 June 1866, no. 238–9; 15 Oct. 1866, no. 279, ANQS; Reg. B, vol. 20, no. 331; vol. 21, no. 239, 259, 260, Sherbrooke Registry Office.

36 Reg. B, vol. 1, no. 480; vol. 6, no. 3397, Cookshire Registry Office.

37 F.S.A. Bélanger, n.p., 16 Aug. 1877, no. 2037, Palais de Justice, St Joseph de Beauce.

38 Channell, *History*, 254. According to the Dun credit reports for the period 1857–62, McIver was doing a steady business and was "good for what he asks." Canada, vol. 21, 739, R.G. Dun & Co. Collection, Baker Library, Harvard University Graduate School of Business Administration.

39 D. Gunn to Lewis McIver, Winslow, 12 Nov. 1867, in *McIver v. Gunn*, Queen's Bench, St Francis, no. 539, ANQS.

40 Reg. B, vol. 20, no. 386, Cookshire Registry Office.

41 Gervais, "Le commerce," 535–6.

42 D. Gunn to Lewis McIver, Stornoway, 5 Feb. 1868, 29 April 1868, in *McIver v. Gunn*.

43 Reg. B, vol. 21, no. 388, Sherbrooke Registry Office; *McIver v. Gunn*; Reg. B, vol. 2, no. 817, Cookshire Registry Office.

44 Reg. B, vol. 10, no. 5935, Cookshire Registry Office.

45 Life of John Leonard, Fonds Leonard, P98–4, ETHS.

46 J.I. Mackie, n.p., 10 June 1871, no. 330, ANQS.

47 Pronovost, "Les marchands," 9. See also St-Georges, "Commerce," 330.

48 On folk remedies and tonics among the local Scots, see Bennett-Knight, "Folkways," 81–9.

49 Macdonald claims that Lewis women were noted for their love of bright colours, but that after 1824 the clergy began to criticize such vanities until black became the dominant hue. See his *Lewis*, 52–3; and *The Tolsta Townships*, 51. A visitor noted in 1838, however, that the Lewis women's dresses were striped and coloured; Mitchell, *Reminiscences*, 232–3.

50 Kesteman, "Une bourgeoisie," 202. On the use of commercial and home-made dyes by the district's Scots, see Bennett-Knight, "Folkways," 72.

51 See Desrosiers, "Un aperçu," 101–4; Michel, "Le livre," 376; Greer, *Peasant*, 156; and Pronovost, "Les marchands," 7.

52 See Greer, *Peasant*, 157–9. The Lewis crofters followed a long tradition of distilling whiskey to help pay their rents, though authorities had clamped down on the smuggling of this product off the island after 1823. Macdonald, *Lewis*, 56, 130–3; *New Statistical Account*, Lewis, 130; Grant, *Highland Folkways*, 303–5.

53 The Gaelic original appears in McLeod, *The Milan Story*, 87–8. The translation was kindly provided by Brian Mearns.

54 On McMinn, see Little, *Nationalism*, 135–40, 146.

55 One merchant operating in the Montreal area during the late eighteenth century balanced the year's accounts each May, allowing debtors another year to settle, then charging 6 per cent interest. The promissory note and mortgage were imposed only as a last resort. Michel, "Endettement," 176. See also McCalla, "Rural Credit," 40; McCalla, "The Internal Economy," 400; Desrosiers, "Un aperçu," 99, 107–8; and Gervais, "Le commerce," 522, 537–44.

56 Non-current accounts for the merchants studied by Pronovost ("Les marchands," 15) were generally of the same magnitude.

57 The court records are too disorganized for a systematic search, but one case was discovered in which Leonard's sons sued a Winslow farmer for failing to pay a promissory note worth $156.85. They won their case by default, for the defendant had left the province. *Hugh Leonard et al. v. John McLeod, dft*, 20 May 1878, no. 527; plumitif, vol. 10, p. 165, Queen's Bench, St Francis, ANQS.

58 Bervin, "Espace."

59 The Crown Lands Office rejected Leonard's claim to one fifty-acre lot adjacent to the village, based on a squatter's transfer (see adjudication 4040, MTF), but as of 1881 that property remained with the Leonard family.

60 Seven years prior to the auction, the original owner of the farm had signed a promissory note to the Leonards for $219.25, and he had subsequently mortgaged the farm to Colin Noble. He had left the province by the time of the sale. Reg. B, vol. 5, no. 2804; vol. 7, no. 666; vol. 9, no. 5344, Cookshire Registry Office..

61 The 1871 inventory, which was taken in June, only a few months after the census, reported two cows, four pigs, four horses, and a colt.

62 Thomas Jr nevertheless had $100 deducted from his salary for doctors' bills and attendance during his sickness of the previous fall.

63 The elder sons, Hugh and Thomas Jr, formed a partnership as "merchants, Hotel keepers, Farmers, Stage proprietors and general traders at Winslow" in 1871. James acquired a 20-per-cent interest in 1882, shortly after Hugh had joined forces with Dominique Morin of Lambton to carry on business as lumber merchants, dealers, and jobbers. The three brothers dissolved their partnership in 1882. Reg. E, Partnership Book, vol. 1, no. 5, 62–3, 75, 92, Cookshire Registry Office.

64 Faillites, vol. 3, 1864–79, no. 13 (1872), Cour Supérieur, St François, ANQS.

65 Channell (*History*, 120–1) claims that Colin and John Noble went to Massachusetts in 1848, but the 1852 Lingwick census lists a John Noble, gentleman, with a nine-year-old American-born son and one two years of age who was born in Canada.

66 Canada, vol. 1, 740, R.G. Dun & Co. Collection, Baker Library. None of the other Stornoway merchants or millers could be located in the Dun records.

67 See Kolish, "Le Conseil législatif," 218–19, and Gagan, "Security," 150. Although hypothecs covered all of a debtor's immovable property, the Winslow contracts always listed the location of specific lot(s) and mentioned whether or not there were buildings and other improvements.

68 On the nature of village merchant relations with farmers in subsistence-oriented communities, see Mutch, "Yeoman," 292.

69 The same point is made in Séguin, *La conquête*, 245. A case in point is the sheriff's auction of the Morisson farm in Whitton, which precipitated the famous "Megantic Outlaw" incident. See Kesteman, *Histoire*, 95.

70 There is no information on Noble's crops because he does not appear in the 1861 agricultural schedule.

71 Channell, *History*, 121. Noble eventually sold parts of the Cookshire property for $750.

72 Reg. B, vol. 37, no. 22673, Cookshire Registry Office.

73 Séguin, *La conquête*, 244. Total profits may be slightly exaggerated: Séguin's Table 2.6 does not list the purchase price of crown land, while apparently including the sale price of all land sold.

74 Picard sold his lots for an average of $284 during the 1870s and $329 during the 1890s, while farms in Hudon's Hébertville ranged from $400 to $800 during the latter half of the nineteenth century. Sevigny, "Le capitalisme," 44; Séguin, *La conquête*, 246.

75 Sevigny, "Le capitalisme," 62.

76 Channell, *History*, 121.

77 Ibid., 43. On Pope's dominant role in the upper St Francis district, see Little, *Nationalism*, especially chap. 5 and 7 and conclusion.

78 Sevigny, "Le capitalisme," 69–70, 77. Picard's hypothecs were effectively "rentes constituées," for the amortization date was ignored as long as the interest was faithfully paid. Lise St-Georges ("Commerce," 341–3) also finds that mortgages in Assomption during the latter half of the eighteenth century did not often result in merchant acquisition of farms, but contrast the case of Rémi Hudon in Hébertville. Séguin, *La conquête*, 243–5.

79 Hamelin and Roby, *Histoire*, 346.

80 There was also a significant increase in Picard's mortgaging activity in Wotton after 1875. See Sevigny, "Le capitalisme," 176.

81 The farmers who lived on this road in Winslow South signed twenty-eight hypothecs prior to 1880, but only eight during the next twenty years. Boulanger, Doyon, and Gagné, "Étude."

82 See Wright, "American Agriculture," 182–9.

83 *Code Civil du Bas Canada*, articles 2047, 2130.

84 There were also three hypothecs signed for $500 each to the Société de Construction de Coaticook, a type of co-operative trust. For the complex arrangements, see Reg. B, vol. 9, no. 5094–5, Cookshire Registry Office.

85 Once again, the situation was essentially the same in the Saguenay parish of St Fulgence. See St-Hilaire, "La structuration," 144.

86 Judd, "Lumbering," 63.

87 Ramsay, *John Ramsay*, 90. Ross was not part of the Lewis migration, for he had been born in Fearn, Rosshire, and immigrated to Lower Canada in 1829 at the age of fifteen. He went to Britain in 1872 and 1873 to recruit immigrants but died a year later. Channell, *History*, 258–9.

CHAPTER SEVEN

1 Stone, "Family History," 71–2, 82–3.

2 *New Statistical Account*, 137–8.

3 MacDermid, "Religious and Ecclesiastical Life," 73–81, 100–3, 108, 126–41, 156, 173–5, 222; Hunter, *Crofting Community*, 95.

4 Quoted in MacDermid, "Religious and Ecclesiastical Life," 170.

5 Macdonald, *Lewis*, 112.

6 MacDermid, "Religious and Ecclesiastical Life," 292–4.

7 Quoted in Hunter, *Crofting Community*, 98–9. See also Wm McGregor to Mrs Mackenzie, Galson, 28 Feb. 1832, Seaforth Muniments, GD 46/13/185, SRO.

8 *Twenty-ninth Annual Report of the Society for the Support of Gaelic Schools* (Edinburgh, 1840), 13–14, NCL.

9 Stanley, *Well-Watered Garden*, 141–2.

10 Hunter, *Crofting Community*, 100–1.

11 MacDermid, "Religious and Ecclesiastical Life," 277–82.

12 Quoted in ibid., 282.

13 Quoted in ibid., 283.

14 Ibid., 286, 302.

15 Ibid., 197–202, 264, 267–9, 284.

16 Ibid., 287–8.

17 Ibid., 273–5.

18 Hunter, *Crofting Community*, 96, 101, 104.

19 Wm McGregor to Mrs Stew't McKenzie, Galson, 10 June 1837, GD 46/11/545/5, SRO. See also Alex. Macleod to Mrs Stewart Mackenzie, Manse at Uig, 28 Aug. 1840, GD 46/12/44, SRO.

20 Quoted in Epps, "Immigrant File."

21 *Thirty-First Annual Report*, 1842, 19–20, NCL.

22 Vaudry, "The Free Church," ix.

23 MacDougall, "The Presbyterian Church," 12–15, 159–62, 174–5. For a useful history of the Presbyterian administrative structure, see Crerar, "Church and Community," chap. 1.

24 Stanley, *Well-Watered Garden*, x; *Home and Foreign Missionary Record for the Church of Scotland* [n.d.], 192, UCCA; John M'Ray, Catechist, and Alex. M'Leod, Schoolmaster, to the Ladies' Society in Edinburgh in aid of the Colonial Mission, Lingwick, 14 Aug. 1844, in *HFMRFCS* (Edinburgh), Dec. 1844, UCCA.

25 Letter to Secretary of Montreal Association, Montreal, 27 Dec. 1845, in *HFMRFCS*, Feb. 1846, 295.

26 Quoted in Rev. John Clugston to the Convener, 26 Jan. 1846, in ibid., March 1846, 320.

27 Same letter continued in ibid., Sept. 1846, 483.

28 Ibid.

29 Extract from Rev. Daniel Clark's Journal, in *HFMRFCS*, Oct. 1846, 506–7.

30 Ibid.

31 Letter from a Christian Friend, Montreal, 29 July 1846, in *HFMRFCS*, Oct. 1846, 507.

32 Letter from Rev. T. M'Lauchlan to the Convener, Stratherwick, 12 Jan. 1848, in *HFMRFCS*, March 1848, 351.

33 Noël, *Competing for Souls*, 156–61.

34 See Weale, "Time."

35 Clark, *Church and Sect*, xii.

36 Letter from a Christian Friend, 29 July 1846, in *HFMRFCS*, Oct. 1846, 507; Clugston to the Convener, Que., 26 Jan. 1846, in ibid., Sept. 1846, 483.

37 Ibid., Nov. 1848, 557. Local tradition later stated that the original money for the church was raised by a settler who went to Philadelphia for that purpose. MacDougall, "The Presbyterian Church," 114–15.

38 Extract from a letter by Rev. John Clugston, late of Quebec, to the Convener, in *HFMRFCS*, Nov. 1848, 557.

39 See Stanley, *Well-Watered Garden*, 142–3.

40 Mrs D. Gordon to Ladies Colonial Association, in *Home and Foreign Record of the Free Church of Scotland*, July 1852, 412, UCCA.

41 Ibid.

42 Ibid., Aug. 1851, 26.

43 *EMR*, July 1851.

44 Presbyterian Church of Canada (Free Church), Presbytery of Montreal, Minutes (notes), vol. 1, 10 March 1852, 164, UCCA. There are two versions of the minutes on microfilm held by the UCCA, one in rough note form, the other a more polished draft. The content is not always exactly the same. They will be distinguished from each other as "Minutes (notes)" and "Minutes," respectively.

45 Ibid., 9 March 1853, 162; 4 May 1853, 173.

46 See, for example, ibid., vol. 2, 31 Jan. 1855; 7 Oct. 1857. Vaudry, "The Free Church," 320–3.

47 Presbytery Minutes (notes), vol. 1, 10 March 1852, 164; 26 Jan. 1853, 155; 4 May 1853, 168; vol. 2, 7 Sept. 1853, n.p.

48 Ibid., vol. 2, 1 Nov. 1854; *EMR*, July 1853, Oct. 1853, Dec. 1854. There were only 113 Scots families in Winslow in 1861, but the congregation clearly included the neighbouring township of Whitton, where 301 adherents to the church resided, according to the 1861 census.

49 Presbytery Minutes (notes), vol. 2, 17 Oct. 1855, 23 Jan. 1856, 2 Aug. 1858, 3 Feb. 1859, UCCA.

50 Ibid., 27 Jan. 1858.

51 *EMR*, 1856. The Free Church in Canada had initially established a common sustentation fund whereby each minister would receive a minimum salary of £100 per year, but resistance to central control had killed it by 1849. Vaudry, "The Free Church," 216–17, 221, 233. References to Home Mission Fund contributions to Winslow and Lingwick can be found in Presbytery Minutes (notes), vol. 2, 5 Aug. 1863; Presbytery Minutes, 27 Sept. 1866, 208, UCCA.

52 Presbytery Minutes (notes), vol. 2, 12 May 1858.

53 Ibid., 11 Aug. 1858.

54 Ibid., 4 June 1860; 1 May 1861.

55 Presbytery Minutes, vol. 2, 7 Aug. 1861, 8, UCCA.

56 Ibid., 16 Oct. 1861, 19–20.

57 Presbytery Minutes (notes), 22 Jan. 1862; Minutes, 14 May 1862, 38, UCCA.

58 Ibid., vol. 2, 22 Jan. 1862; Presbytery Minutes, 14 May 1862, 38–9, UCCA.

59 Presbytery Minutes (notes), vol. 2, 14 May 1862, 6 June 1862, UCCA.

60 Presbytery Minutes, 13 Aug. 1862, 49–52, UCCA.

61 Presbytery Minutes (notes), vol. 2, 8 Oct. 1862; Presbytery Minutes, 6 Oct. 1862, 8 Oct. 1862, 9 Oct. 1862, UCCA. Peter Ward (*Courtship*, 28–30) comments on the sexual improprieties of several New Light preachers in the Maritimes and speculates on "the presence of sexual tensions deeply embedded in evangelical Christianity."

62 Presbytery Minutes (notes), vol. 2, 28 Jan. 1863; Presbytery Minutes, 28 Jan. 1863, 59–61, UCCA.

63 Presbytery Minutes (notes), vol. 2, 6 May 1863; Presbytery Minutes, 6 May 1863, 65, UCCA.

64 Presbytery Minutes, 5 June 1863, 75–6; 10 June 1863, 77; 5 Aug. 1863, 79; Presbytery Minutes (notes), [June 1863], 5 Aug. 1863, UCCA.

65 Presbytery Minutes, 28 Jan. 1864, 96; 25 Feb. 1864, 98–9; 26 Feb. 1864, 100, UCCA.

66 John Leonard, "Speech in Gaelic to Gaelic Society – c.1929," Compton County Historical Society.

67 MacKay, *Donald Morrison*, 56.

68 Presbytery Minutes, 6 Oct. 1869, 354. The original agreement as recorded in the presbytery minutes mentioned only a sum "exceeding" $400 per year; ibid., 25 Feb. 1864, 98.

69 Ibid., 21 Oct. 1869, 364–5.

70 Ibid., 27 Jan. 1870, 376; 5 May 1870, 393–4.

71 Ibid., 6 April 1871, 446. Two of these members had pressed for McDonald's resignation at the presbytery meeting of 5 May 1870, recorded on p. 393 of the Minutes.

72 Ibid., 4 Oct. 1871, 3; 24 Jan. 1872, 9; Record of the Presbytery of Quebec of the Presbyterian Church in Canada (hereafter Quebec Presbytery Record), 8 Dec. 1875, 8, P/11/2, 1875–93, UCCA. Of the three elders in question, Kenneth Campbell's name does not appear as a household head in my Winslow file of reconstituted families, and the only Angus Morrison was thirty-five years old in 1871, rather young to be an elder. However, the seventy-year-old Donald McKay of Winslow may well have been the third individual implicated.

73 Presbytery Minutes, 28 Jan. 1874, 111; 1 April 1874, 119, UCCA.

74 Ibid., 25 Jan. 1872, 13–14.

75 Ibid., 2 Oct. 1873, 99–100; Quebec Presbytery Record, 8 Dec. 1875, 8, UCCA.

76 Quebec Presbytery Record, 8 Dec. 1875, 8, UCCA.

77 Ibid., 9–10; 29 March 1876, 15.

78 Ibid., 8 Dec. 1875, 8; 13 Dec. 1876, 32; 29 March 1876, 15–16. Each congregation was to receive $254 from the Sherbrooke property. Ibid., 12 Sept. 1877, 55.

79 Ibid., 5 July 1876, 20; 13 Sept. 1876, 24–6; 13 Dec. 1876, 32; 20 and 21 March 1878, 65.

80 Ibid., 17 July 1878, 72–3.

81 Ibid., 16 Oct. 1878, 78; 16 April 1878, 88; Minute Book of Synod of Montreal and Ottawa, vol. 1, 90, 15 May 1880, P/7/2, UCCA, Bishop's University.

82 *Hon. J.H. Pope v. Aeneas McMaster*, 1880, no. 36, Court of Queen's Bench, St Francis, ANQS. On political reaction to seizure of McDonald's property, see Little, *Nationalism*, 181.

83 John Moir (*Enduring Witness*, 122) plays down the endurance of the Gaelic element in the Presbyterian church, but Winslow's morning service was held in that language until the church closed its doors for the last time in 1923. MacDonald, *The Family Tree*, 10–11.

84 See Crerar, "Church and Community," chap. 1; Campbell and MacLean, *Beyond the Atlantic Roar*, 57–8; and Bittermann, "Hierarchy," 47.

85 MacDougall ("The Presbyterian Church," 160–2) stresses the democratic nature of Presbyterian lay offices, while proudly identifying prominent members of the bourgeoisie who held such positions.

86 Stanley, *Well-Watered Garden*, 125; Crerar, "Church and Community," 121.

87 *The Home and Foreign Record of the Canada Presbyterian Church*, 1867–9. The Winslow minister did not submit statistics for the other years in the period 1863–74 covered by this journal.

88 *Acts and Proceedings of the General Assembly of the Presbyterian Church in Canada*, 1876, 1880. Again, these are the only two years in between 1870 and 1880 for which Winslow data are available.

89 Session Book of Winslow Congregation, April 1878–Oct. 1880, held by Duncan McLeod, Milan, Que.; Crerar, "Church and Community," 123. Crerar (p. 121) notes the modifying effect of the second generation in his district, and MacDougall ("The Presbyterian Church," 172) claims that discipline became more relaxed in the Quebec presbytery late in the nineteenth century.

90 Stanley, *Well-Watered Garden*, xi; see also pp. 147–8.

91 MacKay, *Donald Morrison*, 52–3. For an excellent description of a communion service on Cape Breton Island in 1886, see Farnham, "Cape Breton Folk."

92 Crerar, "Church and Community," 65–6, 99, 119.

93 W.P. Ward, "Unwed Motherhood," 36–7, 45.

94 Smith, *Lewsiana*, 89–90.

95 Ibid., 68; Smout, "Aspects of Sexual Behaviour," 75.

96 Smout, "Aspects of Sexual Behaviour," 76–8. Flinn's figures for the county of Ross, which included Lewis as well as a sizeable portion of the mainland, where illegitimacy rates were higher, vary from a low of 3.84 per cent in 1855–60 to a high of 4.86 per cent in 1866–70. Flinn, *Scottish Population History*, 350. Ian Carter ("Illegitimate Births," 132) questions the validity of the Scottish statistics largely on the grounds that one cannot know whether different registrars included or excluded children of common-law marriages from the illegitimacy figures.

97 Historians have found few traces of the bundling custom in English Canada. (P. Ward, *Courtship*, 104). A moral dilemma also arose in the western Isles when houses with two or three rooms began to be built. Smout, *Century*, 171, 175; Flinn, *Scottish Population History*, 366.

98 The problem of late baptisms and incomplete burial registers was overcome in Scotland by enactment of civil registration in 1855.

99 Laslett, "Introduction," 41.

100 Crerar, "Church and Community," 95.

101 Flinn, *Scottish Population History*, 363.

102 Smith, *Lewsiana*, 79–81.

103 Macdonald, *The Tolsta Townships*, 64–6.

104 P. Ward, *Courtship*, 105–6. For Laslett's courtship theory of legitimacy, see his "Introduction," 59–61. On the relationship between extramarital conception and socio-economic conditions in Scotland, see Smout, *Century*, 171–2.

105 The temperence movement appears not to have made much impact on the Scots throughout the district until the 1890s. See Channell, *History*, 258, 263, 269, 280; McLeod, *The Milan Story*, 42.

106 See also Macdonald, *Lewis*, 136–9.

107 Session of the Peace – Lingwick – Warrant of Arrest, 17 Sept. 1871, Court Records – Criminal – St Francis District, Sessions of the Peace and Magistrate's Court; Magistrate's Court – Warrant for Arrest, *J.W. Wiggett v. Malcolm McAulay et al.*, 30 June 1880, ANQS.

108 MacKay, *Donald Morrison*, 80.

109 Ibid., 110.

110 Prison Register, District of St Francis, 1882–91, ANQS.

111 On the Morrison affair see Rudin, "The Megantic Outlaw," and Wallace, *Wanted*.

112 See Monet, "French-Canadian Nationalism"; Hardy, "Note"; and Savard, "La vie," 268–9.

113 Philémon Brassard, "Notes sur la paroisse de Saint-Romain de Winslow," 23 Nov. 1888, in Parish Papers, Saint-Romain de Frontenac, Hist. folio 7, AAS; Edmond Langevin to Bishop of Quebec, 25 June 1855, in ibid.; Mgr Cooke to Duhaut, 13 Feb. 1856, RL, II, 13, AETR.

114 Cooke to Duhaut, 13 Feb. 1856, RL, II, 14, AETR.

115 See, for example, the cases described in Little, "The Peaceable Conquest," chap. 11; Nelson, "La guerre," 118–20, 160–6; and Greer, "L'habitant," 20–1.

116 Duhaut to Cooke, 25 March 1856, Parish Papers, Saint-Romain de Winslow, AAS.

117 J.A.H. Gignac, "St Olivier de Garthby," *Annuaire*, vol. 1 (1889–90), no. 15, 503; Cooke to Godbout, 15 Sept. 1857, RL II 164, AETR.

118 Cooke to Duhaut, 5 April 1856, RL II, 33, AETR.

119 Duhaut to Cooke, 26 May 1856, Parish Papers, Saint-Romain, AAS.

120 Cooke to Duhaut, 5 June 1856, RL, II, 43; 14 June 1856, 52–3, AETR.

121 Ibid., 1 Sept. 1856, 68.

122 "Aux fidèles du township de Winslow," 9 Sept. 1856, RL, II, 77, AETR.

123 Duhaut to Cooke, 29 Oct. 1856, G. Duhaut correspondence, AETR.

124 Cooke to Duhaut, 6 Nov. 1856, RL, II, 104, AETR.

125 Cooke to Duhaut, 12 Aug. 1857, 153, ibid.

126 Cooke to Bouchard, 28 April 1858, 165, ibid.

127 "Aux fidèles de la mission de Saint-Romain," 30 Jan. 1861, RL, III, no. 4, AETR.

128 Cooke to Bouchard, 26 Sept. 1862, RL, III no. 37; 8 Nov. 1862, no. 61, AETR; Petition to Bishop of Trois-Rivières, St Romain, 22 Sept. 1862, Parish Papers, Saint-Romain, Hist. folio 7, AAS.

129 Cooke to P. Gagné, Capt., et autres, 26 Sept. 1862, RL, III, no. 38, AETR.

130 Cooke to Bouchard, 8 Nov. 1862, RL, III, no. 61; 30 Sept. 1863, RL, III, no. 50, AETR.

131 Characteristic of clerical historians, Abbé Gravel (*Précis historique*, 18) wrote that there were never any rebels in the population, or any significant troubles.

132 Séguin, *La conquête*, 181.

133 Petition to Bishop of Trois-Rivières, 12 Aug. 1862, Parish Papers, Saint-Romain, Hist. folio 7, AAS. Unless reinforced by a notarized contract, the collection of supplements was not enforceable by civil law. LaBrèque, "La dîme."

134 Procès-verbal de la visite pastorale le 21–23 juillet 1867, Registre des Délibérations des Assemblées de Paroisse et de Fabrique (hereafter Registre de Fabrique), 2, SRP. For the clerico-conservative position, see Pagnuello, *Études*, 357–61; and Mignault, *Le droit*, 17, 19, 25, 181, 221. But prior to 1888, there was some question, at least among the priests of the diocese of Sherbrooke, as to whether a parish had to be civilly incorporated before the vestry could resort to legal sanctions. Because of the bishop of Sherbrooke's initiative, a statute was passed in 1888 stating that the "syndics" of a mission or the "marguilliers" of a parish not civilly incorporated could levy legally enforceable taxes for purposes of construction or maintenance. Petition to Mgr Racine, March 1879, Racine Papers, AAS; Mgr Taschereau to Racine, 22 March 1884, 27 March 1884, 19 May 1888, Archevêché de Québec, II-B-1, AAS; Quebec Statutes, 51 and 52 Vict., cap. XLIV; Pigeon, "Legislation," 97.

135 "Lettre pastorale concernant l'obligation qui incombe aux fidèles de pourvoir au soutien de leurs pasteurs," in *Mandements ... de Sherbrooke*, 20–2.

136 Mgr Taschereau to M. Besset [sic], 23 Jan. 1869; M. Bessette to Mgr LaRocque, Assemblée Législative, 30 June 1869, Archevêché de Québec, II-B-1 (1874–1947), AAS. The transition toward a livestock economy led to the same problem in the older parishes by the later 1880s; J. Roy, "Les revenus," 60.

137 Roy, "Religion," 413; P. Brassard to Mgr Racine, Sherbrooke, 31 Aug. 1877, Curé's Register, SRP.

138 Registre de Fabrique, 24 Oct. 1869, 5, SRP.

139 Savard, "La vie," 270. The average income for a curé in the diocese of Montreal in 1864 was $740; Gagnon, "Le diocèse de Montréal," 121.

140 Pouliot, *Traité*, 787–8; Lemieux, *Histoire*, 161–3; Cooke to Duhaut, Trois-Rivières, 5 June 1856, RL, II, 43, AETR.

141 Benediction of Church, 14 Feb. 1869, Curé's Register, 3, SRP; "St Romain de Winslow," *Annuaire*, vol. 1 (1892–3), no. 9, 121.

142 Livre des Minutes (1870–97), 17 April 1871, 13 June 1872, SRP.

143 Registre de Fabrique, 24 Oct. 1869, 4–5, SRP.

144 Registre de Fabrique, 6 Aug. 1871, 12, SRP.

145 Pastoral Visit for 1873, Registre de Fabrique, 23, SRP.

146 Registre de Fabrique, 20 June 1875, 29, SRP.

147 Report for 1877, Registre du curé, 8, SRP.

148 Report for 1875, Registre du Curé, 10; 18 March 1877, Registre du Curé, SRP. The accounts recorded in the Registre de Fabrique, and relied on here, indicate higher levels of debt than do the curé's annual reports to the bishop.

149 Livre des Minutes (1870–97), 9 Aug. 1875, SRP.

150 Whether by accident or not, the vestry's accounts failed to balance this "loan" with an entry on the debit side.

151 Registre de Fabrique, 46, SRP.

152 Ibid., 47.

153 "St Romain de Winslow," in *Annuaire*, vol. 2 (1892–3), no. 9, 122.

154 Séguin, *La conquête*, 189–91.

155 Petition of Rev. F.X. Vanasse of St Romain, 30 Jan. 1868, art. 871, Correspondance Générale, Municipalités, 1867–80, no. 344, Secrétariat Provincial, E4, ANQQ; F.X. Vanasse to Dept., 17 Aug. 1868, no. 1614; 2 July 1869, no. 3611; [n.d.], no. 3633; 13 Sept. 1869, no. 4543; 28 Sept. 1869, no. 4806, Registres de Lettres Reçues, Agriculture et Travaux Publics, E25; Dept. to James Ross, Quebec, 4 Aug. 1869, I, no. 1619, 194; B. de la Bruère to F.X. Vanasse, 19 July 1870, II, no. 3042, 553, Registres de Lettres Envoyées, E25, ANQQ.

156 E. Moreau to Wm. Sawyer, 1 Sept. 1871, VII, no. 4542, 650; E. Moreau to Rev. P. Brassard at St Romain, 18 Sept. 1871, VIII, no. 4702, 193; 30 Sept. 1871, VIII, no. 4795, 331–2; E. Moreau to Rev. P. Brassard at St Romain, 16 July 1872, X, no. 5918, 490; E. Moreau to P. Brassard, 14 July 1874, XVIII, no. 10464, 250; E. Moreau to Wm Sawyer [1875], XXIII, no. 12775, 400; J.O. Fontaine to Rev. P. Brassard, 8 July 1880, XXXV, [no no.], 673, Registres de Lettres Envoyées, E25, ANQQ.

157 S Lesage to Rev. P. Brassard, Que., 14 Oct. 1880, Register, 19–20, Paroisse de St Romain de Winslow, AAS.

158 André Boucher ("Le rôle," 172) claims that relations between wardens and curés were unfailingly cordial in the parishes he investigated.

159 Cahier d'annonces, Christmas, 1875, SRP.

160 See Greer, "L'habitant," 28–32; Chabot, *Le curé*, chap. 2; Boucher, "La fabrique," 159–61; and Lemieux, *Histoire*, 155–60.

161 Report on Parish for 1872, Registre du Curé, 5, SRP. For conflicting views on who controlled the accounts, see Voisine, *Histoire*, 20, and Boucher, "Le rôle," 166–8.

162 Registre de Fabrique, 24 Oct. 1869, 4, SRP.
163 Greer, "L'habitant," 23–4; Lemieux, *Histoire*, 179–82.
164 Registre de Fabrique, 24 Dec. 1876, 34, SRP.
165 See Rousseau, "La conduite," 273–7.
166 Hardy and Roy, "Mutation," 400–3.
167 Cahier d'annonces, fourth Sunday after Lent, 1872; third Sunday of Lent, 1873, SRP.
168 Ibid., first Sunday of Advent, 1868.
169 The council voted for a liquor licence in 1866 and 1870 but unanimously rejected it in 1871. Michel Audet to Prov. Sec., Winslow North, 1 May 1866, no. 849, vol. 591, RG 4 C1, NA; Livre des Minutes (1870–97), 7 March 1870, 6 March 1871, SRP. The licence issue was frequently mentioned in the curé's sermon notes. See Cahier d'annonces, Septuagesima Sunday, 1867; second Sunday after Epiphany, 1872; third Sunday after Lent, 1875; second Sunday after Easter, 1876, SRP. Neighbouring Lambton banned the sale of alcohol in 1865; Lapointe, *Historique*, 77.
170 Cahier d'annonces, sixteenth Sunday after Easter, 1880, SRP.
171 Ibid., twenty-fifth Sunday after Pentecost, 1871; ninth Sunday after Pentecost, 1873. On the significance of these "transgressions" see Hardy and Roy, "Mutation," 405–7.
172 Registre du Curé, 6 July 1875, 9, SRP. On the seriousness of usury in the minds of the Quebec clergy, see Gagnon, *Mourir*, 30–2.
173 Brassard to Mgr Racine, 27 Nov. 1874, Parish Papers, St Romain, no. 3, AAS.
174 Hardy, "Le greffier" (copy kindly provided by the author).
175 The documents related to this case are in no. 314, vol. 362, RG 4 C1, NA.
176 Prison Register, District of St Francis, 1882–91, ANQS.
177 Langlois, *Histoire*, 253.
178 Laslett, "Introduction," 54–5. For the sixteen English parishes studied by Laslett ("Introduction," 23) for 1800–49, the premarital conception rate was 37 per cent. For the Saguenay region from 1840 to 1869 it was only 4.6 per cent, and from 1870 to 1879, 4.0 per cent (personal communication from Gérard Bouchard). For the St Lawrence Valley prior to 1725 the rate was 6.1 per cent. (Bates, "Les conceptions," 256–8) and for the five Upper Canadian parishes examined by Ward ("Unwed Motherhood," 39) it varied from 7.9 per cent to 19.0 per cent, though Ward includes all births taking place up to eight and a half months after marriage.
179 Bates, "Les conceptions," 269. Lemieux (*Histoire*, 273) states that "les fiançailles solennelles" never existed in French Canada. See also Bouchard, "Sur la dynamique," 479–83.
180 Johnston (*Religion*, 127–9, 134–5) notes the same pattern for eighteenth-century Louisbourg, where there were almost no betrothals and

where premarital conceptions between 1722 and 1757 were 11.2 per cent.

181 Séguin, *La conquête*, 200. See also Audet, "Pouvoir," 64–5.

182 Cahier d'annonces, twenty-sixth Sunday after Pentecost, 1877, SRP.

183 The same general preoccupations appeared more forcefully in the sermon notes of the curé of St Hilarion de Charlevoix, also a poor colonization parish. Audet, "Pouvoir," 65–6. See also Greer, "L'habitant," 26; and Lemieux, *Histoire*, 280–3.

184 Registre de Fabrique, 1873–8, SRP.

185 MacDonald, *The Family Tree*, 11. On the organ controversy in the Presbyterian church, see Vaudry, "The Free Church," 317–19, and Moir, *Enduring Witness*, 131–4. Even St Romain's parent parish of St Vital did not acquire an organ until 1888. Lapointe, *Historique*, 134.

186 See Noel, "God's Scots" and "Dry Patriotism"; Voisine, "Mouvements"; and Rousseau, "Les missions."

187 Parish Report for 1875, Curé's Register, 10, SRP. On this subject, see Voisine, "Jubilés, missions paroissiales," and Lemieux, *Histoire*, 313–16.

188 Érection des 40 heures, Registre du Curé, 18 Jan. 1876, SRP; Cahier d'annonces, Quinquagésima, 1878, 1879, SRP. This participation rate was somewhat higher than that customarily noted for at least one parish in the diocese of Trois-Rivières. G. Trépanier, "Contrôle," 84–5. See also Lemieux, *Histoire*, 312–13.

189 See Hurtubise, "La religiosité"; Cliche, "Les confréries"; Caulier, "Les confréries"; Laperrière, "Religion"; and Tackett, *Priest*, chap. 8.

190 Registre du Curé, 3–4, 6, 9. See Lemieux, *Histoire*, 320–4.

191 G. Trépanier, "Contrôle," 86–92.

192 Little, *Nationalism*, 167; Pépin, "Le phénomène," 96.

193 Parish Report for 1873, Curé's Register, 7, SRP.

194 See, for example, Rodrigue, *Le cycle*, 186–94. Bellavance (*Un village*, 30–1) and Gaffield (*Language*, 87) make the same observation concerning Easter conceptions for the parish of St Thomas de Compton and Prescott County, Ontario, respectively.

195 These ratios are similar to those for seventeenth-century Canada, where 80 per cent of baptisms took place during the first three days. Charbonneau, "Colonisation," 344.

196 See Bourguière, "L'attribution," 47, 64, 67.

197 Bourguière (ibid., 48) notes that the use of Joseph stagnated in eighteenth-century France, while for girls Marie became the most popular name in the country.

198 MacDermid, "Religious and Ecclesiastical Life," 166–8.

199 Lemieux (*Histoire*, 306) makes a similar point.

200 See Gagnon and Hardy, eds., *L'église*, 31; and G. Trépanier, "Contrôle," 100–9.

201 For descriptions of similar intercessions in other parishes, see Audet, "Pouvoir," 50; and G. Trépanier, "Contrôle," 100–5.

202 See Davis, "De la religion," 398; and Tackett, *Priest*, 209–15.

203 Cahier d'annonces, ninth and twelfth Sundays after Pentecost, SRP.

204 Eighteen of Winslow's thirty-three French-Canadian wills included such requests – a considerably lower ratio than the 83 per cent of wills notarized in the rural Quebec district during the nineteenth century. Cliche, "L'évolution," 376–8, 381.

205 Pépin, "Le phénomène," 96.

206 See Laperrière, "Religion," and Hurtubise, "La Religiosité."

CHAPTER EIGHT

1 See, for example, Prentice, *School Promoters*, 20, 180–4.

2 See Darroch, "Class"; Akenson, *The Irish*; and Elliott, *Irish Migrants*.

3 Prentice, *School Promoters*, 20.

4 Houston and Prentice, *Schooling*, x–xi.

5 Ibid., 338.

6 Charland, "Le réseau."

7 B. Curtis, *Building the Educational State*; Gidney and Lawr, "Bureaucracy" and "Who Ran the Schools?"; and Gidney and Millar, "From Voluntarism."

8 Nelson, "La guerre."

9 *Sixtieth Annual Report of the Society for the Support of Gaelic Schools* (hereafter Gaelic Schools Report) (Edinburgh, 1827), 13, NCL.

10 *New Statistical Account*, 168.

11 Sixteenth Gaelic Schools Report (Edinburgh, 1827), 31, NCL.

12 Eighteenth Gaelic Schools Report (Edinburgh, 1829), 33.

13 Seventeenth Gaelic Schools Report (Edinburgh, 1828), 28. He originally wrote great-great-grandmother but corrected himself on p. 21 of the 1829 report.

14 Fifteenth Gaelic Schools Report (Edinburgh, 1826), 31, 50–1.

15 Seventeenth Gaelic Schools Report (Edinburgh, 1828), 29.

16 Twenty-fifth Gaelic Schools Report (Edinburgh, 1836), 28–9.

17 Thirty-third Gaelic Schools Report (Edinburgh, 1844), 32.

18 Twenty-ninth Gaelic Schools Report (Edinburgh, 1840), 25. For further details on the Lewis schools, see Macdonald, *Lewis*, 145–9.

19 For a summary and analysis of school legislation in Lower Canada to 1849, see Nelson, "La guerre," chap. 2 and 4.

20 See ibid., chap. 5, 7, and 8. Similarly, Andrée Dufour ("Diversité," 521–2, 532) argues that the French-Canadian inhabitants of the island of Montreal took advantage of the rather limited educational opportunities during the early nineteenth century.

21 Verrette, "L'alphabetisation," Table 36.

22 Greer, "Pattern," 327, 331.

23 Gaffield and Bouchard, "Literacy," 12.

24 Verrette, "L'alphabetisation," Table 26.

25 Upper Canadian historians do not agree on the relative merits of these two sources. See Mays and Marzl, "Literacy," and Graff, "What the 1861 Census Can Tell Us."

26 Bouchard and Larouche, "Nouvelle mesure," 98, 104–5.

27 Verrette, "L'alphabetisation," Table 36.

28 On the international context, see Greer, "Pattern," 300, 317, 326, 332. Harvey Graff ("Interpreting," 454–5) claims, however, that he has found female literacy to be higher than that of males in rural Ontario.

29 Ten years later, Peel's enrolment ratio did surpass that of the Winslow Scots by a slight margin, and rural Ontario's enrolment reached 86 per cent in 1881. Gagan, *Hopeful Travellers*, 82; Houston and Prentice, *Schooling*, 201.

30 A higher ratio of girls than boys was enrolled in the schools of the Saguenay region until 1931. J. Ouellet, "Le développement," 15.

31 Houston and Prentice, *Schooling*, 200; Katz, *People*, 39.

32 See Gaffield, *Language*, 109–10.

33 Quoted in Bennet-Knight, "Folkways," 48.

34 Ian Davey ("Rhythm," 241) makes the same point for rural Upper Canada.

35 M. Child to J.B. Meilleur, Stanstead, 18 July 1853, no. 1085 (1853); 28 Feb. 1854, no. 346 (1854), Lettres Reçues, E13, ANQQ.

36 Ewen McLean to J.B. Meilleur, Esq., Manse of Winslow, 22 June 1855, no. 1169 (1855), Lettres Reçues, E13, ANQQ.

37 Ewen McLean to Sir E.W. Head, Winslow Manse, 7 November 1855; Petition of inhabitants of Winslow and Whitton, 5 Nov. 1855; Draft reply to Rev. Ewen McLean, Toronto, 21 Nov. 1855, no. 3033, vo. 382, RG 4C1, NA.

38 Alex. Macleod et al. to Mr Chameau [sic], [Winslow, 3 Sept. 1856], no. 1930 (1856); Colin Noble to J.O. Chauveau, Winslow, 25 April 1857; Draft reply, 2 May 1857, no. 1137 (1857), Lettres Reçues, E13, ANQQ.

39 Re enrolment statistics, as recorded in inspectors' reports: many pupils in Winslow South were said to attend two or more schools within the year. Also, those enrolled in dissentient schools were sometimes counted as students in the regular schools as well. H. Hubbard to Giard, Sherbrooke, 2 Dec. 1868, 3 Dec. 1868, no. 3215 (1868), Lettres Reçues, E13, ANQQ. The superintendent of education made it clear in 1860 that reported enrolment was to represent the aggregate number having attended classes during the previous twelve months, not the average

daily attendance. Superintendent to H. Hubbard, Montreal, 9 Feb. 1860, no. 363 (1860), ibid.

40 *JLAC*, xv (1857), Appendix 58. Child was referring to the widely-distributed series of British text books designed during the 1830s to instil loyalty in the Irish, and the values of bourgeois civilization in the working class. See Akenson, *The Irish*, 269–71, and B. Curtis, *Building the Educational State*, 267–73, 286–91.

41 *JLAC*, xvi (1858), Appendix 43.

42 Colin Noble to P.J.O. Chauveau, S. Winslow, 23 Feb. 1858, no. 616 (1858); Colin Noble to M. Childs, Esq., Winslow, 7 June 1858, no. 1428 (1858), Lettres Reçues, E13, ANQQ.

43 Donald MacIver to Sir, Winslow, 17 June 1858, no. 1428 (1858), ibid.

44 M. Child to Sir, Coaticook, 5 July 1858, no. 1428 (1858), ibid.

45 Daniel McIver to Chauveau, Winslow, 5 July 1858; draft reply, 6 Aug. 1858, no. 1428 (1858), ibid.

46 Daniel McIver et al. to Chauveau, Winslow, 6 Dec. 1858, no. 2717 (1858), ibid.

47 Daniel McIver et al. to Chauveau, Winslow, 16 Feb. 1860; H. Hubbard to Chauveau, Danville, 21 July 1860, no. 701 (1860), ibid.

48 *JLAC*, xvii (1859), Appendix 58; H. Hubbard to Chauveau, Danville, 21 July 1860, no. 701 (1860), Lettres Reçues, E13, ANQQ.

49 John Smith to Chauveau, 8 Aug. 1859, 30 Aug. 1859, no. 2005 (1859), ibid. The special tax could be imposed only for erecting, maintaining, and repairing school houses. Draft reply, Montreal, 21 Dec. 1864, no. 2584 (1864); Petition of John Smith et al., rec'd 12 May 1860; draft reply, Montreal, 14 May 1860, no. 1253 (1860), ibid.

50 *SPC*, xx (1862), no. 34.

51 John Smith to Chauveau, Winslow, 8 Aug. 1859, no. 2005 (1859), Lettres Reçues, E13, ANQQ. The grant was supposed to be distributed according to the number of children aged seven to fourteen. Nelson, "La guerre," 66.

52 Hubbard to Chauveau, Danville, 22 Aug. 1861; draft reply, 28 Aug. 1861, no. 2212 (1861), Lettres Reçues, E13, ANQQ.

53 Hubbard to Chauveau, Eaton, 5 July 1862, 29 Sept. 1862, no. 717 (1862); 1 Aug. 1863, 9 Dec. 1863, no. 2193 (1863); Ed. Bélanger to Monsieur, St Romain, 7 Aug. 1863, no. 2296 (1863); Donald Gunn to Hon. Sir, Winslow, 21 Dec. 1863, no. 3142 (1863), ibid.

54 D. Campbell to Chauveau, S. Winslow, 11 Dec. 1862, no. 3006 (1862), ibid. The other letters concerning this case are in the same file.

55 Murdoch McIver et al. to Chauveau, Winslow, 30 March 1864; draft reply, Montreal, 28 April 1864, no. 737 (1864), ibid.

56 *SPC*, xxiv (1865), no. 37.

57 Hubbard to Chauveau, Sherbrooke, 27 June 1864, no. 1276 (1864), Lettres Reçues, E13, ANQQ.

58 Hubbard to Chauveau, Sherbrooke, 9 July 1864, no. 1276 (1864); Petition to Chauveau, Winslow South, 12 July 1864, no. 1511 (1864), ibid. Henry's petition was in English, and all the French names were signed with crosses. While Hubbard stressed that this petition was not his suggestion, he had stated earlier that the best solution was for the commissioners to open a French school and collect the taxes. Hubbard to Chauveau, Sherbrooke, 27 June 1864, no. 1276 (1864), ibid.

59 Gédéon Béliveau et al. to Superintendent, Winslow South, 28 Oct. 1865; M.T. Stenson to Chauveau, Danville, 16 Feb. 1866; draft letter to H. Hubbard, Montreal, 23 Feb. 1866; draft letter to school commissioners of South Winslow, Montreal, 23 Feb. 1866; Hubbard to Chauveau, 2 March 1866, no. 1511 (1864), ibid.

60 Jos. Cormier et al. to G. Ouimet, Winslow S., 28 Sept. 1878; to Monsieur, Winslow, 11 Nov. 1878, no. 2539B (1878); Wm Béliveau to Ouimet, Winslow S., 16 Oct. 1878; draft reply, 25 Oct. 1878, no. 2661 (1878), ibid.; Ouimet to Wm Béliveau, 3 Oct. 1878, 358; Ouimet to MM. les Syndics d'écoles, Winslow-Sud, 16 Nov. 1878, 736, Lettres Expédiées, E13, ANQQ.

61 J. Ferdinand Legendre to Monsieur, Stornoway, 29 Nov. 1880; Wm Béliveau to Monsieur, Winslow-Sud, 6 April 1881; Legendre to Ouimet, Stornoway, 27 Oct. 1881; draft reply, 9 Nov. 1881; Béliveau to Ouimet, Winslow-Sud, 30 Dec. 1881; draft reply, 5 Jan. 1882, no. 1909 (1880), Lettres Reçues, E13, ANQQ.

62 Inspector Hubbard noted that grants had been recorded for both Winslow North and St Romain, even though they were the same place, but no further action appears to have been taken. Hubbard to Chauveau, Sherbrooke, 24 Oct. 1864, no. 2362 (1864), ibid.

63 SPC, xxiv (1865), no. 37.

64 SPQ, 1 (1869), Report of Minister of Public Instruction for 1867 and 1868 (Stenson). Three independent schools remained open until at least 1873. See Table 8.4.

65 A. Gosselin and J. Marceau to Mr le Surintendant, St Romain, 30 March 1866; draft reply, Montreal, 21 April 1866, no. 584 (1866); Jos. Duquet to Monsieur le Surintendant, St Romain, 22 Jan. 1867, no. 140 (1867); draft reply, Montreal, 11 Feb. 1867, Lettres Reçues, E13, ANQQ.

66 Laurent [Gagné] to Ouimet, St Romain, 26 Nov. 1879, no. 2998 (1879), ibid.

67 Cahier d'annonces, Advent Sunday, 1868, SRP; Stenson to Superintendent, Sherbrooke, 4 Feb. 1880, no. 2998 (1879); A. Gosselin and J. Marceau to Mr le Surintendant, St Romain, 16 March 1866, no. 553

(1866), ibid.; Chauveau to J. Marceau, 11 April 1866, 468, vol. 15, Lettres Expédiées, E13, ANQQ.

68 *SPQ*, XI (1877–8), no. 2, 234.

69 Gidney and Lawr, "Who Ran the Schools?" 137.

70 Petition to G. Ouimet, St Romain, 4 July 1880; Order-in-Council, 27 Aug. 1880, no. 1030 (1880), Lettres Reçues, E13, ANQQ.

71 *SPQ*, VIII (1874–5), 129. These observations were reiterated in *SPQ*, XI (1877–8), 233.

72 *SPQ*, XI (1877–8), no. 2, 232–3; Stenson to Ouimet, St Romain de Winslow, 10 July 1877, no. 1751 (1877); draft reply, 20 July 1877, Lettres Reçues, E13, ANQQ.

73 *SPQ*, XIII (1879), no. 5, 102.

74 *SPQ*, XIV (1880), no. 5, 99.

75 *SPQ*, XV (1881–2), no. 5, 57, 120. On the impact of economic recession and crop failure on attendance in Upper Canada, see Davey, "Rhythm," 228–30, and Houston and Prentice, *Schooling*, 216–17.

76 *SPQ*, V (1871), no. 3, 30–6.

77 *SPQ*, XVIII (1874–5), 155.

78 The inspector recommended that Stornoway establish a model school in 1881. *SPQ*, XIV (1880), no. 5, 108; XV (1881–2), no. 5, 133. The curé of St Romain had inquired about the possibility of opening a model school in his parish in 1868, but he apparently dropped the idea after being informed that there was no special fund for such a purpose. F.X. Vanasse to Chauveau, St Romain, 4 Dec. 1868; draft reply, 9 Dec. 1868, no. 3283 (1868), Lettres Reçues, E13, ANQQ.

79 *SPC*, XXIV (1865), no. 37, 110; *SPQ*, XI (1877–8), no. 2, 138; XIII (1879), no. 5, 114; XIV (1880), no. 5, 50; XV (1881–2), no. 5, 132.

80 *SPQ*, XI (1877–8), no. 2, 233.

81 Danylewcz, Light, and Prentice, "Evolution," 89–94, 98, 103.

82 See the Grand Statistical Tables for 1861, 1864, 1866, 1869–70, and 1872–3 in the official reports of the superintendent of education. These salaries presumably included board, at least for the men in 1861, for no teachers were reported as independent householders in the census of that year.

83 "Liste des salaires des enseignants," Art. 2530 (1880), E13, ANQQ. Between 1866 and 1881, teachers' salaries in the Saguenay region were $150 to $160 for men, and $75 to $83 for women. J. Ouellet, "Le développement," 25.

84 Marie-de-Lime Roy to Monsieur, St Romain, 25 Dec. 1864, no. 2692 (1864), Lettres Reçues, E13, ANQQ.

85 Ouimet to School Commisioners of Winslow North [n.d.], vol. 38, 132; 20 July 1877, vol. 40, 377; 22 Sept. 1877, vol. 41, 218; 17 Oct. 1877,

426; 5 Dec. 1877, 980; Ouimet to Mlle D. Hébert, 19 Dec. 1877, vol. 42, 172–3, Lettres Expédiées, E13, ANQQ.

86 Octave Fortin to Delle Marie McKenzie, St Romain, 27 March 1871; Rev. C.A. Sicard de Carufel, St Romain, 15 May 1871; Carufel to Chauveau, St Romain, 6 June 1871; Draft letter to Commissioners, Que., 15 June 1871, no. 965 (1871), Lettres Reçues, E13, ANQQ.

87 Dorion, *Les écoles*, 246–50.

88 See ibid., 252–63; and Le Collectif Clio, *L'histoire*, 213.

89 Laurent [Gagné] to Ouimet, St Romain, 26 Nov. 1879; Stenson to Superintendent, Sherbrooke, 4 Feb. 1880; draft letter to Gagné, Qué., 13 Feb. 1880, no. 2998 (1879), ibid.

90 J. Ouellet, "Le développement," 15.

91 Hardy and Roy, "Encadrement social," 70.

92 *SPQ*, VIII (1874–5), 129–30; X (1876), no. 2, 45.

93 *SPQ*, XI (1877–8), no. 2, 236; XIII (1979), no. 5, 102.

94 See, for example, Ross, "Ethnic Relations," 14–15; and Gmelch, "Social History," 26, 29, 39.

95 Mid-Victorian Ontario is said to have been characterized by a belief in the possibility of earthly salvation, a creed not likely to appeal to the Calvinistic, subsistence-oriented Scots of Winslow. See Westfall, *Two Worlds*, 195, 203, and French, "Egerton Ryerson."

96 There is no evidence that Gaelic was taught in the Scots' schools in the Eastern Townships. Campbell and MacLean (*Beyond the Atlantic Roar*, 131, 141, 147–50) claim that even in Nova Scotia the Highlanders failed to take advantage of the official provision for teaching in their mother tongue.

97 *SPQ*, XIII (1879), no. 5, 102.

98 *SPQ*, XV (1881–2), no. 5, 121.

99 Corrigan and Curtis, "Education."

100 Nelson, "La guerre," chap. 6; Séguin, *La conquête*, 211.

101 Monette, "Groupes dominantes," 84–5.

102 Nelson, "La guerre," 59–60.

103 Joseph Marceau to Minister of Public Instruction, St Romain, 7 Feb. 1872, no. 625 (1872), Lettres Reçues, E13, ANQQ.

104 Colin Noble and Donald McLeod to Chauveau, South Winslow, 18 May 1871, no 790 (1871); Donald N. McLeod to Chauveau, South Winslow, 6 March 1872, no. 899 (1872); Winslow South, 4 Sept. 1875, no. 2289 (1875), ibid.

105 Jos. Marceau to Superintendent, St Romain, 6 July 1872, no. 2035 (1872), ibid. The same practice was followed in the Laurentians; Laurin, *Histoire*, 449.

106 Channell, *History*, 269.

107 St Romain, Minutes, 8 Sept. 1879.

108 Cahier d'annonces, third Sunday after Easter, 1867, SRP.

109 Ibid., Quasimodo Sunday, 1870; Ste Trinité, 1876. For a comparison, see Audet, "Pouvoir," 50, 58–9. On the social role of the Presbyterian church in the Highlands, see MacDermid, "Religious and Ecclesiastical Life," 169.

110 St Romain de Winslow, Livre des Minutes (1870–97), 26 Aug. 1872.

111 Ibid., 2 Dec. 1872; 3 May 1873. A similar point is made in Séguin, La conquête, 189, and Monette, "Groupes dominantes," 80.

112 See, for example, Michel Audet to Provincial Secretary, Winslow North, 26 July 1869; draft reply, 6 Aug. 1869, Art. 873, no. 1039; Murdoch Beaton et al. to Lieut. Gov., Hampden, 3 March 1874; Action, 12 March 1874, Art. 880, no. 350; Louis Turgeon to Prov. Sec., Winslow North, 15 Jan. 1879; Draft Reply, 19 Feb. 1879, Art. 886, no. 84, Correspondance Générale Municipalités, Secrétariat Provincial, E4, ANQQ.

113 Little, "Colonization," 107.

114 St Romain, Minutes, 6 March, 17 April 1871.

115 Ibid., 3, 28 March 1873.

116 Ibid., 5 June 1876, 4 June 1877.

117 For details, see Little, Nationalism, 152.

118 St Romain, Minutes, 3, 13 July 1876, 5, 17 Feb. 1877, 1 March 1879.

119 Ibid., 26 July 1877.

120 Ibid., 1, 6 March, 7 April, 5, 29 May 1879.

121 Ibid., 4, 18 Aug. 1879.

122 Ibid., 23 May 1880, 1 Aug. 1881.

123 Winslow South Municipal Assessment Records, 144, Amounts paid to C.A. Bailey to apply to Railroad Taxes, Stornoway.

124 St Romain, Minutes, [1873], 58.

125 Petition, 8 Feb. 1878, no. 480, Art. 884, E4, ANQQ.

126 Ibid., 17 Jan. 1870.

127 Ibid., 31 Jan. 1876.

128 Ibid., 4 March 1878.

129 This point is made by Richard Beeman ("Social History," 427) in relation to studies on colonial America.

130 Ward (Courtship, 61) claims that in nineteenth-century Ontario two out of three men and women married someone from their own community.

131 P.M. Jones, "Parish," 102.

132 See Deffontaines, "The Rang," and Séguin, La conquête, 182–3.

133 Personal communication from Duncan McLeod.

134 On the various criteria for community identification, and the failure of many of them to overlap even in "traditional" societies, see MacFarlane, Reconstituting Historical Communities, 9–16.

CONCLUSION

1 See, for example, Beeman, "Social History," 426–7; Goubert, "Vingt-cinq ans," 322–3; and Wynn, "Settler Societies," 365–6.
2 Lemon, "Early Americans" and "The Weakness of Place"; Wynn, "Ethnic Migrations," 10. See also Wynn, "Settler Societies," 363, and the historian Gérard Bouchard's "Sur la dynamique."
3 Harris, "Pattern," 369.
4 Harris, "The Simplification of Europe Overseas," 479–80. See also his "The Historical Geography of North American Regions."
5 Harris, "Extension," 43. French Canada is also treated in detail in Harris and Guelke, "Land and Society."
6 Harris, "Poverty."
7 Harris, Roulston, and de Freitas, "Settlement."
8 *New Statistical Account*, 167.
9 Thompson, *Crofting Years*, 33.
10 Ibid., 132.
11 Ostergren, "A Community Transplanted."
12 Overland, *Johan Schroder's Travels*, 11–36, 80–102.
13 Morissonneau, "Genre," 220. A similar view is expressed in Falardeau, "Religion populaire" but contradicted in Hardy and Roy, "Encadrement social," 64. Evidence that religion was not simply forgotten when men entered the woods during the winter can be found in their work songs; see Lacroix and Laforte, "Religion traditionnelle."
14 See Bouchard, "Sur la dynamique," 488.
15 On the distinction between the development of settler societies and that of the Third World, see Denoon, "Understanding Settler Societies," 511–13.
16 See part one of *La conquête*.
17 Little, *Nationalism*, chap. 1 and 5.
18 Bouchard, "Introduction," 22–4.
19 See Little, *Nationalism*, chap. 1.
20 For example, there are suggestive parallels with Winslow to be found in Glenn Lockwood's "Irish Immigrants."
21 On this approach see Darroch and Ornstein, "Ethnicity," 330, and Ramirez, "Ethnic Stucture," 47–8.

Bibliography

MANUSCRIPT SOURCES

ARCHIVES DE L'ARCHEVÊCHÉ
DE SHERBROOKE (AAS)
Correspondance avec Archevêché de Québec (II-B-1)
Mgr Antoine Racine Papers
Papiers des Paroisses, Saint-Romain

ARCHIVES DE LA SOCIÉTÉ
D'HISTOIRE DES CANTONS
DE L'EST (SHERBROOKE)
Fonds Affaire Morrison (P153)

ARCHIVES DE L'ÉVÊCHÉ
DE TROIS-RIVIÈRES
(AETR)
Registres des Lettres, I–III
Correspondance de Rev. G. Duhaut

ARCHIVES NATIONALES
DU QUÉBEC À QUÉBEC
(ANQQ)
Fonds Agriculture et Travaux publics (E25)
    Correspondances reçues, 1867–80
    Registres de lettres envoyées, 1867–80
    Registres de lettres reçues, 1867–80
Fonds Éducation (E13)
    Distribution to poor municipalities, 1870–81
    Lettres expédiées, 1851–81

Lettres reçues, 1855–81
Liste des salaires des enseignants, 1880
Octrois aux nouvelles municipalités, 1851–71
Fonds Secrétariat Provincial (E4)
    Correspondance Générale. Municipalités, 1867–80
Fonds Terres et Forêts (E21)
    Inspector's Report, Winslow, 1885
Registre de paroisse, Saint-Vital de Lambton, 1849–60.

ARCHIVES NATIONALES
DU QUÉBEC À SHERBROOKE
(ANQS)
Court Records – Criminal, St Francis District, 1850–80
    District Magistrate's Court
    Sessions of the Peace, Lingwick
Greffe de E.M. Mackenzie, n.p., 1859–75
Greffe de J.I. Mackie, n.p., 1868–80
Lingwick Register, Presbyterian Church and Church of Scotland, 1849–53
Queen's Bench, St Francis, 1850–80
Registres des Paroisses, Saint-Gabriel de Stratford, 1852–7; Saint-Hyppolite
    de Wotton, 1852–7; Saint-Romain de Winslow, 1858– 80; Saint-Vital de
    Lambton, 1848–51.
Winslow Registers, Presbyterian Church, 1864–80

BIBLIOTHÈQUE NATIONALE,
MONTREAL
Loiselle Index
Rivest Index

BUREAU MUNICIPAL DE ST ROMAIN
Livre des Minutes, 1870–97.

BUREAU MUNICIPAL DE WINSLOW-SUD
Property assessments for 1883

COMPTON COUNTY HISTORICAL
SOCIETY ARCHIVES
(EATON MUSEUM)
Leonard, John. Speech in Gaelic to Gaelic Society of Sherbrooke, c. 1929.

COOKSHIRE REGISTRY OFFICE
Register B, vol. 1–10
Register C, vol. 1
Register E, Partnership Book, vol. 1

DUNCAN MCLEOD, SCOTSTOWN,
QUEBEC
Session Book of Winslow Congregation, 1878–80.

NATIONAL ARCHIVES
OF CANADA (NA)
Canada, Manuscript Census, 1844, 1852–81.
Civil Secretary's Correspondence – Incoming, Canada East (RG 4 C1)
Civil Secretary's Correspondence – Outgoing, Canada East (RG 4 C2)
Colonial Office Papers, Emigration (MG 11, CO 384)
Executive Council, Minute Books (State Matters), 1848–67 (RG 1 E1)
Governor General's Correspondence (RG 7 G14)
Land Petitions, Lower Canada: Winslow Township (RG 1 L3L)
Land Petitions, Upper Canada: "G" Bundle 7, 1853–4 (RG 1 L3)
Lower Canada, Manuscript Census, 1831

PALAIS DE JUSTICE,
ST JOSEPH DE BEAUCE
Greffe de F.S.A. Bélanger, n.p., 1868–80

PALAIS DE JUSTICE,
VALLEYFIELD
Greffe de S.A. Brodeur, n.p., 1875–7

PRESBYTÈRE DE
ST ROMAIN
Cahiers d'annonces pour St Romain et St Gabriel, 1867–80
Livre des Minutes, 1870–97
Registre des Délibérations des Assemblées de Paroisses et de Fabrique,
    1869–80
Registre du Curé, 1870–81

QUÉBEC, MINISTÈRE D'ÉNERGIE,
MINES, ET RESSOURCES
(ARCHIVES OF THE FORMER MINISTÈRE
DE TERRES ET FORÊTS – MTF)
Adjudications, Section Ouest, Winslow
Crown Sales – Western Section
Dossier générale du canton, Winslow
Enregistrements des transports
Free Grants (Index), A – ouest
Orders in Council, Branche Est
Recettes, Branches Est et Ouest
Registry of Assignments

Terrier F, Old Land, Roll no. 6
Terrier no. 2
Vieux Dossiers (correspondances)

ST ANDREW'S SOCIETY OF MONTREAL,
HEADQUARTERS
Minute Book, I

SCOTTISH RECORD OFFICE,
EDINBURGH
Highland and Island Emigration Society Papers (HD 4)
Highland Destitution Records (HD 7)
Mackenzie Papers (GD 403/63/31)
Parish Records, Presbytery of Lewis, 1832–48 (CH 2/473)
Seaforth Muniments (GD 46)

SHERBOOKE REGISTRY OFFICE
Register B, vol. 9–21

UNITED CHURCH OF CANADA
ARCHIVES (UCCA),
BISHOP'S UNIVERSITY
Minute Book of Synod of Montreal and Ottawa, I (1875–1906)
Record of the Presbytery of Quebec of the Presbyterian Church in Canada,
    1875–81

UNITED CHURCH OF CANADA
ARCHIVES (UCCA),
VICTORIA COLLEGE, TORONTO
Presbyterian Church of Canada. Presbytery of Montreal: Minutes, Vol. 1 and
    2, 1861–75; Minutes, vol. 1 and 2, 1844–64 (rough notes)

PRINTED PRIMARY SOURCES

*The Acts and Proceedings of the General Assembly of the Presbyterian Church in
    Canada.* 1875–80.
Annuaire du Séminaire St-Charles Borromée. Sherbrooke: vol. 1 (1887–8), no.
    13; 1889–90, no. 15; vol. 2 (1892–3), no. 9.
Annual Report of the Society for the Support of Gaelic Schools. Edinburgh, 1826–
    61. (NCL).
Bouchette, Joseph. *The British Dominions in North America [..] and a Topograph-
    ical Dictionary of Lower Canada,* 1. London: Longman, 1831.

British Parliamentary Papers. Emigration Series. Shannon, Ireland: Irish University Press, 1968–71.

Canada, Province of. *Journals of the Legislative Assembly*, 1852–66.

Channell, Leonard S. *History of Compton County*. Cookshire: L.S. Channell, 1896.

Code Civil du Bas Canada.

Farnham, C.H. "Cape Breton Folk." *Harpers' New Monthly Magazine*, 72 (Dec. 1885–May 1886): 607–25; reprinted in *Acadiensis*, 8, 2 (1979): 90–106.

Fullarton, Allan, and Charles R. Baird. *Remarks on the Evils at Present affecting the Highlands and Islands of Scotland; With Some Suggestions as to Their Remedies*. Glasgow: William Collins, 1838.

Gauldrée-Boileau, Charles-Henri-Philippe. "Paysan de Saint-Irénée de Charlevoix en 1861 et 1862." Paris: 1875, reprinted in *Paysans et ouvriers Québécois d'autrefois*. Quebec: Presses de l'Université Laval, 1968.

Gérin, L. "L'habitant de Saint-Justin." 1898, reprinted in *Léon Gérin et L'habitant de Saint-Justin*. Montreal: Presses de l'Université de Montreal, 1968.

Great Britain. *Parliamentary Papers*, 1837–58, Annual Reports from the Agent for Emigration in Canada;1844, Report of Royal Commission on the Poor Law (Scotland); 1851, Report to the Board of Supervision by Sir John M'Neill, G.C.B., on the Western Highlands and Islands.

Highland Destitution Reports: Edinburgh Section, Private Papers, 1847. (NLS).

Highland Destitution Reports: Glasgow Section, Reports 8–11, 1848–9. (NLS).

Jones, J.P. "History of Lake Megantic: 1760–1921." Unpublished manuscript at NA (MG 30 H17).

Langelier, J.C. *Liste des terrains concédés par la Couronne dans la Province de Québec de 1763 au 31 décembre 1890*. Quebec: Charles-François Langlois, 1891.

Macdonald, J. "On the Agriculture of the Counties of Ross and Cromarty." Highland and Agricultural Society, *Transactions*, Series 4, 9 (1877): 67–167.

MacDonald, M.N. *The Family Tree and Some Early Reminiscences of Early Days in Winslow and Whitton, Que.* Avonmore, Ont.: n.p., n.d.

MacKay, Angus (Oscar Dhu). *By Trench and Trail in Song and Story*. Seattle and Vancouver: MacKay, 1918.

– *Donald Morrison, The Canadian Outlaw: A Tale of the Scottish Pioneers*. N.p.: n.p., 1892.

MacLeod, M.C. *Settlement of the Lake Megantic District in the Province of Quebec, Canada*, [New York City: n.p., 1931].

Mandements, lettres pastorales, circulaires et autres documents publiés dans le diocèse de Sherbrooke. Sherbrooke: Imprimerie du Seminaire Saint-Charles Borromée, 1878.

Mignault, P.B. *Le droit paroissial étant une étude historique et légale*. Montreal: Beauchemin, 1893.

Mitchell, Joseph. *Reminiscences of My Life in the Highlands* (1883), 1. Edited by I. Robertson. Newton Abbott, 1971.

New Statistical Account of Scotland. Edinburgh, 1835–45.

Pagnuello, S. *Études historiques et légales sur la liberté religieuse en Canada.* Montreal: C.O. Beauchemin & Valois, 1872.

Quebec. *Journals of the Legislative Assembly,* 1867–80.

– *Sessional Papers,* 1869–82.

Smith, W. Anderson. *Lewsiana or Life in the Outer Hebrides.* London: Daldy, Isbister, 1875.

Traill, Catherine Parr. *The Canadian Settler's Guide.* Reprint Toronto and Montreal: McClelland and Stewart, 1969.

Uncorrected Correspondence from February to September 1847 Relating to the Measures Adopted for the Relief of Distress in Scotland, 2nd Report. London: Wm. Clowes and Sons, 1847. (SRO)

NEWSPAPERS

Ecclesiastical and Missionary Record, 1846–60 (microfilm at UCCA).

Free Church of Scotland Monthly Record (Edinburgh), pp. 210–11, no date (microfilm of selected pages at UCCA).

Home and Foreign Missionary Record of the Free Church of Scotland (Edinburgh), 1843–50 (microfilm of selected pages at UCCA).

Home and Foreign Record of the Canada Presbyterian Church, 1862–75.

Home and Foreign Record of the Free Church of Scotland (Edinburgh), 1850– 61 (microfilm of selected pages at UCCA).

Le Journal de Québec, 1848

Stanstead Journal, 1852.

SECONDARY SOURCES

Adams, J.W., and A.B. Kasakoff. "Migration and the Family in Colonial New England: The View from Genealogies." *JFH,* 9 (1984): 24–42.

Akenson, Donald Harman. *The Irish in Ontario: A Study in Rural History.* Kingston and Montreal: McGill-Queen's University Press, 1984.

Anderson, Michael. *Approaches to the History of the Western Family 1500–1914.* London: Macmillan, 1980.

– *Family Structure in Nineteenth Century Lancashire.* Cambridge at the University Press, 1970.

Armstrong, Robert. *Structure and Change: An Economic History of Quebec.* Canada: Gage, 1984.

Atack, Jeremy, and Fred Bateman. *To Their Own Soil: Agriculture in the Antebellum North.* Ames, Iowa: Iowa State University Press, 1987.

Audet, A. "Pouvoir, contrôle social et vie quotidienne à Saint-Hilarion, 1870–1925." In *L'église et le village,* edited by S. Gagnon and Hardy.

Ball, Norman Roger. "The Technology of Settlement and Land Clearing in Upper Canada Prior to 1840." PHD thesis, University of Toronto, 1979.

Baltensperger, B.H. "Agricultural Change among Nebraska Immigrants, 1880– 1930." In *Ethnicity in the Great Plains*, edited by Frederick C. Luebke. Lincoln: University of Nebraska Press, 1980.

Baribeau, Claude. *La seigneurie de la Petite-Nation. 1801–1854. Le rôle économique et social du seigneur.* Hull: Editions Asticou, 1983.

Baron, W.E., and A.E. Bridges. "Making Hay in Northern New England: Maine as a Case Study, 1800–1850." *Agricultural History*, 57 (1983): 165– 80.

Bateman, F. "The 'Marketable Surplus' in Northern Dairy Farming: New Evidence by Size of Farm in 1860." *Agricultural History*, 52 (1978): 345– 63.

Bates, R. "Les conceptions prénuptiales dans la vallée du Saint-Laurent avant 1725." *RHAF*, 40 (1986): 253–72.

Beattie, Susan. *A New Life in Canada: The Letters of Sophia Eastwood, 1843– 1870.* Toronto: Canadian Scholars' Press, 1989.

Beauchamp, C. "Milieu rural et agriculture entre le rose et le noir." *RS*, 23, 3 (1982): 217–26.

Beeman, R.R. "The New Social History and the Search for Community in Colonial America." *American Quarterly*, 29 (1977): 422–43.

Bellavance, Marcel. *Un village en mutation: Compton, Québec, 1880–1920.* Ottawa: Parks Canada, 1982.

Bennett-Knight, M. "Folkways and Religion of the Quebec Hebridean Homes." In *Cultural Retention*, edited by Doucette.

Berkner, L.K. "The Stem Family and the Development Cycle of the Peasant Household: An Eighteenth-Century Austrian Example." *American Historical Review*, 77 (1972): 398–418.

– "The Use and Misuse of Census Data for the Historical Analysis of Family Structure." *JIH*, 5, 4 (1975): 721–38.

Berkner, L.K., and F.K. Mendels. "Inheritance Systems, Family Structure and Demographic Patterns in Western Europe, 1700–1900." In *Historical Studies*, edited by Tilley.

Bernier, Jacques. *La médecine au Québec: naissance et évolution d'une profession.* Quebec: Presses de l'Université Laval, 1989.

Bervin, G. "Espace physique et culture matérielle du marchand-négociant à Québec au début du XIXe siècle (1820–1830)." *MHB*, 14 (1982): 1–16.

Bittermann, Rusty. "The Hierarchy of the Soil: Land and Labour in a 19th Century Cape Breton Community." *Acadiensis*, 18, 1 (1988): 33–55.

– "Middle River: The Social Structure of Agriculture in a Nineteenth- Century Cape Breton Community." MA thesis, University of New Brunswick, 1985.

Blake, J.L. "Distribution of Surnames in the Isle of Lewis." *Scottish Studies*, 10 (1966): 154–61.

Blanchard, Raoul. *Le centre du Canada français*. Montreal: n.p., 1948.

Blouin, C. "La mécanisation de l'agriculture entre 1830 et 1890." In *Agriculture et colonisation*, edited by Séguin.

Booth, John Derek. "Changing Forest Utilization Patterns in the Eastern Townships of Quebec, 1800 to 1930." PHD thesis, McGill University, 1972.

Bouchard, Gérard. "L'agriculture Saguenayenne entre 1840 et 1950: l'évolution de la technologie." *RHAF*, 42 (1990): 353–80.

– "Co-intégration et reproduction de la société rurale: pour un modèle saguenayen de la marginalité." *RS*, 29, 2–3 (1988): 283– 310.

– "La donation entre vifs et la transmission familiale des avoirs fonciers au Saguenay (1870–1940)." Unpublished paper presented to the Colloque d'histoire rurale comparée Québec / France, Montreal, 1990.

– "La dynamique communautaire et l'évolution des sociétés rurales québécoises aux 19e et 20e siècles: construction d'un modèle." *RHAF*, 40 (1986): 51–72.

– "Dynamique des populations locales: la formation des paroisses rurales au Saguenay (1840–1911)." *RHAF*, 41 (1988): 363–88.

– "L'économie agraire et la reproduction sociale dans les campagnes saguenayennes (1852–1971)." *Hs-SH*, 18 (1985): 237–59.

– "Un essai d'anthropologie régionale: l'histoire sociale du Saguenay aux xixe et xxe siècles." *Annales: économies, sociétés, civilisations*, 34 (1979): 106–25.

– "L'étude des structures familiales pré-industrielles: pour un renversement des perspectives." *Revue d'histoire moderne et contemporaine*, 27 (Oct.-Dec. 1981): 544–71.

– "Family Structures and Geographic Mobility at Laterrière, 1851–1935." *JFH*, 2 (1977): 350–69.

– "L'histoire démographique et le problème des migrations: l'exemple de Laterrière." *Hs-SH*, 8 (1975): 21–33.

– "Introduction à l'étude de la société saguenayenne aux xixe et xxe siècles." *RHAF*, 31 (1977): 3–27.

– "Sur la dynamique culturelle des régions de peuplement." *CHR*, 67 (1986): 473–90.

– "Sur la reproduction familiale en milieu rural: systèmes ouverts et systèmes clos." *RS*, 28, 2–3 (1987): 229–51.

– "Les systèmes de transmission des avoirs familaux et le cycle de la société rurale au Québec, du xviie au xxe siècles." *Hs-SH*, 16 (1983): 35–60.

Bouchard, Gérard, and M. Bergeron. "Les rapports annuels des paroisses et l'histoire démographique saguenayenne: étude critique." *Archives*, 10, 3 (1978): 5–33.

Bouchard, Gérard, and I. de Pourbaix. "Individual and Family Life Courses in the Saguenay Region, Quebec, 1842–1911." *JFH*, 12 (1987): 225–42.

Bouchard, Gérard, and A. LaRose. "La réglementation du contenu des actes de baptême, mariage, sépulture, au Québec, des origines à nos jours." *RHAF*, 30 (1976): 67–84.

Bouchard, Gérard, and J. Larouche. "Nouvelle mesure de l'alphabétisation à l'aide de la reconstitution automatique des familles." *Hs-SH*, 22 (1989): 91–120.

– "Paramètres sociaux de la reproduction familiale au Saguenay (1842–1911)." *Sociologie et Sociétés*, 19, 1 (1987): 133–44.

Bouchard, Gérard, and Y. Lavoie. "Le projet d'histoire de la population au Saguenay: l'appareil méthodologique." *RHAF*, 32 (1978): 41–56.

Bouchard, Gérard, R. Roy, C. Pouyez, and R. Thibeault. "Croissance démographique et évolution agraire au Saguenay: xixe–xxe siècles." In *Évolution agraire et croissance démographique*, edited by Antoinette Fauve-Chamoux. Liège: Ordina Editions, 1987.

Boucher, A. "La fabrique et les marguilliers." In *Le Laïc dans l'église*, edited by Hurtubise et al.

– "Le rôle joué par les marguilliers." In *Le laïc et l'église*, edited by Hurtubise et al.

Bouffard, Jean. *Le traité du domaine*. Quebec: 1921; reprint, Quebec: Presses de l'Université Laval, 1977.

Boulanger, Léo, Pierre Doyon, and Yvon Gagné. "Étude socio-économique de Winslow-sud, 1851–1901." Groupe de recherche en histoire régionale, Département d'histoire, Université de Sherbrooke, 1977.

Bourgière, A. "L'attribution du prénom en France: approche historique." In *Société rurale*, edited by Wallot and Goy.

Breen, David. *The Canadian Prairie West and the Ranching Frontier 1874–1924*. Toronto: University of Toronto Press, 1983.

Brookes, A.A. "The Golden Age and the Exodus: The Case of Canning, Kings County." *Acadiensis*, 11, 1 (1981): 57–82.

Bumsted, J.M. "Scottish Emigration to the Maritimes 1770–1815: A New Look at an Old Theme." *Acadiensis*, 10, 2 (1981): 65–85.

Bushman, R. "Family Security in the Transition from Farm to City, 1750–1850." *JFH*, 6 (1981): 238–56.

Byers, E. "Fertility Transition in a New England Commercial Center: Nantucket, Mass., 1680–1840." *JIH*, 13 (1982): 17–40.

Cameron, T. "The Changing Role of the Highland Landlords Relative to Scottish Emigration during the First Half of the 19th Century," *Scottish Colloquium Proceedings*, 4/5 (1972): 77–87.

Campbell, D., and R.A. MacLean. *Beyond the Atlantic Roar: A Study of the Nova Scotia Scots*. Toronto: McClelland and Stewart, 1974.

Campbell, R.H. "Scotland." In *The Scots Abroad: Labour, Capital, and Enterprise, 1750–1914*, edited by R.A. Cage. London: Croom Helm, 1985.

Carr, L.G., and L.S. Walsh. "The Planter's Wife: The Experience of White Women in Seventeenth-Century Maryland." *WMQ*, 3rd series, 34 (1977): 542–71.

Carter, I. "Illegitimate Births and Illegitimate Inferences." *Scottish Journal of Sociology*, 1, 2 (1977): 125–35.

Castelli, M.D. "Le douaire en droit coutumier ou la déviation d'une institution." *Cahiers de droit*, 20 (1979): 315–30.

Casteran, N. "Les stratégies agricoles du paysan canadien-français de l'est ontarien (1870)." *RHAF*, 41 (1987): 23–51.

Caulier, B. "Les confréries de dévotion traditionelles et le réveil religieux à Montréal au XIXe siècle." SCHEC *Sessions d'étude*, 53 (1986): 23–40.

Caya, M. "Henry Caldwell." *Dictionary of Canadian Biography*, v.

Chabot, Richard. *Le curé de campagne et la contestation locale au Québec de 1791 aux troubles de 1837–38*. Montreal: Hurtubise, 1975.

Charbonneau, H. "Colonisation, climat et âge au baptême des Canadiens au XVIIe siècle." *RHAF*, 38 (1985): 341–56.

– "Les régimes de fécondité naturelle en Amérique du Nord: bilan et analyse des observations." In *Natural Fertility: Patterns and Determinants of Natural Fertility / Fécondité naturelle: nivaux et déterminants de la fécondité naturelle*, edited by Henri Leridon and Jane Menken. Liège: Ordina, 1979.

Charbonneau, H., et al. *Naissance d'une population: les Français établis au Canada au XVIIe siècle*. Montréal: Presses de l'Université de Montréal, 1987.

Charland, J.P. "Le réseau d'enseignement public bas-canadien, 1841–1867: une institution de l'État libéral." *RHAF*, 40 (1987): 505–36.

Clark, S.D. *Church and Sect in Canada*. Toronto: University of Toronto Press, 1948.

Clarke, J., and P.K. MacLeod. "Concentration of Scots in Rural Southern Ontario, 1851–1901." *Canadian Cartographer*, 2 (1974): 107–13.

Cliche, M.A. "Les confréries dans le gouvernement de Québec sous le régime français." *RHAF*, 39 (1986): 491–522.

– "L'évolution des clauses religieuses traditionelles dans les testaments de la région de Québec au XIXe siècle." In *Religion populaire*, edited by Lacroix and Simard.

Clio, le Collectif. *L'histoire des femmes au Québec depuis quatre siècles*. Montreal: Les Quinze, 1982.

Cohen, Marjorie Griffin. *Women's Work, Markets, and Economic Development in Nineteenth-Century Ontario*. Toronto: University of Toronto Press, 1988.

Conzen, K.N. "Peasant Pioneers: Generational Succession among German Farmers in Frontier Minnesota." In *The Countryside in the Age of Capitalist Transformation: Essays in the Social History of Rural America*, edited by Steven Hahn and Jonathan Prude. Chapel Hill: University of North Carolina Press, 1985.

Conzen, Michael P. *Frontier Farming in an Urban Shadow*. Madison: Department of History, University of Wisconsin, 1971.

Cooper, Derek. *Road to the Isles: Travellers in the Hebrides 1770–1914*. London: Routledge and Kegan Paul, 1979.

Corrigan, P., and B. Curtis. "Education, Inspection and State Formation: A Preliminary Statement." CHA *Historical Papers*, 1985, 156–71.

Courville, Serge. "La crise agricole du Bas-Canada, éléments d'une réflexion géographique," *CGQ*, 24, 62 (1980): 193–224; 63 (1980): 385–428.

– "Croissances villageoises et industries rurales dans les seigneuries du Québec (1815–1851)." In *Sociétés villageoises*, edited by Séguin and Lebrun.

– "L'habitant canadien dans la première moitié du XIXe siècle: survie ou survivance?" *RS*, 27, 2 (1986): 177–94.

– "Un monde rural en mutation: le Bas-Canada dans la première moitié du XIXe siècle." *Hs-SH*, 20 (1987): 237–58.

– "Rente déclarée payée sur la censive de 90 arpents au recensement nominatif de 1831: méthodologie d'une recherche." *CGQ*, 27, 70 (1983): 43–61.

– "Villages and Agriculture in the Seigneuries of Lower Canada: Conditions of a Comprehensive Study of Rural Quebec in the First Half of the Nineteenth Century." *CPRH*, 5 (1986): 121–49.

Courville, Serge, and Normand Séguin. *Rural Life in Nineteenth-Century Quebec*. CHA Historical Booklet no. 47, Ottawa, 1989.

Couture, C. "La conquête de 1760 et le problème de la transition au capitalisme." *RHAF*, 39 (1986): 369–89.

Craig, Béatrice. "Agriculture and the Lumberman's Frontier in the Upper St John Valley, 1800–70." *Journal of Forest History*, 33, 3 (1988): 125–37.

– "Early French Migrations to Northern Maine, 1785–1850." *Maine Historical Society Quarterly*, 25 (Spring 1986): 230–47.

– "Économie, société et migration: le cas de la vallée du Saint-Jean au 19e siècle." In *L'émigrant acadien vers les États-Unis: 1842–1950*, edited by Claire Quintal. Quebec: Conseil de la Vie française en Amérique, 1984.

– "La transmission des patrimoines fonciers dans le Haut St Jean au XIXe siècle." Unpublished paper presented to the annual meeting of the CHA, 1989.

Craven, P. "The Law of Master and Servant in Mid-Nineteenth-Century Ontario." In *Essays in the History of Canadian Law*, 1, edited by David H. Flaherty. Toronto: Osgoode Society, 1981.

Crerar, Duff Willis. "Church and Community: The Presbyterian Kirk-Session in the District of Bathurst, Upper Canada. MA thesis, University of Western Ontario, 1979.

Curtis, Bruce. *Building the Educational State: Canada West, 1836–1871*. London, Ont.: Althouse Press, 1988.

Curtis, C. "Shanty Life in the Kawarthas, Ontario, 1850–55." *MHB*, 13 (1981): 39–50.

Danylewcz, M., B. Light, and A. Prentice. "The Evolution of the Sexual Division of Labour in Teaching: A Nineteenth-Century Ontario and Quebec Case Study." *Hs-SH*, 16 (1983): 81–110.

Darroch, A.G. "Class in Nineteenth-Century Central Ontario: A Reassessment of the Crisis and Demise of Small Producers During Early Industrialization, 1861–1871." *Canadian Journal of Sociology*, 13, 1–2 (1988) 49–71.

– "Migrants in the Nineteenth-Century: Fugitives or Families in Motion?" *JFH*, 6 (1981): 257–77.

Darroch, A.G., and M.D. Ornstein. "Ethnicity and Occupational Structure in Canada in 1871: The Vertical Mosaic in Historical Perspective." *CHR*, 61 (1980): 305–33.

– "Family and Household in Nineteenth-Century Canada: Regional Patterns and Regional Economies." *JFH*, 9 (1984): 158–77.

Davey, I.E. "The Rhythm of Work and the Rhythm of School." In *Egerton Ryerson*, edited by McDonald and Chaiton.

Davis, N. "'Patriarchy from the Grave': Family Relations in 19th Century New Brunswick Wills." *Acadiensis*, 13, 2 (1984): 91–100.

Davis, N.Z. "De la religion aux cultures religieuses." In *Religion populaire*, edited by Lacroix and Simard.

– "Ghosts, Kin, and Progeny: Some Features of Family Life in Early Modern France." In *The Family*, edited by Alice S. Rossi, Jerome Kagan, and Tamara K. Hareven. New York: W.W. Norton, 1978.

Day, Douglas, ed. *Geographical Perspectives on the Maritime Provinces*. Halifax: Saint Mary's University Press, 1988.

Day, Mrs C.M. *History of the Eastern Townships*. Montreal: John Lovell, 1869.

Dechêne, L. "Observations sur l'agriculture du Bas-Canada au début du xixe siècle." In *Évolution et éclatement*, edited by Wallot and Goy.

Deffontaines, P. "The Rang – Pattern of Rural Settlement in French Canada." In *French-Canadian Society*, edited by Marcel Rioux and Yves Martin. Toronto: McClelland and Stewart, 1964.

Denoon, D. "Understanding Settler Societies." *Historical Studies*, 18 (1979): 511–27.

Dépatie, Sylvie. "Les pratiques de transmission du patrimoine au Canada: le cas de l'Île Jésus au xviiie siècle." Unpublished paper presented to the Colloque d'histoire rurale comparée France / Québec, Montreal, 1990.

– "La structure agraire au Canada: le cas de l'Île Jésus au xviiie siècle." CHA *Historical Papers*, 1986, 56–85.

Desrosiers, C. "Un aperçu des habitudes de consommation de la clientèle de Joseph Cartier, marchand général à Saint-Hyacinthe à la fin du xviiie siècle." CHA *Historical Papers*, 1984, 101–14.

Dessureault, C. "L'égalitarisme paysan dans l'ancienne société rurale de la vallée du St Laurent: éléments pour une ré-interprétation." *RHAF*, 40 (1987): 373–408.

Devine, T.M. *The Great Highland Famine: Hunger, Emigration and the Scottish Highlands in the Nineteenth Century.* Edinburgh: John Donald, 1988.

DeVries, Pieter J., and Georgina MacNab-DeVries. *"They Farmed, Among Other Things..." Three Cape Breton Case Studies.* Sydney, NS: University College of Cape Breton Press, 1983.

Dinet, D. "Statistique de mortalité infantile sous le consulat de l'empire." In *Sur la population française au XVIIIe et au XIXe siècles.* Paris: Société de Démographie historique, 1973.

Dodgshon, R.A. "'Pretence of Blude' and 'Place of Their Dwelling': The Nature of Scottish Clans, 1500–1745." In *Scottish Society 1500–1800*, edited by R.A. Houston and I.D. Whyte. Cambridge: Cambridge University Press, 1989.

Dorion, Jacques. *Les écoles de Rang au Québec.* Montreal: Éditions de l'Homme, 1979.

Doucette, Laurel, ed. *Cultural Retention and Demographic Change: Studies of the Hebridean Scots in the Eastern Townships of Quebec.* Ottawa: National Museum of Man, 1980.

Dufour, A. "Diversité institutionelle et fréquentation scolaire dans l'île de Montréal en 1825 et en 1835." *RHAF*, 40 (1988): 507–35.

Dunkly, Nancy. "Studies in the Scottish Gaelic Folk-Song Tradition in Canada." PHD thesis, Harvard University, 1984.

Dupâquier, Jacques. *Pour la démographie historique.* Paris: Presses Universitaires de France, 1984.

Easterlin, R.A. "Does Human Fertility Adjust to the Environment?" *American Economic Review*, 61 (1971): 399–407.

– "Population Change and Farm Settlement in the Northern United States." *Journal of Economic History*, 36 (1976): 45–75.

Elliott, Bruce. *Irish Migrants in the Canadas: A New Approach.* Kingston and Montreal: McGill-Queen's University Press, 1988.

– "Sources of Bias in Nineteenth-Century Ontario Wills." *Hs-SH*, 18 (1985): 125–32.

Eloi-Gérard, Frère. *Recueil de généalogies des comtés de Beauce-Dorchester-Frontenac, 1652–1946.* Beauceville: Collège du Sacré Coeur [1946].

Emery, G. "Ontario's Civil Registration of Vital Statistics, 1869–1926: The Evolution of an Administrative System." *CHR*, 64 (1983): 468–93.

Epps, B. "Immigrant File: When the First Scots Came from Lewis." *The Record* (Sherbrooke), 21 Oct. 1988.

Falardeau, J.C. "Présentation de Léon Gérin et son oeuvre." In *Léon Gérin et l'habitant de Saint-Justin.* Montreal: Presses de l'Université de Montréal, 1968.

– "Religion populaire et classes sociales." In *Religion populaire*, edited by Lacroix and Simard.

Faucher, A. "The Decline of Shipbuilding at Quebec in the Nineteenth Century." *Canadian Journal of Economics and Political Science*, 23 (1957): 195–215.

Fenton, Alexander. *Scottish Country Life*. Edinburgh: John Donald, 1976.

Flandrin, Jean-Louis. *Families in Former Times: Kinship, Household and Sexuality*, trans. Richard Southern. Cambridge: Cambridge University Press, 1979.

– "Histoire de la famille et histoire des mentalités." CHA *Historical Papers*, 1983, 136–49.

Flinn, M.W. "Malthus, Emigration, and Potatoes in the Scottish North-West, 1770–1870." In *Comparative Aspects of Scottish and Irish Economic and Social History 1600–1900*, edited by L.M. Cullen and T.C. Smout. Edinburgh: John Donald, n.d.

Flinn, Michael, ed., *Scottish Population History from the 17th Century to the 1930s.* Cambridge: Cambridge University Press, 1977.

Fortier, N. "Les recensements canadiens et l'étude de l'agriculture québécoise, 1851–1901." *Hs-SH*, 17 (1984): 257–86.

Fortin, G. "Socio-Cultural Changes in an Agricultural Parish." In *French-Canadian Society*, edited by Marcel Rioux and Yves Martin. Toronto: McClelland and Stewart, 1964.

French, G.S. "Egerton Ryerson and the Methodist Model for Upper Canada." In *Egerton Ryerson*, edited by McDonald and Chaiton.

Friedberger, M. "The Farm Family and the Inheritance Process: Evidence from the Corn Belt, 1870–1950." *Agricultural History*, 57 (1983): 1– 13.

Gadoury, L. "Les stocks des habitants dans les inventaires après décès." *MHB*, 17 (1983): 139–47.

Gadoury, L., Y. Landry, and H. Charbonneau. "Démographie différentielle en Nouvelle-France: villes et campagnes." *RHAF*, 38 (1985): 357–78.

Gaffield, Chad. "Children and Youth in the Changing Calculus of Family Reproduction: Rethinking the Industrial Revolution in Ontario." Unpublished paper presented to the annual meeting of the CHA, 1990.

– *Language, Schooling, and Cultural Conflict: The Origins of the French-Language Controversy in Ontario*. Kingston and Montreal: McGill-Queen's University Press, 1987.

– "Theory and Method in Canadian Historical Demography." *Archivaria*, 14 (Summer 1982): 123–36.

Gaffield, Chad, and Gérard Bouchard. "Literacy, Schooling, and Family Reproduction in Rural Ontario and Quebec." Unpublished paper presented to the annual conference of the Canadian Educational History Association, 1988.

Gagan, David. "Enumerator's Instructions for the Census of Canada 1852 and 1861." *Hs-SH*, 7 (1974): 355–65.

– *Hopeful Travellers: Families, Land and Social Change in Mid-Victorian Peel County, Canada West.* Toronto: University of Toronto Press, 1981.

– "The Indivisibility of Land: A Microanalysis of the System of Inheritance in Nineteenth-Century Ontario." *Journal of Economic History,* 36 (1976): 126–41.

– "Land, Population, and Social Change: The 'Critical Years' of Rural Canada West." *CHR,* 59 (1978): 293–318.

– "The Security of Land: Mortgaging in Toronto Gore Township 1835–95." In *Aspects of Nineteenth-Century Ontario,* edited by F.H. Armstrong et al. Toronto: University of Toronto Press, 1974.

Gagnon, Robert. "La colonisation aux confins de l'Estrie; étude socio-économique." MA thesis, Université de Montréal, 1967.

Gagnon, Serge. "Amours interdits et misères conjugales dans le Québec rural de la fin du xviiie siècle vers 1830 (l'arbitrage des prêtres)." In *Sociétés villageoises,* edited by Séguin and Lebrun.

– "Le Diocèse de Montréal durant les années 1860." In *Le laïc dans l'église,* edited by Hurtubise et al.

– *Mourir hier et aujourd'hui: de la mort chrétienne dans la campagne québécoise au XIXe siècle à la mort technisée dans la cité sans Dieu.* Quebec: Presses de l'Université Laval, 1987.

– *Quebec and Its Historians. The Twentieth Century.* Montreal: Harvest House, 1985.

Gagnon, Serge, and René Hardy, ed. *L'église et le village au Québec 1850–1930.* Leméac, 1979.

Garon, A. "Le Bas-Canada (1792–1838)," and "La mise en tutelle, 1838–67." In *Histoire du Québec,* edited by Jean Hamelin. Montreal: France-Amérique, 1977.

Gaudreau, Guy. *L'exploitation des forêts publiques au Québec, 1842–1905.* Quebec: Institut québécois de recherche sur la culture, 1986.

– "Le Rapport agriculture-forêt au Québec." *RHAF,* 33 (1979): 67–78.

Gauthier, B. "La sous-traitance et l'exploitation forestière en Mauricie (1850–1875)." *MHB,* 13 (1981): 59–67.

Gautier, Etienne, and Louis Henry. *La population de Crulai: paroisse normande, étude historique.* Paris: Presses Universitaires de France, 1958.

Gauvreau, D., and M. Bourque. "Mouvements migratoires et familles: le peuplement du Saguenay avant 1911." *RHAF,* 42 (1988): 169–92.

Gauvreau, D., R. Jetté, and M. Bourque. "Migration in the Saguenay Region: Evidence from Reconstituted Families, 1838–1911." *Historical Methods,* 20, 4 (1987): 143–54.

Gee, E.M.T. "Early Canadian Fertility Transition: A Components Analysis of Census Data." *Canadian Studies in Population,* 6 (1979): 23–32.

Genest, B. "Réflexion méthodologique sur un corpus d'objets funéraires." In *Religion populaire,* edited by Lacroix and Simard.

Gentilcore, R.L. "The Agricultural Background of Settlement in Eastern Nova Scotia." *Annals of the Association of American Geographers*, 46, 4 (1956): 378–404.

Gervais, G. "Le commerce de détail au Canada (1870–1880)." *RHAF*, 33 (1980): 521–56.

Gibson, James R., editor. *European Settlement and Development in North America: Essays on Geographical Change in Honour and Memory of Andrew Hill Clark.* Toronto: University of Toronto Press, 1978.

Gidney, R.D., and D.A. Lawr. "Bureaucracy vs Community? The Origins of Bureaucratic Procedure in the Upper Canadian School System." *Journal of Social History*, 13, 3 (1980): 438–57.

– "Who Ran the Schools? Local Influence in Education Policy in Nineteenth-Century Ontario." *Ontario History*, 72 (1980): 131–43.

Gidney, R.D., and W.P.J. Millar. "From Voluntarism to State Schooling: The Creation of the Public School System in Ontario." *CHR*, 66 (1985): 443–73.

Girard, C. "Familles et patrimoines fonciers dans un canton du Haut-Saguenay depuis la fin du dix-neuvième siècle." *Saguenayensia*, 27, 4 (1985): 146–54.

– "La dynamique de l'échange en milieu rural: Laterrière, Saguenay, 1870–1970." *Saguenayensia*, 27, 4 (1985): 132–7.

Gmelch, S.B. "A Social History of the Quebec Hebridean Settlements." In *Cultural Retention*, edited by Doucette.

Goldring, P. "Lewis and the Hudson's Bay Company in the Nineteenth Century." *Scottish Studies*, 24 (1980): 23–42.

Goodman, David, and Michael Redclift. *From Peasant to Proletarian: Capitalist Development and Agrarian Transitions.* Oxford: Basil Blackwell, 1981.

Gossage, Peter. "Family Formation and Age at Marriage in Saint-Hyacinthe, Quebec, 1845–1891." Unpublished paper presented to the annual meeting of the CHA, 1990.

Goubert, P. "Vingt-cinq ans de démographie historique: bilan et réflexions." In *Sur la population française au XVIIIe et XIXe siècles.* Paris: Société de Démographie historique, 1973.

Graff, H.J. "Interpreting Historical Literacy: The Pattern of Literacy in Quebec – A Comment." *Hs-SH*, 12 (1979): 444–55.

– "What the 1861 Census Can Tell Us About Literacy: A Reply." *Hs-SH*, 8 (1975): 337–49.

Grant, I.F. *Highland Folkways.* London: Routledge and Kegan Paul, 1980.

Grant, J., and K. Inwood. "Gender and Organization in the Canadian Cloth Industry, 1870." *Canadian Papers in Business History*, 1 (1989): 17–31.

– "How Urban Was Cloth Manufacturing in 1870?" Unpublished paper presented to a joint session at the annual meetings of the Canadian Economics Association and the CHA, 1987.

Gravel, Albert. *Les Cantons de l'Est*. Sherbrooke: n.p., 1938.
– *Mélanges historiques, cahier no. 5*. Sherbrooke: n.p., 1968.
– *Précis historique de St Romain*. [Lévis]: Cie de Publication de Lévis, 1934.
Gray, Malcolm. *The Fishing Industries of Scotland 1750–1914: A Study in Regional Adaptation*. Oxford: Oxford University Press, 1978.
– *The Highland Economy. 1750–1850*. Edinburgh and London: Oliver and Boyd, 1957.
– "The Highland Potato Famine of the 1840s." *Economic History Review*, 2nd series, 7 (1955): 357–68.
Greenberg, Michael. *British Trade and the Opening of China, 1800–1842*. London: Cambridge University Press, 1951, reprinted 1969.
Greer, Allan. "Fur-Trade Labour and Lower Canadian Agrarian Structures." CHA *Historical Papers*, 1981, 197–214.
– "L'habitant, la paroisse rurale et la politique locale au XVIIIe siècle: Quelques cas dans la Vallée du Richelieu." SCHEC *Sessions d'études*, 47 (1980): 19–33.
– "The Pattern of Literacy in Quebec, 1745–1899." *Hs-SH*, 11 (1978): 293–335.
– *Peasant, Lord, and Merchant: Rural Society in Three Quebec Parishes, 1740–1840*. Toronto: University of Toronto Press, 1985.
Greven, Philip J. *Four Generations: Population, Land and Family in Colonial Andover, Massachusetts*. Ithaca, NY: Cornell University Press, 1970.
Hajnal, J. "European Marriage Patterns in Perspective." In *Population in History*, edited by D.V. Glass and D.E.C. Eversley. London: Edward Arnold, 1965.
Hamelin, Jean, and Yves Roby. *Histoire économique du Québec 1851–1896*. Montreal: Fides, 1971.
Hamelin, Marcel. *Les premières années du parlementarisme québécois (1867–1878)*. Québec: Presses de l'Université Laval, 1974.
Hardy, René. "Le greffier de la paix et le curé: à propos de l'influence du clergé paroissial en Mauricie." *Annales de Bretagne*, forthcoming.
– "Note sur certaines manifestations du réveil religieux de 1840 dans la paroisse de Notre Dame de Québec." SCHEC *Sessions d'étude*, 35 (1968): 81–93.
Hardy, René, and Normand Séguin. *Forêt et société en Mauricie*. Montreal: Boréal Express / Musée national de l'homme, 1984.
Hardy, René, P. Lanthier, and N. Séguin. "Les industries rurales et l'extension du reseau villageois dans la Mauricie pré-industrielle: l'exemple du comté de Champlain durant la seconde moitié du 19e siècle." In *Sociétés villageoises*, edited by Séguin and Lebrun.
Hardy, René, and J. Roy, "Encadrement social et mutation de la culture religieuse en Mauricie." *Questions de culture*, no. 5, Institut québécois de recherche sur la culture (1983): 61–79.

– "Mutation de la culture religieuse en Mauricie, 1850–1900." In *Évolution et éclatement*, edited by Wallot and Goy.

Hare, John, Marc Lafrance, and David Thierry Ruddel. *Histoire de la Ville de Québec, 1608–1871*. Montreal: Boréal Express, 1987.

Hareven, T.K. "Les grands thèmes de l'histoire de la famille aux États-Unis." *RHAF*, 39 (1985): 185–209.

Hareven, T.K., and M.A. Vinovskis. " Introduction" and "Patterns of Child-bearing in Late Nineteenth Century America: The Determinants of Marital Fertility in Five Massachusetts Towns in 1880." In *Family and Population in Nineteenth-Century America*, edited by Tamara K. Hareven and Maris A. Vinovskis. Princeton, NJ: Princeton University Press, 1978.

Harris, R.C. "The Extension of France into Rural Canada." In *European Settlement*, edited by Gibson.

– "The Historical Geography of North American Regions." *American Behavioral Scientist*, 22, 1 (1978): 115–30.

– "The Pattern of Early Canada." In *People, Places, Patterns, Processes: Geographical Perspectives*, edited by Graene Wynn. Toronto: Copp Clark Pitman, 1990.

– "Of Poverty and Helplessness in Petite Nation." *CHR*, 52 (1971): 23–50.

Harris, R.C., and L. Guelke. "Land and Society in Early Canada and South Africa." *Journal of Historical Geography*, 3 (1977): 135–53.

Harris, R.C., P. Roulston, and C. de Freitas. "The Settlement of Mono Township." *Canadian Geographer*, 19 (1975): 1–17.

Heller, C.F., and F.S. Moore. "Continuity in Rural Land Ownership: Kalamazoo County, Michigan, 1830–1861." *Michigan History*, 56 (1972): 233–46.

Henretta, J.A. "Families and Farms: Mentalité in Pre-Industrial America." *WMQ*, 3rd series, 35 (1978): 3–32.

Henripin, J. "La fécondité des ménages canadiens au début du xviiie siècle." *Population*, 9, 1 (1954): 61–82.

– *La population canadienne au début du XVIIIe siècle: nuptialité - fécondité – mortalité infantile*. Paris: Presses Universitaires de France, 1954.

Henripin, J., and Y. Perron. "The Demographic Transition in the Province of Quebec." In *Population and Social Change*, edited by D.V. Glass and Roger Revelle. New York: Crane, Russak, 1972.

Héroux, A. "Sir John Caldwell." *Dictionary of Canadian Biography*, vii.

Hornsby, S.J. "Migration and Settlement: The Scots of Cape Breton." In *Geographical Perspectives*, edited by Douglas Day.

Hosie, R.C. *Native Trees of Canada*. Seventh edition. Ottawa: Canadian Forestry Service, Department of the Environment, 1975.

Houston, Susan E., and Alison Prentice. *Schooling and Scholars in Nineteenth-Century Ontario*. Toronto: University of Toronto Press, 1988.

Hunter, James. *The Making of the Crofting Community*. Edinburgh: John Donald, 1976.

Hurtubise, P. "La religiosité populaire en Nouvelle-France." In *Religion populaire*, edited by Lacroix and Simard.

Hurtubise, P., et al., eds. *Le laïc dans l'église canadienne-française de 1830 à nos jours*. Montreal: Fides, 1972.

Hutchinson, R. "Emigration from South Uist to Cape Breton." In *Essays in Cape Breton History*, edited by Brian Tennyson. [Sydney, NS]: Lancelot, 1977.

Jarnoux, P. "La colonisation de la seigneurie de Batiscan aux 17e et 18e siècles: l'espace et les hommes." *RHAF*, 40 (1986): 163–91.

Johnson, L.A. "New Thoughts on an Old Problem, 'Self-Sufficient Agriculture in Upper Canada'." Unpublished paper presented to the annual meeting of the CHA, 1984.

Johnston, A.J.B. *Religion in Life at Louisbourg, 1713–1758*. Kingston and Montreal: McGill-Queen's University Press, 1985.

Jones, P.M. "Parish, Seigneurie and the Community of Inhabitants in Southern Central France during the Eighteenth and Nineteenth Centuries." *Past and Present*, 91 (1981): 74–108.

Jones, R.E. "Infant Mortality in Rural North Shropshire." *Population Studies*, 30 (1976): 305–17.

Jones, R.L. "French-Canadian Agriculture in the St Lawrence Valley, 1815–1850." In *Approaches to Canadian Economic History*, edited by W.T. Easterbrook and M.H. Watkins. Toronto: McClelland and Stewart, 1967.

Judd, R.W. "Lumbering and the Farming Frontier in Aroostook County, Maine." *Journal of Forest History*, 28 (1984): 56–67.

Katz, Michael. *The People of Hamilton, Canada West: Family and Class in a Mid-Nineteenth-Century City*. Cambridge, Mass.: Harvard University Press, 1975.

Kelly, K. "Wheat Farming in Simcoe County in the Mid-Nineteenth Century." *Canadian Geographer*, 15, 2 (1971): 95–112.

Kesteman, Jean-Pierre. "Une bourgeoisie et son espace: industrialisation et développement du capitalisme dans le district de Saint-François (Québec), 1823–1879." PHD thesis, Université du Québec à Montréal, 1985.

– *Histoire de Lac Mégantic*. Ville de Lac-Mégantic, 1985.

– "Les travailleurs à la construction du chemin de fer dans la région de Sherbrooke (1851–1853)." *RHAF*, 31 (1978): 525–46.

Keyssar, A. "Widowhood in Eighteenth-Century Massachusetts: A Problem in the History of the Family." *Perspectives in American History*, 8 (1974): 83–119.

Knodel, J., and E. Van de Walle. "Breast Feeding, Fertility and Infant Mortality: An Analysis of Some Early German Data." *Population Studies*, 21 (1967): 109–31.

Kolish, E. "Le Conseil législatif et les bureaux d'enregistrement (1836)." *RHAF*, 35 (1981): 217–30.

Kulikoff, A. "The Transition to Capitalism in Rural America." *WMQ*, 3rd series, 46 (1989): 120–44.

LaBrèque, M.P. "La dîme dans Saint-Frédéric de Drummondville au temps des missionnaires." *Les Cahiers nicolétains*, 4, 1 (1982): 2–12.

Lacroix, Benoît, and Jean Simard, eds. *Religion populaire, religion de clercs?* Quebec: Institut québécois de recherche sur la culture, 1984.

Lacroix, B., and C. Laforte. "Religion traditionelle et les chansons de coureurs de bois." *Laurentian University Review*, 12, 1 (1979): 11–42.

Lafleur, Normand. *La vie quotidienne des premiers colons en Abitibi-Témiscamingue*. Ottawa: Leméac: 1976.

Laforce, Hélène. *Histoire de la sage-femme dans la région de Québec*. Quebec: Institut québécois de recherche sur la culture, 1979.

Laidig, G.L., W.A. Schutjer, and C.S. Stokes. "Agricultural Variation and Human Fertility in Antebellum Pennsylvania." *JFH*, 6 (1981): 195–201.

Langlois, Georges. *Histoire de la population canadienne-française*. Montreal: Éditions Albert Lévesque, 1943.

Laperrière, G. "Religion populaire, religion de clercs? Du Québec à la France, 1792–1982." In *Religion populaire*, edited by Lacroix and Simard.

Lapointe, J. Alphonse. *Historique de Lambton (1848–1948)*. N.p., n.d.

Larouche, D. "Le mouvement de concession des terres à Laterrière." In *Agriculture et colonisation au Québec*, edited by Normand Séguin. Montreal: Boréal Express, 1980.

Laslett, P. "Introduction: Comparing Illegitimacy over Time and between Cultures." In *Bastardy and Its Comparative Perspective*, edited by Peter Laslett, Karla Oosterveen, and Richard M. Smith. London: Edward Arnold, 1980.

Laurin, Serge. *Histoire des Laurentides*. Quebec: Institut québécois de recherche sur la culture, 1989.

Lavallée, L. "La transmission du patrimoine dans la seigneurie de Laprairie, 1667–1760." In *Évolution et éclatement*, edited by Wallot and Goy.

Lawson, Bill. "Emigrants to Ontario and Quebec from the Western Isles." *Seminar Annual* (Ontario Genealogical Society), 1984, 125–34.

– *A Register of Emigrant Families from the Western Isles of Scotland to the Eastern Townships of Quebec, Canada*. Eaton Corner, Que.: Compton County Historical Museum Society, 1988.

Leet, D.R. "Human Fertility and Agricultural Opportunities in Ohio Counties: From Frontier to Maturity, 1810–60." In *Essays in Nineteenth Century Economic History: The Old Northwest*, edited by David C. Klingamen and Richard K. Vedder. Athens: Ohio University Press, 1975.

LeGoff, T.J.A. "The Agricultural Crisis in Lower Canada, 1802–12: A Review of the Controversy," *CHR*, 55 (1974): 1–31.

Lemieux, Denise, and Lucie Mercier. *Les femmes au tournant du siècle, 1880–1940: ages de la vie, maternité et quotidienne.* Quebec: Institut québécois de recherche sur la culture, 1989.

Lemieux, Lucien. *Histoire du catholicisme québécois: Les XVIIIe et XIXe siècles.* Tome 1: *Les années difficiles (1760–1839).* Montreal: Éditions du Boréal, 1989.

Lemon, J.T. "Early Americans and Their Social Environment." *Journal of Historical Geography,* 6 (1980): 115–31.

– "The Weakness of Place and Community in Early Pennsylvania." In *European Settlement,* edited by Gibson.

Leridon, Henri. *Human Fertility: The Basic Components,* trans. by Judith F. Helzner. Chicago and London: University of Chicago Press, 1977.

Levine, D. "The Reliability of Parochial Registration and the Representativeness of Family Reconstitution." *Population Studies,* 30 (1976): 107–22.

Lewis, Frank D., and Marvin McInnis. "Agricultural Output and Efficiency in Lower Canada, 1851." Institute for Economic Research, Queen's University, Discussion Paper No. 451, 1981.

Lithell, U.B. "Breast-Feeding Habits and Their Relation to Infant Mortality and Marital Fertility." *JFH,* 6 (1981): 182–94.

Little, J.I. "Colonization and Municipal Reform in Canada East." *Hs-SH,* 14 (1981): 92–121.

– "Cycles du travail saisonnier dans une zone de colonisation québécoise: les Canadiens-français et les Écossais du Canton de Winslow, Québec, 1852–81." Unpublished paper presented to the Colloque d'histoire rurale comparée Québec / France, Montreal, 1990.

– "Imperialism and Colonization in Lower Canada: The Role of William Bowman Felton." *CHR,* 66 (1985): 511–40.

– *Nationalism, Capitalism, and Colonization in Nineteenth-Century Quebec: The Upper St Francis District.* Kingston and Montreal: McGill-Queen's University Press, 1989.

– "The Peaceable Conquest: French-Canadian Colonization in the Eastern Townships during the Nineteenth Century." PHD thesis, University of Ottawa, 1977.

– "Public Policy and Private Interest in the Lumber Industry of the Eastern Townships: The Case of C.S. Clark and Company, 1854–1881." *Hs-SH,* 19 (1986): 9–37.

Lockridge, Kenneth. "Land, Population and the Evolution of New England Society, 1630–1790; and an Afterthought." In *Colonial America. Essays in Population and Social Development,* edited by Stanley N. Katz. Boston: Little, Brown, 1971.

– *A New England Town: The First Hundred Years, Dedham, Massachusetts, 1636–1736.* New York: W.W. Norton, 1970.

Lockwood, G.J. "Irish Immigrants and the 'Critical Years' in Eastern Ontario: The Case of Montague Township, 1821–1881." *CPRH*, 4 (1984): 154– 78.

Lower, A.R.M. *The North American Assault on the Canadian Forest: A History of the Lumber Trade between Canada and the United States*. New York: Greenwood Press, 1938.

– *Settlement and the Forest Frontier in Eastern Canada*. Toronto: Macmillan, 1936.

McCalla, Douglas. "The Internal Economy of Upper Canada: New Evidence on Agricultural Marketing before 1850." *Agricultural History*, 59 (1985): 397–416.

– "Rural Credit and Rural Development in Upper Canada, 1790 to 1850." In *Patterns of the Past: Interpreting Ontario's History*, edited by Roger Hall, William Westfall, and Laurel Sefton MacDowell. Toronto and Oxford: Dundurn Press, 1988.

– *The Upper Canada Trade 1834–1872: A Study of the Buchanans' Business*. Toronto: University of Toronto Press, 1979.

– "The Wheat Staple and Upper Canadian Development." In *Interpreting Canada's Past*, edited by J.M. Bumsted. Toronto: Oxford University Press.

McCallum, John. *Unequal Beginnings: Agriculture and Economic Development in Quebec and Ontario until 1870*. Toronto: University of Toronto Press, 1980.

McCann, L.D. "'Living a double life': Town and Country in the Industrialization of the Maritimes." In *Geographical Perspectives*, edited by Douglas Day.

MacDermid, Gordon E. "The Religious and Ecclesiastical Life of the Northwest Highlands, 1750–1843: The Background to the Presbyterian Emigrants to Cape Breton, Nova Scotia." PHD thesis, University of Aberdeen, 1967.

Macdonald, Donald. *Lewis. A History of the Island*. Edinburgh: Gordon Wright, 1978.

– *The Tolsta Townships*. Tolsta, Lewis: Tolsta Community Association, 1984.

McDonald, Neil, and Alf Chaiton, eds. *Egerton Ryerson and His Times*. Toronto: Macmillan, 1978.

MacDougall, Alexander G. "The Presbyterian Church in the Presbytery of Quebec, 1875–1925." MA thesis, McGill University, 1960.

MacFarlane, Alan. *Reconstituting Historical Communities*. Cambridge: Cambridge University Press, 1977.

McGuigan, G.F. "Administration of Land Policy and the Growth of Corporate Economic Organization in Lower Canada, 1791–1809." CHA *Report*, 1963, 65–73.

McIlwraith, T.F. "The Adequacy of Rural Roads in the Era before Railways: an Illustration from Upper Canada." *Canadian Geographer*, 14 (1970): 344–60.

McInnis, R.M. "Childbearing and Land Availability: Some Evidence from Individual Household Data." In *Population Patterns in the Past*, edited by Ronald Demos Lee. New York: Academic Press, 1977.

– "Marketable Surpluses in Ontario Farming, 1860." In *Perspectives on Canadian Economic History*, edited by Douglas McCalla. Toronto: Copp Clark Pitman Ltd, 1987.

– "A Reconsideration of the State of Agriculture in Lower Canada in the First Half of the Nineteenth Century," *CPRH*, 3 (1984): 9–49.

– "Some Pitfalls in the 1851–52 Census of Agriculture of Lower Canada." *Hs-SH*, 14 (1981): 219–32.

MacKay, Donald. *Scotland Farewell: The People of the Hector*. Toronto: McGraw-Hill Ryerson, 1980.

Mackenzie, Alexander. *The History of the Highland Clearances*. 1883, revised edition. Glasgow: Alex. MacLaren & Sons, 1946.

MacKinnon, R., and G. Wynn. "Nova Scotian Agriculture in the 'Golden Age': A New Look." In *Geographical Perspectives*, edited by Douglas Day.

Macklam, C. "Patterns of Inheritance in Early Mid-Nineteenth Century French Canada." *Register*, 2, 1–2 (1981): 1–25.

McLean, M. "Achd an Righ: A Highland Response to the Assisted Emigration of 1815." *CPRH*, 5 (1986): 181–77.

– "Peopling Glengarry County: The Scottish Origins of a Canadian Community." CHA *Historical Papers*, 1982, 156–71.

McLeod, Duncan. *The Milan Story*. Privately published [1977].

McMichael, R.N. "The Potato Famine of the 1840s in the Western Highlands and Islands of Scotland." MA thesis, Edinburgh University, 1973.

MacNeil, A.R. "Cultural Stereotypes and Highland Farming in Eastern Nova Scotia, 1827–1861." *Hs-SH*, 19 (1986): 39–56.

Macpherson, A.G. "A Modal Sequence in the Peopling of Central Bonavista Bay, 1676–1857." In *The Peopling of Newfoundland*, edited by Mannion.

– "An Old Highland Parish Register: Survivals of Clanship and Social Change in Laggan, Inverness-shire, 1755–1869." *Scottish Studies*, 11 (1967): 149–92; 12 (1968): 81–111.

Maisonneuve, D. "Structure familiale et exode rurale: le cas de Saint-Damase, 1852–1861." *Cahiers québécois de démographie*, 14, 2 (1985): 379– 408.

Mannion, John J. *The Peopling of Newfoundland: Essays in Historical Geography*. [St John's]: Memorial University of Newfoundland, Institute of Social and Economic Research, 1977.

Marcy, P.T. "Factors Affecting the Fecundity and Fertility of Historical Populations: A Review." *JFH*, 6 (1981): 309–26.

Marr, W.L. "Family-Size Limitation in Canada West, 1851: Some Historical Evidence." *CPRH*, 7 (1990): 273–91.

Mathieu, J. "Mobilité et sédentarité: stratégies familiales en Nouvelle-France." *RS*, 28, 2–3 (1987): 211–28.

Mathieu, J., et al. "Peuplement colonisateur au XVIIIème siècle dans le gouvernement de Québec." In *L'homme et la nature: actes de la Société canadienne d'étude du dix-huitième siècle*, II. Montreal: Société, 1984.

Mays, H.J. "'A Place to Stand': Families, Land and Permanence in Toronto Gore Township, 1820–1890." CHA *Historical Papers* (1980), 185–211.

Mays, A.J., and H.F. Marzl. "Literacy and Social Structure in Nineteenth-Century Ontario: An Exercise in Historical Methodology." *Hs-SH*, 7 (1974): 331–45.

Medick, H. "The Proto-Industrial Family Economy: The Structural Function of Household and Family during the Transition from Peasant Society to Industrial Capitalism." *Social History*, 3 (1976): 291–315.

Merrill, M. "Cash Is Good to Eat: Self-Sufficiency and Exchange in the Rural Economy of the United States." *Radical History Review*, 7 (1975): 42– 71.

Mesnick, G.S. "The Demographic Impact of Breastfeeding: A Critical Review." *Human Biology*, 51 (1979): 109–25.

Michel, L. "Endettement et société rurale dans la région de Montréal au dix-neuvième siècle: premières approches et éléments de réflexion." In *Sociétés villageoises*, edited by Séguin and Lebrun.

– "Le livre de compte (1784–1792) de Gaspard Massue, marchand à Varennes." *Hs-SH*, 13 (1980): 369–98.

Modell, J., and T.K. Hareven. "Transitions: Patterns of Timing." In *The Family and the Life Course in Historical Perspective*, edited by Tamara K. Hareven. New York: Academic Press, 1978.

Moir, John S. *Enduring Witness: A History of the Presbyterian Church in Canada.* Toronto: Bryant Press, 1974.

Molloy, M. "'No Inclination to Mix with Strangers': Marriage Patterns among Highland Scots Migrants to Cape Breton and New Zealand, 1800–1916." *JFH*, 11 (1986): 221–43.

Monet, J. "French-Canadian Nationalism and the Challenge of Ultramontanism." CHA *Report*, 1966, 41–55.

Monette, M. "Groupes dominantes et structure locale de pouvoir à Deschambault et Saint-Casimir, Comté de Portneuf (1829–1870)." *CGQ*, 18, 73–4 (1984): 73–88.

Morel, André. *Les limites de la liberté testamentaire dans le droit civil de la province de Québec.* Paris: R. Pichon et R. Durand-Augias, 1960.

Morgan, R.J. "'Poverty, wretchedness, and misery': The Great Famine in Cape Breton, 1845–1851." *Nova Scotia Historical Review*, 6, 1 (1986): 88– 104.

Morin, D., et al. "Des Cantons-de-l'Est à l'Estrie." *CGQ*, 30, 80 (1986): 249– 69.

Morissonneau, C. "Genre de vie et religion populaire." In *Religion populaire*, edited by Lacroix and Simard.

Mutch, R.E. "Yeoman and Merchant in Pre-Industrial America: Eighteenth Century Massachusetts as a Case Study." *Societas*, 7 (1977): 279– 302.

Nelson, Wendie. "La Guerre des Éteignoirs: Popular Resistance to School Reform in Lower Canada during the 1840s." MA thesis, Simon Fraser University, 1989.

Noël, Françoise. "Chambly Mills, 1784–1815." CHA *Historical Papers*, 1985, 102–16.

– *Competing for Souls: Missionary Activity and Settlement in the Eastern Townships, 1784–1851*. Sherbrooke: Département d'histoire, Université de Sherbrooke, 1988.

– "La gestion des seigneuries de Gabriel Christie dans la vallée du Richelieu (1760–1845)." *RHAF*, 40 (1987): 561–82.

– "Seigneurial Survey and Land Granting Policies." *CPRH*, 5 (1986): 150–80.

Noel, Jan. "Dry Patriotism: The Chiniquy Crusade." *CHR*, 71 (1990): 189–207.

– "God's Scots: Montreal Merchants and the Millenium." Unpublished paper presented to the annual meeting of the CHA, 1984.

Norris, D.A. "Household and Transiency in a Loyalist Township: The People of Adolphustown, 1784–1822." *Hs-SH*, 13 (1980): 399–415.

– "Migration, Pioneer Settlement, and the Life Course: The First Families of an Ontario Township." *CPRH*, 4 (1984): 130–52.

O'Bready, Maurice. *De Ktiné à Sherbrooke: esquisse historique de Sherbrooke, des origines à 1954*. Sherbrooke: Université de Sherbrooke, 1973.

– *Histoire de Wotton*. Sherbrooke: Messager, 1949.

Ommer, R.E. "Highland Scots Migration to Southwestern Newfoundland: A Study of Kinship." In *The Peopling of Newfoundland*, edited by Mannion.

– "Primitive Accumulation and the Scottish Clann in the Old World and the New." *Journal of Historical Geography*, 12, 2 (1986): 121–41.

Ostergren, R.C. "A Community Transplanted: The Formative Experience of a Swedish Immigrant Community in the Upper Middle West." *Journal of Historical Geography*, 5 (1979): 189–212.

– "Land and Family in Rural Immigrant Communities." *Annals of the Association of American Geographers*, 71 (1981): 400–11.

Ouellet, Fernand. "Libéré ou exploité! le paysan québécois d'avant 1850." *Hs-SH*, 13 (1980): 339–68.

– *Lower Canada 1791–1840: Social Change and Nationalism*. Toronto: McLelland and Stewart, 1980.

Ouellet, Fernand, J. Hamelin, and R. Chabot. "Les prix agricoles dans les villes et les campagnes du Québec d'avant 1850: aperçus quantitatifs." *Hs-SH*, 15 (1982): 83–128.

Ouellet, J. "Le développement du système scolaire au Saguenay – Lac-Saint-Jean depuis 150 ans." *Saguenayensia*, 21, 1 (1988): 6–36.

Overland, Orm, ed. and transl. *Johan Schroder's Travels in Canada, 1863*. Montreal and Kingston: McGill-Queen's University Press, 1989.

Paquet, Gilles, and Jean-Pierre Wallot. "Crise agricole et tensions socio-ethniques dans le Bas-Canada, 1802–1812: éléments pour une réinterprétation," *RHAF*, 26 (1972): 185–238.

– "Les habitants de Montréal et de Québec (1790–1835): contextes géo-économiques différents, même stratégie foncière." In *Sociétés villageoises*, edited by Lebrun and Séguin.

– *Lower Canada at the Turn of the Nineteenth Century: Restructuring and Modernization*. CHA Booklet no. 45, Ottawa, 1988.

– "Stratégie foncière de l'habitant: Québec (1790–1835)." *RHAF*, 39 (1986): 551–82.

– "Structures sociales et niveaux de richesse dans les campagnes du Québec: 1792–1812." *MHB*, 17 (1983): 25–43.

Parker, W.H. "A Revolution in the Agricultural Geography of Lower Canada, 1833–1838." *Revue canadienne de Géographie*, 11 (Dec. 1957): 189–94.

Pentland, H. Clare. *Labour and Capital in Canada 1850–1860*. Toronto: James Lorimer, 1981.

Pépin, G. "Le phénomène religieux populaire dans les Cantons de l'Est: premier inventaire des sources écrites." In *Recherches et religions populaires*, edited by Andrée Désilets and Guy Laperrière. Montreal: Bellarmin, 1976.

Perron, Marc. *Un grand éducateur agricole: Edouard-A. Barnard 1835–1898*. Montreal: privately published, 1955.

Perron, N. "Genèse des activités laitières, 1850–1960." In *Agriculture et colonisation*, edited by Séguin.

Pigeon, L.P. "Législation civile des paroisses." SCHEC *Rapport*, 1947–8, 93–9.

Pouliot, Jean-François. *Traité de droit fabricien et paroissial*. Montreal: Wilson et Lafleur, 1956.

Pouyez, Christian, and M. Bergeron. "L'étude des migrations au Saguenay (1842–1931): problèmes de méthode." *Hs-SH*, 11 (1978): 26–61.

Pouyez, Christian, and Yolande Lavoie. *Les Saguenayens: introduction à l'histoire des populations du Saguenay XVIe–XXe siècles*. Sillery: Presses de l'Université du Québec, 1983.

Pouyez, Christian, R. Roy, and G. Bouchard. "La mobilité géographique en milieu rural: le Saguenay, 1852–1861." *Hs-SH*, 14 (1981): 123–56.

Prentice, Alison. *The School Promoters: Education and Social Class in Mid-Nineteenth Century Upper Canada*. Toronto: McClelland and Stewart, 1977.

Pronovost, Claude. "Les marchands de la Rive Nord du Saint-Laurent au XIXe siècle." Unpublished paper presented to the colloque d'histoire rurale comparée France / Québec, Montreal, 1990.

Pronovost, Claude, and L. St-Georges. "L'identification des marchands ruraux dans six paroisses de la plaine de Montréal, 1831 à 1861." *RHAF*, 42 (1988): 241–51.

Pruitt, B.H. "Self-Sufficiency and the Agricultural Economy of Eighteenth Century Massachusetts." *WMQ*, 3rd series, 41 (1984): 333–64.

Ramirez, B. "Ethnic Structure and Working-Class History." *Labour / Le travail*, 19 (1987): 45–8.

Ramirez, B., and J. Lamarre. "Du Québec vers les États-Unis: l'étude des lieux d'origine." *RHAF*, 38 (1985): 409–22.

Ramsay, Freda. *John Ramsay of Kildalton.* Toronto: Peter Martin [1969?].

Ribordy, G. "Le choix des prénoms à Sudbury au tournant du xxe siècle." *RHAF*, 43 (1989): 179–201.

Rice, J.G. "The Role of Culture and Community in Frontier Prairie Farming." *Journal of Historical Geography*, 3, 2 (1977): 155–75.

Richards, Eric. *A History of the Highland Clearances: Agrarian Transformation and the Evictions, 1746–1886.* London and Canberra: Croom Helm, 1982.

Roach, T.R. "Farm Woodlots and Pulpwood Exports from Eastern Canada, 1900–1920." In *History of Sustained-Yield Forestry: A Symposium*, edited by H.K. Steen. Santa Cruz, Calif.: Forest History Society, 1984.

Robert, J.C. "The City of Wealth and Death: Urban Mortality in Montreal, 1821–1871." In *Essays in the History of Canadian Medicine*, edited by Wendy Mitchinson and Janice Dickin McGinnis. Toronto: McClelland and Stewart, 1988.

– "Un seigneur entrepreneur, Barthélemy Joliette, et la fondation du village d'industrie (Joliette), 1822–1850." *RHAF*, 26 (1972): 375–96.

Rodrigue, Denise. *Le cycle de Pâques au Québec et dans l'ouest de la France.* Quebec: Presses de l'Université Laval, 1983.

Roelens, J., and K. Inwood. "'Labouring at the Loom': A Case Study of Rural Manufacturing in Leeds County, Ontario, 1870." *CPRH*, 7 (1990): 215–35.

Ross, Aileen D. "Ethnic Relations and Social Structure: A Study of the Invasion of French-Speaking Canadians into an English-Canadian District." PDH thesis, University of Chicago, 1950.

Rousseau, L. "La conduite pascale dans la région montréalaise, 1831–1865: un indice des mouvements de la ferveur religieuse." In *L'église de Montréal: aperçu d'hier et d'aujourd'hui.* Montreal: Fides, 1986.

– "Les missions populaires de 1840–42: acteurs principaux et conséquences." SCHEC *Sessions d'étude*, 53 (1986): 7–21.

Roy, J. "Religion et vie quotidienne à Saint-Boniface au xIxe siècle: une contribution à l'étude de la piété populaire en Mauricie." In *Sociétés villageoises*, edited by Séguin and Lebrun.

– "Les revenus des curés du diocèse de Nicolet, 1885–1904." SCHEC *Sessions d'étude*, 52 (1985): 51–67.

Roy, J. Edmond. *Histoire de la Seigneurie de Lauzon*, I–V. Lévis: n.p., 1897–1904.

Roy, R., Y. Landry, and H. Charbonneau. "Quelques comportements des Canadiens au xvIIe siècle d'après les registres paroissiaux." *RHAF*, 31 (1977): 49–73.

Ruddell, D.T. "The Domestic Textile Industry in the Region and City of Quebec, 1792–1835." *MHB*, 17 (1983): 95–125.

– *Quebec City, 1765–1831: The Evolution of a Colonial Town.* Ottawa: Canadian Museum of Civilization, 1987.

Rudin, R. "The Megantic Outlaw and His Times: Ethnic Tensions in Quebec in the 1880s." *Canadian Ethnic Studies*, 18, 1 (1986): 16–31.

St-Georges, L. "Commerce, crédit et transactions foncières: pratiques de la communauté marchande du bourg de l'Assomption, 1748–1791." *RHAF*, 39 (1986): 323–43.

St-Hilaire, M. "Origines et destins des familles pionnières d'une paroisse saguenayenne au xixe siècle." *CGQ*, 22, 85 (1988): 5–26.

– "La structuration foncière en milieu de colonisation agro-forestière: Saint-Fulgence, 1852–1898." *Saguenayensia*, 27, 4 (1985): 138–45.

Santerre, Renaud. "La sécurité de vieillesse au Québec: de la donation de ferme à l'hypothèque inversée, 1850–1990." Unpublished paper presented to the Colloque d'histoire rurale comparée Québec / France, Montreal, 1990.

Savard, P. "La vie du clergé québécois au xixe siècle." *RS*, 8, 3 (1967): 259–73.

Schulze, D. "Rural Manufacture in Lower Canada: Understanding Seigneurial Privilege and the Transition in the Countryside." *Alternate Routes: A Critical Review*, 7 (1984): 134–67.

Seccareccia, M.S. "Immigration and Business Cycles – Pauper Migration to Canada, 1815–1874." In *Explorations in Canadian Economic History*, edited by Duncan Cameron. Ottawa: University of Ottawa Press, 1984.

Segalen, Martine. *Love and Power in the Peasant Family.* Chicago: University of Chicago Press, 1983.

Séguin, Normand, ed. *Agriculture et colonisation au Québec.* Montreal: Boréal Express, 1980.

– *La conquête du sol au 19e siècle.* Sillery: Boréal Express, 1977.

Séguin, Normand, and François Lebrun, eds. *Sociétés villageoises et rapports villes-campagnes au Québec et dans la France de l'Ouest, XVIIe-XXe siècles.* Trois-Rivières: Centre de recherche en études québécoises, Université du Québec à Trois-Rivières, 1987.

Sevigny, Daniel. "Le capitalisme et la politique dans une région québécoise de colonisation: le cas de Jacques Picard à Wotton, 1828–1905." MA thesis, Simon Fraser University, 1982.

Sherman, Annie Isabel. *History of the Families of Sherman-MacIver: With Stories of People and Places in the Eastern Townships.* Sherbrooke: Page-Sangster, 1971.

Short, R.V. "Breast Feeding." *Scientific American*, 250, 4 (1984): 35–41.

Shorter, Edward. *The Making of the Modern Family.* New York: Basic Books, 1975.

Skelton, Oscar Douglas. *Life and Times of Sir Alexander Tilloch Galt.* Toronto, 1920, reprint Toronto: McClelland and Stewart, 1966.

Smith, D.B. "The Study of the Family in Early America: Trends, Problems, and Prospects." *WMQ*, 3rd series, 39 (1982): 3–28.

Smith, D.S. "Parental Power and Marriage Patterns: An Analysis of Historical Trends in Hingham, Massachusetts." *Journal of Marriage and the Family*, 35 (1973): 419–28.

Smith, David C., et al. "Climate Fluctuation and Agricultural Change in Southern and Central Maine, 1765–1880." *Maine Historical Society Quarterly*, 21 (spring 1982): 179–200.

– *A History of Lumbering in Maine 1861–1960.* Orono: University of Maine Press, 1972.

Smout, Christopher, and Ian Levitt. *The State of the Scottish Working Class in 1843.* Edinburgh: Academic Press, 1979.

Smout, T.C. *A Century of the Scottish People 1830–1950.* London: Fontana, 1987.

– "Aspects of Sexual Behaviour in Nineteenth-Century Scotland." In *Social Class in Scotland: Past and Present*, edited by A. Allan MacLaren. Edinburgh: John Donald, n.d.

La Société généalogique des Cantons de L'Est. *Les mariages de Saint-Romain de Winslow 1865–1970.* [Sherbrooke: 1970].

Sorg, M.H., and B.C. Craig. "Patterns of Infant Mortality in the Upper St John Valley French Population: 1791–1838." *Human Biology*, 55, 1 (1983): 100–13.

Stanley, Laurie. *The Well-Watered Garden: The Presbyterian Church in Cape Breton, 1798–1860.* Sydney, NS: University College of Cape Breton Press, 1983.

Stone, L. "Family History in the 1980s: Past Achievements and Future Trends." *JIH*, 12 (1981): 51–87.

Stornoway 1858 / 1983. Sherbrooke: Gauvin et Associés [1983].

Tackett, Timothy. *Priest and Parish in Eighteenth Century France: A Social and Political Study of the Curés in a Diocese of Dauphiné, 1750–1791.* Princeton, NJ: Princeton University Press, 1977.

Temkin-Greener, H., and A.C. Swedlund. "Fertility Transition in the Connecticut Valley: 1740–1850." *Population Studies*, 32 (1978): 27–41.

Tepperman, L. "Ethnic Variations in Marriage and Fertility: Canada, 1871." *Canadian Review of Sociology and Anthropology*, 11 (1974): 324–43.

Thibeault, R. "Les unités de mesure dans les documents officiels du dix-neuvième siècle au Bas Canada et au Québec." *RHAF*, 43 (1989): 221–32.

Thomas, Peter. *Strangers from a Secret Land: The Voyages of the Brig "Albion" and the Founding of the First Welsh Settlements in Canada.* Toronto: University of Toronto Press, 1986.

Thompson, Francis. *Crofting Years.* Barr, Ayrshire: Luath, 1984.

Tilley, C. "The Historical Study of Vital Processes." In *Historical Studies of Changing Fertility*, edited by Charles Tilley. Princeton, NJ: Princeton University Press, 1978.

Treckel, P.A. "Breastfeeding and Maternal Sexuality in Colonial America." *JIH*, 20 (1989): 25–51.

Trépanier, G. "Contrôle social et vécu religieux dans la paroisse de Champlain, 1850–1900." In *L'église et le village*, edited by Gagnon and Hardy.

Trépanier, P. "Les influences le playsiennes au Canada français, 1855–1888." *Journal of Canadian Studies*, 22, 1 (1987): 66–84.

Vaudry, Richard W. "The Free Church in Canada, 1844–1861." PHD thesis, McGill University, 1984.

Verdon, Michel. *Anthropologie de la colonisation au Québec: le dilemme d'un village du Lac-Saint-Jean*. Montreal: Presses de l'Université de Montréal, 1973.

Vermette, L. "Les donations: activités domestiques et genre de vie 1800–1820 et 1850–1870." In *Évolution et éclatement*, edited by Wallot and Goy.

Verrette, M. "L'alphabétisation au Québec, 1660–1899." Unpublished paper presented to the annual meeting of the CHA, 1989.

Vinovskis, M.A. "From Household Size to the Life Course: Some Observations on Recent Trends in Family History." *American Behavioral Scientist*, 21, 2 (1977): 263–87.

– "Recent Trends in American Historical Demography: Some Methodological and Conceptual Considerations." *Annual Review of Sociology*, 4 (1978): 603–27.

Voisine, Nive. *Histoire de l'église catholique au Québec (1608–1970)*. Montreal: Fides, 1971.

– "Jubilés, missions paroissiales et prédication au XIXe siècle." *RS*, 23, 1–2 (1982): 125–38.

– "Mouvements de tempérance et religion populaire." In *Religion populaire*, edited by Lacroix and Simard.

Wallace, Clarke W. *Wanted: Donald Morrison. The True Story of the Megantic Outlaw*. Toronto: Doubleday Canada, 1977.

Wallot, Jean Pierre. "L'impact du marché sur les campagnes canadiennes au début du XIXe siècle." In *Société rurale*, edited by Wallot and Goy.

Wallot, Jean-Pierre, and Joseph Goy, eds. *Évolution et éclatement du monde rural: France-Québec XVIIe-XXe siècles*. Montreal: Presses de l'Université de Montréal, 1986.

– *Société rurale dans la France de l'Ouest et au Québec (XVIIe-XXe siècles)*. Montreal: École des Hautes Études en Sciences sociales, Université de Montréal, 1981.

Ward, Peter. *Courtship, Love, and Marriage in Nineteenth-Century English Canada*. Montreal and Kingston: McGill-Queen's University Press, 1990.

Ward, W.P. "Courtship and Social Space in Nineteenth-Century English Canada." *CHR*, 68 (1987): 35–62.

– "Unwed Motherhood in Nineteenth-Century English Canada." CHA *Historical Papers*, 1981, 34–56.

Waters, J.J. "Family, Inheritance, and Migration in Colonial New England: The Evidence from Guilford, Connecticut." *WMQ*, 3rd series, 39 (1982): 64–86.

Weale, D. "The Time Is Come! Millenarianism in Colonial Prince Edward Island." *Acadiensis*, 7, 1 (1977): 35–48.

Westfall, William. *Two Worlds: The Protestant Culture of Nineteenth-Century Ontario*. Kingston and Montreal: McGill-Queen's University Press, 1989.

Whyte, Donald. *A Dictionary of Scottish Emigrants to Canada before Confederation*. Toronto: Ontario Genealogical Society, 1986.

Wien, T. "Les travaux pressants: calendrier agricole, assolement et productivité au Canada au xviiie siècle." *RHAF*, 43 (1990): 535–58.

Willigan, J. Dennis, and Katherine A. Lynch. *Sources and Methods of Historical Demography*. New York: Academic, 1982.

Wright, G. "American Agriculture and the Labor Market: What Happened to Proletarianization?" *Agricultural History*, 62, 3 (1988): 182–209.

Wrigley, E.A. "Family Reconstitution." In *An Introduction to English Historical Demography from the Sixteenth to the Nineteenth Century*, edited by E.A. Wrigley. New York: Basic Books, 1966.

– *Population and History*. Toronto: McGraw-Hill, 1969.

Wynn, Graeme. "Ethnic Migrations and Atlantic Canada: Geographical Perspectives." *Canadian Ethnic Studies*, 18, 1 (1986): 1–15.

– "Settler Societies in Geographical Focus." *Historical Studies*, 20, 80 (1983): 353–66.

– *Timber Colony: A Historical Geography of Early Nineteenth Century New Brunswick*. Toronto: University of Toronto Press, 1981.

Youngson, A.J. *After the Forty-Five: The Economic Impact on the Scottish Highlands*. Edinburgh: Edinburgh University Press, 1973.

Index

Crofters and Habitants